Bristol Radical Pamphleteer #15

Votes For Ladies

The Suffrage Movement 1867 – 1918

GW00707556

Sheila McNeil

ISBN 978-1-911522-16-4

Bristol Radical History Group. 2nd Edition 2014.
1st Edition 2010.
www.brh.org.uk ~ brh@brh.org.uk

Introduction

The suffragette movement is one of the best known stories in the struggle for further emancipation of the people in Britain. Almost everybody has heard about when Emily Davison went under the King's horse at the Derby wearing her suffragette colours of White, Purple and Green. This is one of the most famous images of the movement organised by the well known Emmeline Pankhurst, whose work towards female enfranchisement earned her fame across the globe.

The suffragettes are widely seen as the pinnacle of women's radical action in the early twentieth century. However, beyond the passion and drive of such unladylike militancy, were the organisation and aims of this movement as radical as the means used to try to obtain it? Were the suffragettes alone in the struggle for female emancipation? And how far can the granting of limited female suffrage in 1918 be attributed to the exploits of these women? This pamphlet will analyse this iconic "women's" movement and question how far it can really be seen as part of radical history.

Democracy At The Turn Of The 20th Century

The suffragette movement emerged from a political landscape which had seen much change in the preceding years, particularly in terms of the size and composition of the electorate. Following the 3 Great Reforms (the Representation of the People Acts or RPAs) of 1832, 1867 and 1884 ,the majority of males

Emily Davison's fatal collision with Anmer, the King's horse, during the Derby at Epsom, 4 June 1913.

in Britain could vote. The beginnings of formal constitutional opposition to female suffrage were laid out in the terms of the 1832 reform act which stated specifically that it would enfranchise certain "male persons" but not women even if they met the high qualifications of property, wealth and status. By 1884, whether a man could vote or not depended upon a property qualification; you either needed to own a house or be a lodger paying at least £10 a year and you also needed to have been living in a residence for at least a year. The prevailing ideas of franchise were based upon property and taxation from which the vast majority of women were excluded (unless they had inherited property from their families) and therefore women had very limited legal status.

As a growing proportion of the male population could exercise the right to vote, political parties now had to try to win support by passing measures that pleased the population and to avoid supporting those which would endanger their chances in upcoming elections. Throughout the Victorian period, the prevailing attitude of the public towards the question of female suffrage was hostile. Overbearing Victorian gender stereotypes and ingrained ideas about separate spheres for men and women meant that not only was the idea of a woman voting seen as inappropriate by a population within which a woman's primary role was as a mother and a wife, it was also seen by many as unnecessary, dangerous and ridiculous. If women were to remain within the domestic sphere they would have no need to vote as they could be represented by their fathers and husbands. The notion of women becoming involved in politics was seen as a threat to the patriarchal Victorian interpretation of the family unit. Prime Minister William Gladstone often gave this as his reason for opposing female suffrage, as he said that it would damage the sanctity of the family.

Of course, these enforced ideologies were only relevant to women of a certain status as working class women had no choice but to diverge from this idyllic image of womanhood and the family because it was necessary for them to work to make ends meet. Despite this, ideas about a woman's place were enforced throughout all walks of society. Due to the fact that much of the population stood against female suffrage, the two main parties, the Conservatives and the Liberals (Tories and Whigs) were wary of showing support for this controversial issue in case it lost them popularity.

Beginning Of Campaigning

The campaign for the woman's right to vote began in 1867 around the time of the second reform act. The MP John Stuart Mill suggested an amendment to this reform to allow some measure of female suffrage, again based upon property. When this amendment was declined, women decided to start campaigning themselves for the right to vote. The Suffragists were a peaceful body who used constitutional and nonviolent methods in their campaigning such as lobbying MPs, rallies and petitions. Although there were many suffrage groups across the country, the majority of these were coordinated under the National Union of Women's Suffrage Societies (NUWSS), run by Millicent Fawcett. Small steps were made towards the vote using these methods.

By the turn of the century women were allowed to vote in municipal and local elections and also became more involved in the public sphere, sitting on school boards and becoming poor law guardians.

The Women's Social And Political Union

Emmeline Pankhurst was the widow of the socialist MP Richard Pankhurst who had campaigned for measures such as universal adult suffrage, payment of salaries for MPs, disestablishment of the Church of England, free compulsory elementary education, Irish Home Rule, land nationalization and the abolition of the House of Lords. In 1903 she, with the help of three of her daughters Christabel, Sylvia and Adela, set up the Women's Social and Political Union (WSPU) in Manchester. The initial aim of the organisation was to recruit more working class women into the fight for female enfranchisement.

To begin with, the group operated similarly to other suffrage organisations but 1905 saw the first use of more extreme action when Christabel Pankhurst and her friend Annie Kenney interrupted a Liberal Party rally by heckling Winston Churchill and Edward Grey, shouting for votes for women. The women were removed from the building by police who they spat at and kicked and after refusing to pay their fine, they were sentenced to 3 days in prison. This sparked the beginning of the suffragette militant campaign to get the vote. Tired of conventional methods failing to achieve the vote even after 40 years, these women began destroying ballots, chaining themselves to parliamentary railings and even carried out a widespread series of arson attacks at the homes of politicians who stood against the cause of votes for women.

Emmeline Pankurst, 1913.

Christabel Pankhust, 1913.

Sylvia Pankhurst, 1927.

Annie Kenney, 1909.

Christabel Pankhurst in Manchester, 1909.

The militancy employed by the WSPU was not only a more extreme approach, it was a sensationalist tactic. Newspapers at the time had not previously given much attention to the suffrage movement. Such public militant actions were published in both local and national newspapers, which brought the cause of votes for women onto the national stage and the question of female suffrage into the consciousness of the public. The very word 'suffragette' was coined by the *Daily Mail* as a derogatory nickname for the militant campaigners who, rather than being perturbed by this, adopted the title, and even named one of their magazines after it. It is this militancy, combined with the contemporary controversial nature of the movement that earned the WSPU and the suffragette's their 'radical' name in history.

Between 1903 and 1906 the introduction of militancy was not the only change to the WSPU. Christabel Pankhurst, Emmeline's eldest daughter, was made the official leader of the WSPU. In 1903 the society had strong ties with the Labour Party, especially with the party leader Keir Hardy, which is not surprising given the political history for this family. Between these dates however, the WSPU began to distance itself from being a working class, inclusive campaign and became increasingly elitist. In 1906 the organisation moved its central base from Manchester to London. This geographical change seems to physically represent the shift in the ideals and approach of the Women's Social and Political Union at this time.

Structure

The Women's Social and Political Union was essentially a hierarchical and autocratic organisation. An unelected central committee comprising of members of the Pankhurst family - Emmeline, Christabel, Adela and Sylvia (who was secretary) - and their close friends Emmeline Pethick-Lawrence (treasurer) and Annie Kenney, made the decisions. They were aided somewhat by a sub-committee again comprising of close family friends, but the society was essentially a top down organisation with rank and file members having little or no say in decision making. Once these decisions had been made, they were relayed to the national branches of the WSPU by eleven (unelected) regional officers.

This lack of democracy within the organisation faced criticism from within. Teresa Billington-Grieg and Charlotte Despard were members of the WSPU who wanted it to be more democratic. In 1907, they drafted a new 'constitution' which they presented at a national conference which included amendments to the way the society was run in order to make it more democratic and allow members to take part in decision making. Emmeline dramatically tore it up and said "Our women should walk in step and take their instructions like an army". These women were described as "socialist suffragettes" and broke away from the WSPU to form a different, democratic suffrage organisation, the Women's Freedom League. They were the first of many to split away from the organisation. Not only were many women annoyed that they didn't have any input in decision making, the lack of democracy was seen as hypocritical. The WSPU were campaigning to allow some women to be involved in the British democratic system, yet they did not have democracy within their own movement.

Aims

The initial aim of the Women's Social and Political Union was to recruit more working class women into the struggle for the vote. Rather than campaigning for universal suffrage which would enfranchise all men and women over 21, the movement fought for votes for women on equal terms to men. That meant that the women who would gain the vote would be those who met the property qualification which therefore excluded working class women and many middle class women. As it was unusual for a woman to own property around this time, only a very small proportion of women would gain the vote. If the campaign was to succeed in gaining suffrage on equal terms to men, it was estimated that women would make up a sixth of the total electorate. This was seen by

Joan of Arc, the 'patron saint' of the Suffragettes, taken from a WSPU poster.

many women as not very productive as women would not be able to force significant change if they made up such a small minority of voters.

When the movement began, the Pankhurst family's political outlook was fairly liberal, with Sylvia Pankhurst in particular harbouring very similar political opinions to those of her father before her. Many members who became involved in the movement early on were also of a more socialist leaning and some were displeased by the WSPU's decision not to fight for universal adult suffrage. The society however, felt that it was more likely to be successful campaigning for this single cause.

The Split From The Labour Party

Between 1903 and 1906, Christabel cut all official ties with the Labour Party. The reason she gave was that she didn't want the movement to be party aligned and that it should be politically neutral in terms of any allegiance. However, there were other motives behind this. Distancing themselves from the Labour Party would make it easier for the WSPU to recruit women from the social elite. Christabel wanted to attract more middle class women to the movement as 1) they were able to contribute financially to the WSPU which had the aim of raising £20,000 and 2) she believed that the House of Commons would be "more impressed by the demonstrations of the feminine bourgeoisie than of the female proletariat." She wanted to disassociate the group from working women and keep it exclusively middle class.

This break from the party was described by Sylvia as an example of her sister's "incipient Toryism". The sisters were politically opposed in many respects and this is how Sylvia described Christabel's attitude towards working women's participation:

a working woman's movement is of no value; working women are the weakest position of the sex; how could it be otherwise? Their lives are too hard, their education too meagre to equip them for the contest. Surely it is a mistake to use the weakest for the struggle. We want picked women, the very strongest and the most intelligent.

Difficulties For Working Women

Working class women were never asked to leave the organisation, but in some ways they were alienated. Not only were working class women distanced by the fact that the main organisers of the group were more interested in recruiting middle and upper class women, some of the methods of campaigning used and the times and places of meetings and events made it difficult for working women to become involved.

WSPU meetings were a social event. They were often held in member's houses and the women would not only talk politics but they would drink tea, eat cake and get to know one another. These meetings were rarely held at times which working class women were available. As middle class women didn't need to work, meetings were often held in the day time. Even when working class women were at home, they had very little time for themselves. Juggling working, child care and domestic tasks meant that they were only available, if at all, for short periods in the evenings. Another problem for working women with the meetings being held at middle class homes was that working class women were not expected to be in middle class areas.

Militancy And Hypocrisy

Militancy also alienated working class women in that they found it very difficult to partake in such activities because they, unlike the middle class members, did not have maids or servants to care for their families if they were to be put in prison. The WSPU began trying to gain sympathy from the public. Middle class women would deliberately get themselves arrested and put in prison and would play the victim. The public were horrified by the treatment of respectable women, which distanced working women further. This tactic did in some ways set back the cause. On 'Black Friday', for example, when suffragette demonstrators were beaten up by plain clothes policemen, the suffragettes tried to gain sympathy from the public by imposing the idea that they were middle class respectable women who were being victimised by men. However, this was hypocritical as it played on the idea that women were not equal to men but needed to be protected from them and thus reinforced the hegemony of gender stereotypes. They were campaigning to be recognised as being as strong, responsible, mature and worthy of respect as men, and then undermining it by playing on the patriarchal perception that women were frail, helpless creatures who had to be treated with greater care and special consideration.

Splits From The WSPU

When you look further into the class construction of the suffragettes you can begin to see that as time passed, the more exclusively middle class they became. The WSPU's early alliance with the Independent Labour Party (ILP) was not welcomed by all members of the ILP. As the women were not campaigning for Adult Suffrage, many Labour Party members saw supporting the movement as counterproductive as it would essentially only benefit and further empower the middle classes. The break from the party confirmed that their aims were limited and again the WSPU faced criticism from within their own ranks, this time about their class composition and elitism.

'Black Friday', 18 November 1910, was the first time Suffragettes were met with physical violence and abuse by the police. Two thirds of the 300 women protesters were arrested during a 6 hour battle as they tried to force their way to parliament. Two women died as a result of their injuries. This photograph shows Suffragette Ada Wright on the floor after being beaten by police.

Dora Montefiore was an adult suffragist who set up the first London Canning Town branch of the WSPU. When she attempted to expand her branches within London without the Pankhursts' prior consent, they decided she was becoming too independent. She broke away from the WSPU in 1908 as she too disagreed with their aim of enfranchising middle class women and not including working class women and men. She was also perturbed by the Pankhursts' will to dominate decisions about where to set up new branches of the movement. There was continuing conflict between

Emmeline Pankhurst being arrested,1910.

the WSPU and its Canning Town branch as it advocated universal adult suffrage not female suffrage on the same grounds as men, and the secretary of the branch Adelaide Knight also resigned due to the elitist aims of the WSPU and because they weren't "keeping their promises to the working woman".

As Christabel wanted to attract more women from the social elite into the movement, many members of the WSPU who had joined the society in its early stages were made to keep their political convictions quiet in order not to offend any of the new middle class or more conservative women. Adela Pankhurst was the youngest Pankhurst sister involved in the organisation of the movement. Among the organisers, she was known as the 'black sheep'. She, like Sylvia, still held on to the socialist convictions that she had grown up with and believed ultimately in adult suffrage, rather than equal suffrage.

In 1910, the level of militancy had risen to widespread arson attacks and attacks on the homes of politicians. Adela attempted to advise her sister and mother that this level of militancy was loosing the suffragette's support from the public. She left the WSPU in 1911 for this reason. Emmeline Pankhurst was frightened that Adela would publicly speak out against and humiliate the organisation, and after she made a speech advocating adult suffrage, her mother bought her a

**One of many cartoon postcards that played on the violent image of the Suffragettes.
Probably published by Millar and Lang c 1910.**

one way ticket to Australia, banishing her own daughter to the other side of the world and forbidding her to ever speak in public in England again.

Adela was not the only member of the family to face estrangement by Christabel and Emmeline. In October 1912 Sylvia Pankhurst travelled to London with her American friend Zelie Emmerson to set up a further branch of the WSPU in Bow, East London. Christabel was strongly against setting up a branch in such a working class area but Sylvia elected to speak on behalf of working class women, against the wishes and advice of her mother and sister. In 1913 she founded the East London Federation of Suffragettes (ELFS) This branch of the WSPU was not only working class in its composition but it was far more democratic than many other branches of the organisation and so conflicted with the ideals set down by Christabel and Emmeline.

In 1913, Christabel was in Paris in hiding from the police who had imprisoned her on several occasions. She summoned Sylvia there and told her either to dissolve the ELFS or be expelled from the organisation. Sylvia refused, and thus she and the branch in Bow were cut off from the main suffragette movement.

Sylvia realised that the fight for he vote was inextricably linked with the fight against poverty and destitution. Later in life, Sylvia set up the Communist Party. She spent much of her time in Ethiopia fighting against the Italian fascists. When she fell pregnant with the baby of an Italian communist, her mother never spoke to her again as she refused to marry the man or give the child his name.

Another criticism of the WSPU was that it saw gaining a measure of equal franchise as the be all and end all of campaigning. Emmeline Pankhurst said:

> Our members are absolutely single minded; they concentrate all their forces on one object, political equality with men. No member of the WSPU divides her attention between suffrage and other social reforms.

Political equality with men was a much deeper issue than a question of the vote, and even if the WSPU were to be successful, the fact that women would make up such a small portion of the electorate would mean that there would still be over-whelming inequality.

The Women's Social and Political Union began as a society which aimed to include working women in the struggle for the vote. By the end of 1913 the movement had become one in which the ladies were respectable and fashionable. The narrow aims of the WSPU, its autocratic structure and overbearing middle class composition had led to the estrangement of many campaigners, even members of the Pankhurst family. Theresa Billington Grieg summed up her views when she left the organisation:

> It has cut down its demand from one of sex equality to one of votes on a limited basis. It has suppressed free speech on fundamental issues. It has gradually edged the working class element out of the ranks. It has become socially exclusive, ultra-respectable and narrowly religious.

Radical Suffragists

The suffrage movement was not only made up of the militant suffragettes, and other methods of campaigning still continued during the period in which they were active. The radical suffragists are a group barely acknowledged for their effort in campaigning for female suffrage. Only one book exists about their efforts, despite the many years they devoted to the cause. *One Hand Tied Behind*

Us by Jill Liddington and Jill Norris tells the story of the factory women in the north of the country who even risked their livelihoods for the cause. Although they were not militant, they were still a radical group of women, as they have been dubbed by Liddington and Norris. Their methods included petitioning and meetings. Women would stand outside the factory gates with petitions, often enduring much abuse from the women that passed them.

Women, Trade Unions And Support From The TUC

They also worked closely with trade unions and attempted to get them on side. One of their great successes was succeeding in gaining support from the Trades Union Council (TUC) for a measure to bring about universal adult suffrage for men and women. In 1901, a factory girl from Ashton-under-Lyne named Helena Silcock made a speech to the TUC pointing out many of the flaws in the arguments against women being allowed to vote. One of the most important points for her, and many other young women like her, was that many women were unmarried meaning that they had little or no legal status. The argument that women were adequately represented by their husbands was therefore redundant in this respect:

> It is said that women are sufficiently protected by their husbands. I would point out that not all women are wives. There are in fact 5 million working women in this country who have to earn their own livelihood, some protection should be extended to them, so that by means of the vote they may assist in bringing about legislation which will enable them to live and not merely exist.

In the 19th and early 20th centuries, trade unions were very hostile towards women. Due to the huge gender pay gap, employers often favoured offering a woman a job as she would be much more easily exploitable than a man and cheaper to employ. This threatened men's chances of employment and so trade unions were naturally wary of allowing women into the ranks. Gaining support from the TUC was therefore a big achievement. In some ways it was very hard for the radical suffragists to campaign. If they were to go to meetings, it often took up the very limited time which they had for themselves in between working and household duties. Many of these women also faced great hostility from their husbands. The radical suffragists said that the burdens of work, child care and domestic chores meant that they were campaigning with one hand tied behind them.

Selina Cooper And What The Vote Could Mean

Selina Cooper was a notable figure head in the movement. When a petition of over 60 000 names was presented to parliament for female suffrage, she had collected over one thousand herself. Selina was elected as the first working class poor law guardian. She was very critical of the WSPU in that they concentrated all their efforts into gaining the vote. For Selina and the other factory women the vote was seen as a stepping stone towards further reform and greater emancipation of women in Britain. WSPU ladies did not have to endure the hard conditions which working women were subjected to. The vote, to these women, would allow them a voice to try to better their lifestyles and gain better rights and protection, especially in terms of health and work.

> Women do not want their political power to enable them to boast that they are on equal terms with men. They want it for the same purpose as men – to better conditions … make the lot of the worker pleasanter … We do not want it as a mere plaything!

The radical suffragists were not only breaking the stereotype that women could not be involved in politics, they were also disproving the idea that it would be dangerous and harmful to enfranchise them. One of the problems with the militancy of the suffragettes was that there was a contemporary idea in some circles that allowing women to immerse themselves in the political sphere would mean that they would lose their femininity and become distorted figures of womanhood. To those who thought this, the violence portrayed by the WSPU was to them a confirmation of the dangers of women mixing in politics. The radical suffragists were showing that women could operate in the democratic system in which they were trying to gain influence. They were also a pillar for the working classes. Many of the radical suffragists were also involved in other campaigns such as worker's co-operatives, campaigns for birth control and better rights in the work place. For them, the fight for the vote and the fight against exploitation were intertwined and could not be seen as separate entities as they were by the WSPU. Many of the women did not see the point of campaigning for the vote if they did not know how it could be used.

"*Votes for Women*," November 20, 1914.

Registered at the G.P.O. as a Newspaper.

The War Paper for Women

VOTES FOR WOMEN

OFFICIAL ORGAN OF THE UNITED SUFFRAGISTS

VOL. VIII. (Third Series), No. 350.   FRIDAY, NOVEMBER 20, 1914.   Price 1d. Weekly (Post Free 1½d.)

HAVING IT BOTH WAYS

THE PRIME MINISTER: "Here is seven-and-sixpence for you because your husband died fighting for his country. If you cannot live on it you must go out to work."
SOLDIER'S WIDOW: "Not me! My place is the home. You always told me so when I asked you for a vote. You can't have it both ways, you know!"

(*The proposed Government pension for the childless widow of a man killed in action is fixed at seven-and-sixpence a week, on the assumption that if able-bodied she will go out to work.*)

The cover of *Votes For Women* from 20 November 1914.

The Reaction To World War One

The WSPU's reaction to the outbreak of the First World War shows the difference in its politics from when it was originally founded. In 1914, Christabel made a deal with the government to end all suffragette campaigning in return for the release of the suffragettes who were in prison. Her autocratic control allowed her to do this, despite objections from many suffragettes such as Kitty Marion. The WSPU, who had burned down the houses of MPs, and whose women had suffered imprisonment and even force feeding at the hands of the government, were now working side by side with the state. The organisation began a vigorous patriotic campaign. They changed the name of the magazine *Suffragette* to *Britannica* and led and organised great rallies in the street. They were also involved in the 'white feather' campaign. During World War One, conscientious objectors were often anonymously given white feathers as a symbol of their 'cowardice'. Many women from the WSPU travelled to Russia to speak to the women there to try to keep their men fighting.

The National Union of Women's Suffrage Societies was split over the war. Many of the women wanted to campaign for peace rather than support the war effort, but the leader Millicent Fawcett decided to support the government as she believed that if England was to be invaded by Germany, women would face much worse conditions under the Kaiser than they did with the British government.

The East London Federation however, campaigned to protect working class families from the ravages of war. It campaigned against price rises, for equal pay and a moratorium on debt. They sought to unionise and support women at work.

The Representation Of The People Act 1918

In 1915 a coalition government was formed. Previous attitudes and worries held by the Labour and Liberal Parties that enfranchising women would be dangerous, as the women considered for the franchise (women of higher social statuses) would be more inclined towards voting conservative, vanished. David Lloyd George replaced the anti-suffrage Asquith during the war and again the fact that the WSPU had ceased their militant campaigns were all reasons why parliament was more willing to consider votes for women. The decision to give women the vote may have been affected by the fact that most other commonwealth countries had enfranchised women, as did the USA at the same time as it was being debated in British parliament.

In 1918, the fourth Representation of the People Act was passed which enfranchised some women in Britain. Women over 30, who met property qualifications, were married and on the local government register could vote. Many factors led to this decision including the long term work of suffrage groups, the outbreak of World War One, changes in the running of the country and a changing international scene. The work of suffrage groups was important as it had taught women how to operate and without this previous experience, the women would not have been able to exploit the situation so effectively. The political environment also changed during the war and with the end of the militant campaign, parliament became more sympathetic towards the votes for women cause.

The granting of limited female suffrage in 1918 is often attributed to the First World War. During the war, women began to take on roles in the work place which were previously dominated by men. They also contributed heavily with their work in munitions factories. These new work positions challenged contemporary gender stereotypes; however, this was not seen as permanent by employers, the government or the media. It also physically represented the gap between men and women as while women were at home, men were fighting in France. Although women did gain the vote soon after the war, those who were able to vote were over 30 and had to be on the local government electoral register. This suggests that women's contribution to the war effort was not such a great factor in parliament's decision to include some women in the franchise as, most of the women, for example, who worked in the munitions factories, were under the age of 30 which would infer that the vote was not given to women in recognition of the work they did during the war.

Additionally, the reason for passing the Representation of the People Bill was to ensure that men fighting for their country had the right to vote. Men who had been fighting abroad would not be able to vote under the previous system because they had not been living in a British residency for at least a year. Women's contribution to the war effort did allow them the chance to show that they were capable of performing tasks that would previously have only been given to men. However, the extension of the franchise in 1918 excluded many of the women who had carried out this important work for the country.

"Votes for Women," December 10, 1915.   Registered at the G.P.O. as a Newspaper.

The War Paper for Women

VOTES FOR WOMEN

OFFICIAL ORGAN OF THE UNITED SUFFRAGISTS

VOL. IX. (Third Series), No. 405.   FRIDAY, DECEMBER 10, 1915.   Price 1d. Weekly (Post Free 1½d.)

WHY NOT VOTES FOR TWO AS WELL AS JOBS FOR TWO ?

WOMAN (just off to drive a 4-ton motor lorry): "Now that we've exchanged jobs and your vote will be used to protect my interests in the Home, don't you think you had better give me a vote, too, in order to protect your interests in the Labour market?"

(In the course of a question in the House of Commons, last week, Mr. Jowett asked the Under-Secretary of State for War if he was aware that young men who had joined the Royal Army Medical Corps, and whose civilian posts had been filled by women, were now being employed as charwomen in British hospitals.)

The cover of *Votes For Women* from 10 December 1915.

Conclusions

The Women's Social and Political Union or the 'suffragettes' fought for nearly a decade for the cause of Votes for Women but the contribution of other suffragists seems to have been ignored and marginalised. The work of groups such as the East London Federation of Suffragettes and the Radical Suffragists, not only contributed towards the fight for the vote, but were instrumental in educating women about issues within the work place and of health, which were very important in terms of the further emancipation of women. As Dora Monteiore said, the WSPU were not interested in "Votes for Women" but they fought for "Votes for Ladies".

Bibliography

One Hand Tied Behind Us – Jil Liddington and Jil Norris

Rebel Girl – Jil Liddington

The Ascent of Woman – Melanie Phillips

The Suffragette Movement – Sylvia Pankhurst

The Pankhursts – Martin Pugh

The Non-militant Militant – Teresa Billington Grieg

Women's and Gender History 1860 - 1914 – Paula Bartley

The Changing Position of Women and the Suffrage Question 1860 – 1930 – Rosemary Rees

In Letters of Gold - Rosemary Taylor

http://marxists.org/archive/montefiore/index.htm

http://marxists.org/archive/pankhurst-sylvia/index.htm

The Suffragettes are widely seen as the pinnacle of women's radical action in the early twentieth century. However, beyond the passion and drive of such 'unladylike' militancy, were the organisation and aims of the movement as radical as its methods? Were the Suffragettes alone in the struggle for female emancipation? And how far can the introduction of limited female suffrage in 1918 be attributed to the exploits of these women?

Votes For Ladies analyses this iconic women's movement and questions how far can really be seen as part of radical history.

VOTES FOR WORKING WOMEN

ISBN 978-1-911522-

£3

9 781911 522164

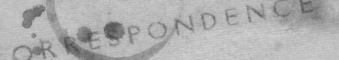

Dominic's France
The Cool Climate

D. G. Ruggim

Dominic's France
The Cool Climate

Dominic Rippon

BEAUTIFULBOOKS

First published 2007.

Beautiful Books Limited
117 Sugden Road
London SW11 5ED

www.beautiful-books.co.uk

ISBN 9781905636051

9 8 7 6 5 4 3 2 1

Book design and artwork by Dan Fear.
Cover design and artwork by Ian Pickard.
Photography by Dominic Rippon.
Printed in Dubai by Oriental Press.

the cool climate

Acknowledgements

Special thanks to Philippe Wibrotte and Françoise
Peretti of the CIVC (Comité Interprofessionnel
des Vins de Champagne), and to Cécile
Mathiaud, of the BIVB (Bureau Interprofessionnel
des Vins de Bourgogne). Thanks also to Pierre
Jochem at the ADT (Association Départementale
du Tourisme) in the Haut-Rhin, Alsace.

I would like to thank all of the winemakers,
restaurateurs and others who feature in this
book, and who made it possible.

Thanks to my family, and especially my mother,
for all of their support. Thank you to the team at
Beautiful Books and particularly my good friend and
designer Dan Fear. This really is Dan's book too.

In memory of my grandfather, "Phil" Rippon.

Contents

Introduction   8

Champagne   16

Loire Valley   92

Burgundy   **176**

Alsace   **266**

Glossary   354

Index   358

Introduction

What is Dominic's France?

Dominic's France is both a travel guide and a story. It is the tale of how, in spring 2006, I left a comfortable job in the British wine trade, to embark on a six-month cycle odyssey in the four northernmost – 'cool climate' – wine regions of France.

This book is a distillation of my experiences into an honest, personal travel guide; the result of a quest to find the finest wine estates and best local restaurants in Champagne, the Loire Valley, Burgundy and Alsace. The focus is on those places where visitors can expect the warmest welcomes, with a generous helping of other highlights along the way.

Each chapter outlines a week's itinerary, for the motorist or the cyclist, through exciting winemaking country and some of France's most beautiful landscapes. The itineraries are detailed, personally researched, and flexible enough that the traveller can set his or her own agenda.

This is a guide for the independent traveller, so your journey begins where mine finishes.

The experience of a lifetime

I have spent many exciting years in France over the last decade, but as spring 2006 approached I had little idea just what a challenge I had set myself.

Things began at the London Waterloo Eurostar terminal on the 15th May. The train got as far as Brixton, and broke down. As it limped back into London, hurried telephone calls from passengers ensured that flights to Paris were soon fully booked. I had abandoned my phone in London, thinking that I wouldn't need it. Meanwhile, my bike had arrived in Paris by train the previous day.

When I eventually made it to Champagne, the cold winter gave way to the warmth of summer, and as vineyard work got underway my own journey began.

As summer became hotter and the café terraces filled up, I reached the Loire Valley, the *Jardin de France*, with its deliciously crisp wines and beautiful Renaissance châteaux. When the grape harvest was announced I was on Burgundy's Côte d'Or, or 'Golden Slope', amongst the vineyards of Gevrey-Chambertin, Puligny-Montrachet and the region's other world-famous wine villages.

As autumn set in, the vine leaves turned golden red and began to fall. I was in Alsace, the most fascinating (if least French) of the northern regions, pedalling hard to avoid the onset of the continental winter.

ABOVE
May 2006

A word on cycling

This is not a guide only for cyclists. There are obvious advantages to travelling on four wheels, but I decided to undertake the trip by bike because this is the best way, in my view, to experience all of the sights, smells and tastes of the French countryside.

As I cycled through the vineyards, however, I learned that the bicycle provided one further benefit: its capacity to bring out the best, as well as the worst, in the people I met. The bike thus became a litmus test for France's 'good eggs', those winemakers, restaurateurs and hoteliers who welcomed a sweaty, dishevelled British cyclist, rather than setting the dogs on him!

What is the cool climate?

The 'cool climate' is the winemaking world's Holy Grail. The Aussies, Kiwis, South Africans and Americans all talk about their cool climate vineyards, where the grapes ripen slowly, developing fresh, complex flavours. These vineyards are contrasted with the hotter regions, where grapes rush to ripeness, producing wines that are higher in alcohol, and can have coarse, cooked flavours.

The northern part of France is the international template for this fresher, 'cooler' style of wine. In New Zealand's Marlborough region, for example, Sauvignon Blancs are made in imitation of those from France's Loire Valley. Washington State, in the U.S.A., is renowned for its Pinot Noirs, which are flatteringly described as "very Burgundian". And most winemaking nations use their coolest vineyards to produce sparkling wines, in the hope of eventually rivalling the best from Champagne. So far, none has succeeded.

The 'cool climate' is not merely wine jargon, however. In this context, it refers to the northern part of France, *La France septentrionale*. 'Septentrional' is a Latin-derived word that still just about exists in English (it appears in James Joyce's Ulysses). It is usually translated as 'northern', but I prefer 'cool'.

Not as cool as all that...

When I say cool, however, I certainly do not mean chilly. When I arrived in the Loire Valley in July 2006, daytime temperatures were soaring to 40 degrees. Rather, these are the regions where weather, and particularly temperature, variations are greatest: between night and day, season to season, and from one vintage to the next.

It is the unpredictability of wine growing at this latitude that makes the wines so fascinating. Vines and vignerons struggle against the elements to produce wines that are the purest reflections of the most French idea of them all: *terroir*!

This word 'terroir'

Terroir is essentially a mystical concept, a philosophy of the relationship between man, the environment, the earth and its fruits. The *goût de terroir*, or the taste of terroir, is its evidence in wine.

Terroir derives from the French word for the soil or earth, '*la terre*'; it is an idea that seems natural in a culture with a strong, enduring rural tradition. In the Anglo-Saxon wine world, however, terroir is still something of a hot potato. For many, terroir is explained simply in terms of environmental and physical factors in a given vineyard. For others, it is a mythical beast, whose very existence is debatable.

At its simplest, the French invoke the term to mean things like 'rustic' or 'natural', and it is applied to all manner of culinary and libationary products. But terroir has a specific and deep-rooted meaning for the French winemaker; to understand the concept, one must know a little about the history of wine growing in France.

Terroir and the history of French wine

The Romans are generally cited as the fathers of French viticulture. When they arrived in the land that is now France, in the 1st century AD, the Romans planted vines along many important trade routes. But the wines would almost certainly have been rather unpleasant and vinegary, served diluted as a way of purifying the often dangerous drinking water.

When Europe was christianised, churches needed better wines for use in the Mass. These were imported from the south of Europe, the Near East and North Africa. They were rich wines, made from sun-baked grapes, and often cut with olive oil to preserve them for the voyage north.

By the early middle ages, France's own religious houses were growing vines for the Eucharist and, increasingly, for pleasure. The Emperor Charlemagne encouraged good wine growing, and the Benedictine monastic order became notorious for its alcoholic revelries.

In the early 12th century, things changed, with the appearance of an extraordinary monk named Bernard. Saint Bernard, as he would become known, created the ascetic Cistercian order at the Abbey of Cîteaux, in Burgundy. When he died in 1153, Saint Bernard had established more than 500 Cistercian monasteries, all of which had one important thing in common: the practice of refined viticulture.

The wines made in these monasteries were very different from the thin, vinegary brews of the Roman settlers, and from those jammy blends brought from the south. Saint Bernard applied his religious zeal, with all the austerity of the Cistercian order, to monastic winemaking. The vines were to live in the image of the monks who tended them; only in this way would they bear divine fruit.

The shallow vineyard soils were a fertile bed of luxury, a breeding ground fungus and bacteria. To find truth, mankind must transcend worldly goods; to make fine wine, the vines must suffer. Vineyards were farmed within walled enclosures, called *clos*, and the vines were planted barely 15 centimetres apart, forcing them to dig deep roots in their search for nutrients.

The sites chosen by the monks were those hillsides where exposure to the sun was best, allowing the grapes to ripen in the cool northern vineyards. But the soils in these vineyards were poor and stony, making the vines work hard to find water and nutrients. The result was low yields of small, concentrated grapes, giving wines with complex flavours, each wine bearing the unique sensory imprint of the parcel of land on which they were grown.

Such things as mesoclimate (climate specific to a vineyard), sun exposure, soil type and drainage can help explain differences in terroirs, but it is the spiritual quest of the Cistercian monks that adds the mystery to an idea that, despite extensive studies, is still not fully understood.

Terroir and sustainable viticulture

I did not set out with an eco-project in mind, but the more winemakers I met who worked their land and made their wines naturally, the more convinced I was of the positive effects this had on the wine.

In the 1970s many French growers were wooed by the agrochemical industry, persuaded that chemical pesticides, herbicides and other synthetic nasties equalled easy vineyard management. Most shocking of all is in Champagne, where the Parisian authorities managed to dump large amounts of shredded dustbin waste onto the vineyards "as fertiliser". The scattered remnants of plastic and glass between vine rows are still embarrassingly visible today.

Apart from their deleterious effects on the environment, synthetic products in the vineyard spoil the plants, overfeeding them and disrupting their natural rhythms. As the plants' ecosystems are destroyed, so are their relationships with the soil and their environment. The vigneron plays a less important role in working the soil. Terroir ceases to leave its mark on the wines, which become dull and standardised.

Fortunately, the last ten years have seen something of an ecological revival amongst France's best winemakers. Sustainable vineyard practices are increasing, and more winemakers are converting to organic viticulture. This is nothing new; it is a return to the way the land has been worked for centuries.

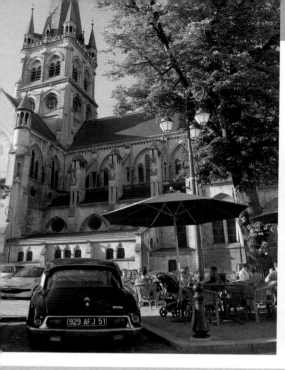

Organic vineyards and life beyond

Organic viticulture is, quite simply, natural vineyard farming, avoiding toxic herbicides, pesticides and synthetic fertilisers. Instead, natural manure and compost are used to nourish the soils. The vineyard ecosystem is encouraged, and cover crops are planted between vine rows to help stabilise the soil.

A handful of official bodies are authorised to award organic status to vineyards. Many winemakers adhere to sustainable vineyard practices, or *lutte raisonnée*, but are not certified as organic. There are sometimes political reasons for opting out, but more often the winemaker does not have the manpower to avoid using chemical herbicides when weeds become a problem.

The most extreme and philosophical form of organic viti-viniculture is biodynamics, which encompasses not only vine growing, but also the entire winemaking process.

Biodynamics is the radical theory proposed by Austrian scientist and philosopher Dr Rudolph Steiner in the 1920s. Steiner argued that the plant and the earth are living things, functioning according to cosmic rhythms. Rather than trying to manipulate and curtail the plants' energies with synthetic substances, Steiner claimed, the aim of the farmer should be to liberate the spirit of the organism, creating a harmonious balance between soil, plant and the universe.

In the abstract, biodynamics might sound confusing, but its practical application has yielded superb results. Many of France's finest winemakers subscribe to Steiner's theory, whether or not they are certified as biodynamic.

Organic, or even biodynamic, certification is far from a guarantee of wine quality, but all good winemakers farm their vines naturally. These winemakers are also, in my experience, the most interesting people, and always have a fascinating story to tell.

Tasting wine and judging quality

Any professional wine tasting in Britain is filled with distinguished-looking folk earnestly nosing small samples, pausing for thought, swilling the wine around the mouth, before producing a thin, carefully aimed arc of spit, and a technical opinion.

A winemaker wants to hear how his wines make the *amateur* 'feel'. Analysis is for scientists and critics. Wine drinking, surely, is about pleasure. Likewise, when people read books, they do so for enjoyment, rather than to check for spelling mistakes.

I am always impressed by the views of people who have no professional experience of wine tasting. They so often get it right! The enjoyment of wine is, however, like that of literature, music, art or sport; it is enriched by greater knowledge and experience.

There are few rules for wine tasting. The range of possible aromas and flavours is vast, and everyone has their own preferences. In general, a cheaper wine should be immediately pleasant; a more expensive one should be interesting and complex. If a wine is neither of these things, then it is probably either a dud bottle, or a badly made wine.

One thing to look out for is a wine's aftertaste, or its 'finish'. This, if anything, is the most reliable sign of a wine's quality. A good cheaper wine might have a short, well-balanced finish. A great wine should have a long, lingering aftertaste, with complex flavours that dance on the palate.

Whether a wine has the ability to age is a trickier subject. A wine's ageing potential derives from a particular balance of fruit flavour, acidity, body, alcohol and, principally in red wines, tannin.

The ability to tell the difference between a wine that can age, and one that cannot, requires years of practice. Nothing gives a winemaker greater pleasure than to dig out an old vintage from his cellar and pour a sample for a visiting wine critic; amid the critic's rapturous exclamations, the winemaker slyly produces the magazine article that the same critic wrote ten years earlier, declaring the wine "very pleasant, but not for the long haul"!

My own notes are descriptions of wines that I tasted in 2006. You may get to try the same wines with further bottle age, or from later vintages, as an interesting comparison.

What the officials say

Winemaking is more tightly regulated in France than anywhere else on the planet. And the rules are, predictably, the subject of fierce disputes. In 1936, the system of *appellation d'origine contrôlée* (AOC) was created, to regulate the production of quality wine in France, at a time when falsification in wine labelling was rife.

About 40% of French wines now have AOC status, which guarantees their geographical origins, the grape variety or varieties used, their style, and even regionally permitted methods of viticulture, such as pruning systems and maximum vine yields.

Many argue, however, that the one thing AOC status does *not* guarantee is quality. Here the human element is to blame. The regional authorities have tended to favour their winemaking chums when handing out the honours. The most famous examples of such corruption were in Bordeaux and Burgundy, although new reforms are making classifications more reliable.

Even so, many quality-conscious winemakers have chosen to opt out of the appellation system. Thus, many great wines are 'de-classified' by their own producers, to the lower rank of *vins de pays*, or even as basic *vins de tables*. This allows the vigneron greater winemaking flexibility, but is more common in the south of France, where *vin de pays* is a recognisable brand. In the northern regions, a rebellious winemaker is more likely either to bend the *appellation contrôlée* rules, or to ignore them completely.

Eating, drinking and staying in France

France is the best place on earth to plan a gastronomic holiday. Wine is made to go with food, and most French regions' winemaking cultures have developed in tandem with the local culinary traditions.

One of the remarkable things about France is just how cheap great food can be. It is quite possible to eat a midday meal at a Michelin-starred restaurant for only €30 (without drinks). You might pay that for a single course in a British 'gastro-pub'.

I have concentrated on those restaurants where delicious, fresh food is served in an unpretentious, friendly environment. Michelin stars mean that you can expect clean knives and forks with every course!

Wine and food matching is highly personal. Certain general rules of logic apply at the poles: big tannic red wines tend to like red meats, whilst light whites with firm acidity go well with fish. On the other hand, a light fruity red Pinot Noir from Burgundy's Hautes-Côtes is delicious with a rare-cooked tuna steak, whilst a firm white Burgundy or Alsatian Pinot Gris can marry with rich meat dishes. My advice is simply to experiment; or ask the sommelier, the chef, or the winemaker, for advice.

Having spent six months on the road in France, my advice on accommodation is rather more conservative: stick to personal recommendations and reliable hotel chains. A gorgeous rural *gîte* or *chambre d'hôte* (B&B) completes a perfect holiday, but a bad-tempered or deranged host can easily spoil it.

How to use this book

From Champagne to Alsace, select any of the tours and decide how far you wish to stick to it. Every tour is suitable for driving or cycling, or a combination of both, with suggested strolls along the way.

Gastronomes will be able to use this book as a specific, personal restaurant guide. For the amateur enthusiast, it is a way of combining the alluring pleasures of France's food and wine with the tranquillity of the French countryside. This book will also inform those aficionados who already know what they're looking for, where to find it.

I have concentrated on winemakers and restaurants in a very personal way. Many of the vignerons offer discounts, and restaurants will frequently give something 'extra' on presentation of this book. This is a bonus, rather than an entitlement. Restaurants' owners change, wineries pass from father to son, and people are forgetful. In any case, it cannot do harm to show this book where indicated, or at least to leave it visible.

Getting your wine home

The proximity of 'the cool climate' to Great Britain makes it an easy drive. This way you can stock up with as many of your favourite wines as you can fit in the boot.

Otherwise, the easiest way to buy the wines you have tasted is through a UK importer. I have given names of importers with featured wine estates. Or, you can import in small quantities directly from the producer.

Bon voyage!

Champagne

PARIS

FRANCE

Champagne: May & June 2006

Rising stars and bursting bubbles

I once ordered "un bouteille de vin" in a Paris restaurant. "UNE bouteille," the waiter corrected, with a grimace that said "Fumble with our language if you must, Monsieur, but please leave our genders alone!" English speakers know that assigning genders to inanimate objects is, well, a bit silly, and in this case the waiter knew exactly what I wanted. But there are occasions when mastery of French noun genders can avoid confusion. Walk into a Reims wine bar and ask for *le* champagne, and you will be served a flute of something delicious and fizzy; the taking of *la* Champagne (with a capital 'C') was Kaiser Wilhelm's military objective in 1914!

For most visitors to la Champagne (the region), le champagne is a drink associated with the large merchant houses of Reims and Epernay. In their cavernous cellars, a host of subterranean railways, video suites and light shows skilfully reinforce the image of champagne as an elegant, sophisticated and aspirational wine.

But le champagne as we know it has a fairly short history and the region's widespread prosperity an even shorter one. Today, Champagne is flourishing as never before, with too little wine to sell to an ever-thirstier world market, and not enough land left to plant. But at the heart of la Champagne, I found an enduring rural, familial culture, made up of the 15,000 or so growers who supply the large houses with their base wines.

A growing number of these *récoltants-manipulants* (nearly 3000) are handcrafting delicious cuvées and selling them under their own labels.

After exploring the large cellars of Reims and Epernay, followed by a succession of bike-related hold-ups, I decided to follow the Grand and Premier Cru villages through the heart of Champagne country, and into the cellars of some of the region's best family estates. This is where you get to taste how champagne is really made, usually for free; and the wines in these smaller village wineries sell for as little as 13 euros a bottle (little more than 8 quid!).

The terms 'Grand' and 'Premier Cru' have a variety of meanings in France. In Bordeaux they apply to individual châteaux, in Burgundy they delimit small parcels of land, and in both the wines are likely to be expensive. In Champagne none of these things applies. Grand Cru champagne is simply a wine made from grapes grown in one of seventeen villages, each supposedly blessed with superior, unique growing conditions. Premier Cru champagnes come from a further forty-two villages, and a slightly lower classification.

Simplicity helps explain the global success of champagne. Drinkers might not know exactly where the wine comes from or how it is made, let alone get to grips with terms like *blanc de blancs* or Grand Cru, but these are all what ad-men call "hooray words". You don't need to understand them to know that they're good.

Brand Champagne has drawn its strength from the big names in the business: Moët & Chandon, Ruinart, Veuve Clicquot and many others. But

as more of the *récoltants-manipulants* are successful in marketing their own products, the traditional relationship of mutual dependence between them and the Champagne houses becomes more fragile.

Keen to expand their empires, but with no land left to buy or plant in Champagne, three of the region's biggest players are rumoured to have invested in the chalky slopes of England's South Downs, a terroir that is considered similar to that in Champagne.

Getting There

There are dozens of daily trains and flights from London to Paris. The journey from Paris to Reims is only an hour by car or taxi, or one and a half hours by train. A 45-minute Paris-Reims TGV connection should be in place by the time of publication.

Cars are easily hired from either Paris Charles de Gaulle airport or Paris Gare du Nord Eurostar terminal. From the airport, take the A1/E19 towards Paris, fork left onto the A3/E15, then follow signs for Marne la Vallée and the E50/A4. From the Gare du Nord, head east towards Place de la République, then follow signs to Charenton, joining the E50/A4 to Reims.

The ferry makes most sense if you're planning to restock your cellars. Champagne's proximity to the UK has long made this a favourite option amongst Brits. From Calais simply follow the autoroute signs for Reims, a 170-mile journey.

For cyclists travelling with their own bikes, the Eurostar will carry them for an extra £20, or you can wheel them onto ferries at no extra cost. Air travel is not recommended, as baggage handlers will show little respect to your beloved machine. Check the timetables on the net to see which French trains take bicycles. ⑂ www.sncf.com

If you wish to hire a bike once in France, be warned that you cannot do so in Reims. Either organise things in Paris, or reserve one in advance from Champagne's only suitable bike hire centre, in Epernay: Espace Aquatique Balléo (The Swimming Baths). ✉ **Parc Roger Menu (off avenue Maréchal Foch)** ① **03 26 53 35 60** ⑂ **www.ccefc.fr**

Weather, climate and the best time to visit

By arriving in Champagne in mid-May, I had missed the departure of the bitterly cold *champenois* winter – *les saints de la glace* – by a mere few days. I decided to begin my tour of France's cool climate in Champagne partly as it has a surprisingly low spring rainfall. Unfortunately, by the beginning of June 2006 the weather was still unusually chilly.

The Champagne countryside has a deceptively tranquil complexion in spring. As the buds burst on the vines and leaves start to appear, so the worries of the growing season begin. The risk of rot and even of frost at this time of year is still great, so a glance at most vineyards reveals energetic spraying of the vines. The plants also need to be pulled upright and brought within their training wires as their growth becomes more vigorous, and any branches not destined to produce fruit must be removed.

In the second week of June the cloudy skies suddenly made way for a sun hot enough to make a Bedouin swoon. Muttering began in the vineyards about the infamous 2003 heatwave, in which grapes cooked on the vines, yields were dramatically reduced and the juice lacked acidity. Grape prices were forced up, and Champagne houses needed to dig deep into their precious stocks of reserve wines.

2003 was an exceptional year all over France, but the climate of Champagne is generally a harsh one. Feeling the dramatic seasonal temperature variation of its northern continental situation, and the cool wind and the rain from the Atlantic, the winemakers regard this as both Champagne's Achilles' heel and her unique strength, essential for the slow but sure ripening of grapes needed for champagne production.

It is worth braving the weather's unpredictability at this time of year, since you will share the place with fewer Belgian tourists than from late June, and find more wineries and restaurants open than in August. There is a festive feel in September and October around harvest time, but many of the smaller wineries will be short of the time necessary to provide an unhurried welcome.

Landscape, terroir & grape varieties

Previous visits to the Champagne vineyard had left me with fond memories of soft sunshine, greenery and…"rolling hills". So it was with mild apprehension that I pedalled towards the Montagne de Reims, south of the city. But at under 300 metres at its highest point, this "mountain" is a more kindly adversary than it sounds, and the wine villages are mostly bunched together along its lower slopes.

The Montagne de Reims is the beginning of Pinot Noir country in Champagne. On the less well exposed north facing slopes nearest Reims, this black-skinned grape produces delicate, headily perfumed wines, with a strong backbone of acidity. Further south around Aÿ and Bouzy, the southern exposure permits greater ripeness, giving wines with a fuller body. The latter of these villages is well known for the production of still Côteaux Champenois wines, particularly of the red variety. Rarely exported, largely on the grounds of its expense, Côteaux Champenois Rouge from a fine producer can be a deliciously light, cherry-scented wine. The powerfully fruity, but less ageworthy black Pinot Meunier grape is also planted in smaller quantities, as is the Chardonnay. This last gives champagnes with delicate floral aromas when planted on the Montagne de Reims.

South of Epernay the east-facing slopes of the Côte des Blancs are uniquely suited to growing Chardonnay vines. Although Chardonnay represents only about a quarter of all Champagne grapes, which fetch a correspondingly high price, this is the only grape grown in the area between Epernay and Le Mesnil-sur-Oger. Here it produces wines with crisp citrus and mineral flavours, which in time develop hints of biscuit, brioche and honeycomb.

The ripest, fullest Pinots Noir and Meunier are planted on the mainly south-facing slopes of the Marne Valley, following the river west from Cumières and Hautvillers towards Dormans and Château-Thierry.

The secret of Champagne's grape cultivation is the chalk, or *la craye*, which forms the subsoil for the entire region. This is the same chalk that continues northwest under the English Channel, rearing up in Dover as its famous white cliffs. The chalk retains valuable moisture and warmth needed by the vines during the growing season, and provides a source of nitrogen for the grapes, which aids yeast activity during fermentation.

Topsoils vary in depth and type throughout Champagne. Deeper soils contain more clay and alluvial matter nearer the River Marne, and are stonier and shallower on the hillsides. But it is vineyard aspect and gradient, rather than soil variation, that best explains differences in terroir, and therefore wine styles, in Champagne.

The history of champagne wine

Vines have been grown in Champagne since the 1st century AD, although champagne as we know it dates only from the late 1600s. Before then the still wines of Champagne enjoyed considerable renown in the nearby royal court of Paris, but were dogged by the habit of prematurely ending their fermentations following the harvest with the onset of the cold Champagne winter. The residual yeast and sugar would cause the fermentations to fire up again the following spring after the wine was bottled. The trapped carbon dioxide created bubbles in the finished wine, often causing the bottles to explode.

It was the Benedictine monk Dom Pierre Pérignon, cellarmaster of the abbey at Hautvillers, who first studied the wine's second fermentation in bottle. Pérignon's important legacy to the region was the art of blending wines from different vineyards, grapes and vintages to give balance to the finished product. Only later did he develop a taste for the bubbles, deliberately provoking the wine's second fermentation, or *prise de mousse*.

The 17th century also saw the introduction of tougher glass bottles from northern England and the revolutionary new cork stopper from Portugal. It was the combination of these new technologies that allowed the immense pressure created by the wine's *prise de mousse* to be harnessed, yielding a relatively safe method of creating the wine we now know and love.

It was another Benedictine monk, Dom Ruinart from Reims, who introduced his nephew, Nicholas Ruinart to this new sparkling brew. Noting the downturn in his family's drapery business, the young Ruinart decided to invest in the production of this new style of wine, creating the first champagne house in Reims in 1729.

By now, the wine's second fermentation in bottle was encouraged by the addition of *liqueur de tirage*, a solution of cane sugar and yeast, to the light, acidic still wine following its first fermentation. The bottles were then carefully stacked in the Roman chalk pits 30 metres beneath the streets of Reims and Epernay. A constant temperature of 11 degrees in these cellars caused the *prise de mousse* to take place slowly, allowing the development of fine, delicate bubbles in the wines.

In the early 19th century, Madame Clicquot-Ponsardin or La Veuve (the widow) Clicquot, made the final crucial advance in the development of modern champagne. Until then, the deposit of dead yeast cells caused by the second fermentation had been removed haphazardly and somewhat ineffectively, by simply resting the bottles on their necks and waiting for the sediment to collect there for removal, or 'disgorgement'. La Veuve invented the process of *remuage*, by having her kitchen table chopped in half, hinged and bored with holes. The result was the first *pupitre*, the device still used in many of the region's cellars, which allows the bottles to be diagonally inverted and given a quick twist to-and-fro every few days for up to eight weeks by a *remueur*. This ensures that all of the sediment is pushed towards the neck of the bottle ready for its disgorgement.

The champagne-making process has changed very little in the last three centuries, except that it is now more or less automated in most cellars. The extent of its automation depends on the winery's size and on the principles by which the winemaker works. Stainless steel vats frequently sit alongside old oak ones, from which wine is drawn and bottled. A precise measure of *liqueur de tirage* is added, and the bottles are aged in cellars often with computerised temperature control systems.

The romantic but labour-intensive practice of *remuage* in *pupitres* has been replaced in most wineries by huge *gyropalettes*. Each one of these enormous swivelling cuboids is able to prepare 500 bottles for disgorgement within a week. The sediment in the bottleneck is neatly collected within a plastic crown cap, and the neck of the bottle is frozen in brine solution. When the cap is removed, the pressure in the bottle forces out the frozen sediment. The wine is then given its *dosage*, the addition of wine and cane sugar (*liqueuer d'expedition*) to achieve the desired level of sweetness.

The champagne industry today

Ask any champagne house what makes the perfect champagne, and they will proudly quote you the number of different vineyards, villages and vintages from which their wines are blended. For them, as for Dom Pérignon, this is what gives the wines their balance and consistency of style. But as I talked to the growers making and bottling their own champagnes, a different story began to emerge. Their view is that the wines produced from

grapes grown only in specific villages and in single years are the ones that best represent the differences in Champagne's terroir.

The growers' argument continues that the climate in Champagne today is both warmer and more predictable than it was in the 17th century, allowing the grapes to ripen more or less reliably every year in the best sites. Nobody knows which grape varieties Dom Pérignon would have used, but since 1935 champagne wines have been made only from Pinot Noir, Pinot Meunier and Chardonnay. These three superior varieties have, moreover, benefited from rigorous clonal selection, further reducing the need for blending as a means of ironing out imperfections.

Since the 18th century, growers and merchant houses have co-existed and co-operated in a state of uneasy inter-dependence. In the early 20th century, the phylloxera louse arrived in Champagne, decimating its vineyards; and in 1910 the growers' plight worsened when the harvest failed completely. The houses reduced the price they were prepared to pay for grapes by more than half, buying cheaper grapes from outside the region with which to make their champagnes. The poverty-stricken growers duly rioted in the streets of Epernay.

The modern relationship is indeed a complex one, and is in a constant state of flux. The merchant houses, or *négociants-manipulants*, have brought the region its renown, allowing the smaller *récoltant-manipulants* to sell their own wines successfully under the Champagne umbrella. The latter group recognises their debt to the houses, and most still rely on them to buy the majority of their grape harvests. Conversely, without the growers, the houses would have few or no grapes from which to make wine for their champagne brands.

Another group, the co-operative cellars, completes the trio of champagne producers. Co-ops began to develop in the hard days of the 1930s as a means by which individual growers could combine to make, label and sell their own wines. Today, co-ops like Jacquart in Reims, Nicholas Feuillatte in Chouilly and Champagne Mailly Grand Cru rank among the best-respected producers.

All three groups are represented by Champagne's all-encompassing and extremely dynamic trade body, the Comité Interprofessionel des Vins de Champagne (CIVC).

Champagne and style

The majority of champagnes are the grower's or the house's non-vintage 'brut', generally a blend of the three permitted champagne grapes. *Blanc de blancs* wines must be made exclusively from white Chardonnay grapes, whilst *Blanc de Noirs* are white champagnes made only from Pinots Noir and Meunier. Brut simply means that the wine is dry.

White champagne can be made from red grapes because the pigment is in the grape skins rather than the pulp. The grape bunches are handpicked and placed carefully into small boxes, then pressed quickly so that the juice has no contact with the skins and is therefore not stained.

Champagnes that are dosed with a greater concentration of sugar before bottling are labelled *sec*, *demi-sec*, dry or rich. But for many, the purest expression of champagne is in its *brut zéro*, or *brut sauvage* incarnation, in which no sugar is included in the wine's *dosage*.

An elite minority of champagnes carry the date of a single year, when the growing conditions that year are thought to justify the bottling of such a wine. These vintage, or *millésimé*, wines must be matured on their lees, the dead yeast cells from their second fermentation, for at least 3 years, compared with only 15 months for non-vintage wines. To confuse, however, many of the best producers mature even their non-vintage wines for 3 or more years, and plenty of small growers bottle single vintage wines with less than 3 years lees ageing, which therefore cannot bear a vintage date.

The roller-coaster fashion for rosé champagne will mean that, in many cellars, vignerons may even be short of tasting samples to show you! Champagne is the only French region in which a rosé wine can be made by blending white base wines with red. But an increasing number of producers are making champagne rosés by the *saignée* or 'bleeding' method, using only Pinot grapes, macerated for a short time on their skins before pressing.

Only in Champagne

Virtually unheard-of on foreign markets are Champagne's once more famous still red and white wines, sold under the Côteaux Champenois appellation. These are fresh and light-bodied wines, mostly sold in local restaurants. Further south in the Aube *département*, the full-bodied still dry Rosé de Riceys is made from Pinot grapes, and is a fine partner for rustic *champenois* cuisine.

A popular apéritif is Ratafia de Champagne, a blend of unfermented grape must and grape spirit. Marc de Champagne is the fiery local *eau-de-vie*, distilled from pressed grape skins. Fine de Champagne is the rather gentler distillation of the juice from the final pressing of champagne grapes and the disgorged sediment from the wine's bottlenecks.

Wine & food

The chefs of Champagne are divided between the ones who 'cook local', and those who use fresh ingredients from the region, but deny the worth, or even the existence, of *cuisine champenoise*.

Champagne's prosperity came fairly recently, so the region has

TOP
Riddling racks, or
pupitres, beneath
the streets of Reims

traditionally served a very rustic table. Smoked ham and rich, pungent tripe sausages called *andouillettes* are supplemented around harvest time by *potée champenoise*, a hearty stew made with several different meats, sausages, autumn vegetables and potatoes.

Fresh river fish are a big part of the *champenois* diet, particularly pike, pikeperch and trout. The best restaurants change their menus in harmony with the seasons, and during my visit in May and early June the smell of local white asparagus filled the Champagne kitchens.

When *haute cuisine* arrived in the region, it introduced gastronomic wonders from diverse areas of France. Many distinguished chefs did greet my request for '*cuisine champenoise*' with a shrug, whilst using Côteaux Champenois wines and Ratafia as a base for delicious sauces, serving locally reared *champenois escargots* and *lentillons roses*, the local pink variety of lentil which, confusingly, turns brown when it is cooked.

The Champagne region is famous for its soft, creamy cow's cheeses. The best known, *brie de Meaux*, does not actually come from Champagne, but its proximity and its heritage (it was said to be a favourite at the table of the Emperor Charlemagne) make it a popular choice on restaurant cheese boards. *Chaorce*, from the Aube in the south of Champagne, is a delicious mild oozing cheese; the more pungent *Langres* is often flavoured with the fiery Marc de Champagne.

The people of Reims indulge their sweet teeth with the city's famous *biscuits roses*, delicious pink oblong macaroons, which you can buy in most patisseries. But why not visit Maison Fossier, Reims's main producer of this speciality, at their boutique near the Cathedral. ✉ **25, cours Jean-Baptiste Langlet** ✆ **03 26 47 59 84**

Champagne is an excellent apéritif; further

stimulating the appetite of the touring cyclist, but it can also pair well with food. Light non-vintage champagne is best kept with salads and subtly flavoured fish dishes, although fuller wines from villages south of the Montagne de Reims and the Marne Valley partner with correspondingly full-flavoured foods. Vintage wines can cope with varying intensities of meat, but their complex flavours are often best expressed on their own.

Blanc de blancs is traditionally a fish wine. The highly fashionable *champagne rosé* goes well with richer, sweet sauces as well as the local red fruit-based desserts, often incorporating *biscuits roses de Reims*.

Driving, cycling or walking

You will encounter fewer cyclists in Champagne than in many French regions, as the area has been slow to exploit this form of tourism. In Reims particularly, I would advise the use of pavements: you might hurt a pedestrian, but at least you won't be killed by a car! But the wider Champagne region has plenty to offer the cyclist, with pretty villages, rolling vineyards and tranquil forests to pedal through.

If it's flat land you're looking for, however, you may be in for a surprise. Whilst Champagne is no Alpine cyclo-purgatory, the Montagne de Reims and the Côte des Blancs will in places challenge the novice rider. Champagne makes sense as a short week's tour, but the daily itineraries are amongst the most challenging in this book, ideal for the more energetic wine lover!

The advantage of arriving by car is that you can stock up on the stuff, with a substantial saving on UK prices. Added to which, a car provides greater flexibility, allowing the tour to be extended or shortened with ease. You will not have to book the rural accommodation so far in advance, since the lack of any in one village will simply require driving to another nearby or back to Reims or Epernay.

Signposted vineyard trails are not so common in Champagne as they are in many wine regions, but there are plenty of vineyards to amble around and pretty villages to discover on foot. The nature reserve of the Montagne de Reims is a particular treat for wildlife enthusiasts.

Summary itinerary

A tour of Champagne should begin in Reims, the region's capital and birthplace of the champagne industry. You should plan to spend a day or two here before visiting the villages and vineyards.

The Champagne itinerary is shorter than the others in this book, to leave time for a discovery of Reims and its famous merchant houses.

Days 1 & 2
The Montagne de Reims

Champagne's Grand Cru villages begin just south of Reims at Sillery, then arc round the eastern slopes of the Montagne de Reims to the south through Ambonnay and Bouzy, joining the Marne Valley at Tours-sur-Marne.

From the village of Verzy north of the Montagne, the route leads through the forest where some of Champagne's most surprising hidden wonders are to be found. The Faux de Verzy are the startling twisted trees that have inspired so many local yarns, whilst Distillerie Guillon is one of only two French producers of single malt whisky!

From Tours-sur-Marne, the River leads west through the pretty Grand Cru village of Aÿ, home to Champagne Bollinger, and into Epernay, capital of champagne wine.

Tips for cyclists

This entire section is about 40 miles. The first day's itinerary is about ten miles longer than the one that follows, and includes an energetic climb into the Forest of the Montagne de Reims.

Day 2 is shorter and follows the Marne's course to Epernay along a pleasant riverside cycle path. The only real hill is the one that leads to the essential vineyard walk in the village of Mutigny, above Aÿ.

Days 3 & 4
The Côte des Blancs, the Marne Valley west of Epernay & over the mountain to Reims

South of Epernay, the Côte des Blancs begins and the Grand Cru villages continue where the Chardonnay grape is king. Cramant, Avize and Le Mesnil-sur-Oger are three of Champagne's most famous villages, each one quietly nestling between vineyards below and the forest above.

There is an optional foray into the Marne Valley west of Epernay, where some of the region's most beautiful countryside and best value wines are to be found.

The final day's itinerary leads through the best Premier Cru villages, beginning with Cumières and Hautvillers, Dom Pérignon's own village. Beyond the Forest of the Montagne de Reims, you emerge in Ludes, Chigny-les-Roses and Rilly-la-Montagne, three excellent Premier Cru villages, on the way back to Reims.

Tips for cyclists

This is potentially the toughest two-day ride in this book. Both days' itineraries depart from Epernay, so there is much scope for combining parts of both.

The final day is a beautifully tranquil but physically challenging 30 miles, and requires a reasonable level of fitness. Failing that, cars can be hired and trains can be caught from Epernay.

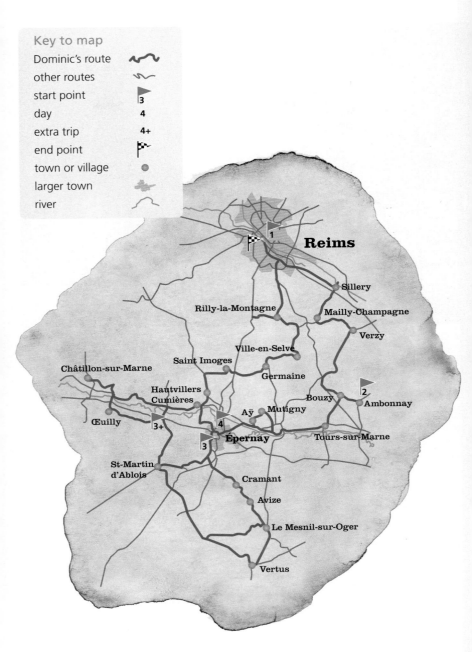

Key to map

Dominic's route

other routes

start point

day

extra trip

end point

town or village

larger town

river

Reims

Sillery

Rilly-la-Montagne

Mailly-Champagne

Verzy

Ville-en-Selve

Saint Imoges

Germaine

Châtillon-sur-Marne

Hautvillers

Cumières

Bouzy

Ambonnay

Aÿ

Mutigny

Œuilly

Epernay

Tours-sur-Marne

St-Martin
d'Ablois

Cramant

Avize

Le Mesnil-sur-Oger

Vertus

Reims

First stop, Reims

Pronounced "ranz", or sometimes "reems" by well-meaning tourist information staff, Reims is more a civilised burg than an exuberant bohemia, but its people are generous with smiles, and 'bonjours' are plentiful. The city also boasts an excellent tourist office, beside the Cathedral. So make sure you pick up a free comprehensive map with directions to the Champagne houses and other sites of interest.

My own 'press tour' of the city began inauspiciously, with an introduction to the equally French qualities of courtesy and intransigence. In this situation, British irony is the only option.

"Can I chain my bike to the railings outside the tourist office?" I asked.

"Non," said my lady guide-to-be, "Oui," said the nice girls behind the information desk.

"Surely I can leave my helmet at the desk," I joked with the guide, back outside.

"Non," came the deadpan response. "Bien sur," sang the cuties inside.

So, with the bike safely chained and my helmet under cover, I went back outside and grinned. "Tout est possible, Madame. Tout est possible!" Then I hopped on the road train with the rest of the tourists.

Ville des Sacres

Reims suffered considerably during the First World War, after which a mere sixty of its houses were left inhabitable. The rebuilt Reims is a fascinating architectural mix of reconstructed medieval, Renaissance and Art Deco; a great place just to wander round, from shop to terraced café, marvelling at a city whose spirit has survived so many assaults.

There is plenty to see in Reims, but you should start with the Cathedral of Notre-Dame. Begun in 1211, it was intended that it should become the largest cathedral in Christendom (which, sadly, it never did). The Cathedral was the site of French coronations for six centuries until 1825, including that of the Dauphin Charles VII in 1429, with the support of Joan of Arc. The stone statues carved into the Cathedral's intricate façade are more amazing each time you behold them, with their better-preserved smaller counterparts just inside the main entrance. Don't miss the 20th century stained glass window on the Cathedral's north side, depicting the history of the champagne making process.

Reims's heritage dates back to Roman times, when its quarries were dug; the same chalk pits that now serve as underground cellars for the city's Champagne houses. The only other remnants of Roman rule are the triple archway of *Porte Mars*, on the large roundabout between the *Hautes Promenades* and the *Cimetière du Nord*, and the wonderfully preserved 3rd century underground grain store on Place du Forum. Visits to this latter are free throughout the summer. ① **03 26 50 13 74**

The other 'unmissable' sight in Reims is its Basilica of St. Rémy. On the way out of town towards the vineyards (see Day 1 itinerary), the Romanesque Basilica predates the Cathedral by two centuries, and was made a World Heritage site by UNESCO in 1991. It contains the remains of St. Rémy who converted Clovis to Christianity and crowned him King of the Franks in 496.

Amongst its other many attractions, Reims includes a Museum of the Surrender in the building where the Third Reich signed the unconditional peace with Allied Forces on Monday 7th May 1945; a Planetarium; and an Automobile Museum. All these and more are worth the extra day or two you should plan to spend in Reims.

Reims at a glance

Itinerary	30 – 35
Restaurants	36 – 37

BELOW
Summer begins in Reims

BOTTOM
Splendid: Reims Cathedral

Visiting Champagne houses in Reims

Thousands of thirsty tourists flock to Reims every year to visit the city's prestigious wine cellars. Each Champagne house has thought long and hard about where they stand on welcoming these people. The rule is that either they do, or they don't. And there isn't much in between.

I remember visiting the Louis Roederer stand just outside the main exhibition hall at VINEXPO (Bordeaux) 2005. As we approached, we were greeted by two surly bulldogs behind a small desk-display cabinet containing dummy bottles of the famous Roederer vintage cuvée Cristal. "Can we help you?" they asked uninvitingly. As it happened, yes they could. My companion was a Roederer customer; someone the house regards as a 'regional ambassador' for the Roederer brand in the UK. This was explained, the chief exec was summoned, the curtains parted and we entered a world of champagne, caviar and go-go dancers.

Houses like Louis Roederer, Krug and Charles Heidsieck are exclusive crews. You're either in or you're out. Hence their embarrassing appeal to the American hip-hop scene. I would stick to the houses that advertise with the tourist office. They all make good wines, and have well organised (paying) cellar tours. Each is instructive, slick and propagandist. If nothing else, you will leave understanding why champagne is so enormously successful.

So where do you start?

I would head for Champagne Ruinart, the region's oldest négociant house and cradle of the Champagne industry. In the early 18th century the young Benedictine monk Dom Thierry Ruinart observed the pioneering work on blending undertaken by fellow scholar Dom Pérignon in the Abbey of Hautvillers. The Ruinart family had been successful drapers in Reims, but foreseeing problems in that industry, Dom Ruinart's nephew Nicholas Ruinart decided to invest in the production of champagne wine. His first sales date from 1st September 1729.

Nicholas's son Claude moved the premises to their current site, making use of the pre-existing Gallo-Roman chalk pits for the maturation and storage of the wine.

The 8 km of Ruinart cellars are some of the most impressive in Champagne, and the Ruinart tour is one of the most personal. Now the jewel in the crown of the mighty Moët Hennessy group, Ruinart retains its autonomy and its unique style. The wines are classy but expensive, based on Chardonnay from the house's own Grand Cru vines in the village of Sillery.

The tour in English is free and includes a tasting of one champagne, but it is worth paying a little more for an instructive comparative tasting with food partnering suggestions. ✉ **4, rue des Crayères** ✆ **03 26 77 51 51** 🖥 **www.ruinart.com**

The other house of great historical interest is Champagne Veuve Clicquot Ponsardin. Philippe Clicquot founded the business in 1772 and his champagnes quickly enjoyed enormous popularity amongst the Moscow aristocracy. His son François died young in 1805, leaving his widow (veuve) Nicole-Barbe Ponsardin in charge of the estate. In the sixty years that followed, the widow Clicquot expanded the business and invented the *pupitre*, or riddling rack, to ease the collection of dead yeast cells in

ABOVE
Champagne Ruinart

BELOW
Fairytale:
Champagne
Pommery

champagne bottle necks following its second fermentation, to facilitate their removal from the wine.

The visit gives a fascinating insight into the history of the family business, although the house is now also owned by the Moët Hennessy group. Make an appointment to visit. ℐ **03 26 89 53 90**
🖰 **www.veuve-clicquot.com**

Another Champagne widow whose story echoes that of the Veuve Clicquot's is Madame Pommery. In 1858, her husband died leaving her with two children, a recently established company and little winemaking knowledge. Madame Pommery set out to learn the trade from scratch, and by the time of her death in 1890, she had established Champagne Pommery as one of the world's leading brands. The Russian market held the key to Pommery's initial success, but the canny widow developed the 'brut' style for the growing British market.

The Pommery cellars are contiguous with those of Champagne Ruinart, and are amongst the region's most impressive. Above stands the house's fairytale neo-Gothic château. Visits are without appointment.
ℐ **03 26 61 62 55** 🖰 **www.pommery.com**

Many of the Champagne houses were originally founded by German rather than French merchants. The Mumm family, for example, made wine in Germany's

Rhine Valley before setting up in Reims in 1827. Champagne G.H. Mumm remained a family business until its seizure by the French government in 1914 when its owner, Georges-Hermann Mumm, was ousted as a German national at the beginning of the Great War.

In 1945 René Lalou took over and had the incredible foresight to buy vineyard land in California seven years later. The company has been passed between rival corporate empires over the last decade, finally bought by Pernod-Ricard following the break-up of the British-owned Allied-Domecq group in 2004. Once considered something of a supermarket discount brand, the Mumm label has grown in prestige in the last five years, and is increasingly recognised as a fine champagne.

Visits are without appointment, but phone in advance to join a vineyard tour, finishing in the house's famous windmill in Verzenay (see page 39).

① 03 26 49 59 70 ⌁ www.mumm.com

My final suggestion is Champagne Piper-Heidsieck, another house that makes pleasantly floral and, for a Champagne house at least, good value wines. This is where you get to taste the glitzy side of Champagne as you travel through the chalk pits in Reims's only automated cellar train. Piper has always been a favourite at the tables of Hollywood. Marilyn Monroe and Humphrey Bogart are just two big screen stars who called the house's champagnes their favourites. The Piper-Heidsieck train takes you through familiar film sets, recreated underground and always supported by a few bottles sporting the bright red and gold Piper label.

① 03 26 84 43 44 ⌁ www.piper-heidsieck.com

TOP
Philippe Thieffry:
winemaking wizard
at Champagne
Veuve Clicquot

**MIDDLE &
BOTTOM**
June festivities
celebrate the
beloved Joan of Arc

Château les Crayères
Phone 03 26 82 80 80
www.lescrayeres.com

l'Assiette Champenoise
Phone 03 26 84 64 64
www.assiettechampenoise.com

Le Millénaire
4, rue Bertin

Phone 03 26 08 26 62
www.lemillenaire.com

La Vigneraie
12/14, rue de Thillois

Phone 03 26 88 67 27
www.vigneraie.com

Reims restaurants

Of all of the French provincial capitals, Reims has one of the finest selections of restaurants, brasseries and cheerful streetside cafés. The two jewels in its crown are Château les Crayères, and l'Assiette Champenoise just west of the city at Tinqueux. Both are breathtakingly posh châteaux-hotels with double Michelin-starred restaurants. As far as these two are concerned, it has all already been said. The first particularly is a regular feature on the CVs of France's best chefs. Both are for millionaires and their buddies.

Back in the real world, Reims' centre has some fabulous gastronomic possibilities that will leave you change for the journey home. My first choice is Le Millénaire, "the Millennium". This small restaurant has a stylishly modern, relaxed feel, and is blissfully free of any pomp or stuffiness. Laurent Laplaige took over in 1999, and in 2005 the restaurant won back a well-deserved Michelin star. Seafood is the speciality here; the lobster is possibly the finest I've tasted. Set menus start at €28, and the average per-head spend is €75-€100. Closed for Saturday lunch and all day Sunday.

Get a free glass of champagne on presentation of this book.

LEFT
Fashionable:
Restaurant
Le Millénaire

BELOW
Chef Hervé Badier,
of Restaurant La
Vigneraie

Another fantastic option is La Vigneraie, just off Place Drouet d'Erlon. Chef Hervé Badier claims not to cook 'champenois', but his recipes show more than a hint of terroir. Hervé trained at Château les Crayères and his cooking retains the same high culinary standards, but at main course prices which range between €22 and €35. Champagnes too are very reasonable, starting at €35 per bottle, with a good range served by the glass.

House specialities include pan-fried pikeperch and an excellent *Filet de Boeuf Rossini*, both cooked in red Côteaux Champenois wine sauces. Call me greedy, but I enjoyed one followed by the other, washed down with a bottle of René Geoffroy's delicious Cumières Rouge.

Closed Sunday evening, Monday, and Wednesday lunchtimes. Annual closure is for the first three weeks of August.

Get a free ratafia apéritif on presentation of this book.

Something a little simpler

The city's most popular brasserie is **Le Boulingrin**, which seems to have been teleported straight from the chic end of Paris in the early 20th century, complete with sulky waitresses. If you can learn to love these, and you can't resist a big plate of fresh oysters, then this is the place to eat.

Varied set menus start at €17.50 including drinks, and change every three weeks. Closed: Sunday.

Take this book along and get a free apéritif.

At the top of Place d'Erlon on Boulevard Foch, **Côté Cuisine** serves good food for a modest price. The restaurant has its own garden for summer dining. **Show the book here for a free apéritif.**

Place d'Erlon is the (gently) beating heart of Reims's nightlife. The two most fashionable places here are **L'Apostrophe** and **Les 3 Brasseurs**. The first serves good exotic fusion-style cuisine; the second is part of an Alsatian chain that does pretty ordinary food but brews its own very good beer, which it serves in proper Alsatian-sized glasses.

The place to sip a cool glass of champagne or a hot cup of coffee while watching the Reims afternoon go by is the **Café du Palais**. Opposite Le Grand Thèatre on Place Myron Herrick, this is a beautifully decorated popular lunchtime venue which cannot have changed much since the Vogt family took it over in 1930.

Le Boulingrin
48, rue du Mars

Phone 03 26 40 96 22
www.boulingrin.fr

Côté Cuisine
Phone 03 26 83 93 68

L'Apostrophe
Phone 03 26 79 19 89
www.restaurant-lapostrophe.com

Les 3 Brasseurs
Phone 03 26 47 86 28
www.les3brasseurs-reims.com

Café du Palais
Phone 03 26 47 52 54
www.cafedupalais.fr

RIGHT
Café du Palais

FAR RIGHT
Brasserie du
Boulingrin

Day 1 itinerary (17 miles)

Leaving Reims

The Reims one-way system can be a little confusing, so the easiest way to get your bearings is to begin in place Cardinal Luçon in front of Cathédrale Notre-Dame. Join rue Chanzy one block in front of the Cathedral, which becomes rue Gambetta as you follow the road east, and then rue du Grand Cerf as you approach the Basilica of St. Rémy on your right.

Turn right after the Basilica, and right again past the Museum, then left into rue du Châtelet, which leads over the bridge Pont Fléchambault. Pass under the AutoRoute (A4) and turn left immediately into Rue Ledru Rollin. Follow this road (which becomes the D8) out of Reims.

Entering the vineyards

The D8 continues uninterrupted until the village of Sillery, just under ten miles from Reims's centre. Sillery is not a big winemaking centre, but Champagne Ruinart is one house that has important holdings here, growing fine Chardonnay for its blends. These vineyards saw the worst of the cruel hailstorm that swept through the vineyards in mid-June 2006, destroying much of the village's fruit. Sillery is also home to the first of the excellent rural restaurants, the Relais de Sillery (see page 48). For an early lunch beside the river, cross the town until you see the cemetery on your right, turn left over the canal and the restaurant is ahead on your left.

Further on, past the Relais, is the fascinating Fort de la Pompelle, with its own military museum. Built between 1880 and 1883 to protect the city of Reims from German invasion, the fort was disarmed in 1913, only to be taken without a fight by the Kaiser's army on the 4th September 1914. It was then recaptured by the French twenty days later following their victory in the Battle of the Marne.

Conquering the fort

As a cyclist, my sympathy is with any soldier who has ever approached La Pompelle with a mind to penetrating its interior. In a ridiculous parody of those brave souls, my own efforts to find a way into the fort avoiding the uncyclable N44 led to the third of my spoke-breaking incidents. Not to be defeated, I abandoned the bike and continued on foot. When I hit the fort's perimeter fence, I made my way stealthily towards its northern flank, sliding down a ravine straight onto the dual carriageway, which I was forced to follow to the fort's entrance. I will spare you the epilogue, which included rain, miles of bike wheeling and lots of swearing. Cyclists should probably give it a miss. Open most days from 10 till 5. ☎ **03 26 49 11 85**

Wine and windmills

From Sillery, double back past the cemetery and take the first left turn, signposted 'Mailly-Champagne'. The vinescape begins quite suddenly about a mile later, with the rolling hills of the Montagne de Reims ahead and the first views of the windmill at Verzenay.

On approaching Mailly-Champagne, fork right at the war memorial and then turn right again towards Champagne Mailly Grand Cru (see page 44). Past the cellars, continue along the road for about half a mile to admire Bernard Pages's bizarre totem-like sculpture, *La Terre*, in the vineyards to your left. Cross the vineyards on foot to see the sculpture up close and for a panoramic view of your route so far, north beyond the vineyards towards Reims.

Back past Mailly Grand Cru, follow the road up a moderate hill to the Champagne Mumm-owned windmill above the Village of Verzenay. This is only open for visits as part of the Champagne Mumm vineyard tour from Reims

Day 1 at a glance

Itinerary	38 – 43
Wineries	44 – 47
Restaurants	48 – 49

ABOVE
The Phare de
Verzenay

BELOW
Anne-Marie Lefèvre,
of Verzy

(see page 35). After the windmill, descend and turn right on entering the village, following the sign to the 'Phare de Verzenay'. Another right opposite the church, and a short climb takes you to the Phare (lighthouse) de Verzenay. This far from the sea, the Phare was clearly never built for those in peril on it, but served as a chic restaurant from 1909 to advertise the champagnes of the now non-existent house of Joseph Goulet. The building was abandoned after World War I, but now houses a multimedia museum of viticulture, where you can learn about the region's turbulent winemaking history, and follow the entire Champagne growing season up the spiral staircase. Audio tours are in English. ☏ **03 26 07 87 87** 🖱 **www.lephareverzenay.com**

A descent and a short climb lead over the brow of the hill into the pretty village of Verzy. Vine growing here can be traced back to the year 700, although Verzy suffered as much as anywhere in Champagne from the 20th century's wars.

Tasting in Verzy

The biggest name in Verzy is Champagne Louis de Sacy, which is on your left as you enter the village. An important house with a fine reputation, the business has been family-run since 1633, and today has its own 20 hectares of vines in five different villages. Under the auspices of young director Alain de Sacy, the house range includes an excellent Grand Cru blend, a particularly firm rosé and the complex nutty vintage wine, Grand Soir. ☏ **03 26 97 91 13** 🖱 **www.champagne-louis-de-sacy.fr**

For a very different experience, call on the much smaller Champagne Etienne Lefèvre at the other end of the village, towards Villers-Marmery. Anne-Marie and Etienne Lefèvre's 8 hectares of 80% Pinot Noir and 20% Chardonnay vines are all planted on Grand Cru Verzy soil. Natural viticultural methods, an average vine age of 25 years, and the loving touch of a small family estate allow the production of pleasant, exuberant Pinot-style wines.

Anne-Marie (sister of La Vigneraie chef Hervé Badier, in Reims) organises fascinating tours of the family cellars, where half of the village was apparently forced to camp during WWI, when the village was almost razed to the ground. Visits are free, and if you're lucky, you may get to taste the wines with some of Anne-Marie's *biscuits roses de Reims*. ☏ **03 26 97 96 99** 🖱 **www.champagne-etienne-lefevre.com**

A good rustic country restaurant to try in the centre of Verzy is Au Chant des Galipes. ☏ **03 26 97 91 40**

Spirits of the forest

Whilst eating at Au Chant des Galipes, I was asked by a couple of English tourists what on earth there was to do around Verzy. A more pertinent question is: "Where do you start?"

Opposite Champagne Louis de Sacy, a one-kilometre climb leads into the forest of the Montagne de Reims to the famous Faux de Verzy. The Faux are a bizarre scattered collection of misshapen beech trees, the final remains of the 6th century Abbey of Saint Basle that stood on the site, and was destroyed during the French Revolution. In local myth, these trees are the writhing forms of villagers-that-were, transformed by the spell of an enraged monk.

The second surprise awaits a few miles beyond the brow of the hill, after the nature reserve. Any field in Champagne not filled with grapevines is likely to be planted with grain, and a few further miles through the forest reveals why. Distillerie Guillon is one of only two French single malt distilleries, and the whisky produced here is a delicious artisanal product, very different from Scotch.

Thierry Guillon started out as a winemaker before discovering a greater love for the harder stuff. So in 1997, he established Champagne's own whisky distillery in the forest of the Montagne de Reims. Open every day 10-12 and 14.30-18.00, the tour and tasting are interesting, relaxed and free of charge.

Thierry also hosts various art exhibitions and events at the distillery. Check the website for details.
① 03 26 51 87 50 ⏁ www.whisky-guillon.com

Further down the hill, the forest ends in the small hamlet of Vertuelle, in which you can visit La Ferme Vertuelle. This is a perfectly preserved post-war French farm, complete with chicken-infested Citroëns. For a few euros, you can eat your picnic or wander among the farm's animals (free for under-13s). Farmer Jerome and his wife also sell an assortment of homemade country foods.
① 03 26 57 07 02 ⏁ www.fermevertuelle.com

Vineyards with a difference

As you re-enter the vineyards south of La Montagne, the northern exposure of the slopes around Mailly-Champagne, Verzenay and Verzy turns to face the south, improving ripening conditions and giving fuller-bodied wines.

Carry on through Louvois, and then turn left at the first crossroads to take the vineyard road towards Bouzy, the wine village that has inspired more British snickering

ABOVE
Ghostly trees:
the Faux de Verzy

ABOVE
Thierry Guillon,
Champagne's only
single malt whisky
distiller

than any outside of Gascony's famous Condom. Pinot Noir accounts for most of the plantings here, and the champagnes produced are characteristically full and fruity. But Bouzy is perhaps even more famous for a wine that doesn't sparkle, and is red. Bouzy Rouge is also made from the Pinot Noir which, to ripen sufficiently to make this style of wine, has to be grown on the best vineyard sites. Consequently, the wines have to be sold at the same price as a good bottle of bubbly, something that explains their absence from export markets.

But a good bottle of Bouzy Rouge is simply delicious, tasting something like a light-bodied red Sancerre, with intensely pure Pinot aromas of roses and fresh raspberries. A great place to try this local speciality, as well as the village's finest champagnes, is at the cellars of Champagne Pierre Paillard (see page 46).

Eating and bedding down

The place to eat, and possibly to stay, is the Auberge St-Vincent in Ambonnay, the next village (see page 49).

Otherwise, an excellent B&B option in Bouzy is Marie-Thérèse Bonnaire's wonderful *chambres d'hôte* Les Barbotines, part of the old wine estate Paul Clouet. Although the wine is now made at her husband's domaine, Champagne Bonnaire in Cramant (see page 70), you will be greeted with a glass of the estate's Grand Cru Bouzy on arrival, and you can, if you wish, taste the entire range from both estates here. Room prices start at €64; **breakfast is free on presentation of the book.** Advance booking is essential.
① 03 26 57 07 31 🖑 www.lesbarbotines.com

Ferme de Vertuelle
51150 LOUVOIS

Champagne Mailly Grand Cru

28, Rue de la Libération Mailly-Champagne

Phone 03 26 49 41 10
Contact@champagne-mailly.com
www.champagne-mailly.com

The Estate

Fifteen years ago, Champagne Mailly was a good co-operative cellar. Since the extraordinary 1996 vintage, it has been regarded as one of Champagne's finest producers. Mailly Grand Cru's champagnes now feature on the wine lists of the region's two most exclusive restaurants: Château les Crayères in Reims and L'Assiette Champenoise at Tinqueux. It also has the rare distinction of exporting fully half of its annual sales of 500,000 bottles.

All this is the result of an uncompromising quest for quality amongst Champagne Mailly's 75 growers. Established in 1929, Mailly is one of Champagne's oldest co-ops, now controlling 70 hectares of local vineyard, a third of the village's Grand Cru plantings. Vines are tended naturally (*culture raisonnée*), with meticulous experimentation including the trial planting of different kinds of grass between vine rows. Plantings are split between 75% Pinot Noir and 25% Chardonnay, making rounded, mineral wines with extraordinary fruit character. The non-vintage wines receive a minimum of 3 years' lees ageing; the vintage wines are aged for 4.

The winery tour reveals the guts of a spotlessly modern winery, and you are free to speak to the winemaking team as you follow the young wine on its journey. Commercial director Patrig Morvezen has played a key role in Mailly-Champagne's rise to brilliance. A proud Breton (is there any other kind?) and expert on all things Celtic, Patrig will have retired by the time of publication, so Welsh visitors will have to take the tour in French or English rather than their own language.

Appointments are not strictly necessary, but if you phone ahead you may receive a more personal welcome. There is no charge.

UK importer:
Ellis of Richmond

LEFT
Rosé champagnes ready for riddling

FAR LEFT
Proud Breton, Patrig Morvezen

Choice wines:

Extra Brut NV

A blend of 75% Pinot Noir and 25% Chardonnay, this wine has no *dosage* of sugar added following its disgorgement. It expresses the full purity of a healthy harvest, with ripe citrus and dried fruit aromas. A lively mousse fills the mouth and gives life to the wine's intense mineral flavours.

Try with oysters, caviar or white fish.

Blanc de Noirs NV

Champagne Mailly began making this wine in 1988. It is a white champagne made from 100% Pinot Noir grapes, a traditional champagne style in the Montagne de Reims.

It is now considered to be the benchmark for the rare Blanc de Noirs style of Grand Cru champagne, showing intense, creamy strawberry and raspberry flavours.

The reintroduction of this champagne style to the Mailly range was the brainchild of Patrig Morvezen, who wanted to make a wine that would partner well with the seafood of his native Brittany.

Brut Rosé

Made by macerating red Pinot Noir grapes on their skins for a short time (the *saignée* method), rather than blending white wine with red, this rosé is something of a luxury. It combines a gentle delicacy of colour with the pure raspberry flavours absorbed during the juice's contact with its grapes' skins.

An excellent accompaniment to rich red fruit desserts, or fruit cheesecake.

Les Echansons 1996

The finest of Mailly's Grand Cru vintage champagnes, this is an incredibly complex and ageworthy wine, of which only 6,800 bottles are made in a year. The blend is 75% Pinot Noir and 25% Chardonnay, and is described by Mailly as "a champagne of passion and ecstasy".

An almost exotic nose of freshly baked bread, spice and honey, retains the marked freshness of the house's style. The palate is both fresh and exotic, with spiced dried fruits emerging on a finish that lasts forever.

Mailly's promotions department recommends game dishes with Les Echansons. I think this is pushing it. Try poultry, lobster or seafood risotto.

Champagne Pierre Paillard

**2, rue du XXe Siècle
51150 Bouzy**

Phone 03 26 57 08 04
Fax 03 26 57 83 03
www.champagne-pierre-paillard.fr

The Estate

Half an hour late and dripping with sweat is no way to introduce yourself to any French winemaker. And Benoit Paillard is a big man. Reserved at first, and even a little intimidating, Benoit reveals himself by turns as a vigneron, a poet and a philosopher. He edits his own monthly news review on Champagne, telling stories about the region's latest events and developments.

Benoit is the seventh generation of Paillards to make wine on the family's 11 hectare estate. He explains what makes the champagnes of Bouzy unique, and how until the mid-19th century, still red wines were the village's biggest sellers. The estate is proud of its fabulous red Pinot Noir, patiently maturing in old oak *barriques* in the underground cellars. I tasted the 2004 still in barrel, which was already displaying supple, delicate cherry fruit flavours.

Sustainable vineyard management enhances the quality of the Paillard wines, as only natural fertilisers are used. In consequence, the champagnes are exceptionally well balanced, showing great purity of flavour. The estate has an unusually high proportion of Chardonnay vines on the Montagne de Reims, giving the wines greater finesse and ageing potential, and balancing the full, fruity character of Bouzy Pinot. Even the non-vintage Brut receives four years' lees ageing, adding further complexity to the blend.

Take time to look at the ancient family photographs and vineyard machinery in the small museum that is also the estate's tasting room.

Contact to arrange a visit. Closed 10th to 25th August.

LEFT
Benoit Paillard draws
samples of red wine
from barrel

OPPOSITE PAGE TOP
Benoit in his small
family museum

Choice wines:

Brut N.V

Made from 60% Pinot Noir and 40% Chardonnay, this is a blend from the 2000 and 2002 vintages. The nose shows delicate aromas of white flowers and *tilleul*, with ripe green apple flavours developing onto a full, mineral finish.

This wine has enough body and freshness to partner well with fish.

Millésime 2000

Chardonnay represents 60% of this blend, with Pinot Noir adding the remainder, giving a paler, more delicate wine.

The bubbles are fine and the nose extremely complex, with aromas of honeysuckle and minerals. The palate is a model of balance, mouth-filling but elegant, with flavours of ripe apples and flowers.

Drink as an apéritif or with light meat dishes.

Bouzy Rouge 2002

This red wine is made entirely from the Pinot Noir grape, bottled unfiltered after seven months' ageing in tank, followed by fourteen months in old oak barriques.

The result is a wine that is light in colour, with exceptionally pure cherry and red berry fruit aromas. On the palate, the initial impression is of sweet red fruits, followed by a long dry finish.

Wonderful drunk on its own, try also with feathered game.

Le Relais de Sillery

3, rue de la Gare
51500 Sillery

Phone 03 26 49 10 11
Fax 03 26 49 12 07

Le Relais de Sillery was opened almost a century ago by a female lion tamer turned chef. She left behind the career but was unable to part with her animals, so diners would apparently eat in some rather fearsome company!

Things are more civilised today, and it was on the peaceful riverside terrace overlooking the restaurant's garden that I enjoyed an unforgettable meal with Patrig Morvezen, then the commercial director of Champagne Mailly Grand Cru. The Relais, Patrig explained, is where Champagne houses north of the Montagne de Reims invite their clients for meals, and twice daily their Mercs litter the road all the way from the village centre.

"This place *will* get its Michelin star," Patrig assured me; and Philippe Vazard's light, stylish cooking certainly deserves one. In spring, a fresh asparagus *fricassée* and *crèmée de morilles* is a sublime starter, followed by another fricassée, of sole and *langoustines*, served on a bed of fresh pasta.

The cheese board is a real education, and a great opportunity to taste the delicious creamy cheeses of the Champagne region, such as *Chaorce* and *Langres*.

Menus are excellent value at between €20 and €50.

Don't call Sunday evening, Monday or Tuesday evening. This is when the chef goes fishing!

Jean-Claude Pelletier is something of a legend in the Montagne de Reims for his delicious brand of refined country cuisine. Ambonnay's vignerons might grumble about the generous selection of *Grandes Marques* champagnes on his wine list, but no one would question Jean-Claude's fantastic talent as a chef.

In a region where chichi is the rule and "cuisine champenoise" is almost a taboo, Jean-Claude is a self-proclaimed *terroir-ist*. Most vignerons learn their trade from their fathers, bringing the knowledge of generations to their work. Jean-Claude is a rare example of a chef who can claim the same. Many of his specialities are based on traditional recipes, passed from generation to champenoise generation, creatively adapted and beautifully presented.

Rustic meets refined here, but the two are separated between a Menu de Terroir for €30, and a more gastronomic Menu du Marché for €70. There is even an unexpected vegetarian ensemble at €35.

L'Auberge had been recently renovated when I visited; its décor is tastefully traditional, with a relaxed familial feel and excellent service. Jean-Claude's wife Anne-Marie offers her wealth of advice about the local area, and suggests various deals if you fancy staying in one of their comfortable rooms for a couple of nights. Rooms are between €50 and €70.

Closed: Sunday evening, Monday and Tuesday lunchtime. The chef's holidays are February and the second half of August.

L'Auberge Saint-Vincent
1, rue Saint-Vincent
51150 Ambonnay

Phone 03 26 57 01 98
Fax 03 26 57 81 48
www.auberge-st-vincent.com

RIGHT
Warm welcome:
Jean-Claude and
Anne-Marie Pelletier

ABOVE
The village of
Ambonnay

Day 2 itinerary (15 miles)
The Marne Valley to Epernay

A morning in Ambonnay

Ambonnay is an unusually well preserved medieval market town, in a region that has been roughly treated over the centuries. Stretching outwards from its market place into the narrow lanes of the village, many of the buildings are enclosed within stone courtyard walls, accessed through their ornate, typically champenois porches.

The village was an important religious settlement from Roman times; its Romanesque-Gothic style church built by the Templar monks of the Commanderie Saint-Jean de Jerusalem, who began its construction at the beginning of the 11th century. Vine growing was part of village life from around this period, and branches of grapevines are carved into many of the church's stone pillars.

Today Ambonnay is amongst the best-reputed wine villages in Champagne, the vineyards sharing the south and southeastern aspect with those of neighbouring Bouzy, making similarly full-bodied wines. The village's 370 hectares of vines make it a larger area than Bouzy.

Its slopes rise to an altitude of 130 metres, affording protection from the hazards of spring frosts. A thin clay-limestone topsoil gives perfect conditions for the Pinot Noir grape, so Ambonnay Rouge, although less renowned than Bouzy, can be a fine elegant red wine.

My favourite of Ambonnay's winemakers is the iconoclastic Jacques Beaufort (see page 56). But another essential visit is Champagne Marguet Père & Fils. This estate developed from Champagne Marguet-Bonnerave, the first estate in Champagne to be awarded the Institute of Masters of Wine Certificate of Excellence. The young Benoit Marguet is in charge of the new domaine: an exciting and ambitious winemaker to look out for. His marriage to the daughter of Bernard Launois (see page 65), in Le Mesnil-sur-Oger, is sure to have interesting consequences for both estates.
① 03 26 57 01 08 ⑦ www.champagne-marguet.fr

Day 2 at a glance
Itinerary	50 – 55
Wineries	56 – 59
Restaurants	60 – 61

Into the Valley

Double back through Bouzy, bearing left through the village, then turn left in place A Collard towards Tours-sur-Marne. Continue over the mini-roundabout, turn right briefly onto the D34, where *l'Escargot des Grands Crus* is almost immediately on your left. Here you can meet the relatives of yesterday's repast, at the snail-breeding centre from which Jean-Claude Peletier of l'Auberge Saint Vincent buys for his restaurant menu! ① 03 26 64 29 06 ⑦ escargotdesgrandscrus@wanadoo.fr

Tours-sur-Marne is home to the great Laurent-Perrier estate. Established in 1812, L-P is the largest family-owned Champagne house, and head of an empire that today includes Champagne de Castellane in Epernay (see page 55), as well as Champagnes Delamotte and Salon in Le Mesnil-sur-Oger. The last of these is considered by many to make the finest of all champagnes.

The Laurent-Perrier wines typically contain a high proportion of Chardonnay, and show an elegance that has long made them popular amongst Brits. But the house is possibly best known for its delicious 'skin-contact' rosé champagnes. "The benchmark for rosé champagne around the world," is L-P's self-proclaimed, but justified, eulogy for its Cuvée Rosé Brut.

Visitors to the estate are greeted by its cheeky stone cherub, symbolically weeing into a pool whilst advising: "Ne buvez jamais d'eau!" (Never drink water!). Phone to arrange a visit. ① 03 26 58 91 22 ⑦ www.laurent-perrier.com

In the centre of Tours-sur-Marne, the Church of St Mary Magdalene stands beside the village's picturesque

BELOW
Young talent:
Benoit Marguet

riverbank. Opposite the loch is hotel-restaurant La Touraine Champenoise. This place is a little on the stuffy side, but it is hard to resist the building's beautiful flower-bedecked façade.

Following the Marne and tasting in Aÿ

In Tours-sur-Marne, cyclists can cross the river opposite La Touraine Champenoise and turn right onto the cycle path that leads along the river's south bank opposite Mareuil-sur-Aÿ, to the village of Aÿ. Motorists rejoin the D1, then carry on over the next mini-roundabout, through Mareuil-sur-Aÿ and into the centre of Aÿ. The big name in Mareuil is Champagne Philipponnat, which owns 17 hectares of mainly Pinot Noir vines, producing fine, ageworthy, gutsy cuvées. But the one to visit in Mareuil if you have time is Champagne Billecart-Salmon, whose champagnes are some of the finest south of the Montagne (and not as expensive as they sound). Visits are by appointment during the week. ➀ **03 26 52 60 22** ⁂ **www.champagne-billecart.fr**

The next stop is the village of Aÿ (pronounced *aye-ee*), home to Champagne Bollinger.

There is no mistaking the Bollinger style: big, oak-aged, Pinot Noir-dominated and capable of ageing gracefully for years in bottle. But generalities aside, the Bollinger range is decidedly eclectic. RD, for example, is a "recently disgorged" wine, made only in great vintages and aged on its lees for between eight and twenty five years. Vieilles Vignes Françaises is made from a few inexplicably healthy parcels of ungrafted vines in the village of Aÿ, offering a rare glimpse of how champagne tasted more than a century ago before the arrival of phylloxera.

Another taste of the past is Bollinger's rare La Côte aux Enfants, a red Pinot Noir wine from grapes grown on a small parcel in Aÿ. Indeed, the village was once renowned above all others in Champagne for its red wines, apparently rivalling those of Burgundy at the royal court. But that's enough about Bolly, you won't be able to visit unless you're already buying trade quantities of the house's wines, and the same is true of their (fairly) recent acquisition in Aÿ, Champagne Ayala.

Your best bet is to plan a visit to Champagne Roger Brun (see page 58), a small family estate that is well geared up to receive visitors. Champagne Goutorbe is Aÿ's biggest winemaker and an important nurseryman, providing vines for the region's other growers. The Goutorbe estate offers a welcome of sorts, complete with arcane technical video (in French) about the work of a nursery. ➀ **Tel. 03 26 55 21 70** ⁂ **www.champagne-henri-goutorbe.com**

The town of Aÿ

Aÿ is an attractive, lively little place, its characterful main street running parallel to the D1 and boasting a good selection of restaurants. By far the best of these is Le Vieux Puits (see page 60), and this is the place to stop for a gastronomic lunch.

In Aÿ you will also find the Villa Bissinger Champagne School, for those wanting to learn a little more about the wine. ① **03 26 55 78 78**  **www.villa-bissinger.com** If you simply want to take a relaxed stroll around town, ask at the Mairie for the explanatory leaflet, which guides you between information plaques, in French and English.

Aÿ must have been an impressive sight at the end of the 16th century when its fortified walls were built, but the town took its present form in the two hundred years that followed, when the walls were demolished to build houses and roads. Aÿ's hitherto peaceful history was disturbed on the 12th April 1911, when the growers' riots in Epernay spilled over into the town, and many buildings owned by négociant houses were burned.

Once every two years on the first weekend of July, all of the champagne producers of Aÿ open their doors to the public. This is next due for 2008, so you may just get to visit Bollinger after all.

Walking in the vineyards

Well-organised vineyard walks are something of a rarity in Champagne, so the carefully prepared itinerary in the village of Mutigny, above Aÿ, is a must.

Go back east along the main street in Aÿ, into Rue Jules Blondeau, and turn left at the sign for Mutigny. After a steep climb into the village (altitude 250 metres), ask at the *Mairie* for details of the walk. Either follow the friendly explanatory signs (in French and English) in the vineyards on your own or join one of the guided tours organised from April to the end of October.

ABOVE & TOP
Vineyard walk
in Mutigny

From Tuesday afternoon to Sunday, tours begin at 9.30 am, 2 and 4 pm. Phone in advance at the weekend, or for a tour in English. ① **03 26 52 31 37**  **www.mutigny-en-champagne.com**

On to Epernay

The main street through Aÿ leads back onto the road towards Epernay, which is a quick two-mile hop. As you cross the bridge on entering Epernay you will see the tower of Champagne de Castellane looming on your left. Follow the road right towards the centre of town.

Epernay

If Reims is the capital of Champagne, Epernay is happy to be known as "capital of champagne wines". The combined vineyard holdings of the town's powerful négociant houses amounts to 20 000 hectares, their elegant neo-classical and Renaissance headquarters surmounting some 110 kilometres of subterranean cellars. Epernay's best-known houses are largely to be found along Avenue de Champagne, and here there are plenty of opportunities to taste.

I would plan to spend less time in Epernay than in Reims. Much of the town was flattened by the 20th century's two World Wars, which together damaged its patrimony more than the tourist authorities care to admit. Apart

from wine and food, what Epernay does very well is… swimming. Winemakers excepted, Epernay's public baths are probably the town's greatest attraction, and this is also the place to hire bikes (see page 20).

The houses to visit in Epernay

The two largest and most obvious addresses in Epernay are those of Mercier and Moët & Chandon. Both are part of the Moët Hennessy group. Visits are without appointment, in several languages, and will cost you money. I first visited Mercier as a child, and still remember the famous gargantuan oak *foudre*, the construction of which began in 1871 and lasted 16 years. Designed to hold 16 000 hectolitres of wine, the equivalent of 200 000 bottles, this iconic barrel was transported to the Exposition Universelle de Paris in 1889 and played a pivotal role in promoting the wines of Champagne outside the region. I remember enjoying the Disneyland train visit of the 18 kilometres of Mercier cellars, and being less impressed with the glass of champagne I was handed at the end. The Mercier visit is still fun, but in twenty years the wines haven't much grown on me.
① 03 26 51 22 22 ⁂ www.champagnemercier.fr

The same is essentially true of the standard blends chez Moët & Chandon. Now at the head of the multinational Moët Hennessy group, Moët is the largest and most famous of the champagne houses. The visit is slick and well organised, although you are unlikely to get a taste of Moët's prestige brand Cuvée Dom Pérignon. ① 03 26 51 20 20 ⁂ www.moet.com

A more illustrious range of wines comes a little further up the Avenue de Champagne at number 44, once described by Sir Winston Churchill as "the world's most drinkable address". These are the cellars of Champagne Pol Roger. In 1855, Pol Roger was one of the first houses to produce brut style champagnes, especially for the British market, where the wines still enjoy enormous popularity. So enamoured was Sir Winston with the house's wines that he named one of his winning racehorses after it. In return, the house named their prestige vintage cuvée after him, and when Sir Winston died in 1965, a black line was added to all of the Pol Roger labels. Cuvée Winston Churchill is only made in the best years, and is one of the finest of all vintage champagnes. ① 03 26 59 58 00 ⁂ www.polroger.com

You will have to make an appointment to taste at the Pol Roger cellars, as you will at the other house worth visiting on the Avenue, Champagne Perrier-Jouët. In 1858, Perrier-Jouët became the first house to show the names of villages, or *crus*, on its bottle labels. In the

decade that followed, the house continued its innovations as the first champagne producer to show vintage dates on their bottles. Chardonnay from the Côte des Blancs is an important ingredient in the Perrier-Jouët wines, which have a characteristic finesse and lightness of touch.
① 03 26 53 38 00 ⌁ www.perrier-jouet.com

But for the overall best visit in Epernay, continue along the Avenue de Champagne towards the enormous tower of Champagne De Castellane. Standing sixty-six metres above the Epernay skyline, the tower was designed by August-Mareus Toudoire of Paris Gare de Lyon fame. You can climb its 237 steps as part of the excellent De Castellane cellar tour, giving panoramic views north from Epernay towards the Montagne de Reims, east and west along the Marne Valley, and south into the Côte des Blancs.

Champagne De Castellane was established in 1890 by the Viscount Florens de Castellane, head of one of France's most powerful families. The house's characteristic bottle labels sport the red cross of Saint-André, the standard of Champagne's oldest military regiment. Now owned by Laurent-Perrier, the De Castellane cellar tour still has a personal feel – following the entire champagne-making process into the house's impressive cellars. There is an inevitable collection of vineyard machinery and a more unusual museum of old printing presses.

No appointment is necessary, and what you pay depends on how much you taste (how many wines, not how many flavours!). The quality of the De Castellane wines is increasingly impressive; and it is certainly worth paying the extra Euro asked for the pleasure of trying the prestigious Cuvée Commodore. This is made from 35% Chardonnay and 65% Pinot Noir grapes, from Premier and Grand Cru vineyards. It spends over 5 years maturing in the cellars before being riddled by hand and disgorged.
① 03 26 51 19 19 ⌁ www.castellane.com

Biodynamics gone mad in Epernay

The first house I visited in Epernay was Champagne Leclerc-Briant. I was seduced by the story of an important négociant house dating from the 17th century that has made its wines biodynamically since 2002. The tour allows the visitor to abseil into the cellars, down a shaft once used for lowering bottles into the cellars for ageing. You even get to open a bottle of champagne in the ceremonial way by cutting off neck, cork and all with a sabre!

But the wines are expensive and increasingly disappointing. Pascal Leclerc is the only Champagne magnate who has attempted to run a large *négociant* business along such rigorous lines. It will be interesting to watch this one develop over the next decade, to see whether biodynamics is ultimately feasible in Champagne on this scale. ① **03 26 54 45 33**
⌁ www.leclercbriant.com

ABOVE & TOP
Looming: the De Castellane tower

OPPOSITE PAGE TOP
Church of Notre Dame, Epernay

BOTTOM
St. Martin's Gate

Champagne André Beaufort

1, rue de Vaudemange
51150 Ambonnay

Phone 03 26 57 01 50
Fax 03 26 52 83 50
www.champagne-beaufort.sup.fr

The Estate

Just as Frank Zappa was too weird even for the hippies, Jacques Beaufort is viewed with curiosity even by his organic neighbours and with suspicion by the authorities. Having developed an allergy to all synthetic vineyard treatments in 1969, Jacques had converted his six hectares of vines entirely to organic viticulture within two years. He is therefore the father of this movement in Champagne, a region where there are still no more than 20 organic wine estates.

Jacques now works around eight hectares of vines with the help of his five sons, and their champagnes could not be more different from those of a large *négociant* house. Some of the estate's vines are in Ambonnay, but the majority are planted nearly 100 miles south in the village of Polisy in the Aube. In contrast to the full, fruity wines of Ambonnay with which they are blended, the grapes from these more southerly vineyards give wines with elegant aromas and a satisfying bitterness on the palate. Concentrated and vinous, these are some of the region's most gastronomic wines.

Often in trouble with the INAO (Institut National des Appellations d'Origine) for allowing the vineyards' own ecosystems to develop (called "weeds" by the authorities), this is an estate whose vintage wines are regularly rated the equals of Krug's and Bollinger's. Prices are, as you might expect, a tiny fraction of these bigger names.

These wines are not widely available in the UK.

LEFT
The rebellious
Jacques Beaufort
and his son Amaury

Choice wines:

The Beaufort wines are all *assemblages* of 80% Pinot Noir and 20% Chardonnay. Amaury Beaufort, Jacques's eldest son, recommends oysters with many of the wines, but I think they are versatile enough to allow experimentation with a range of rich seafoods and white meat dishes.

Brut Reserve Polisy Vintage 2001

From tiny vine yields of only 15 hectalitres per hectare, this wine was aged in large oak *tonneaux* before being taken to Ambonnay for its second fermentation.

Intense, ripe pear and passion fruit aromas show a mineral, almost candied creaminess. On the palate, fresh apples and citrus fruit give onto a long, structured tannic finish.

This is a young wine that has yet to develop its true brilliance.

Brut Grand Cru Ambonnay 1992/93 blend

The estate had only just released this champagne when I tasted it. "It wasn't ready for drinking until now," Amaury told me.

Ripe citrus aromas show hints of cinnamon and spiced pears. At fifteen years of age, the wine is clearly in its adolescence. With excellent concentration and weight on the palate, its extraordinary freshness hints at a further ten years ageing potential.

Brut Vintage 1989

This wine is a rare treat, hinted at by its beautiful straw colour and fine, persistent bubbles.

The grapes in 1989 achieved an impressive level of ripeness by the time of the harvest (13° potential alcohol), and the wine combines power and freshness in equal measure and perfect balance. Ripe apples are complimented on the nose by the earthier, more complex effects of bottle age.

The palate is a marvel of richness and complexity, revealing a wine that is drinking beautifully, but could age for longer.

RIGHT
Amaury Beaufort in
the family's organic
vineyards

Champagne Roger Brun

10, rue Saint-Vincent
51160 Aÿ

Phone 03 26 55 45 50
Fax 03 26 54 09 40
info@champagne-roger-brun.com
www.champagne-roger-brun.com

BELOW
Philippe Brun serves
a generous helping

The Estate

The Brun family has grown vines in Aÿ since the time of the French Revolution, but until the 20th century the wines they made were red and did not sparkle. It was Roger Brun's great grandfather who learned the champagne-making process in the early 1900s whilst working for Moët & Chandon. Today, Philippe and Caroline Brun run the family estate as brother and sister, and are always happy to show visitors how their wines are made.

Caroline and Philippe are both generous, amusing personalities. In a refreshing reversal of the norm, Philippe wasn't impressed by the visit of a wine writer. "Oh no, you're not one of those *Masters of Wine*, are you?" he asked wearily. It wasn't until the unannounced arrival of a couple of Belgian tourists that Philippe perked up and reached for the reserve bottlings. Then began a provocative dialogue about politics, the battles between champagne growers and houses, and Philippe's general mistrust of journalists.

The estate owns about six and a half hectares of Premiers and Grands Crus vines, from which they make their best cuvées; also buying Pinot Meunier grapes for their basic blends.

Like so many winemaking families, the Bruns have grown, diverged, rifted and developed different estates over the past century. Another to look out for in Aÿ is Champagne Edouard Brun.

Phone 03 26 55 20 11
www.champagne-edouard-brun.fr

Contact to arrange a visit any time except during the harvest. Philippe and Caroline both speak excellent English.

Present this book for a 5% discount on cellar door prices.

The Brun family runs a reasonably priced B & B, next to their winery opposite the church in Aÿ.

UK importer:
Liberty Wines

Choice wines:

Réserve Grand Cru 'La Pelle' NV

An *assemblage* of 85-90 % Pinot Noir, with a seasoning of Chardonnay, this wine is made from 50% older reserve wines and aged for 3 years on its lees.

The wine is pale in colour but powerfully ripe on the nose, with youthful aromas of apple, peach and yellow flowers.

Rounded and full on the palate, drink with exotic fish dishes and white meats.

Brut Rosé Premier Cru NV

A 100% Pinot Noir blend, this rosé is something of a house speciality; a vintage wine in all but name, it is only ever produced from grapes grown in the finest harvests.

A beautiful salmon-colour, the wine is made by the *saignée* method of skin maceration, imparting ripe, young and intense strawberry aromas. The palate is just as lively, with good body and length.

Best drunk as an apéritif or with berry fruit desserts.

Cuvée des Sires Grand Cru 2000 Extra Brut

Bright gold in colour, with a delicate effervescence, this superb vintage champagne is made from 70% Pinot Noir and 30% Chardonnay.

Prior to the second fermentation, the base wines are aged in old oak barrels, giving open and intense aromas of honeyed quince and spiced pear. In the mouth, this is a big wine, with powerful fruit, firm acidity and an extremely long finish.

Philippe Brun recommends grilled lobster, sushi and even creamy cheese as food partners.

RIGHT
Caroline Brun with one of the estate's traditional 'basket' grape presses

Restaurant Le Vieux Puits
18, rue Roger Sondag
51160 Aÿ

Phone 03 26 56 96 53
Fax 03 26 56 96 54
www.perso.orange.fr/levieuxpuits

Hidden in a discreet enclosed courtyard near the centre of Aÿ, young chef-patissier Eric Aubert and his wife Sylvie run the relatively new but already much-acclaimed restaurant Le Vieux Puits ("the old well").

"We're already in dozens of guide books," Eric told me, proudly indicating a bookshelf in the corner of the dining room. This struck me as rather like tempting a potential suitor by boasting of past romantic exploits, but my appetite returned when Eric brought in the platter of fresh mullet he had bought from market earlier that morning. Eric is clearly a chef for whom fresh, seasonal products are indispensable, and this is the reason for the restaurant's considerable popularity.

The wine list begins with the 'Sélection du Sommelier', a choice of delicious champagnes from the villages around Aÿ, each at a very reasonable €38. Set menus start at €30, with a choice of fresh meat or fish.

Le Vieux Puits has an interesting shop where you can buy rare local specialities such as Bollinger's Aÿ Rouge *La Côte des Enfants*, at retail prices.

Closed all day Wednesday and Thursday.

Present this book for a free digestif *Marc de Champagne* from the Aÿ distillery Jean Goyard, if you dare!

Epernay restaurants
My favourite eateries in Epernay are two charming, low-key establishments near the town centre. Very different in style, both are friendly and informal, serving great food without a hint of pretentiousness.

La Cave à Champagne is the more rustic of the pair. A mere €16.50 buys a quintessentially Champenois 3-course meal, from the aptly named *Menu Sympa*. The more gastronomic *Menu Gourmand* comes in at €32; or you can choose from another 3-course selection for €40, which includes a different glass of champagne to match each course.

Chef Bernard Ocio is a fanatical champagne lover, and his passion is expressed in a wine list that features an entire explanatory page on each one of his favourite producers. Bernard likes to leave the kitchen when he can, to meet his guests, so you will probably get to compliment him on his culinary creations.

Epernay's other great restaurant, **La Table Kobus**, is where the town's champagne houses entertain their guests. But the beauty is that everyone is equally welcome here: locals, tourists, children, and even sweaty cyclists.

Owner Serge Hercher adds a unique warmth to La Table, always keen to offer his advice on the wine list and menu; always with a beaming smile. Serge's right-hand-man Thierry Sidan prepares delicious dishes that are both traditional and progressive. Having worked at, amongst others, the legendary Hôtel de Crillon in Paris, Thierry is a chef of outstanding pedigree. He nonetheless ignores the fashion for "sculpture-cuisine", believing that food is about gastronomic pleasure rather than artistic decoration.

Menus start at €20, and, extraordinarily, you are free to bring your own wine. The idea is that if the winemakers do it, why shouldn't anyone else? This practice has inevitably put the wind up other restaurateurs within a 50-mile radius!

Present the book and receive a free ratafia apéritif (although this might be pushing it if you arrive brandishing your own plonk).

Closed Sunday evening, all day Monday and Thursday evening; also for 15 days in August.

Two further, gastronomic options are **Les Cépages** and **Les Berceaux**. The former is particularly well appreciated for its excellent wine list; the latter incorporates a bistro, gastronomic restaurant and a good value hotel (see page 91).

La Cave à Champagne
16, rue Gambetta
(Off Place de la République)

Phone 03 26 55 50 70
www.la-cave-a-champagne.com

La Table Kobus
3 rue Dr Rousseau
(Behind Eglise Notre-Dame)

Phone 03 26 51 53 53
www.latablekobus.com

Les Cépages
16, rue de la Fauvette

Phone 03 26 55 16 93
www.lescepages-epernay.com

Les Berceaux
13, rue des Berceaux

Phone 03 26 55 28 84
www.lesberceaux.com

RIGHT
Serge Harcher with right-hand-man Thierry Sidan, on his left

OPPOSITE PAGE TOP
Chef Eric Aubert

OPPOSITE PAGE BOTTOM
Bernard Ocio chats with customers at La Cave à Champagne

Day 3 itinerary (30+ miles)
The Côte des Blancs

Leaving Epernay and climbing the Côte

From Place de la République in Epernay, take rue Eugène Mercier out of the town centre. Stay in the left lane, cross the mini-roundabout and turn right in front of the Church of St. Peter and St. Paul, then left onto avenue Maréchal Foch.

Continue over the first mini-roundabout, then before turning right at the next one into the village of Pierry, turn left instead and pay a visit to La Chocolaterie Thibaut where guided visits (in French and English) show how artisanal products can be crafted from chocolate alone.
☎ 03 26 51 58 04 ⌂ www.chocolaterie-thibaut.com

Continue to the centre of Pierry, and don't miss the left turn signposted 'Cuis' and 'Avize' off place Henri Leblanc. Over the crossroads at the top of the hill, the rolling slopes of the Côte des Blancs appear ahead beneath the forest that follows the vineyards all the way to Vertus.

Turn left at the next junction, then right at the mini-roundabout towards Cramant. A moderately tough two-and-a-half-mile climb takes you through the village of Cuis and into the centre of Cramant.

Famous names, ghostly streets

Cramant is the first of the prestigious village names of the Côte des Blancs. This is the start of Chardonnay country, and the spiritual home of *blanc de blancs* champagne. In short, a strange place to find neither shop nor decent restaurant! The winery to visit in Cramant is Champagne Bonnaire (see page 70). Pass the village post office and take the next right, followed by a left turn down the hill and another right as the road forks in two. Champagne Bonnaire is the large building on your right.

The next village is Avize. At least as famous as Cramant, and for the same reasons, Avize would teach me not to judge a wine village by its size on the map. I had planned to spend a week in Avize, and arrived late on a June afternoon with tumbleweed blowing through my spokes. Avize is the size of a small town, but its only eatery, a pizza takeaway, closed for a week the day I arrived. There was rumoured to be a gastronomic restaurant in the planning at the time of writing, so watch this space.

Champagne in Avize

My lodgings in Avize were some rough digs occupied mainly by students of the village's famous *Lycée Viticole de la Champagne*, the training ground for some of France's top winemaking talent. The lycée owns its own nine hectares of vines, mainly on the Côte des Blancs, and every year sells a part of its Chardonnay crop to the houses of Veuve Clicquot Ponsardin and Pommery in Reims. The lycée bottles and markets its own wines under the Champagne Sanger label and these are, as you might expect, very well made.

The students organise various tasting weekends, and details of these are posted on the lycée's website. Cellar visits are possible at other times on request. The Champagne Sanger shop is open all week, and can be found just off the D10 in Avize on Rampart du Midi. ① 03 26 57 79 79 ⑦ www.lycee-avize.fr ⑦ www.sanger.fr

The winery of serious interest in Avize is Domaine Jacques Selosse. The show is run by Anselme Selosse, a man I have heard described as "the best known of the unknown champagne producers". Anselme's cult popularity has made him a very busy man, so advance appointments are essential here, as is an open mind vis-à-vis organic and biodynamic viticulture. But Anselme is

Day 3 at a glance

Itinerary	62 – 67
Extra Itinerary	68 – 69
Wineries	70 – 73
Restaurants	74 – 75

BELOW & BOTTOM
Entering the Côte des Blancs

ABOVE
Cult winemaker
Anselme Selosse
disgorges a bottle
by hand

**OPPOSITE PAGE
TOP & MIDDLE**
Oger

BOTTOM
Champagne Launois,
Le Mesnil-sur-Oger

not interested in certification for his troubles; his is a thoroughly individual approach to winemaking, and the wines he creates have very few comparisons in the region.

Anselme belongs to the laissez-faire school of natural viticulture. Nature is more powerful than man and should be allowed to take its course, explains Anselme. My interest whetted, I asked a question that provoked a surprising response:

"Why not use the residual sugar in your ripest grapes for both the first and the second (bottle) fermentations, instead of adding cane sugar to provoke the latter?" This is, after all, a common practice amongst winemakers in the Loire Valley.

Anselme was way ahead of me. "I already have," he replied, and added that this was the technique advised by France's most famous viticulturist, Dr. Guyot, for making the purest of champagnes. Anselme then produced the letter he had received from the authorities forbidding the commercialisation of such wines as *appellation contrôlée Champagne*. His method is apparently considered un-champenois by the region's own representatives, who yet again, seem frightened of rocking such a buoyant vessel!

The estate is "hidden" at 22, rue Ernest Vallé, a one-way street below the main square in Avize. ① **03 26 57 53 56**

Europe's prettiest village

A mile after Avize is the smaller village of Oger, where the blood returns to the pale face of the Côte des Blancs. Oger was the proud winner of a gold medal in the 2005 *Concours Européen des Villes & Villages Fleuris* (European towns and villages in bloom). Take time to climb Oger's small cobbled streets amongst its ornamental fountains, up towards the village's 400 hectares of Chardonnay vines. The flower boxes from which the village's fame derives are crafted from old wash basins, wine barrels and other things close to its heritage. The 12th and 13th century Church of Saint-Laurent is particularly interesting, with its Romanesque porch and bell tower and a later Gothic choir.

On entering the village, a winery worth visiting is Champagne Jean Milan, a small grower-turned-négociant whose wines epitomise the elegant Côte des Blancs style, and are very keenly priced. Within its small courtyard, the winery also has a couple of good B&B rooms, which require advance booking. ① **03 26 57 50 09** ⏺ **www.champagne-milan.com**

Another Oger champagne house, Henry de Vaugency, owns the recently renamed Museum of Love and its 19th Century Traditions in the village centre. This is not the sort of museum you expect to be interactive, but you can admire some 600 jewels, gifts of courtship and items of nuptial clothing.

The estate also owns several decent *chambres d'hôte* rooms.
① **03 26 57 50 89** ⏺ **www.mariage-et-champagne.com**

Le Mesnil-sur-Oger

This next village is surely the most famous of the Côte des Blancs. Home to the Krug-owned Clos-de-Mesnil vineyard, the village also boasts the residency of Salon, that most prestigious of all Champagne houses. Laurent-Perrier bought Salon in 1989, but the house still only produces vintage wines, and then only in the very best years, preferring to sell its grapes rather than make a wine that falls anywhere short of perfection. Salon is, I'm afraid, out of bounds for tourists. The estate to visit in Le Mesnil-sur-Oger is Champagne Launois Père & Fils, which is on your right as you enter the village.

Bernard Launois makes fresh, full-flavoured champagnes from his 22 hectares of Chardonnay vines in the Côte des Blancs, as well as a further 12 hectares further south in Sézanne. He sells grapes to the big houses such as Moët & Chandon and Lanson, then picks those for his own cuvées a week later, adding complexity and structure to the wines.

Champagne Launois also houses an excellent museum, which is constantly being extended into the cellars beneath the estate. Here you will find a large collection of manual juice pumps, gigantic ancient wine presses and various eclectic viticultural artefacts, bought as junk forty years ago and now worth a fortune! The guided tour finishes in Champagne's most elegant underground tasting room. ① 03 26 57 50 15 ⊕ www.champagne-launois.fr

But there are countless excellent small growers in Le Mesnil. Pierre Moncuit is not well known in the UK, but this estate has long dazzled the French market with its gorgeous *blanc de blancs* champagnes. ① 03 26 57 52 65 ⊕ www.pierre-moncuit.fr

Another great vigneron I found in the town centre is Champagne Michel Turgy, an estate that produces exceptional wines of surprising value. ① 03 26 57 53 43 ⊕ www.champagne-turgy.com

Le Mesnil-sur-Oger breaks the spell of hunger and forms an oasis in the gastronomic desert of the Côte des Blancs, with Restaurant Le Mesnil (see page 74). If you need somewhere to stay, the charming Madame Baradon of Champagne Baradon-Michaudet runs an excellent B & B in a small courtyard just off the village's Grande Rue, and somehow still finds time to make the estate's wine! ① 03 26 57 19 70 ⊕ www.champagne-baradon-michaudet.com

A stroll around Le Mesnil

Continue up the road past the restaurant until you reach the village church on your right. Directly opposite is the opening to the church's peaceful grotto, accurately modelled on the one at Lourdes. This is a perfect place to relax for a while, or even to take a picnic.

Beyond the church you can either climb left into the vineyards for a view of the town – a road which leads out towards Villers-aux-Bois (see below) – or turn right back into the town centre where you will pass the well-renowned village co-operative cellar Champagne Le Mesnil Grand Cru. ✉ **32, rue charpentier Laurain** This opens its doors to the public for free tastings on certain Saturdays in June and July. Check the website for details. ☎ **03 26 57 53 23** 🕐 **www.union-champagne.fr**

To the (virtuous) end of the Côte

If you still have time and energy to spare, a further three miles from Le Mesnil-sur-Oger is the village of Vertus, or "Virtues". There is a minor, quite hilly road that leaves Le Mesnil south through the vineyards, although this is forbidden for motorists and a little rough for road bikes in wet conditions. The easiest thing is to bite the bullet and take the D9.

ABOVE
Le Mesnil's peaceful grotto

**LEFT
TOP, MIDDLE &
BOTTOM**
The Launois cellars and underground wine museum

The Vertus vineyard is big, at 520 hectares, and this is split fairly equally between plantings of Pinot Noir and Chardonnay. The town is less well known than those further north on the Côte; the only two large houses that own any land here are Louis Roederer and Veuve Clicquot. Duval-Leroy is the biggest name in Vertus, and Pierre Larmandier is the town's most interesting grower (see page 72). The Larmandier-Bernier winery is on the outskirts of town in the direction of Bergères-les-Vertus – check the domaine's excellent website for further details.

If the Côte has left you tired and hungry, the Hostellerie de la Reine Blanche (The White Queen) is a pleasant chalet-style hotel with a decent restaurant. Rooms are available from €75. ☎ **03 26 52 20 76**
⌂ **www.hotel-reine-blanche.com**

Back through the Forest of Vertus

Climb the hill on the D36 towards the Forest from Vertus, towards Villers-aux-Bois. Continue through Villers and follow the D36 as it forks right towards St-Martin d'Ablois.

A right turn here takes you back towards Epernay through Pierry on the D11. The first village you pass through is Vinay, where you can eat at the Hostellerie la Briqueterie, one of Champagne's best hotel-restaurants (see page 75).

The alternative is to continue through St-Martin d'Ablois along the D22 towards Vauciennes and into the western Marne Valley (see below).

Day 3 extra trip (15-20 miles) the Marne Valley west of Epernay

This added loop is short but hilly. It works well as an extra day by bike, or as part of one by car. In the latter case, it is also worth visiting the town of Dormans west along the N3 south of the River or on its north bank following the D1. Dormans has an excellent tourist office, housed within the town's splendid château.

The south bank

The trip begins in the village of Vauciennes, which spreads outwards from its small church: a fascinating higgledy-piggledy of preserved archways, reconstructed walls and filled-in windows. The direct road to Boursault does not allow cars, so motorists will have to turn right towards Damery and, instead of crossing the River, turn left onto the N3 and then left again back up the hill to Boursault.

Boursault is best known for its neo-Renaissance Château, built for the widow Veuve Clicquot in 1843. Used as a military hospital during the 2nd World War, the Château is now owned by the Fringhian family. You can taste the wines the family produces (except on Tuesday and Wednesday), but the Château itself is a private residence and not open to the public. ① **03 26 58 42 21** ⌂ **www.champagnechateaudeboursault.fr**

A few miles further along the D222 is the village of Œuilly. Pronounced as an exclamation of something between surprise and revulsion, this village is where my trip began in mid-May 2006, at Champagne Tarlant, where I waited days for my bike to arrive.

This part of the Marne Valley is Pinot Meunier country, giving the wines an intense immediate fruitiness and a pleasantly rounded palate. Apart from making wonderful champagnes, the Tarlants offer Champagne's best welcome. And their *chambres d'hôte* rooms, housed in the one-time grape pickers' digs, are worth the advance booking they require.
① **03 26 58 30 60** ⌂ **www.tarlant.com**

Another essential visit is the Ecomusée d'Œuilly. The theme here is the 19th century; the friendly guided visit takes you around a preserved vigneron's house, the old village school and a distillery. Amazingly, this museum is open all year round. ① **03 26 57 10 30** ⌂ **www.ecomusee-ecole.com**

Champagne TARLANT

Across the River

Follow the road down through Œuilly, cross the N3 and then the bridge to Binson-et-Orquigny. In the centre of the village, a left turn leads up to Villers-sous-Châtillon. This is where I found Champagne Jacky Charpentier, the producer of some of the region's best-value wines. The estate also runs a comfortable *gîte*, and provides good value rustic meals to complement the family's champagnes. ☎ 03 26 58 05 78
✆ champagnejcharpentier@wanadoo.fr

Just beyond Villers-sous-Châtillon is Châtillon-sur-Marne, where La Porte Oubliée (the Forgotten Door) is a pleasant country restaurant in the Village Square. Closed Tuesday evening and Wednesday.
☎ 03 26 58 37 58

Châtillon is also home to an example of the lesser-spotted champenois tourist office, on rue de l'Eglise. ☎ 03 26 58 32 86 The village was the birthplace of Pope Urban II, and his statue stands proud on the hill above the village where its ancient castle once stood. This park gives the most magnificent views of the Marne Valley, from where you can imagine the importance of Châtillon as a crossroads for trade and for history's advancing armies – observations which explain the castle's significance as well as its eventual destruction.

Back through Binson-et-Orquigny, follow the D1 through the rustic village of Venteuil to Damery. In Damery you will find the producer with the least likely name, Champagne Jeeper. In 1944, winemaker Armand Goutorbe returned handicapped from WWII. The state provided him with a jeep to help with vineyard work, enabling the estate to expand to its present day area of 32 hectares. Noting also how closely his name resembled that of half the Valley's other vignerons, Goutorbe created the Jeeper brand so as to distinguish his own estate's wines. The name's appeal to an Anglo-Saxon clientele cannot have been entirely lost on the canny Goutorbe. ☎ 03 26 58 41 23
✆ www.champagne-jeeper.com

From Damery, continue along the D1 to Cumières, or cyclists can take the path that skirts the riverbank to Cumières' picturesque quay. Cross the River in Cumières. Follow the road to Mardeuil and turn left in the village centre back towards Epernay (see beginning of day 4 itinerary).

ABOVE
Vineyard work

OPPOSITE PAGE TOP
Jean-Marc, son of Jacky Charpentier

OPPOSITE PAGE MIDDLE
Work in the vineyards

OPPOSITE PAGE BOTTOM
Where my trip began

Champagne Bonnaire

120, rue d'Epernay
51530 Cramant

Phone 03 26 57 50 85
Fax 03 26 57 59 17
Info@champagne-bonnaire.com
www.champagne-bonnaire.com

The Estate

Accompanying the energetic Jean-Louis Bonnaire on a tour of his cellars feels a bit like taking a stroll around a Formula 1 pit lane with Mr Frank Williams. The wine must be tested, and tasted, at every stage to ensure a perfect balance in the finished product.

With a total of 22 hectares, Jean-Louis cultivates a majority of Chardonnay vines in and around the Grand Cru village of Cramant, supplemented by Pinots Noir (5%) and Meunier (35%) from the town of Fossoy in the Marne Valley. His philosophy lies in the marriage of traditional vineyard practices – using organic fertilisers and minimal treatment of the vines – with modern precision vinification in the winery. The wines are full, creamy and thoroughly individual; the medals they win every year speak volumes.

Jean-Louis also makes the wines from his wife Marie-Thérèse's Bouzy estate Champagne Paul Clouet, now a charming B&B (see page 42). So this is a unique opportunity to compare two very different styles of Grand Cru champagne. The wines from both estates age very well. I was lucky to taste a 1988 Bonnaire *Blanc de Blancs* next to a Paul Clouet blend from the 1992 vintage. As Jean-Louis justifiably claims, you will find different champagnes to these, but not better!

Contact to arrange a visit. A nominal fee may be requested, but is well worth it for the tasting alone.

UK importers:
Wine Merchants Ltd, Warwick
Park Lane Champagne, East Grinstead

LEFT
Jean-Louis Bonnaire
monitors the wine's
fermentation

Choice wines:

Bonnaire Blanc de Blancs Grand Cru NV

Chardonnay grapes give this wine a pale, delicate colour. The nose is floral and mineral, with a subtle exoticism, and an attractive pure intensity.

On the palate, the flavours are creamy and concentrated, with notes of honey and almond.

Drink as an apéritif, with salads or with white fish.

Paul Clouet Grand Cru NV Brut

Made from 75% Pinot Noir and 25% Chardonnay, this Bouzy Grand Cru has a more intense golden colour. The nose is powerfully intense, with aromas of exotic peach, raspberry, ripe pear and jasmine.

Apricots, peaches and dried fruits make for a weighty, mouth filling wine, with a very long finish.

Try as a partner for poultry dishes in rich sauces.

Bonnaire Brut Blanc de Blancs Grand Cru Vintage 2000

With a pale colour and lively effervescence, this is an extraordinary wine still in its infancy. On the nose it shows great complexity, with fresh butter, minerals and spiced apple tea.

The palate is fresh, with a super-concentrated mix of cinnamon spice, dried fruits and creamy minerality.

This vintage champagne will age gracefully for up to 15 years. Drink on its own to fully appreciate the complex character of Côte des Blancs Chardonnay as it matures.

RIGHT
Very civilised

TOP
Jean-Louis in his
Cramant vineyards

Champagne Larmandier-Bernier

19, avenue du Général de Gaulle
51130 Vertus

Phone 03 26 52 13 24
Fax 03 26 52 21 00
www.larmandier.com

The Estate

Champagne making is a process, but champagne is a wine, and it is for this reason that Pierre Larmandier insisted that I visit his vineyards, to see where the work really happens. We got stuck behind tractors towing trailerloads of wood chippings ready to dump between vine rows to prevent soil erosion. Pierre released a sigh. These chippings are the bane of modern viticulture, he explained, and are unnecessary in an organic vineyard. Every time you add something foreign to an environment, it doesn't come alone, but with friends. Dead wood is a part of the forest, a breeding ground for mushrooms – the one thing you don't need in the vineyard!

The Larmandier-Bernier estate has been organic for over twenty years. Cover crops in the vineyards hold together the soil, preventing erosion in a natural way. These plants also drink excess rainwater, preventing rot rather than causing it. Pierre Larmandier and his wife Sophie are common sense winemakers, practising biodynamic viticulture with the aim of enhancing the influence of terroir in their wines. You won't find the 'bio' symbols on their wine bottles – Pierre doesn't believe in using this as a marketing tool – but the purity and concentration in the wines speak for themselves.

The wines are quite different in style to the more powerful, almost rustic brews of Jacques Beaufort or the more oxydic style of Anselme Selosse in Avize. The Larmandier champagnes are crisp, austere and squeaky clean. The flavours are unmasked by residual sugar, allowing full expression to the Côte des Blancs terroir. The estate includes 15 hectares of Chardonnay (85%) and Pinot Noir (15%) vines in Vertus and the more famous Grand Cru villages of Cramant, Avize, Chouilly and Oger.

Visitors are welcome, preferably by appointment.

UK importer:
Vine Trail, Bristol
Harvey Nichols

Choice wines:

Premier Cru Brut Tradition NV

This is the estate's "battle horse" (the wonderful French equivalent of the English expression 'work horse'), made from 80% Chardonnay from the Côte des Blancs and 20% Pinot Noir from Vertus. It is disgorged manually and dosed with only 5 grammes per litre of sugar – effectively making it an 'extra brut' wine.

The nose shows savoury aromas of brioche and ripe citrus fruits, with a hint of raspberry from the Pinot Noir. The Pinot also adds structure and roundness to the palate, on which pure flavours combine in a satisfying finish.

An apéritif wine par excellence.

Terre de Vertus Premier Cru NV

The epitome of a "grower's champagne", this comes from Chardonnay vines grown on a single terroir in Vertus, and is made exclusively from the 2004 vintage. It is undosed and therefore contains no residual sugar.

The aromas are immediately individual and contrasting: white flowers and minerals. The palate too is austere yet fruity, with citrus flavours and a hint of rhubarb flower on a long finish.

Try with oysters.

Vieilles Vignes de Cramant 2000

This vintage wine is made from the finest Cramant Chardonnay grapes, grown on vines aged between 50 and 70 years – the latter of which somehow survived the last war!

The wine has benefited from a few years in bottle, and has started to develop savoury aromas of brioche and fresh cream cheese.

Mineral, broad and uncompromisingly dry on the palate, this champagne will continue to age gracefully for many years, developing in richness and complexity.

Drink with white meats in rich sauces.

ABOVE
Pierre Larmandier in his vineyards, with grass underfoot

Restaurant Le Mesnil

2, rue Pasteur
51190 Le Mesnil-sur-Oger

Phone 03 26 57 95 57
Fax 03 26 57 78 57
www.chez.com/mesnil

For nearly thirty years, Claude and Yvette Jaillant have run this gastronomic gem in Champagne's most famous wine village. Claude has published recipe books in France and Norway, and has developed a loyal gastronomic following both at home and abroad. As the best – sorry, the only – restaurant for miles around, and with such an illustrious name, you would expect Le Mesnil to be pricey. But because this is France and not Britain, it isn't.

A formidable wine list features over 500 different labels, including many halves and magnums, as well as a page devoted entirely to the village's *blanc de blancs* wines. Local vigneron Pierre Moncuit's non-vintage blend is a house favourite and a must-try! But the Jaillants are sensitive to the price of champagne, and so Yvette proposes an interesting selection of local (-ish) *vins de pays* that you will probably never have heard of, but which taste great and won't leave a hole in your wallet.

The cuisine is seasonal, with a leaning towards fish dishes that partner well with the Chardonnay-based champagnes of the Côte des Blancs. The chef's Champenois *escargots*, cooked in a delicately creamy garlic and parsley sauce, make an excellent starter.

Set menus begin at €22; the average per-head spend is around €45.

Present this book to receive a free ratafia apéritif.

Closed Monday and Tuesday nights, and all of Wednesday.

LEFT
Claude Jaillant
in his kitchen

Don't you just hate it when you forget what a vegetable is in a foreign language? You look at the menu, master the meat or the fish, and your rumbling belly somehow conjures images that persuade you to overlook the fact that *betterave* means beetroot, that spectre of force-feeding from so many chlorinated school canteens.

But I knew what *betterave* was, which was why, having ordered it, I decided to finish my plate as a punishment for my own lack of concentration. And something amazing happened. I actually liked it. I did the same thing years earlier in a Sancerre restaurant with kidneys, and this was yet another proof that something horrible in the hands of a brilliant chef can show new and exceptional sides to its nature.

I didn't get to meet Gilles Goess, to thank him for saving a vegetable in my estimation by serving it with some delicious "wafer thin" scallops, but a chat with sommelier Amaury Emrchez was a fascinating introduction to some of Champagne's talented unknown growers.

You can expect to pay a hundred euros à la carte at La Briqueterie by the time you include drinks, but turn up at lunchtime and the three course menu costs the price of your main dish: between €34 and €43.

The hotel is as elegant as the restaurant, with rooms that look out into the beautiful hotel gardens and the vineyards beyond. These cost €200+.

Closed for 2 weeks at the end of December.

Hostellerie La Briqueterie
4, route de Sézanne
51530 Vinay

Phone 03 26 59 99 99
Fax 03 26 59 92 10
www.labriqueterie.fr

RIGHT
La Briqueterie's
service team

ABOVE
The Marne Valley

Day 4 itinerary (30 miles)
Rivers deep, mountains high

Crossing the Marne to Cumières

To reach Cumières from Epernay, follow signs to Reims until Place Léon Bourgeois. Then take the second exit off the roundabout and turn left across the dual carriageway opposite the *Eglise Notre-Dame*. This road leads towards the village of Mardeuil.

Continue over the first crossroads, then turn right into Avenue de Mardeuil. Follow the road for a mile or so and, just before you reach the centre of Mardeuil, turn right into rue Pasteur, which leads across the Marne and into Cumières.

Cumières

The limestone soils of Cumières are topped by a thick layer of clay, making them ideal for growing the two Pinots, Noir and Meunier. The champagnes made here are full and powerful, and Cumières is another village that is renowned for its red wines. These tend to be earthier and slightly more rustic than those from Bouzy,

Ambonnay and Aÿ further east, and are therefore good partners for country cuisine.

The name you will see in all the restaurants is Champagne René Geoffroy, whose cellars are just below the village's main street near the school (see page 82). The organic producer to look out for in Cumières is Champagne Georges Laval. ① **03 26 51 73 66**

Cumières also boasts an excellent restaurant in Le Caveau (see page 86), which is on your right just before the road leaves the village towards Hautvillers and Dizy.

Beside Le Caveau is the *Bateau Champagne Vallée*, which organises a range of daily cruises along the River Marne. These run from the beginning of March to mid-December (except on Monday), although the commentary is in French. ① **03 26 54 49 51**
⤶ **www.champagneetcroisiere.com**

Hautvillers, the cradle of champagne

If Reims is the birthplace of the champagne industry, Hautvillers is where the wine was invented. This is Dom Pérignon's own village, and its church contains the tomb of Champagne's most famous son.

Leave the village of Cumières east along the D1, and turn left almost immediately up the hill at the signpost for Hautvillers. This steep climb takes you up what is known locally as the "Côte des Morts". Nothing to do with any ill-fated cycling expeditions, the name derives from a time when Hautvillers lacked its own cemetery, and the townspeople therefore had to descend the coffins via the steep slope to the villages below for burial. The Tour de France sometimes passes by here, and the professionals apparently scale the hill with condescending nonchalance, hands behind heads. I got off and pushed, and if you're carrying heavy panniers, you might want to do the same!

Hautvillers is the prettiest of the Champagne villages, twinned with a host of European towns including the beautiful Eguisheim in Alsace (see page 344). A typically Alsatian village, Eguisheim boasts more than twenty restaurants. Hautvillers only has the one, but its Restaurant de l'Abbaye is a great dining spot nonetheless (see page 88).

Take a stroll through the streets of Hautvillers to admire the village's wood-beamed houses, its fountains and its stone washbasins. Outside many of the village's homes, wrought-iron signs depict the trade practised by their inhabitants in the 1950s: the brainchild of Jean Couten, mayor of Hautvillers in that decade; and another nod towards the villages of Upper Alsace.

The Hautvillers Abbey is the site of Dom Pérignon's

Day 4 at a glance
Itinerary   76 – 81
Wineries   82 – 85
Restaurants   86 – 89

BELOW
The village of
Cumières

BOTTOM
Rue Dom Pérignon,
Hautvillers

ABOVE
Jean Bliard and his
wife, with the
lettuces they grow
between grape vines

BELOW
Hautvillers

historic wizardry (1668-1715), but is now owned by Moët & Chandon and unfortunately not open to the public. Hautvillers has a good tourist office, in Place de la République, where you can pick up further information on the village and its surroundings, as well as a map.

Tasting in Hautvillers

You just cannot visit Dom Pérignon's own village without tasting any wine, and here there are various options, depending on your tastes and humour.

By far the biggest name in Hautvillers is Champagne J.M. Gobillard & Fils. The wines' production now takes place on an industrial estate at the bottom of the hill in Dizy, but you can still taste the champagnes, which are very good, in the Gobillard boutique opposite the Abbey of Hautvillers. ① **03 26 51 00 24**
ⓦ **www.champagne-gobillard.com**

The village's most interesting wines come from Champagne Vincent Bliard. This was until recently Champagne Jean Bliard, Vincent's father's estate. Jean finally retired in his 70s, but is still very much involved in vineyard work. Jean has practised organic viticulture since 1970; his love for the earth persuading him to eschew the use of vineyard chemicals when they came into fashion at that time. He now claims to be the only geriatric in the village who doesn't need medication! If you're lucky, you might still get to buy wines under the Jean Bliard label. Visits are by appointment.
① **03 26 59 44 38**

The simplest and most friendly experience is at the cellars of Champagne G. Tribaut, perched on the edge of the village with fabulous views into the *Grande Vallée de la Marne*. The Tribaut family has been a pioneering force in promoting wine tourism in Hautvillers, and the cellar tour is friendly and personal, revealing a very manual process; the wine's disgorgement, for example, is still largely undertaken by hand. ① **03 26 59 40 57**
ⓦ **www.champagne.g.tribaut.com**

Through the forest to Saint-Imoges

Leave Hautvillers along rue Dom Pérignon from place de la République and follow the road up the hill onto the D386. A short, steep climb takes you into the forest.

A mile and a half along the D386, take the right turn to Saint-Imoges. After two further miles, turn right in the centre of the village and continue towards the intersection with the N51.

A gastronomic crossroads

There are two dining options around Saint-Imoges. The first is La Maison du Vigneron just before the N51. This is an excellent rustic diner. Don't be put off by the Belgian coaches lined up outside: the dishes are superbly presented and the service excellent when you consider the restaurant's enormous 300-cover potential. Set menus start at a worthy €22.

Present this book and receive a free apéritif. Book well in advance at weekends to beat the Belgians! ① 03 26 52 88 00 ⌖ www.lamaisonduvigneron.com

The real Relais & Château is a mile south along the N51 in the hamlet of Bellevue. Le Royal Champagne**** is the classiest hotel outside of the Reims belt, and its traditional Michelin-starred restaurant one of the region's best respected. The very cheapest rooms here – low season – still cost more than €200, but the restaurant serves delicious lunchtime menus from about €35. ① 03 26 52 87 11 ⌖ www.royalchampagne.com

ABOVE
Tasting with Valérie Coudrain-Tribaut, at Champagne G. Tribaut

BELOW
The view from Hautvillers

ABOVE
Chef André Bougy,
of La Maison du
Vigneron at
Saint-Imoges

Fresh Mountain air

Cross the N51 towards Germaine, where the forest feels somehow wilder and more tranquil. This is a popular spot for ramblers, but a lack of signposts and trails makes orientation difficult and getting lost surprisingly easy. As you approach Germaine the forest clears a little, and for the first time it does feel like you are on a mountain rather than just a big hill.

In Germaine, turn left in front of the Mairie and then left again to visit La Maison du Boucheron, "the lumberjack's house", a small museum containing a collection of ancient woodcutting and crafting tools. La Maison is open in the afternoon on Sundays and bank holidays from Easter to mid-November. Contact to arrange a guided tour during the week. ① **03 26 59 44 44** ⌐ **www.parc-montagnedereims.fr**

Take the second right turn in Germaine, cross the railway lines and then climb towards Ville-en-Selve. Part way up the hill, you will notice a handful of vineyards with a rather strange complexion. This is one for viticulture geeks. Some of the champagne houses are experimenting with the taller lyre-shaped method of vine training, which has apparently shown some advantages over the narrow-spaced low-trellised pruning system used in most of Champagne's vineyards. Moët & Chandon is one name you will see on the plaques beneath these vines; Mercier is another.

Follow the road past the Mairie through the village and take the left turn signposted 'D33 Ludes' and 'Sillery'. A challenging half-mile climb flattens out, followed by a hair-raising descent out of the forest and into the village of Ludes. Here the famous name is Canard-Duchêne, where visits to the château-estate take place throughout the week (except on Sunday) from April to October. ① **03 26 61 11 60** ⌐ **www.canard-duchene.fr**

Double back through Ludes and follow the sign to Chigny-les-Roses.

Chigny-les-Roses and Rilly-la-Montagne

An enormous oak cask marks the entry to Chigny-les-Roses, another pretty, typically Champenois Premier Cru village with some extraordinary winemakers. The house I would visit is Champagne Georges Gardet, for which turn left into rue Georges Legros before entering the village square (see page 84). If you forgot to make an appointment, drop in on Jacky Dumangin, a producer of fresh, natural wines who is well used to receiving visitors. ① **03 26 03 46 34** ⌐ **www.champagne-dumangin.com**

Barely a mile from Chigny-les-Roses is Rilly-la-Montagne, home to the excellent Champagne Vilmart. The Vilmart estate owns about 11 hectares of vines, of which 60% is Chardonnay and 40% Pinot Noir. The wines are very traditional in style: well-structured, elegant and only showing their best after several years in bottle. The Chardonnay-rich oak-aged vintage Coeur de Cuvée is the finest expression of the estate's craft.

Champagne Vilmart isn't really geared up for visits, but I would drop in anyway. You might just get to taste something special. ☏ **03 26 03 40 01**
🖳 **www.champagnevilmart.com**

Back to Reims, or one last feast

In Rilly-la-Montagne, either turn right at the signpost for 'Cormontreuil', which leads back to Reims; or continue straight, then through Villers-Allerand to the N51, where you will find Restaurant Le Grand Cerf on the opposite side of the road a little way up the hill (see page 89).

Returning to Reims, pass the church in Rilly-la-Montagne and follow the D409, which joins the D9 to Reims. At the roundabout on the outskirts of the city, take the second exit to 'Cormontreuil centre', and then turn right on the corner. You should recognise the crossroads when you reach the centre of Cormontreuil; a left turn takes you back into Reims along the same road by which the tour begins.

Champagne René Geoffroy

150, rue du Bois des Jots
51480 Cumières

Phone 03 26 55 32 31
Fax 03 26 54 66 50
Info@champagne-geoffroy.com
www.champagne-geoffroy.com

The Estate

This is a grower who should by now need no introduction, as he appears on most of Champagne's best restaurant wine lists. The estate only makes wine from its own grapes, and has the rare luxury of needing to sell none to the Champagne houses – such is the demand for Geoffroy's wines.

René's son Jean-Baptiste is progressively taking over the reins of his father's 28-hectare estate, and immediately puts you at your ease with the warmest of welcomes. Indeed, the Geoffroy cellars seem to double up as a social centre for an eclectic mix of champagne fanatics. Jean-Baptiste explains how he employs only natural methods of pest and weed control, using wild plants as ground cover and organic materials to fertilise his vines. After the harvest, he vinifies the grapes from every one of his 35 parcels of vines separately before beginning the complex process of *assemblage*, so as to achieve the perfect balance in the wines.

For Jean-Baptiste as for René, it is the expression of the unique terroir of Cumières that is important. This is the village in which the Champagne vintage starts, its well-exposed south-facing vineyards ripening the grapes more fully than anywhere else in the region. These are consequently the fullest-bodied of champagnes.

The estate's highly reputed reds can, in a good year, represent ten per cent of its entire production.

UK importer:
Amphora Wines Ltd, Leicestershire

Choice wines:

'Empreinte' Grand Cru Brut

A blend of 75% Pinot Noir and 25% Chardonnay, this wine's nose shows extraordinary life, with aromas reminiscent of strawberries and rosy red apples.

Oak barrel ageing has left no trace of wood flavour, but has given the wine a rounded mouth feel, adding richness to its flavours. With a full body and good acidity, Empreinte is a good partner even for lamb dishes.

'Volupté' Grand Cru Brut

This wine's name really does speak for itself. Made from 80% Chardonnay and 20% Pinot Noir, fresh butter and cream show on the nose, with hints of white flowers.

The palate has a creamy fullness of body, the effect of ageing in old oak barrels; its long finish is balanced with a firm thread of acidity.

An excellent partner for sea bass or turbot; try also with goat's cheese.

Brut Rosé Grand Cru

Made by the 'skin contact' method, from 100% Pinot Noir grapes, this rosé has a delicate pale ruby colour and persistent bubbles. Candied cherries and raspberries show on the nose, whilst the palate is full, grippy and long.

Given a year or two, this wine develops very different flavours, of darker fruits like prunes and dried cherries.

Drink with lobster, crab or scallops.

Cumières Rouge NV

Made from 100% Pinot Noir and aged for a year in oak, Geoffroy's red wine is a blend of 3 different years, adding balance and making it ready to drink soon after bottling.

The nose reveals developed aromas of spiced plums, cherries and prunes. Cherry flavours on the front palate develop into dark fruits on a long dry finish.

Fuller-bodied than the region's other reds, this wine drinks well with white or red meats, but also with fish cooked in rich red wine sauces.

RIGHT & TOP
Jean Baptiste
Geoffroy tastes
alone and with
friends

Champagne Gardet

13, rue Georges Legros
51500 Chigny-les-Roses

Phone 03 26 03 42 03
Fax 03 26 03 43 95
Info@champagne-gardet.com
www.champagne-gardet.com

The Estate

You will need to book in advance to visit the Gardet cellars, and to taste the estate's characterful wines on the veranda that was once part of the Gardet family home. There is no team dedicated to cellar visits, but Nadine Meyer's impeccable cellar tour is amongst the most instructive in the region. She made even the bottling process fascinating.

Champagne Gardet dates back to the end of the 19th century, at which time Charles Gardet established the house in Epernay. In the twenties, his son Georges moved the family cellars to the pretty village of Chigny-les-Roses to allow the expansion of the business. Little more than a decade later, the German army arrived and plundered the house, and the family's back garden was picked as the favourite site for a V2 rocket launch pad!

Champagne Gardet today is one of the region's most dynamic and modern négociants, owning 7 hectares of local Premier Cru vineyard, and buying the rest of its grapes from 30 different growers covering around 100 hectares across the region. Its range is constantly evolving, and it is no surprise that Champagne Gardet exports over half of its annual production.

The non-vintage wines have long been favourites of mine; all have a proportion of reserve wines added, top cuvées from each vintage which are set aside and aged in huge 100-year-old oak vats.

The visit is free, fascinating and in excellent English.

Present this book for a 5% discount on cellar door prices.

UK importer:
Michael Peace is the UK agent. The wines find their way into, amongst others, London's Dorchester Hotel.

Choice wines:

Brut Special NV

Made from Premier and Grand Cru grapes (one third each of Chardonnay, Pinot Noir and Pinot Meunier) from across the region, 20% of this blend comes from wines aged for 1 to 2 years in oak barrels. The wine is then matured on its lees for 5 years.

An intense, expressive nose marries developed red fruit with a soft creaminess. A complex, weighty palate makes the wine a good partner for white meats.

Rosé Charles Gardet 2001

A recent addition to the Gardet range, this Premier Cru rosé is made from old vine Pinots Noir and Meunier, which are allowed between 8 and 24 hours contact with their skins before pressing.

The result is a powerfully fruity wine with intense aromas of cranberry and cherry, and a deliciously full-flavoured palate to match.

This rosé could be enjoyed with savoury exotic foods or red fruit desserts.

Cuvée Charles Gardet Vintage 1999

This prestige cuvée is made from two-thirds Chardonnay and a third Pinot Noir grapes, all of which come from Premier and Grand Cru vineyards. The Pinot gives the wine body and weight, whilst the Chardonnay lends freshness in youth and a bready complexity as it develops in bottle.

Following its second fermentation, the wine ages slowly on its lees for five years in the depths of the Gardet cellars, before being disgorged and going to market.

There are honeyed lemons on a youthful nose and a stony minerality coupled with a lemony bite on the palate. This is a wine that needs some time to develop, and can be enjoyed as an apéritif or with white fish.

TOP
Champagne tasting
in the Gardet gardens

Restaurant Le Caveau

**Rue de la Coopérative
51480 Cumières**

Phone 03 26 54 83 23
Fax 03 26 54 24 56
www.lecaveau-cumieres.com

"You're a very, very naughty boy," exclaimed an American voice as Chef Jean-Claude Rambach presented me with one of his waitresses in full service attire, complete with coquettish twirl. Political correctness can wait at the door of this restaurant, as Jean-Claude dresses all his waitresses in *bagnolet* hats and other charming garments traditionally worn in Champagne during the harvest.

"Naughty boy," repeated the chef.

As its name suggests, Le Caveau is an ancient wine cellar, a full 17 metres underground at its farthest point so you can eat surrounded by the precious chalk that gives life to the vines in Champagne, and flavour to its wines. The wine list here is particularly fine, and this is just one reason why it is a favourite amongst many of the region's chefs.

Jean-Claude Rambach is a real local personality; regularly taking part in cookery fairs in the region, he has also participated in events as far afield as the Ivory Coast and Singapore. Jean-Claude's recipes are traditionally French, with a strong hint of *terroir*, often incorporating Côteaux Champenois wines as a base for recipes he has been perfecting for over 40 years.

Set menus are in French and English, and are some of the region's best value at €16 and €42. A Gourmet Menu is served for €55, and an extra €17 buys you a different glass of wine with every dish.

Present this book to receive a free flute of champagne as an apéritif.

Closed Sunday, Monday and Tuesday evening, and all of Wednesday.

LEFT
Caveau chef Jean-Claude Rambach

OPPOSITE PAGE TOP LEFT
Traditional harvest dress

OPPOSITE PAGE TOP RIGHT
Jean-Claude shares a bottle with restaurant staff and customers

OPPOSITE PAGE BOTTOM
Ancient wine cellar

Restaurant de l'Abbaye
Rue de l'Eglise
51160 Hautvillers

Phone 03 26 59 44 79
Fax 03 26 59 45 36
www.abbayehautvillers.org

BELOW
Thierry Ladragin

Opposite the abbey in which Dom Pérignon conducted his famous blending experiments, Chef Thierry Landragin works his own magic in Restaurant de l'Abbaye. Full of good humour, Thierry prides himself on the contact he has with his customers, regularly emerging from his kitchen for a joke or a quick glass of bubbly.

Things have changed dramatically since Thierry took over l'Abbaye in the early 1980s. It started out as an open-air truck stop, famous for its rowdy summer barbecues. At that time Thierry had no training as a cook, but whenever he recognised chefs in his restaurant, he would collar them and ask to work unpaid in *their* restaurants during the winter months. Gradually Thierry became esteemed as a chef himself, and today he serves some of Champagne's most delicious rustic dishes.

The restaurant gained a roof in the 1990s. The authorities forbade Thierry from building an extravagant exterior for the restaurant, so he made up for it inside. The restaurant may have gained in gastronomic pedigree, but its familial ambience is undiminished, and summer barbecues are still a regular occurrence.

Set menus cost between €16 and €40.

Present this book and receive a free flute of champagne with your meal.

Closed Sunday evening, Monday and Tuesday all year round; Wednesday and Thursday evening from November to March. Also closed at the beginning of January and for the second half of August.

Le Grand Cerf is a civilised, elegant gastronomic establishment of the old school, providing flawless service and an outstanding, continually evolving menu. Michelin stars come and go in most places, but Le Grand Cerf has held onto its own for over 20 years.

Chef-proprietor Dominique Gireudeau came to the region in 1979, when he worked with the legendary Gérard Boyer at Château les Crayères. Taking on Le Grand Cerf in 1992, Dominique's aim was to provide simple, classic dishes to complement the wines of Champagne, in which fresh seasonal ingredients are allowed to speak for themselves.

Set menus start at €34, with the priciest costing €88. Try the *Homard* (lobster) *melon en vinaigrette aigre-douce* as a starter, or the *St-Pierre* (John Dory) *Breton rôti sauce verjutée* as a main course. Although these dishes don't work perfectly one following the other, both are excellent partners for fine Pinot-based champagnes.

If visiting in the summer, ask to be seated outside in the beautiful leafy garden behind the restaurant. This is a sublime place to cool off after climbing the hill to the restaurant, with the **free glass of house champagne you will receive on presentation of this book.**

Closed Tuesday evening, Wednesday and Sunday.

Le Grand Cerf
51500 Montchenot

Phone 03 26 97 60 07
Fax 03 26 97 64 24

RIGHT
Chef Dominique
Gireudeau prepares
something delicious

Staying in Reims

Budget

CIS de Champagne
Chaussée Boquaine
51100 Reims
Phone 03 26 40 52 60
Fax 03 26 47 35 70
www.cis-reims.com

More like a university residence than a youth
hostel: clean and friendly, with simple single
rooms from around €20. A buffet breakfast is
included, which is better than in most hotels.
Reims's centre is a 10-minute walk. Parking
and wifi are both free.

Hotels

Hotel Crystal ★★
86 Place Drouet d'Erlon
51100 Reims
Phone 03 26 88 44 44
Fax 03 26 47 49 28
www.hotel-crystal.fr

Set in a peaceful garden away from the bustle
of Place Drouet d'Erlon, Hotel Crystal is
comfortable and well kept. **Prices start at
€50 for ensuite rooms with a 5% discount
for book holders.** English is spoken.

Hotel Porte Mars ★★★
2 Place de la République
51100 Reims
Phone 03 26 40 28 35
Fax 03 26 88 92 12
www.hotelportemars.com

Reputed for its superb breakfasts, the rooms
are quiet and well equipped, starting at €69.
Patronne Nathalie Denys and her husband are
full of advice and information about the local
area. Wifi is free, as is the car park opposite.
The town centre is a 10-minute walk.
**Show Nathalie the book and receive a
free welcome glass of champagne.**

For something a little swankier, try the
recently refurbished, ultra-modern **Best
Western Hotel de la Paix ★★★** where visiting
wine merchants are schmoozed by the
champagne houses. Prices start at €105, and
on-site parking is free.
9, rue Buirette
51100 Reims
Phone 03 26 40 04 08
Fax 03 26 47 75 04
www.bestwestern-lapaix-reims.com

And if money is no object, there is no
substitute for the elegant grandeur of
Chateau les Crayeres ★★★★
64, bd Henry Vasnier
Phone 03 26 82 80 80
Fax 03 26 82 65 52
www.lescrayeres.com
Prices start at €280.

Bed & breakfast

M & Mme Philippon
21 Place du Chapitre 51100 Reims
Phone 03 26 91 06 22
claude.philippon@tele2.fr

Hidden in a small courtyard a stone's throw
from the cathedral, M Philipon's place is
excellent value. Prices start at €35 including
breakfast. He only has two rooms, so
advance booking is strongly advised. Email
or phone Mme Philippon in the evening
for spoken English.

Mme Claudine Larcher
11 Rue Ponsardin 51100 Reims
Phone 03 26 47 32 50
cllarcher@yahoo.fr

Immaculate rooms and a warm welcome
from Mme Larcher make this Reims's finest
B&B. Rooms are about €40. Breakfast is
served on the terrace in summer.

Mme Larcher speaks some English and
parking is free on the road outside the house,
a 10-minute walk from the centre of Reims.

Epernay Accommodation

Hotels

Les Berceaux***
13, rue des Berceaux
51200 Epernay
Phone 03 26 55 28 84
Fax 03 26 55 10 36
www.lesberceaux.com

Situated in the centre of Epernay, Les Berceaux is a reasonably priced smart hotel. Patrick Michelon's bistro and his gastronomic restaurant are both popular dining options.

Room prices start at €77.
Bicycle parking is for groups of 5 at most.

Le Clos Raymi***
3, rue Joseph de Venoge
51200 Epernay
Phone 03 26 51 00 58
Fax 03 26 51 18 98
www.closraymi-hotel.com

The epitome of champenois elegance, Clos Raymi, is set in its own peaceful gardens only two blocks from Avenue de Champagne.
A double room is €100.
Advance booking is essential at weekends.
Free parking inside the garden.

Bed & Breakfast

Parva Domvs
27, avenue de Champagne
51200 Epernay
Phone 03 26 32 40 74
Fax 03 26 52 97 56
rimaire@wanadoo.fr

On Epernay's most famous street, Monsieur & Madame Rimaire's B & B is the best place to stay in town, if you can get a room. Brush up on your French, because no English is spoken.

Prices start at €70, including breakfast.
Advance booking is essential.
Free parking inside the garden courtyard.

Au Coeur des Vignes
2, chemin des Crepons
51200 Epernay
Phone 03 26 55 44 74
Fax 03 26 55 44 74
Mobile 06 85 61 64 04

Overlooking the town, just off avenue Maréchal Foch, leading into Epernay from the Côte des Blancs, this chambre d'hôte is situated where the houses end and the vines begin.

With 3 bedrooms, prices start at €45.
Advance booking is essential. Free parking is inside the garden.

Loire

The Loire Valley:
June – July 2006

The Middle Loire: The Garden of France

The Loire River flows nearly 300 miles across France, from the vineyards of Pouilly-Fumé in western Burgundy through a dizzying array of winegrowing areas, climates and terroirs, to Brittany's own Muscadet appellation, where it debouches into the Atlantic.

For centuries, the Loire Valley has served as France's national garden, or *Le Jardin de France*. Its picturesque verdant countryside and dense forests made it a perfect country retreat for French royalty and their favourites until the Revolution. Their legacy is over 120 châteaux, many beautiful gardens, and an incredible richness of history. In November 2000, UNESCO made the Loire Valley France's largest World Heritage Site.

Unless you have a full year to spend, you cannot hope to 'do' the Loire, and neither, I was forced to accept, could I.

The relatively straight line I had drawn through the map became increasingly serpentine as distraction after attraction drew me in. Many of the towns along the route could happily do for a week's sojourn in themselves. The range of wines produced by a single estate is often more varied than those from an entire region.

My proposed itinerary is based on the area between Amboise and Saumur, in the middle Loire, where the highest concentration of fine wine villages, fairytale châteaux and beautiful scenery is to be found.

It has always puzzled me why the Loire's wines are not better known outside France, but more surprising still is that even most Frenchmen seem unaware of just how much this region has to offer. The happy result is that, even at the highly reputed estates, you can find excellent wines at incredibly fair prices.

The winemakers of the middle Loire are amongst the most generous and good-natured anywhere in France. Their cellars are hewn from the soft, chalky *tuffeau* rock that is so characteristic of the region, and many local dwellings and country restaurants are also to be found in these small caves, or *maisons troglodytiques*.

As I arrived in Touraine from Champagne, the vines had just finished a healthy week of flowering. This is a crucial period in the growing season, since it determines the regularity of fruit set for the harvest, which takes place around 100 days later. Having sensed unsettled weather conditions in the previous weeks, the vines held their horses, then flowered quickly, to avoid any unwelcome rain or strong winds.

The storms raged briefly a week or two later, but the fruit set was excellent, prompting the quality-conscious growers to begin their 'green harvests' in July. The sheer quantity of healthy fruit made the removal of excess grapes essential, to preserve the concentration of fruit flavours and to aid ripening in the remaining bunches.

Getting there

The obvious place to begin a visit of the middle Loire is Tours. Flights are from London Stansted to Tours airport, which is a stone's throw from Tours centre. If hiring a car, leave the Airport along rue de l'Aéroport. Continue over two roundabouts, and then bear left onto Boulevard du Maréchal Juin, which takes you over the River Loire into the city centre.

Alternatively, Tours is just over an hour from Paris on the TGV, to which you can connect directly from the Eurostar. This is the best option if you want to bring your own bicycle (which you can do for an extra £20); otherwise it is easy to hire a decent bike either in Tours or in one of many towns and villages the length of the Loire.

If you feel like stocking up on wines that you may not find outside the region, a better bet is to bring your own vehicle on the ferry. From Calais, follow the *autoroute* (A1) to Paris, then continue from Paris along the A10 to Tours, via Orléans. This is a 330-mile journey.

Arriving in Tours

Tours was the capital of France in Gallo-Roman times, and an important royal city until the French Revolution. Situated at the centre of Loire châteaux country, Tours is also said to be where the purest form of the French language is spoken – whatever that means. The city is home to an important university, and has a young, dynamic feel.

Vieux Tours is the city's well-signposted old town, where crowds of people gather in the medieval place Plumereau to eat and take photographs. The area between here and the 'artisanal quarter', across rue Bretonneau, is a pleasant place for a stroll, or to grab a bite in one of the streetside bistros.

Within the old town, the Musée du Gemmail is the most idiosyncratic of Tours' museums. This 'museum' is an interesting exhibition of images made from multiple shards of stained glass, superimposed one upon another, and illuminated from behind. ➀ 02 47 61 01 19 ⁀ www.gemmail.com

For those already thirsty for wine knowledge, the Museum of the Wines of Touraine is near the bridge 'Pont Wilson', east of the old town. ➀ 02 47 61 07 93

A colourful, vibrant market takes place in the old town every Wednesday until well into the evening. Here you can buy everything from local wines and cheeses, to your own herb garden.

Restaurants

The city's finest hotel-restaurant is Château Belmont****. The famous Jean Bardet runs the double-Michelin-starred restaurant, and is widely acknowledged to be one of France's finest chefs. Quality and repute at this level are things you pay for, and pay for it you will. The cheapest menu is €60; hotel rooms start at €150. ✉ 57, rue Groison, 37100 Tours ➀ 02 47 41 41 11 ⁀ www.jeanbardet.com

For an outstanding gastronomic experience at a lower price (€35 at lunchtime), take the N10 over the River Cher south of the city and join Alain Couturier at La Roche Le Roy. Here you can enjoy creative fish dishes whilst relaxing on the terrace, or inside the 18th-century manor house. ✉ 55, route de St Avertin, 37200 Tours ➀ 02 47 27 22 00 ⁀ www.rocheleroy.com

But *Vieux Tours* is the place you will want to visit. The star restaurant in this quarter is **Restaurant La DeuvaLière.** ✉ 18, rue de la Monnaie, 37000 Tours ① 02 47 64 01 57 ⏣ Ladeuvaliere@wanadoo.fr

A stone's throw from the old town's crowded streets and pricey bistros, Servane and Emmanuel created La DeuvaLière in 2003.

Emmanuel's cooking is wonderfully inventive, marrying French traditions with influences from every corner of the globe.

Eclectic starters on the summer menu include *Gambas tandoori* and *Avocado gaspacho*. An exquisite tuna steak is cooked rare and tender, served with goat's cheese and vegetables wrapped in light pastry, and finished with an arabesque red pepper *coulis*. For dessert, the house speciality is the *Moelleux tiède au chocolat et framboises fraîches à coeur*, a recipe Emmanuel learned on his travels, from a much-admired Brazilian chef.

Both the menu and the wine list are reassuringly short, with à la carte meals for between €25 and €35 . Lunchtime ensembles are €10 and €15.

Show Servane this book to receive a free apéritif. Closed Saturday lunchtime, Sunday and Monday.

Staying in Tours

FUAJ ' Vieux Tours' ✉ 5, rue Bretonneau, 37000 **Tours** ① 02 47 37 81 58 ⏣ www.ajtours.org This youth hostel provides wifi access and bike rental, and it couldn't be better situated. Individual rooms are available for less than €20.

3-star hotels in Tours are mainly corporate affairs, but there are some very pleasant 2-star establishments in the city centre. Two are listed below; both provide rooms for €50-€60.

Hôtel des Châteaux de la Loire** ✉ 12, rue Gambetta, 37000 Tours ① 02 47 05 10 05 ⏣ http://hoteldeschateaux.fr

Hôtel du Manoir** ✉ 2, rue Traversière 37000 Tours ① 02 47 05 37 37 ⏣ http://site.voila.fr/hotel.manoir.tours

For unparalleled luxury and refinement, however, there is only one choice – see Château Belmont****, opposite.

RIGHT
A summer
evening in Tours

ABOVE & TOP
Vieux Tours

Weather, climate and the best time to visit

A week after arriving in the Loire, I began to ask myself a troubling question: "Cool climate, what cool climate?" Midsummer in northern France is undoubtedly hotter than it is in the UK, but it is also hotter than it used to be in northern France.

By the last week of July 2006, midday temperatures were soaring to 40 degrees, and grapes were showing signs of scorching in the more exposed vineyards. Many vignerons learned their lessons from the hot vintage of 2003, and held back from removing the leaves around grape bunches, allowing them some protection from the sun's rays. But the increasing drought meant that the size of individual grapes was well below average, threatening potentially tiny yields for vignerons who had already finished their 'green harvests'.

Climate change is a big talking point amongst Loire vignerons, who have experienced uncommonly warm weather since the Millennium.

Vintage variation at this latitude has always been great, with fascinating differences in wine styles from year to year. The vineyards of Touraine and Anjou-Saumur are influenced both by the continental climate to the east and by the wind and rain from the Atlantic. The rain can cause problems when it arrives at vintage time, but cool winds are an essential moderating influence. 2005, for example, was a warm, very dry year; the grapes ripened as quickly and as fully as they had in 2003, but the wines turned out very differently. The 2003s are ripe and pleasant, but often lack acidity and therefore ageing potential. The difference came in August 2005, when a cool wind blew in from the Atlantic, causing the grapes to contract, concentrating sugar, flavour and acidity. The result is a fascinating vintage: the 2005 wines are supple and ripe, but with deliciously fresh flavours. The best will develop for many decades.

The heat in this part of the Loire is rarely stifling and my advice, contrary to that elsewhere, is to visit during high season, preferably in July. The Loire Valley is well equipped to deal with its summer tourist population, and you are unlikely to have serious problems finding accommodation. Add to which, most tourist attractions open for longer during July and August, and some only open for these two months. Conversely, outside of high season, you will have great flexibility in where you stay, and the possibility of negotiating discounts.

The weather in the first week of February might not be so conducive to holidaymaking, but this is when one of France's most exciting wine fairs, the *Salon des Vins de Loire*, takes place, in Angers. ☎ **02 41 93 40 40** 🖰 www.salondesvinsdeloire.com

A royal history

This tour broadly covers the Touraine area of the middle Loire, continuing west into the vineyards of Saumur-Champigny. This is the heart of the royal *Jardin de France*. To the west is the region of Anjou, which shares much of its eastern neighbour's history, and where excellent wines are made from similar grapes.

Touraine is so named after a Celtic tribe, the Turones, which populated the area some 2000 years ago. The Romans arrived in the 1st century AD, bringing with them the tools and techniques of winemaking. By the Middle Ages, wines were shipped from the Loire Valley to the Low Countries; and the merchants of Anjou exported red wines by sea to England.

English royal history merged with that of Touraine when, in 1044, the province came under the control of the house of Anjou, from which the Plantagenet kings of England are descended. Henry II Plantagenet became king of England in 1154, and chose Château de Chinon as his main military stronghold in the Loire Valley.

Most of the Loire's châteaux were built as fortified military barracks during the violent Middle Ages. Chinon appears again in 1429, when Joan of Arc visited the Château to pledge her support for the Dauphin, the future Charles VII of France, against English claims to the French throne.

The region's medieval châteaux were converted into grand, luxurious country homes during the Renaissance, when the Loire became a convenient country retreat for French royalty and their powerful aristocratic allies.

The Loire's proximity to Paris, and its access to export markets via the Atlantic, made for a prosperous wine trade until the 19th century, when the railways arrived, and wines from the south of France came within easy reach of Paris and northern Europe.

At the end of the 19th century, the phylloxera vineyard pest hit the Loire Valley with particular ferocity. Many vineyards were grubbed up, and the land was replanted with the apples, pears and soft fruits that are still an important part of the region's agriculture.

Challenges ahead

The extensive geographical area of the Loire's vineyards makes any cohesion between the various appellations extremely difficult. Why should a successful vigneron in Sancerre be concerned with an impoverished one 300 miles away in Muscadet?

The differences in wine styles the length of the Loire is matched only by the notorious variation in their quality. Gone are the days when the Parisians would mop up any surplus wine of mediocre quality. So the Loire's winemakers are now forced to make some tough choices.

ABOVE & TOP
Tours market

A trend is beginning to emerge, in which the failing winemakers are gradually disappearing, and their assiduous, quality-conscious brothers are increasing in renown. The second half of the 20th century saw the replanting of vineyards in appellations like Sancerre, Bourgueil, Chinon and Vouvray, all of which had suffered for decades following the devastation caused by phylloxera.

The best of the Loire's vignerons have fought to distinguish themselves, and have become powerful forces for natural winemaking. Despite the unpredictability of its weather, the middle Loire is developing into one of France's most important centres for organic and biodynamic winemaking.

Terroir, grape varieties & a plethora of wine styles

The middle Loire produces every imaginable style of wine, from refreshing sparklers to delicious cherry-scented red wines; and sweet whites that can age for as long as a century. The secret to fine winemaking in this part of the Loire is in two of its grape varieties: the white Chenin Blanc, which is native to the region, and the red Cabernet Franc.

The Chenin Blanc is naturally high in acidity, making it an excellent candidate for the production of sparkling wine. The finest fizz is made in the town of Vouvray, where it can show rich, honeyed bready aromas similar to those of vintage champagne. The region's most common sparkling wine is the often-excellent Crémant de Loire, which can come from any of the middle Loire's vineyards.

If picked slightly later, the Chenin Blanc gives firm, full-bodied dry (*sec*), off-dry (*sec-tendre*), and medium-dry (*demi-sec*) wines, which show complex aromas of quince and apple. In warm years, or when noble rot develops in the vineyards, sweet (*moelleux*) wines are made from late harvested grapes; these are honeyed, luscious dessert wines, with good acidity and superlative ageing potential. The finest of these sweeties are made in Vouvray, and its near neighbour Montlouis.

The Cabernet Franc is the great red grape of the middle Loire, the main ingredient in the wines of Chinon, Bourgueil and Saumur-Champigny. Perhaps more famous as an ingredient in Saint-Emilion, on Bordeaux's 'right bank', the Cabernet Franc ripens earlier than its more famous descendant, the Cabernet Sauvignon, and produces softer wines, with cherry and raspberry aromas.

The Loire's reds were traditionally light-bodied wines, with refreshingly high acidity and delicate red fruit flavours. But recent warm vintages, and the fashion for later-picked, fuller-bodied wines mean that they now tend to be deeper in colour, with more intense, spicy flavours. Cabernet Sauvignon is increasingly used to add further muscle to these reds.

Other red grapes are blended with the Cabernets to make pleasant, country wines from the wider Touraine appellation. These grapes include the tannic Côt variety, the light fruity Gamay of the Beaujolais, and the thin-skinned Grolleau. The last two of these, together with the two Cabernets, are ingredients in the region's delicious rosés. The Loire's other celebrity red grape, the Pinot Noir, is only grown in tiny quantities in Touraine, as an ingredient in, for example, the rosés of the tiny Touraine-Noble-Joué appellation.

ABOVE
The view of Chinon from the Château

TOP
Tours market

The Sauvignon Blanc is the Loire's other important white grape. Its most famous incarnations are as Sancerre and Pouilly-Fumé, around 100 miles east of Tours. It is also the main grape for Touraine Blanc, which tends to be a lighter, more floral wine than either Sancerre or Pouilly-Fumé. Although this grape is more fashionable internationally than the Chenin Blanc, the opposite is true amongst winemakers in the middle Loire, for whom Chenin is the undisputed king of white grapes.

The area's *appellations contrôlées* are many, and will be explored as a part of the itineraries that follow. My advice is simply to try lots and to be prepared to make discoveries.

The terroir of the middle Loire is extremely varied, and individual vineyard microclimates are essential to grape ripening. The best vineyard sites are on the south-facing slopes near the banks of the River Loire and its tributaries, the Cher, the Indre and the Vienne. The soil is based on the area's soft, porous chalk soil, called *tuffeau*. Further from the riverbanks, clay is mixed with limestone, allowing the production of firmer red wines; sandy soils give lighter wines; and pebbles of flint store and reflect heat in many sites, helping to ripen the grapes.

The Loire is unusual in having no 'Grand Cru' classification, although Vouvray's Clos du Bourg and Chinon's Clos de l'Echo, for example, would be obvious choices if one were ever agreed. The difficulty is in imposing any

general standard on such a large and diverse viticultural area. However, the best winemakers in the middle Loire are increasingly bottling the wines from different vineyard sites separately, and farming their land naturally to highlight these fascinating differences in terroir.

Wine & food

The massive variety of Loire wines, combined with their often low prices, has two happy consequences for the gastronome. The first is their extensive use as a base for almost every kind of cooking sauce; the second is the pleasure that can be derived from finding a wine to match your choice of dish.

The Loire's cuisine is most fundamentally French, but many chefs revel in subtle influences from further afield, notably the Orient. The local Chenin-based white wines, in particular, make extremely versatile food partners, marrying as well with exotically spiced foods as with refined French recipes, or simple rustic cuisine.

Freshwater fish is the Loire speciality, and locally caught *sandre* (pikeperch) takes pride of place on most good restaurant menus. This is traditionally cooked in a simple butter sauce. *Brème* (bream), *brochet* (pike), and home-smoked salmon are other staples of the Loire diet, with *anguilles* (eels) and *lamproie* (lamprey) served in a thick, rustic sauce made with local red wine.

Tasty chunks of pork, called *rillons*, are cooked in their own fat, and make a great base for filling lunchtime salads. Don't confuse these with the coarse pâté, known as *rillettes*, which is made all over France.

The Loire is rich in the wildlife necessary for haute cuisine. The region's extensive forests are home to various game beasts; you will find venison on the more refined autumn menus, and you may well also encounter *sangliers*, or wild boars. The Richelais, in southern Touraine, is truffle country, and dogs are trained to sniff these out in winter.

If you are lucky, you may happen upon the *Géline de Touraine*, or *Dame Noire*, a rare breed of hen which, at the time of writing, had just received the prestigious *Label Rouge* culinary award. The rich, complex flavours of dishes such as these are perfectly matched by the region's supple Cabernet Franc-based red wines, particularly those with some bottle age.

The most talented chefs I met in the Loire shared a singular pride in their herb and vegetable gardens, whether planted in an extensive walled enclosure or an overgrown urban back yard. The movement among Loire winemakers towards natural viticulture is matched by the desire of local chefs to cook with fresh, seasonal vegetables.

Fine local goat's cheeses dominate restaurant cheeseboards; *Ste-Maure-de-Touraine* recently joined the *Crotin de Chavignol* in Sancerre with its own *appellation d'origine contrôlée*. Just as Crotin is complemented by a glass of white Sancerre, *Ste-Maure* partners wonderfully with Touraine's Chenin and Sauvignon-based wines.

For years, following the phylloxera vineyard epidemic in the late 19th century, apples and pears replaced grapes as the region's most important fruit crop. *Tarte Tatin* is the Loire's classic dessert, but orchard fruits are used creatively in a variety of other puds. *Pommes* and *poires tapées* are made by dehydrating the fruits in stone ovens following their harvest. They are then crushed and either eaten straight away or marinated in local red or white wine, with a little cinnamon and sugar. These desserts are delicious partners for the sweeter wines made from the Chenin Blanc grape.

Fresh seasonal red fruits and melons are grown locally, and the macaroons from the village of Cormery, between Bléré and Esvres, are particularly prized. In the pretty town of Chinon, a speciality worth looking for is the delicious local wine jam.

Driving, cycling or walking

The Loire's interesting centres of wine production are more widely dispersed than those of any other region in this book, though the terrain is relatively forgiving.

The Loire Valley is, more than anywhere else in France, made for the cyclist. Touraine in particular has been active in promoting cycle tourism for more than a decade. And the first impression on arriving in Tours is of bicycles, and lots of them. Motorists are, moreover, astonishingly courteous to cyclists in the Loire.

Every town, village and hamlet has its own network of proposed cycle and pedestrian routes, and bike hire and repair is ubiquitous. Cycle lanes are common on main roads. *'La Loire à Vélo'* is the region's official guide for the cyclist, but it only occasionally brings you into contact with the vineyards. The *'Route des Vignobles'* is Touraine's pre-defined vineyard trail, but it can be rather confusing, and is inevitably the product of local vineyard 'pitchfork politics'.

Tours is close enough to the UK that many Brits choose to arrive in their own cars. And, seemingly, plenty never make it back home! This method of transport has the advantage that you can fill up the boot, and you will want to. The wines are some of France's most refreshingly delicious, and their reasonable prices make this a great way to stock up for the year's drinking. The ageing potential of many of the wines also means you can build up a good small cellar without breaking the bank.

Summary itinerary

Days 1 & 2
Chenin & Châteaux

This stage begins in Tours, and loops round from Vouvray to its little brother appellation Montlouis, south of the Loire. Here the Chenin Blanc grape is king, producing every style of white wine, from 'traditional method' sparklers to super-concentrated dessert sweeties capable of ageing for 100 years.

En route, you will pass two of the Loire's most magnificent châteaux, Amboise and Chenonceaux. In the Touraine-Amboise appellation, excellent white wines are made from Chenin and Sauvignon Blanc; Touraine Rouge is produced from the Cabernet Franc, Gamay and Côt (Malbec) grapes.

Tips for cyclists

This first stage includes a hilly initial 7 miles through the vineyards from Tours to Vouvray. The alternative is the flatter – but less cycle-friendly – D751 road, south of the Loire. The route through the vineyards from Vouvray to Amboise is 15 further miles.

The 25-mile loop back to Montlouis, via Chenonceaux, is fairly gentle, after an initial climb. Between Amboise and Chenonceaux, an official 'cycle path' leads through some of the Loire's most characterful villages.

Days 3 & 4
The obscure and the famous

From Montlouis, the journey south takes you into the vineyards of Noble-Joué, the Loire's smallest *appellation d'origine contrôlée*. The fresh, full-bodied rosés made from these vines are difficult to find outside Touraine.

The town of Azay-le-Rideau is an ideal place to spend a night. It is home to some excellent vignerons, who produce an enormous range of excellent value wines. The local Grolleau grape

makes light, fruity rosés of uncommon charm.

Through the forest is the wonderful town of Chinon, with its commanding Château. The town's red wines are amongst the Loire's most famous.

Tips for cyclists

This is the longest stretch in the Loire itinerary. Day 3 is a fairly flat 30 miles (except in the vineyards of Noble-Joué). The road from Azay-le-Rideau to Chinon is only 18 miles, allowing time to explore Chinon, the region's most characterful town.

Days 5 & 6
The town of Bourgueil
& the vineyards of
Saumur-Champigny

From Chinon, the small villages lead past the Eco-museum at Véron, across the Loire to the market town of Bourgueil. This town is also famous for its red wines; the best vineyards are found to its north, where winemakers' cellars are dug deep into the rocks beneath their vines.

Crossing the Loire again to the south, the small riverside town of Montsoreau is a wonderful place to stay the night before heading south to the Abbey at Fontevraud.

From here, it is a short hop to the vineyards of Saumur-Champigny, the most fashionable red winemaking appellation in the Loire, before descending into the town of Saumur, famous for its sparkling wine production.

Tips for cyclists

Day 5 allows you to either stay the night in Bourgueil, or continue to Montsoreau. The latter option allows more time to explore Fontevraud-l'Abbaye and the Saumur-Champigny vineyards the following day. Day 6 is a shorter, but slightly hillier 15-20 miles, through the Fontevraud Forest to Saumur-Champigny.

Key to map

Dominic's route	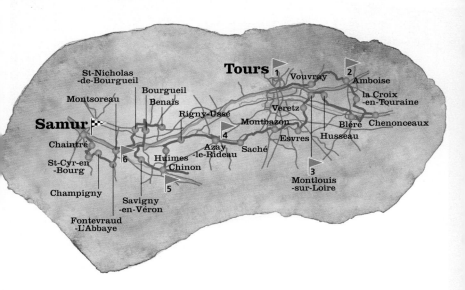
other routes	
start point	
day	4
extra trip	4+
end point	
town or village	•
larger town	
river	

Day 1 itinerary (15-22 miles)
Vouvray to Amboise (from Tours)

Entering the vineyards of Vouvray

Leave the centre of Tours east along Avenue André
Malraux, which skirts the south bank of the Loire. This
road becomes the D751, the officially recommended cycle
route to Vouvray and Montlouis. This is the flattest road,
but it is quite narrow, and is used throughout the day by
juggernauts. If taking this route, follow the second exit off
the first roundabout, and the first exit off the second, to
reach Vouvray.

Alternatively, cross the river in Tours, and join the
N152 north of the Loire towards Vouvray. The route that
follows is the hilly, prettier one through the vineyards to
Vouvray. Follow signs over the large roundabout to
'Rochecorbon' and 'Vouvray'; then take the second left
off the N152 into the village of Rochecorbon.

A little way up the hill in Rochecorbon, the
Romanesque Chapel of Saint George is on your left. Built
in the 11th century, the Chapel boasts a 12th century
stained glass window and some wonderfully restored

frescoes depicting Jesus washing the feet of the Apostles.

Free guided visits are on Sunday and bank holiday afternoons, from mid-May to the end of October. Contact the Rochecorbon Tourist Office for details.
ⓘ **02 47 52 80 22**

Take the next right at the sign for the hamlet of 'La Cholterie', and continue into the vineyards. Descend into the centre of Rochecorbon, and continue over the crossroads, bearing right after the church. Turn left into rue du Peu Boulin, and climb the narrow, steep hill that takes you into the vineyards of the Vouvray appellation. This is the most picturesque way to reach the first of Touraine's famous wine villages.

Back on the N152, below Rochecorbon, is the excellent restaurant Hostellerie de la Lanterne.
ⓘ **02 47 52 50 02**

Vouvray

In Vouvray, the Chenin Blanc grape produces every conceivable style of white wine, from the bone dry and austere, to the sweet and luscious. Vintage variation is the key to the huge range of wines made in Vouvray, a weakness that the village's best winemakers have turned into a unique strength. In warm years, the grapes reach incredible levels of ripeness, favouring the production of sweet, or *moelleux*, wines. Vouvray is where the River Cisse flows into the Loire, creating autumn mists, which help the development of *botrytis*. This 'noble rot' further concentrates the sugar, flavour and acidity in the grapes, making Vouvray's sweeties some of the world's longest lived white wines.

In less warm years, or when 'noble rot' does not develop, *demi-sec* (medium-dry), *sec-tendre* (off-dry) and *sec* (dry), wines are made. In cool years, when the Chenin grapes ripen less fully, the vignerons make sparkling Vouvrays, which are, in my view, the finest fizzy wines made anywhere in the Loire Valley. Since the style of wine produced depends on the weather conditions of a given year, it seems absurd to talk about good vs. bad vintages in Vouvray!

Any Vouvray from a good producer has the potential to age well, thanks to the firm acidity of the Chenin grape. The *tuffeau* chalk soils that form the white cliffs beside the Loire are perfectly suited to the Chenin; the cellars, wineries and homes of many villagers are cut into this soft, porous rock beneath the vineyards. Some of the best vineyards are situated on the south-facing slopes above the village, on soils containing more clay and gravel.

The village of Vouvray is widely dispersed, built on the flat land near the Loire, and on a series of slopes and

Day 1 at a glance

Itinerary	106 – 111
Wineries	112 – 115
Restaurants	116 – 117

BELOW & BOTTOM
Vouvray's houses: built into the soft chalky cliffs

plateaux, surrounded by vines. Rue du Commerce is Vouvray's ancient main street, on which its 13th century church stands just beneath the vineyards. From beside the church, you can climb the footpath 'Allée de la Cimetière', for an outstanding view of the village and the Loire below.

The helpful Vouvray tourist office has details of various vineyard walks. ☎ 02 47 52 68 73

Vouvray is also home to André and Jacques Hardouin, possibly France's finest charcutiers. The production is based in the vineyards north of the town, but the Hardouins have two shops in Vouvray, as well as one in Tours. ☎ 02 47 40 40 40 ∽ www.hardouin.fr

Discovering Vouvray's best winemakers

Some of the Loire's most revered winemakers are to be found in Vouvray, many of whom also produce wines from Vouvray's sister appellation, Montlouis. But the extended nature of Vouvray's streets can make these tricky to find.

Domaine Huët is the most famous name in Vouvray, a biodynamic estate that makes superlative wines (see page 114). To visit, take rue des Ecoles (D46) east from the village centre, and turn left into rue de la Croix Buisée. The estate is on your right.

Domaine Champalou is my other top choice (see page 112), but this one is hidden a little further away, in the vineyards. Follow the D47 north through Vouvray (rue Victor Hugo), over the mini-roundabout. Then turn left, ignoring the sign for 'Champalou' directing you straight on. Follow rue de la Bonne Dame and take the right fork after the crossroads. On your left, you will see Domaine Champalou's finest vineyard, Clos Portail, in front of the estate.

Near the Champalou estate is Vouvray's friendliest restaurant, La Cave Martin (see page 116).

Another vinous name to conjure with is Domaine du Clos Naudin, just down the road from the Huët estate. This estate is less well known than Domaine Huët, but vigneron Philippe Foreau's wines are in a similar league to his neighbour's. ☎ 02 47 52 71 46

Château Moncontour, on rue du Petit Côteau, makes less illustrious wines, but its cavernous cellars house a fascinating, and enormous, museum of viticulture. The celebrated writer Balzac tried repeatedly, and unsuccessfully, to buy the Château in the 19th century. The Château today is the private residence of the Feray family, and only its cellars are open to the public. ☎ 02 47 52 60 77 ∽ www.moncontour.com

Through the vines into 'Touraine-Amboise'

Follow rue des Ecoles east from Vouvray, along the D1 to Amboise. Then follow signs to Vernou-sur-Brenne, turning right towards the centre of the village. In Vernou, you will find François Pinon, another fantastic Vouvray producer.

I discovered the delicious Pinon wines in one of my favourite restaurants in Tours. François, a former child psychologist, took over the estate from his father in 1987. The wines are certified organic; all grapes are hand-harvested and no cultured yeasts are used in the fermentations. The estate's vines are situated in the vineyards above Vernou, considered some of the finest in the Vouvray appellation. For François, it is essential that the estate's wines

express this terroir and, above all, the vintage conditions in which the grapes are grown. ① 02 47 52 16 59
✉ 55, Vallée de Cousse

To follow the vineyard road to Amboise, turn right in front of the church in Vernou, and follow the road out of the village, turning right again at the sign for 'Chançay'.

Turn left at the junction with the D78, then immediately right onto the D79 at the sign for 'Nazelles'. After half a mile, a turn left leads to the stunning Italian terraced gardens of the Renaissance Château de Valmer.

The Château also owns 20 hectares of vines, from which it produces and bottles its own wines. Don't miss the 16th century *troglodytique* chapel, hewn from the chalky hillside within the Château's grounds.
① 02 47 52 93 12 ⬧ www.chateau-de-valmer.com

Continue along the D79, and follow the road straight at the next sign, for 'Nazelles'. The village of Vallée de Rayée leads into a patch of woodland, which clears after a mile or so, giving wonderful views of the fields and vines as you enter the Touraine-Amboise appellation.

The wines of Touraine-Amboise

Created in 1954, and represented by its own robed brotherhood, Touraine-Amboise is a smaller and less famous appellation than Vouvray. Like those of its neighbour, the white wines from Touraine-Amboise are made from the Chenin Blanc grape; they cover the same range of styles as Vouvray, although never quite achieving the same concentration, or the longevity. Light, fruity red wines and rosés are made from the Cabernet Franc, Gamay, and Côt grapes.

Descend the hill to join the D1, turning left at the sign for 'Nazelles', and turn right at the crossroads in Nazelles onto the D5. Take the second exit off the roundabout onto Boulevard des Platanes and continue over the next crossroads, under the railway line. Follow the bridge over the Loire into the centre of Amboise.

ABOVE & TOP
The viticulture museum at Château de Moncontour

Amboise

I have heard Amboise described as "the Loire's own San Tropez", and although this is the kind of hyperbole of which only French tourist authorities are capable, Amboise is one of the Loire's most important touristic and historical centres.

High above today's postcard shops and ice-cream parlours in the town square, Château Royal d'Amboise was a centre for the French royal court in the 15th and 16th centuries. Following the untimely death of King Charles VIII, who is said to have whacked his head on one of the castle's doorframes, his successor Louis XII moved the court upstream to Blois.

Amongst the Château's attractions are the magnificently restored King's

ABOVE
The grounds of
Château d'Amboise

TOP
Amboise town
square

**OPPOSITE PAGE
BOTTOM &
TOP LEFT**
Château d'Amboise

**OPPOSITE PAGE
TOP RIGHT**
Amboise from
the Château

Bedroom, and St. Hubert's Chapel, which contains the tomb of Leonardo da Vinci. ☎ 02 47 57 00 98
🔗 www.chateau-amboise.com

From June to August, there is a dazzling nocturnal recreation of the King's Renaissance court in the grounds of the Château. ☎ 02 47 57 14 47
🔗 www.renaissance-amboise.com

Another of Amboise's must-see attractions is Château du Clos Lucé, the house in which Leonardo da Vinci spent the last years of his life. Inside the Château is a fascinating exhibition of models of da Vinci's inventions, built by IBM. ☎ 02 47 57 00 73
🔗 www.chateaux-france.com/closluce

Just outside Amboise, La Pagode de Chanteloup is a beautifully preserved 18th century Chinese-style folly, built by the duke of Choiseul, and surrounded by a semi-circular lake. This is all that remains of the duke's once-marvellous château, destroyed by marauding bands in 1823. ☎ 02 47 57 20 97
🔗 www.pagode-chanteloup.com

Wine tasting in Amboise

An excellent place to begin the discovery of Amboise's wines is the Caveau de Vignerons d'Amboise, in front of the Château. ☎ 02 47 57 23 69
🔗 http://caveauvins-amboise.monsite.wanadoo.fr/

This is not a co-operative cellar, but the tasting centre and sales depot for thirteen of the township's best winemakers. These include Domaine de la Grange Tiphaine (see Day 2 itinerary); and Xavier Frissant, who grows some of the area's finest Sauvignon Blancs, on the flinty soils of the Touraine appellation east of Amboise.

You can find Xavier Frissant's estate in the village of Mosnes, around ten miles east of Amboise along the D751. ☎ 02 47 57 23 18 🔗 www.xavierfrissant.com

Maison Champalou

7, rue du Grand Ormeau
37210 Vouvray

Phone 02 47 52 64 49
Fax 02 47 52 67 99
Champalou@wanadoo.fr
www.champalou.com

The Estate

My first meeting with the Champalou family was in the torrid heat of late June 2006, but as the sun radiated in the vineyards, harmony and *joie de vivre* emanated from the family cellars. Maison Champalou was the creation of a young couple, who fell in love whilst studying viticulture together. Catherine and Didier are both children of vignerons, and their union produced a new quest for wine quality and a fierce desire to evolve.

The Champalous bought their first two hectares of vines in 1984, and have since carefully sought the most interesting vineyards, as they have become available. Today, the estate's twenty hectares of Chenin Blanc vines are split between forty individual parcels of vines in Vouvray.

Didier is responsible for the vineyards, which he works, as he has for more than twenty years, according to the principles of 'reasoned viticulture', without the use of chemical herbicides. Every crop is hand-harvested. Catherine is mistress of the cellars, making sure that the wines are vinified and bottled so as to preserve the pure fruit flavours of the Chenin grape. The year before writing, Catherine and Didier had invested in a new modern subterranean cellar system, allowing them to undertake the entire winemaking and bottling process on site.

The couple's daughter Céline had joined Catherine in the cellars months before my visit, following vinous travels in South Africa and New Zealand. She had been impressed by the meticulous practices of the New World winemakers, but returned to Vouvray convinced of the magic of its unique terroir.

In summer 2006, the estate was selling mainly dry wines from the cool 2004 vintage. The 2005s are sure to be fantastic, but were still patiently maturing in the cellars at the time of writing.

UK importers:
Les Caves de Pyrene
Enotria Wine Cellars
Great Western Wines, Bath

LEFT
Catherine Champalou
in the vineyards

Choice wines:

Vouvray Brut NV

Like the traditional method sparklers of Domaine Huët, this wine's second fermentation, in bottle, feeds off the residual grape sugar from its first alcoholic fermentation. It then matures on its lees for two years before it is corked.

Made from Chenin grapes grown on the clay-limestone soils on the plateaux above the village, the wine has delicate bubbles and a pale colour. The nose is creamy and mineral, with aromas of freshly mown grass and hints of spiced citrus and pear. On the palate, it is creamy and fresh, with a medium body and firm acidity.

An excellent partner for langoustines, scallops or even white meats, Catherine nonetheless claims to drink this wine with almost every meal!

La Cuvée des Fondraux 2004

This blend issues from Chenin vines with an average age of 45 years, planted on the flinty clay slopes descending from above Vouvray towards the banks of the Loire.

The juice passes straight into old oak barrels and undergoes a slow fermentation, until the wine reaches a perfect balance of sugar, acidity and alcohol. It then ages in its barrels for between 9 and 12 months.

The wine is still very young, but already showing attractive acacia and mineral aromas. A taste reveals a full-bodied off-dry palate, with firm acidity and a long mineral finish.

This wine could age gracefully for 15 years, and needs a couple of seasons yet to show its best; drink with poultry dishes, soft cheeses or fruit salad.

La Cuvée Moelleuse 2003

This sweet cuvée is made from individually selected nobly rotten grapes, only possible in certain years. It consequently has 85 grammes per litre of residual sugar.

The hot 2003 growing season has given the wine intense, exotic aromas of honeysuckle and apple compote; 35-year-old vines grown on sandy clay soil have added concentration and a rounded peachiness to a palate that is both luscious and elegant.

This wine marries beautifully with *foie gras* and sweet desserts.

TOP
Catherine Champalou and
daughter Céline

RIGHT
Winemaking couple: Didier
and Catherine Champalou

Domaine Huët
l'Echansonne

11-13, rue de la Croix-Buisée
37210 Vouvray

Phone 02 47 52 78 87
Contact@huet-echansonne.com
www.huet-echansonne.com

The Estate

Victor Huët created this estate in 1928, and was succeeded first by his son Gaston, then by Noël Pinguet, Gaston's son-in-law. Noël took over the estate thirty years ago and, since then, has become an inspiration for many of France's most exciting young winemakers.

Noël has run Domaine Huët since 1990 according to biodynamic principles, the strictest and most philosophical of all organic methods of viticulture. But far from promoting biodynamics as a self-evident recipe for great winemaking, Noël's approach is experimental, founded on a conviction that there is always more to learn.

Almost two decades after the estate's biodynamic conversion, Noël is careful to explain the positive effects on wine quality as observations, rather than as necessary, causal links. Indeed, the estate was already making great wines prior to 1990.

Domaine Huët owns three of Vouvray's finest terroirs: Le Mont, Le Haut-Lieu and Le Clos du Bourg. The Chenin Blanc is the only grape used by the estate, and the styles of wine depend completely upon the vintage. In 2004, for example, wonderful dry and sparkling wines were produced; whilst 2003 was a great year for sweet, or *moelleux* wines, and no fizz was made at all.

The Huët winery is state-of-the-art; the newly crushed grape nectar makes its way through the winemaking process using gravity alone. The estate's large cellars are cut beneath the Haut-Lieu vineyard, and hold a large number of old vintages, dating back over 100 years.

The estate's spirit of openness is reflected in the unusually generous wine tastings it offers. If you make an appointment at Domaine Huët, you are likely to try wines of several different vintages terroirs and styles.

UK importer:
The Wine Society

LEFT
The Huët cellars

Choice wines:
Brut Pétillant 2000
This is a fine *méthode traditionnelle* sparkling wine, made like a champagne, but with one crucial difference: it re-ferments in bottle with the residual grape sugar from its first fermentation, rather than with added cane sugar. It then spends at least three years maturing on its lees before the dead yeast cells are disgorged and the wine is corked.

The wine's character is like to a good, full-bodied vintage champagne: small delicate bubbles, a nose reminiscent of brioche, honeycomb and ripe apple. The palate is crisp, rich and full of ripe apple flavours.

An excellent partner for creamy fish dishes.

Le Mont 2001 Demi-Sec
Le Mont is the famous 8-hectare parcel of vines planted on flinty clay soil on the hills rising from the Loire.

The 2001 Demi-Sec is youthful, but exuberant, with an elegant but rich nose of lime and honeycomb. On the palate, the wine shows its full richness, with a firm bite of acidity and good length.

This wine is drinking well, but will continue to improve. This is an extremely versatile food wine; try with roast pork and apple sauce.

Le Haut-Lieu 2005 Moelleux
The heavy, deep clay soil of this 9-hectare parcel gives a wine that is exotic and aromatic on the nose, with a predominance of fresh white peach aromas.

On the palate the wine is supple and sweet with open, exotic flavours and a long, intense and elegant finish.

Drink with *foie gras* or exotic fruit desserts.

Le Clos du Bourg 1996 Moelleux 1ère Trie
Jewel in the crown of Huët's holdings, Le Clos de Bourg is Noël Pinguet's own favourite terroir. It is a small limestone parcel surrounded by a stone wall, above the town of Vouvray, near the church.

The wine comes from super-ripe grapes, individually harvested on the pickers' first passage through the vineyard. It is golden in colour, with intensely ripe honeyed citrus fruits on the nose.

On the palate, it is intense and luscious, with 68 grammes per litre of residual sugar. Its flavours are of rich grapefruit, pineapple and ginger. The finish is long and satisfying.

Drink with sweet caramel desserts.

Auberge La Cave Martin, Vouvray

**66 rue de La Vallée Coquette
37210 Vouvray**

**Phone 02 47 52 62 18
Fax 02 47 52 79 34**

The day before eating at Auberge la Cave Martin, I had asked vigneronne Catherine Champalou where Vouvray's winemakers come to eat. She had left me in little doubt that this was the place.

Hidden away in the vineyards above Vouvray, La Cave Martin is the town's most pleasant inn, but is also the most difficult one to find. It is just off La Vallée Coquette, a road that leads off rue de Sens, into which you can turn left as you approach Vouvray through the vineyards from Tours.

Charming lady-owner Martine Lenoble serves simple country dishes, in a characterful restaurant dining room hewn from the *tuffeau* rock face that supports the vineyards above. On sunny days, you can enjoy your meal on the restaurant's beautiful shaded terrace.

The wines at La Cave Martin only come from the Loire Valley, and most are made by Vouvray's vignerons, from their vineyards within the commune and in nearby Montlouis. Martine will serve any wine on her list by the glass for only a few euros. So why not try several?

The 3-course lunch menu, with a choice of either meat or fish, is only €15, and à la carte main courses cost this much at most.

Martine speaks some English.

Closed Sunday and Monday. Reservation is advised

ABOVE
Choiseul chef Pascal Bouvier

Eating in Amboise

Amboise's most prestigious, and expensive, hotel-restaurant is Le Choiseul.

This restaurant is a very serious affair, with well-trained waiters serving traditional French gastronomic cuisine, and looking irritated at hyperactive American children hanging off the curtains.

The set evening menu is about €60, with main courses à la carte around €30. At these prices the food tastes a little expensive, although at lunchtime, the new bistro-style menu 'Le 36' is better value at between €15 and €30.

But Le Choiseul has been upstaged, and considerably undercut, by the opening of the dynamic Pavillon de Lys in Amboise. This is, in my view, the finest of the town's restaurants.

Gifted young chef Sébastien Bégouin arrived in Amboise in 2004, and bought a large bourgeois town house, with a mind to creating a stylish hotel-restaurant. Within a year, **Le Pavillon des Lys** was a huge local hit and a darling of the Paris media.

The key to Le Pavillon's success is its dynamic menus, delicious flavours and a beautiful simplicity of presentation. All of the food is fresh, light and elegant, marrying well with the crisp, light-bodied local wines.

There are two menus from which to choose: a *Menu Dégustation* for €35 and a vegetarian *Menu Légumes* for €23. The former includes no fewer than three successive starters, a fish course, then a meat course, and three desserts. The vegetarian menu proposes six creative dishes based on cooked vegetables. If this isn't enough, you can choose from a cheese board that features more than thirty different cheeses. The menus change twice weekly, and in harmony with the seasons, the market, and the inspiration of the inscrutable Sébastien.

Book well in advance for weekends in the summer.

Closed Tuesday evening and all of January.

If you are travelling east of Amboise towards Mosnes, the splendid country hotel-restaurant **Château de Pray** is just beyond the village of Chargé on the D751, and certainly well worth a visit.

Le Choiseul

36, quai Charles Guinot
37400 Amboise

Phone 02 47 30 45 45
Fax 02 47 30 46 10

Le Pavillon des Lys

9, rue d'Orange
37400 Amboise

Phone 02 47 30 01 01
Fax 02 47 30 01 90
www.pavillondeslys.com

Château de Pray

Route de Chargé
37400 Amboise

Phone 02 47 57 23 67
Fax 02 47 57 32 50
http://praycastel.online.fr

BELOW
Restaurant Le
Pavillon de Lys

ABOVE
Awe-inspiring:
Château de
Chenonceaux

Day 2 itinerary (25 miles)

Amboise to Montlouis, and the Loire's most famous château

Amboise's finest winemaker

Pass the Château on your left, and leave Amboise along rue Victor Hugo. Then fork right along rue du Clos Lucé, past Château du Clos Lucé. Continue over the crossroads at the bottom of the hill, and follow the bicycle sign towards Chenonceaux.

This 'cycle route' is the most interesting way to reach Chenonceaux, site of the Loire's most famous château. It is well sign-posted and perfectly suitable for cars.

Turn left at the mini-roundabout and then immediately right, and follow the road up a moderately steep hill for a mile. The winery to visit is Domaine La Grange Tiphaine, on the right just before the junction with the D31 (see page 122). Here the vineyards are planted amongst various crops, in between patches of forest, which shelters the vineyards and gives the area its unique micro-climate.

Across the D31, you can explore the châteaux of the

Loire in miniature, at the Parc des Mini-Châteaux, which is on your right. ① **02 47 23 44 57**
⤶ www.mini-chateaux.com

Day 2 at a glance	
Itinerary	118 – 121
Wineries	122 – 125
Restaurants	126 – 127

Hamlets, vines and hot-air balloons

Follow the road downhill along the D81, through the Forest of Amboise. After three miles, turn right at the sign for 'La Croix-en-Touraine', and then take the first left.

As the Forest clears, you enter the best of the Loire's picturesque open farmland, that which has made hot-air-balloon flights such a successful local industry. This is an industry in which, years ago, I played my own very brief part.

I was never a pilot, but a ground crewman, and the combination of early-morning starts and an exploitative management would make this my shortest ever career. But the month I spent chasing balloons through these lanes in a Mercedes Sprinter left me with memories of wild vineyards and fields, and rustic villages in which time has stood still. The pilots work hard on the burners to avoid landing in the trellised vineyards, but supplies of sparkling Vouvray are essential to mollify angry farmers when the inevitable happens. Only pleasure and wonder can fix such vivid memories.

The road to Chenonceaux, and its extraordinary Château

After the hamlet of Les Bergeries, the road to Chenonceaux is well signposted by little bicycle signs, which guide you through the vineyards and small farming villages until the descent into the valley of the River Cher.

Once in the village of Civray-de-Touraine, turn right into rue des Ecoles, then left onto the D40 for a short mile into Chenonceaux. The Château is on your left as you enter the village. One of Touraine's most memorable restaurants, the Auberge du Bon Laboureur, is in the village centre (see page 126).

If you only mean to visit one of the Loire's châteaux in your life, that one should be Château de Chenonceaux. This is the château on all the postcards, the one over which the hot-air balloonists and their clients hope to drift. Château de Chenonceaux encapsulates all the beauty and grandeur of the French Renaissance; its many arches straddle the River Cher, and the splendid gardens, designed by Diane de Poitiers and Catherine de Medici, greet you as you enter the estate. The Château also owns 30 hectares of vines, and produces its own wines.

Every weekend in June, and every evening in July and August, the gardens are lit up between 9.30 and 11pm, to the sound of Corelli's musical compositions. Entry is around €10. ☏ 02 47 23 90 07
🖱 www.chenonceau.com

Through Bléré, into the wild vineyards of Montlouis

Double back along the D40 towards Civray-de-Touraine. Then turn left at the crossroads at the sign for 'Bléré'. Cross the railway lines and then the River Cher, and take the third exit off the roundabout a mile later into Thoré. Climb into the vineyards, and then turn right before entering the village of Argy. Another mile finds you in Bléré.

At first sight, Bléré is just another pretty French market town, but it has been an important historical crossroads since before the Middle Ages, when its fortifications were erected. Henry II Plantagenet of England built its first bridge in the 12th century, to facilitate the passage of his troops to the south of France. Bléré is not renowned for its wines today, but it was an important port and trading post for the wine trade until the beginning of the 20th century.

Bléré also has a fine Michelin-starred restaurant in Le Cheval Blanc, in place de l'Eglise. ☏ 02 47 30 30 14
🖱 www.lechevalblancblere.com

Cross the bridge back over the Cher in Bléré, and continue to the centre of La Croix-en-Touraine. Then turn left at the crossroads back onto the D40 at the sign for 'Montlouis-sur-Loire'.

Continue along the D40 through the centre of Saint-Martin-le-Beau. After a further mile, just past the sign indicating that you have left the village, turn right opposite the picnic area. This small country road leads through the depths of the Montlouis appellation, into vineyards that suddenly feel very wild and isolated. The countryside here is beautiful, but I got lost and ended up asking directions from a group of farmers who definitely looked capable of recreating some of the more frightening scenes from the 1970s film 'Deliverance'.

It is therefore essential to turn right at the first junction, then left 100 yards later. This is called rue des Marronniers, after the *lieu-dit* vineyard of the same name, and leads into the hamlet of Husseau.

The Montlouis terroir

Montlouis is the sometimes forgotten little brother of Vouvray, making the same range of wine styles, from dry sparkling to sweet and luscious. The soils of Montlouis are sandier than those of Vouvray, and its situation on the north bank of the Loire means that fewer of Montlouis' vineyards benefit from the southern exposure enjoyed by those of its more famous sibling. The wines tend to be a little less intense, and consequently often cheaper, than those of Vouvray. Many of Montlouis' producers own land in both appellations.

The hamlet of Husseau

Husseau is where all of Montlouis' finest winemakers live. The most famous is Jacky Blot, of Domaine de la Taille aux Loups (see page 124). Jacky is glad to be situated off the main tourist trail, and clearly prefers to welcome genuine wine fanatics than their barrel-kicking counterparts. To visit the estate, turn right at the crossroads above the village, into rue des Aîtres. The inconspicuous entrance to the estate is on your left after 100 yards.

Yves Chidaine runs the other famous estate in Husseau, Domaine François Chidaine. Yves was not encouraging visits at the time of writing, but this, I was told, might change.

The estate is at 5 La Grande Rue, the road leading from rue des Aîtres. ① **02 47 45 19 14**

Otherwise, you can taste the wines in Chidaine's shop, La Cave Insolite, in Montlouis-sur-Loire (see below).

The other name to look out for in Husseau is Dominique Moyer. The estate is at 2, rue de la Croix des Granges. ① **02 47 50 94 83**

Montlouis-sur-Loire

To reach Montlouis, continue west through Husseau along rue du Volagré, which leads directly into the town.

In a region so popular with tourists, Montlouis-sur-Loire feels refreshingly like a real working town. In the upper part of town is its square, with pubs, shops and a tourist office. On the route down through the old streets towards the Loire, the Romanesque church of St-Laurent overlooks the river. Its small square was the village cemetery between the 12th and 16th centuries.

As you continue down to the quay, evidence of Montlouis' trading history becomes more apparent; the cellars, cut into the *tuffeau* cliffs opposite the Loire, were once the warehouses and homes of the town's merchants.

The quay is where Montlouis' co-operative wine cellar, the *Cave des Producteurs*, is based. Created in 1961, the *Cave* is run by 25 of Montlouis' growers, and produces one third of the town's wines. There is a small – free – cellar visit throughout the week, including Sunday; the wines are well-made and extremely good value. ① **02 47 50 80 98** www.cave-montlouis.com

Also on the quay is the retail outlet of Domaine François Chidaine (see above). Here you can discover not only the Chidaine wines, but also a range of other greats from all over the Loire. 'La Cave Insolite' is open all week except Sunday. ① **02 47 45 19 14** www.cave-insolite-chidaine.com

The excellent Restaurant La Tourangelle is also on the quay (see page 127).

ABOVE
Grape bunches forming

TOP
Vines in flower

Domaine La Grange Tiphaine

37400 Amboise

Phone 02 47 57 64 17
Fax 02 47 57 39 49
lagrangetiphaine@ifrance.com
www.lagrangetiphaine.com

The Estate

Walking amongst his vines above the town of Amboise, vigneron Damien Delecheneau picks up one of the many large pebbles of flint from the ground. It is hot to touch.

"These stones store the sun's heat during the day," Damien explains, "then act as radiators during the cool nights, helping to ripen the grapes."

The vigneron proudly scratches below the dusty surface of the sandy clay to reveal moisture. The soil retains valuable water in periods of drought, he claims, because he never uses chemical herbicides. Thus, when rain falls, it is absorbed, rather than running away across the bare soil.

Damien took over the reins of his family estate in 2001, after travelling extensively in the vineyards of France, California and South Africa. Domaine La Grange Tiphaine includes 6 hectares of vines in the Touraine-Amboise appellation, and 4 hectares in Montlouis, where the famous Jacky Blot, of Domaine de la Taille aux Loups, regards Damien as one of the region's most accomplished young winemakers.

Damien's additional work as oenology professor at the Amboise viticultural college means that he is extremely busy, but the Delecheneau family believes in welcoming visitors to the estate, by appointment.

The whites are made exclusively from the Chenin Blanc grape; the reds come from the Côt (Malbec), Cabernet Franc and Gamay. The wines share a characteristic freshness, with ripe fruit flavours, making them fascinating food partners. These wines are, however, equally quaffable on their own on a warm summer's day.

Present this book for a 5% discount, if buying Touraine-Amboise Rouge 'Ad Libitum'.

UK importer:
Stone, Vine & Sun

Choice wines:

Touraine-Amboise Blanc 'Bel Air' Sec 2005

Grown on clay-limestone soils, scattered with the large flint pebbles typical of Amboise, this is dry Chenin Blanc at its finest.

The nose is subtle and mineral, with aromas of ripe lemons and fresh celery. The wine's minerality is more intense on the palate, where lemon flavours are mixed with grapefruit and supported by a firm thread of acidity.

This is a medium-bodied wine that could age for up to ten years. Drink as an apéritif or with goat's cheese.

Touraine-Amboise Rouge 'Ad Libitum' 2004

'Ad Lib' is a blend of 25% Gamay, grown on fine clay soils, with 25% Côt and 50% Cabernet Franc, both from clay-limestone vineyards.

The wine's colour is deep purple; its nose is intensely spicy with hints of minerals, redcurrants and anise. The flavours are more intense still, with a fresh acidity and good tannic grip. A few years bottle age will soften the wine, and give it a broad spicy palate.

This wine would be a wonderful partner for roast lamb, or spicy North African dishes.

Touraine-Amboise Rouge 'Clef de Sol' 2004

This is a blend of 35% Côt and 65% Cabernet Franc grapes; the latter were harvested as late as 24th October to ensure full ripeness. The vines are 60 years old, giving small yields of concentrated juice, which is fermented and aged in *barriques* for twelve months, and bottled with only a light filtration.

The result is a deeply coloured wine, with aromas of concentrated ripe plums and cherries. The palate shows freshness and vivacity, backed up by a good structure and a long finish. This is a wine that could benefit from ten years in bottle.

Damien recommends red meat as a food partner, "with just a sprinkling of black pepper".

Côt 'Vieilles Vignes'

French vignerons may legally call their vines 'old' after their twentieth birthdays, and many do just that. Damien Delecheneau's Côt vines, however, have lived 115 years, making them amongst the oldest in production.

The wine is dark and concentrated, with a deep colour and powerful, earthy aromas of plum and black cherry. On the palate, the tannins are firm, but ripe and refined; the fruit concentration is extraordinary.

Old vines' Côt can age gracefully in bottle for many years, but low vine yields, and a massive demand from customers, frequently leave the estate short of bottles of this fantastic wine.

**ABOVE &
OPPOSITE PAGE**
Young talent
Damien
Delecheneau
amongst his vines

Domaine de la Taille aux Loups

8, rue des Aîtres, Husseau
37270 Montlouis-sur-Loire

Phone 02 47 45 11 11
Fax 02 47 45 11 14
www.jackyblot.com

Domaine de la Butte

La Butte
37140 Bourgueil

Phone 02 47 97 81 30
Fax 02 47 97 99 45

The Estate

Jacky Blot is the man behind Montlouis' famous Domaine de la Taille aux Loups. A warm, charming character, Jacky modestly describes himself as a farmer rather than an artist, "or an artisan, perhaps…"

Like any uncompromisingly hands-on winemaker, Jacky's renown has made him a very busy man, as he juggles his roles of vigneron and wine personality. When I met Jacky, we began tasting alone, but within half an hour others had arrived. Jacky's delicious wines and infectious personality attract wine lovers from many countries, like bees to a honeypot. Mick Jagger, Jacky told me, is a regular visitor and a keen customer.

For Jacky, the finest wines must be made from perfect grapes, and so the land is tilled manually, and grapes are picked selectively by hand. Eschewing the modern hurried tendency, Jacky's wines undergo a slow maturation. They are bottled when they are ready; the styles of wine faithfully represent the weather conditions in which the grapes were harvested. The domaine's 20 hectares of old Chenin Blanc vines are shared between the appellations of Montlouis and Vouvray, on opposite sides of the Loire.

In 2002, Jack Blot began producing red wines at his newly acquired Domaine de la Butte in Bourgueil, with its 14 hectares of hillside vineyards. The domaine's impressive cellars are dug deep beneath the vineyards, north of the town. The wines are already considered some of Bourgueil's finest, and are available for tasting either at the Montlouis estate, or in Bourgueil, where cellar visits are, if anything, more practical.

Phone in advance to visit either estate. Genuine lovers of the region's wines will receive a warm welcome.

UK importers:
Justerini & Brooks
Fields, Morris & Verdin

Choice wines:

Montlouis Pétillant Naturel 'Triple Zéro' NV

This wine comes from 50-year-old vines, grown on flinty clay soils, on a limestone bedrock. Bunches are individually harvested and vinified without the addition of any sugar.

Triple Zéro thus means that there is no initial sugar enrichment of the grape must; the wine's second, bottle, fermentation feeds off the natural grape sugars left after the first fermentation; and no *liqueur d'expedition* is added to sweeten the wine before it is corked. This is a thinly disguised sideswipe at the Champenois, many of whom add sugar to their wines three times during the winemaking process!

The wine is rich, pure and intense on the nose, with fresh apple and brioche aromas. On the palate, it is bone dry and mouth filling.

A perfect apéritif wine, Triple Zéro is also a great partner for white fish dishes.

Montlouis Liquoreux 'Cuvée des Loups' 2003

This rich, sweet cuvée comes from 80-year-old Chenin vines grown on south-facing flinty clay slopes near the village of Husseau. 'Nobly rotten' grapes were harvested early in October, at a level of ripeness which allowed a full 100 grammes per litre of residual sugar in the finished wine, which was aged for a year in small oak *barriques*.

On the nose, the wine is exotic and peachy, yet fresh, with a palate that is at once intense, honeyed and elegant. The finish is long and extremely complex.
Drink as an apéritif or with *foie gras*.

Montlouis Liquoreux 'Romulus' 2003

Completely 'botrytised' grapes were picked individually from two separate vineyard selections, late in the growing season. A further rigorous selection took place at the sorting table. The result is a wine with an enormous residual sugar level of over 200 grammes per litre.

TOP
Jacky Blot serves wine to customers faithful

The wine's colour is an intense, bright gold; its nose betrays its extreme youth, with subtly exotic and honeyed aromas overlaid with toasty hints. On the palate, the concentration of pure fruit, acidity and sugar is astonishing, and the wine has an incredible length of flavour.

This wine could age for at least 50 years. Drink with rich fruit desserts.

If you are lucky, you might get to taste Montlouis Liquoreux 'Romulus Plus'. From even lower yields of more shrivelled and yet more concentrated grapes, this wine could age for a full century!

Auberge du Bon Laboureur, Chenonceaux

Hôtel****-Restaurant
37150 Chenonceaux

Phone 02 47 23 90 02
Fax 02 47 23 82 01
Info@bonlaboureur.com
www.bonlaboureur.com

In the centre of Chenonceaux, four generations of the Jeudi family have created a leafy haven of tranquillity and refinement in the Auberge du Bon Laboureur. A former coaching inn, the hotel and restaurant are, together, the epitome of country chic, with a relaxed, unpretentious atmosphere.

Antoine Jeudi is the chef. His cooking is simple, refined and traditional. Most of the herbs and vegetables used in his dishes are picked from the restaurant's own garden, and other ingredients are bought fresh from the market. Antoine earned the restaurant a Michelin star in the year 2000, but menus have stayed affordable, at between €20 and €70. The wine list is extensive and varied, with many old vintages, and good bottles for less than €20.

General manager Fabrice is Madame Jeudi's "right hand man", and has an excellent knowledge of the best local winemakers.

"The fantastic thing about the Loire," Fabrice enthused, "is that there are great wines everywhere, even outside the villages you associate with the great names."

And with that, Fabrice produced a bottle of Sauvignon Blanc from the nearby village of Bourré (which, in French, means 'plastered'!). The producer was a young winemaker named Levin; the wine was clearly inspired by the intensely flavoured, crisp Sauvignons from New Zealand, making a great partner for the restaurant's wonderful seafood *entrées*.

After a hearty meal and a relaxing *digestif* on the terrace, you may be tempted to stay in one of the hotel's characterful rooms for the night, but disappointment awaits those who have not booked well in advance.

Excellent English is spoken by all.

Present this book to receive a free apéritif.

This small restaurant is certainly Montlouis' finest. Bruno Delagneau's cooking is gastronomic and imaginative; delicious flavours simply presented. The chef's wife and her small team are not looking for stars and accolades, but take obvious pride in offering a fantastic welcome, with a service that is impeccable.

Bruno is the archetypal French chef: large, surly, and extremely talented. The sort of chap you wouldn't pick a fight with after a long service. Bruno is originally from Champagne, where he learned his trade under the famous Gérard Boyer, of Château des Crayères, in Reims. Consequently, it is hard to fault Bruno's cooking, which is traditionally French, but flavoured with Oriental spices and Italian herbs.

Fresh fish is the house speciality. The chef's king prawn salad is a fine starter, followed by fresh sea bream in a creamy mushroom sauce. The 'Menu Suggestion' is €30, with a 2-course lunchtime option for €20. The full menu, which allows you to choose à la carte, is €40.

The wine list is as interesting as Bruno's cooking, with a large local selection, and a thoughtful range from other regions of France, particularly Bordeaux.

The restaurant's garden nestles in a small enclave under the *tuffeau* rock-face, a wonderfully peaceful place to sit and enjoy a summer lunch.

Closed Sunday evening and Monday.

The restaurant staff speak good English.

Restaurant La Tourangelle
47, quai Albert Baillet
37270 Montlouis-sur-Loire

Phone 02 47 50 97 35
Fax 02 47 50 88 57

ABOVE
A drink beside the
river in Azay-le-Rideau

Day 3 itinerary (30 miles)

Montlouis to Azay-le-Rideau: the forgotten heart of Touraine

Leaving Montlouis

In Montlouis, at the top of place du 11 Novembre 1918,
fork right at the sign for 'Véretz', and follow the road to
the left out of town, and over the mini-roundabout.

Cross the bridge in Véretz, then turn left and
immediately right at the sign for 'Esvres'. This road leads
through the old streets of Véretz, past its 16th century
church and under its reconstructed Renaissance château.

Turn right at the roundabout at the top of the hill,
and follow the road through fields and forest for about
7 miles to the centre of Esvres. Turn right into the village
past the church, and take the next right opposite the
railway station, into rue de Tours. This road leads uphill
into the vineyards of 'Touraine-Noble-Joué'.

Touraine's forgotten wine

Touraine-Noble-Joué is the smallest, and most recently

created, of Touraine's *appellations contrôlées*. Noble-Joué is a *vin gris*, or a pale rosé; the grapes used in its production are pressed almost as soon as they are picked, with no skin maceration. The grape varieties are unique in the region, and are similar to those used to make *blanc de noirs* champagne. It is the three Pinots that lend the wine its 'noble' nomenclature: a majority of the red Pinot Meunier gives the juice a fruity freshness, Pinot Gris (Malvoisie) adds body and structure, whilst Pinot Noir brings finesse to the blend.

The place to discover the distinguished history of Touraine's 'forgotten wine' is at the cellars of its star producer, the Rousseau Frères (see page 132). Head out of Esvres, up rue de Tours, and follow the vineyards for about a mile, until the turning left for 'Réunica' and 'Château de la Dorée'. The estate is on your right in the tiny hamlet of Le Vau.

Day 3 at a glance
Itinerary 128 – 131
Wineries 132 – 135
Restaurants 136 – 137

Just don't get lost!

The heat of the sun in July 2006 was stifling, rendering cycling, wine tasting and route planning a difficult trio of activities. After a longer lunch than I had planned with the charming Rousseau family in Vau, I set off through the woods to Azay-le-Rideau, tired and slightly inebriated. My inability to concentrate on Michel's directions was the first of a series of errors that landed me in Azay-le-Rideau at dusk, with nowhere to stay.

I decided on the quickest route back to my lodgings in Tours, in near darkness, along what proved to be a dangerous trunk road; one which nonetheless ran straight through the suburb of Joué-lès-Tours, birthplace of Touraine-Noble-Joué. I'm not sure what I had expected of Joué-lès-Tours, perhaps a civilised middle-class satellite town, with a couple of scattered garden vineyards planted for curiosity. Instead, I was met by one of those *banlieux*, or suburbs, that you hear about on the news: no place for a tired, lost-looking British cyclist.

The correct way is to rejoin the road through Le Vau outside the Rousseau estate, and follow it to the right where the one-way system obliges you to do so. Turn left at the next crossroads into the forest, and continue straight until you cross the railway lines. Then turn left briefly onto the N10 into Montbazon.

It sounds so simple now.

A bite to eat, and the road to Azay-le-Rideau

Montbazon is the first of a series of sleepy, colourful towns bordering the River Indre that beg you to stop for

BELOW
"I'm lost too!"

BOTTOM
Le Château d'Artigny

ABOVE
Château de Saché

OPPOSITE PAGE
Reflected glory:
The Château at
Azay-le-Rideau

a glass of wine or a beer on the riverside 'beach'. The best place to eat is Château d'Artigny, a mile beyond Montbazon, along the D17 towards Azay-le-Rideau (see page 136).

The last village before Azay-le-Rideau is Saché, with the peaceful, intimate Château de Saché at its centre. Within the Château is a museum dedicated to the life and works of 19th-century novelist and playwright Honoré de Balzac. It is within this château that Balzac conceived and wrote many of his most famous works.

The Château was first built in the Middle Ages, but adopted its present form during the Renaissance; its interior is decorated in the 19th century style, as Balzac would have known it. One can imagine the inspiration the writer found in the Château's verdant gardens, the perfect place for an afternoon stroll or a romantic tête-à-tête.

Balzac-related art exhibitions are regularly held at the Château, which is open all year. Moreover, you are sure to encounter fewer tourists here than in the larger, more famous châteaux of the Loire. ① **02 47 26 86 50** www.cg37.fr

The Auberge du XII Siècle, in the centre of Saché, is a wood-beamed country inn once frequented by Balzac; now a Michelin-starred restaurant, which serves delicious regional dishes. ① **02 47 26 88 77**

From Saché, simply follow the D17 to Azay-le-Rideau.

Azay-le-Rideau

Azay-le-Rideau is one of the Loire's most picturesque towns, and there is little immediate evidence of wine production, since the town's winemakers are relatively few and mostly live in the surrounding villages.

Azay is most famous for its Château, constructed on the site of a medieval stronghold, and surrounded by a moat designed to double the grandeur of its Renaissance architecture in its reflection. Gilles Berthelot, secretary of the treasury to King François I, built the Château in the 16th century, and its intricate landscape gardens were added some 300 years later.

There is a sound and light show in the Château's grounds every evening in July and August, and every Friday and Saturday in September. ① **02 47 45 42 04** www.monum.fr

Appellation Touraine Azay-le-Rideau

Like Amboise, Azay-le-Rideau can suffix its name to that of the 'Touraine' appellation, in labelling its white wines. These are made only from the Chenin Blanc grape and are usually dry, but can be *demi-sec* or even *moelleux*, in years when the grapes ripen sufficiently to make these sweeter styles. The wines of Azay-le-Rideau are never as rich as those from Vouvray or Montlouis, since 'noble rot' is rare in the vineyards of Azay. The appellation's dry whites, however, can show a distinctive delicacy, coupled with an impressive ageing potential.

The red wines are simply called 'Touraine Rouge', and are based on Cabernet Franc, the Gamay of the Beaujolais, and the powerfully tannic Côt variety (Malbec). The sandy clay soils of Azay-le-Rideau give generally lighter wines than those from nearby Chinon and Bourgueil, with pleasantly rustic flavours.

Very fine traditional method sparkling wines are made from the Chenin Blanc, with small amounts of Cabernet Franc and the red Grolleau grape. These, like many wines from Azay-le-Rideau, can be unbelievably good value.

A charming local speciality is a light, fruity rosé made exclusively from the thin-skinned Grolleau grape. Sparkling rosés also come from blends of Grolleau and Cabernet Franc.

The attack of phylloxera in the late 19th century wiped out most of the area's vineyards. Since then, its agriculture has been mixed, and many winemakers still grow cereal crops, apples and pears, as well as vines.

One of the town's exceptional winemakers is Pascal Pibaleau (see page 134), two miles out of Azay-le-Rideau along Rue Carnot from the town centre (D57 to Langeais).

Bedding down in Azay, or a further exploration

There are few better places than Azay-le-Rideau for simply sitting in a riverside bar, or on a peaceful restaurant terrace, with a cold drink. But the D39 leads north, a temptingly short six miles, to the famous Château de Villandry.

Built in the same century as Château d'Azay-le-Rideau, Château de Villandry is most famous for its magnificent English-style gardens, which date from the 19th century. ① 02 47 50 02 09 ⟐ www.chateauvillandry.com

And en route to Villandry, in the hamlet of Vallères, is possibly Azay-le-Rideau's most meticulous winemaker. Guillaume Decroix is a young and dynamic force for natural winemaking in Azay, and is always happy to welcome visitors to his cellars. ① 02 47 45 97 79 ✉ Les Caves du Château de Fouchault, Route de Lignières

Rousseau Frères – Touraine-Noble-Joué

Le Vau
37320 Esvres

Phone 02 47 26 44 45
Fax 02 47 26 53 12
Rousseau-freres@wanadoo.fr

The Estate

When I pedalled into the Rousseau brothers' estate in late July, the weather was hot but the sky was ominously dark. Michel Rousseau had just received an automated call from the weather office announcing the threat of hail, so he was firing up his anti-hail machine. Michel is part of a pan-regional group of vignerons who, when a hail warning arrives, look out for each other by burning a harmless silver-based gas which enters the clouds, breaking down the hailstones.

Michel began by talking not about his estate, but of Touraine-Noble-Joué. At only 35 hectares, this is the Loire's smallest *appellation contrôlée*. It was only in 2001 that it received its 'AOC' status, yet Michel proudly recounts the history of a wine that was once a favourite at the table of King Louis XI. Indeed, by the end of the 19th century, this was one of Touraine's most important wine-growing areas.

The attack of phylloxera, a couple of World Wars and the 20th century urbanisation of Joué-les-Tours, the wine's ancient centre of production, all heralded the wine's decline. And until the mid-1970s, vignerons were unwilling to resurrect the area's capricious grape varieties.

The Rousseau brothers work their vineyards, as far as possible, as self-regulating ecosystems, the wild grasses between the vines forcing their roots deep into the soil in their search for nutrients. These grasses, Michel explains, also soak up excess rain around harvest time, preventing the grapes from swelling with water and diluting their flavours.

Contact Michel or Bernard to arrange a visit.

The Rousseau Frères have no UK importer, as they do not produce sufficient quantities of wine to satisfy the demands of a foreign wholesaler!

Instead, the wines are eagerly quaffed in the restaurants of Touraine.

Choice wines:

Touraine-Noble-Joué 2005

This is the estate's signature rosé wine, made from 50% Pinot Meunier, 35% Pinot Gris and 15% Pinot Noir. These different grapes are grown on sandy clay soils interspersed with pebbles of flint. The varieties are vinified separately, spending three months on their lees after fermentation, to develop more intense fruit aromas.

The wine's colour is a characteristically pale *oeil de perdrix*, or 'eye of partridge'; on the nose there are strawberries and wild red berry fruit aromas, with a delicate underlying minerality.

Intense red berry flavours appear on a fresh, rounded palate with good length of flavour. The wine is extremely versatile with food, and an excellent partner for richly flavoured fish, white meats, or more exotic, spicy dishes.

Touraine Malvoisie Moelleux 2005

In the Loire Valley, the name 'Malvoisie' is a synonym for the Pinot Gris grape, and Noble-Joué is the only place in the region where it is grown. The wine is similar in style to some wines produced in the Savoie region, in the alpine foothills, and the Swiss Valais.

2005 is the product of two separate harvests in the same vineyards, one at the beginning of October, the other towards the end, to ensure that individual bunches of grapes had achieved optimum levels of maturity. By the time of the second passage through the vines, 'noble rot' was well developed on the grapes. The wine shows honeyed aromas, which are unmistakably reminiscent of *Poire William*.

On the palate, the wine is sweet, intense and exotic. An excellent apéritif wine; try also with *foie gras*, or rich apple pie.

The brothers Rousseau bottled a tiny quantity of the 2005 Malvoisie exclusively from the *deuxième trie*: grapes picked during the second passage through the vineyard, in late October. This rare wine shows pure *Poire William* and honey on the nose; its palate is sweet and super-concentrated, with 120 grammes per litre of residual sugar.

TOP
A tasting chez
Michel Rousseau

Domaine Pascal Pibaleau

68, route de Langeais
37190 Azay-le-Rideau

Phone 02 47 45 27 58
Fax 02 47 45 26 18
Pascal.pibaleau@wanadoo.fr
www.vins-pibaleau.com

The Estate

Two generations ago, the Pibaleau estate was a polycultural farm; Pascal Pibaleau's father and grandfather grew apples and mixed cereal crops as well as grapes. The domaine passed to Pascal from his father in 1996, and now includes 16 hectares of flinty clay vineyards devoted exclusively to wine production.

Pascal and his wife Christine have farmed organically since the late 1990s, although it will be 2008 before the word 'biologique' appears on their bottle labels. The juice from which the wines are made is not enriched with sugar, as the styles of wine produced depend entirely on vintage conditions.

The eclectic range includes dry, sparkling and sweet whites made primarily from Chenin Blanc grapes. The estate makes still and sparkling rosés, and various interesting reds from the Cabernet Franc, Gamay and Côt varieties, including an experimental blend of all three. Pascal insists on undertaking the entire winemaking process on site, even carrying out the maturation of his own traditional method sparkling wines.

The smiling Pascal was keen to show me the family cellars, dug by his father and grandfather, before proudly presenting his new winery. This building is cut into the hillside beneath the vineyards, so that grapes can be received directly from the vines above, and fed down by gravity into the winery, rather than be pumped roughly through a hose.

Phone in advance to visit. Pascal and his wife speak some English.

UK importers:
Waterloo Wine Co, London
3D Wines Ltd, Swineshead
The Wine Warehouse, Tetbury

LEFT & OPPOSITE PAGE
All smiles:
Pascal Pibaleau

Choice wines:

Touraine Azay-le-Rideau Rosé 2005

This unique rosé is made exclusively from the local Grolleau grape which, according to appellation regulations, must be pressed immediately without maceration on its skins.

The thin-skinned Grolleau thus gives a rosé that is light in colour, with a pretty raspberry-and-redcurrant nose. The flavours are pure summer fruits, with the pleasant softness that comes from fully ripe grapes.

An excellent accompaniment to summer barbecues or charcuterie.

Crémant de Loire Blanc Brut NV

This is a fantastic Loire *crémant*, based on the Chenin Blanc grape, with 10% Grolleau, to add fruity freshness, and 10% Cabernet Franc, to give body and intensity. The wine's second, bottle, fermentation uses the residual grape sugar left after its first fermentation in vat; it then ages on its lees for two years.

The wine has a delicate nose of ripe apples, with strong hints of red fruits. Rich strawberry and apple flavours dominate the palate, in a well-structured, pleasant summer sparkler.

Drink as an apéritif or with light desserts.

Touraine Azay-le-Rideau Blanc
"La Noblesse d'Axiaum" 2003

A relatively new addition to the Pibaleau range, this is 100% old vine Chenin Blanc, which undergoes a slow fermentation and ages in wood *barriques* for eleven months before bottling.

The nose is complex and mineral; its oak influence is barely noticeable. Aromas of white flowers dominate, with hints of what the French call *bonbons anglais* (boiled sweets). The palate is full and rich, yet subtle, floral and honeyed, with excellent length of flavour.

A great match for white meats, fish in creamy sauces, or to accompany the cheese board.

Touraine Rouge "l'Héritage d'Axiaum" 2003

Made from the powerful red Côt grape, from the hot 2003 vintage, this is a wine that requires time and patience. Pascal fermented the juice at a maximum of 23 degrees, then aged the wine in *barriques* for 9 months, to tame the savage tannins of the Côt.

The wine is deeply coloured, with a rich spiced plum nose. The concentration is evident on the palate, as is the tannin, which is ripe but still needs to soften. This wine would benefit from eight years' bottle age to show its true potential.

A good partner for roast lamb, rich game dishes, or strong, hard cheeses.

Le Château d'Artigny★★★★
37250 Montbazon

Phone 02 47 34 30 30
Fax 02 47 34 30 39
www.artigny.com

This grand 18th century Château houses an elegant restaurant, with large windows overlooking the forest within its grounds. The menu is based on traditional French recipes, but is creatively influenced by oriental flavours. The Château is a great place to have lunch, since full midday menus are available for only about €30.

On the first Saturday of each month, Chef Francis Maignaut organises culinary workshops from 9am until noon, focussing each time on a different gastronomic theme. Contact in advance for details.

The four-star hotel rooms cost €160 to €320. The hotel employs an arcane price reductions system that, if you can navigate it, may win you a substantial discount. Bike hire features among the hotel's many services, and cyclists are most welcome in what is otherwise a very posh hotel.

The restaurant is open every day of the year.

In the centre of Azay-le-Rideau, cyclists get a special welcome at Le Grand Monarque, from owner Jean-Michel Forest. A sports journalist turned restaurateur, Jean-Michel specialised in cycling, covering no fewer than 18 Tours de France; he owns a collection of bicycles ridden by the race's winning riders.

A gastronome by passion and an impeccable connoisseur of Loire wines, Jean-Michel maintains an 800-strong wine list, with a focus on the Loire and plenty of old vintages. Jean-Michel has additionally sourced fascinating wines from regions all over the world.

Gastronomic menus in the evenings are between €30 and €60. At lunchtimes, you can relax on the airy restaurant terrace and choose from a stylish 3-course bistro menu at €15, with plenty of wines available by the glass or pitcher.

Some English is spoken. Book in advance for evenings and weekends.

Present this book to Jean-Michel to receive a free apéritif.

The restaurant is never shut between Easter and mid-October. In low season, it is closed Sunday evening, all day Monday, and Tuesday lunchtime. Annual closure is from December to mid-February.

Le Grand Monarque*** Hôtel-Restaurant

3, place de la République
37190 Azay-le-Rideau

Phone 02 47 45 40 08
Fax 02 47 45 46 25
www.legrandmonarque.com

ABOVE
Jean-Michel Forest:
sports journalist
turned restaurateur

Ghislaine and Jean-Luc Fèvre's warm, traditional Restaurant L'Aigle d'Or is the other fine place to eat in Azay-le-Rideau. It too has a pleasant garden and a great wine list, but the real treat here is Jean-Luc's exceptional brand of regional cooking.

Unusually for the Loire Valley, the speciality here is homemade duck *foie gras*, which Jean-Luc incorporates into a delicious king prawn salad starter. *Foie gras* is also served with *poires tapées* from the farms in nearby Rivarennes. An essential main course is the chef's *Blanquette de Sandre*.

Menus are from €20 to €60; the most expensive includes a different glass of wine to match each course.

Closed: Wednesday and Sunday evenings all year, Tuesday evening except in July and August, and Monday evening from December to March.

Annual closure is in November and February.

Restaurant L'Aigle d'Or

10, rue Adelaïde Riché
37190 Azay-le-Rideau

Phone 02 47 45 24 58
Fax 02 47 45 90 18

Day 4 itinerary (18 miles)

Azay-le-Rideau to Chinon: entering red wine country

Grapes & pears

Leave the centre of Azay-le-Rideau along rue Nationale and cross the bridge south of the town. Turn right onto the D17 at the sign for 'Rivarennes' and 'Rigny-Ussé'. Four miles from Azay-le-Rideau, in the hamlet of Armentières, a sign on your left points to Domaine James & Nicholas Paget, another of Azay's fine wine estates.
② 02 47 95 54 02 ⁀ N_paget@club-internet.fr

The next hamlet is Quinçay, home to the Herins, who claim to be the only family still to use nothing but love and log fires in the production of *poires tapées*, the local sweet speciality. When the pears from their orchards ripen in autumn, they are picked and slowly dehydrated in a wood-burning stove for a week. They are then crushed and either eaten straight away or marinated in local red or white wine, with a little cinnamon and sugar.

With the arrival of the phylloxera louse in the 19th

century, apple and pear orchards became crucial to the area's farmers, who had previously relied on the grape harvest for their income. In a spirit of enterprise born of necessity, *poires tapées* and other fruit-based desserts were increasingly made, and exported as far afield as the Low Countries and even Great Britain.

Christine and Yves Herin's daughter Coraline speaks some English and is otherwise "good with hand gestures", as she put it.

A tasting of the product range costs about €2. Open daily from 10 till 6. ① **02 47 95 45 19** ⌁ **www.poirestapees.com**

Day 4 at a glance
Itinerary 138 – 143
Wineries 144 – 147
Restaurants 148 – 149

The Castle of the Sleeping Beauty

Beyond Quinçay, turn left onto the D7 at the signpost for 'Château d'Ussé'. Three further miles through the peaceful forest leads to the village of Rigny-Ussé.

The fairytale Château d'Ussé was built between the 15th and 17th centuries. It is the one that inspired Charles Perrault's 17th-century yarn *La Belle au Bois Dormant*, or the Tale of the Sleeping Beauty.

The estate is family-owned, and the visit is interesting, if a little pricey at €11. Particularly impressive are the exhibition of period garments and weapons, and the collection of horse-drawn carriages in the castle stables. ① **02 47 95 54 05**

The road to Chinon

Three kilometres beyond the Château, turn left onto the D16 to Chinon. Continue through Huimes, the first village of the Chinon appellation, and into the hamlet of La Grille, home to its first excellent wine estate.

Château de La Grille owns 28 hectares of vines in the hamlet of La Grille, once part of a much larger farm estate. The Gosset family of Champagne bought the Château in 1951, improving the already great reputation that its wines enjoyed. ① **02 47 93 01 95** ⌁ **www.chateau-de-la-grille.com**

On entering Chinon, you pass its most famous and picturesque vineyard, Clos de l'Echo, on your right opposite the castle. This vineyard is wholly owned by Couly-Dutheil, Chinon's largest wine producer (see below).

Chinon

Built largely on the north bank of the River Vienne, the sleepy town of Chinon is perched on the hillside around its ruined medieval Château. Chinon has a friendly, relaxed feel that has already persuaded a small number of wise Brits to make it their home. With an abundance of

ABOVE
Poires tapées in Quinçay

BOTTOM
Château d'Ussé

ABOVE & BELOW
The Castle of the
Sleeping Beauty

excellent wine estates and three fine restaurants, you may well decide to spend more than a single night in Chinon.

The town's history dates from the Iron Age, but its period of prosperity and expansion really began under Henry II Plantagenet, crowned King of England in 1154.

During France's Hundred Years War with England, Château de Chinon became a key base for the French heir apparent, the future Charles VII, and it was here in 1429 that Joan of Arc famously swore her support to 'the Dauphin'. Many of the buildings in Chinon's medieval quarter date from this, the town's historical heyday, and you can wander along the cobbled streets that once played host to a thriving market.

The Château is open all year. Inside the restored clock tower is a rather basic museum devoted to Joan of Arc; more interesting are the lively festivals that take place in the Château's grounds in summer, recreating its folklore and history. The views of the town and river from the Château's high battlements are magnificent. ☎ 02 47 93 13 45

The wines of Chinon

In common with the Loire's other vineyards, those of Chinon suffered decimation by the phylloxera louse at the end of the 19th century. But Chinon's wines have enjoyed considerable renown since before phylloxera, and today they benefit from a cult following that frequently leaves its best producers short of wine to sell.

Styles of wine vary depending on whether grapes are grown on the flat sand and gravel soils beside the River, or on the limestone *côteaux*, or slopes, above the town and the surrounding villages. These slopes produce red wines with a firmer structure and greater ageing potential than those from the river valley.

Chinon's red wines are made from the Cabernet Franc grape, with up to 25% Cabernet Sauvignon; delicious full-bodied rosés are made from the same grapes. Much rarer is Chinon Blanc, a white wine made from the Chenin Blanc.

Chinon Rouge was once quite an acquired taste: high in acidity, with astringent, 'stalky' flavours that needed time to soften. The tendency over the last decade has been towards a fuller-bodied, softer style, as grapes are picked later to give riper fruit flavours. This trend has been helped along by a run of warm vintages since the Millennium. The best red Chinons show fresh red fruit flavours, with an earthiness often likened to the smell of fresh pencil shavings. With time in bottle, they can even resemble fine 'right-bank' clarets, and at a fraction of the price.

Chinon's winemakers

The town's largest producer is Couly-Dutheil, owner of the prestigious Clos de l'Echo vineyard beside the Château. Disputes are alleged to be raging in the Couly-Dutheil clan and, for many, the wines themselves have rather lost their way in recent years. Visits to the estate's impressive cellars are possible, by appointment, and with a charge.
① 02 47 97 20 20 ⁀ www.coulydutheil-chinon.com

Beneath the foundations of Château de Chinon are the cellars of Marc Plouzeau, whose wines have improved immeasurably over the last decade (see page 144). But the highest concentration of winemaking talent is a few miles to the east of Chinon in the tiny village of Cravant-les-Côteaux.

Cravant's most fashionable producer is Philippe Alliet, who will almost certainly have few wines to sell; such is the demand for his delicious creations. ① 02 47 93 17 62

By far the best vigneron to visit in Cravant-les-Côteaux is the fantastic Bernard Baudry (see page 146).

To reach Cravant-les-Côteaux, leave Chinon along rue du 11 Novembre, from place Jeanne d'Arc. Turn left in front of the railway station, and continue into the village of Cravant. Domaine Bernard Baudry is on the main road (D21), just beyond Château de Sonnay.

Another of Chinon's finest vignerons, Domaine Charles Joguet, is barely more than a mile from Cravant-les-Côteaux, in the village of Sazilly. Sazilly is, however, on the other side of the River Vienne, so unless you're an Olympic long jumper, you will need to return to Chinon, cross the River and take the D749 back east. ① 02 47 58 55 53 ⁀ www.charlesjoguet.com

Living well in Chinon

Chinon's most famous son is François Rabelais, author of the 16th-century comic novels *Gargantua* and *Pantagruel*. A notorious bon vivant, Rabelais' writing is as bawdy as that of his English forerunner Geoffrey Chaucer. His books were banned by the Catholic Church and placed on the *Index librorum prohibitorum*, or Index of Forbidden Books.

The *Confrérie des Bons Entonneurs Rabelaisiens* is Chinon's own robed wine brotherhood. In common with the *Chevaliers de Tastevin* in Burgundy, it is the *confrères* job to protect and promote the reputation of Chinon wines – with a lot of Rabelais thrown in for fun. Indeed, to become *confrères*, they have to prove their devotion to the cause by downing half a bottle of Chinon without taking a breath, or throwing up!

ABOVE
Wine from Chinon chef Jean-Claude Rigollet's tiny parcel of vines within Clos de l'Echo

The subterranean headquarters of the *Confrérie* are the Caves Painctes de Chinon, which are open to visitors in July and August. ① **02 47 93 30 44**

Chinon's other attractions

Chinon's wine museum, the Musée Animé du Vin, is pretty awful, and having watched its owner/chef pick dirt from beneath his fingernails, I couldn't stomach the thought of eating at the attached restaurant. But the Chinon Museum of Art and History, on rue Haute Saint-Maurice, is well worth a visit. ① **02 47 93 18 12**
⊕ www.chinon-histoire.org

Otherwise, have a wander in the Maison de la Rivière, an exhibition of the area's aquatic traditions, including a reconstructed boat-building workshop and aquaria containing fish from the Vienne. ① **02 47 95 93 15**
⊕ www.cpie-val-de-loire.org

If you feel like a relaxing paddle along the river in a canoe or kayak, you can rent one from Chinon Loisirs Activités Nature, across the bridge on the Vienne's south bank. ① **06 23 82 96 33**

Open from the 1st March until mid-October. Bike rental and organised wine-related river tours are also offered. **Present this book for a 10% discount.**

THIS PAGE
TOP
Folk festivities at Château de Chinon

MIDDLE
The Château from the town

LEFT
The town from the Château

OPPOSITE PAGE
TOP LEFT
The *Confrérie des Bons Entonneurs Rabelaisiens*

TOP RIGHT
Chinon's medieval streets

BOTTOM
Home to the *confrères*: the Caves Painctes de Chinon

Caves Plouzeau

94, rue Haut Saint-Maurice
37500 Chinon

Phone 02 47 93 16 34
Fax 02 47 98 48 23
Info@plouzeau.com
www.plouzeau.com

The Estate

Ten years ago, the wines of the Plouzeau family estate, Château de la Bonnelière, were sold as entry-level house blends in Chinon's restaurants. The wines were light and fruity, but fairly insubstantial. However, since Pierre Plouzeau's dynamic son Marc took over in 1998, things have changed dramatically.

Marc set to work immediately improving the estate's vineyards and, within a few years, all of the estate's 15 hectares of vines were grown organically. The wines from different parcels are hand harvested and vinified separately, so as to preserve the characters of different terroirs, in individual wine bottlings.

The wines are supple and show intensely pure fruit flavours. The oak-aged cuvées have an impressive ageing potential, something Marc believes is the result of natural viticultural methods. All of the estate's wines are transferred into wood *barriques* to finish their fermentations, so that the wood tannins are well integrated with the wines' flavours.

In the centre of old Chinon, the Plouzeau cellars are as impressive as the estate's recent wines. Dug in the 12th century to provide rocks to build the Château, you can walk beneath the wells through which the rocks were once hoisted, and under the Château itself to where Marc Plouzeau now ages his wines.

Free cellar visits and tastings are possible from Tuesday to Saturday, from April to September: 11 till 1pm and 3 till 7pm.

No appointment is necessary.

Present this book for a 5% discount on wines purchased

UK importer:
General Wine Company, Hants

LEFT
Ambitious: Marc
Plouzeau

Choice wines:
Chinon Rosé 'Rive Gauche' 2005
This rosé is made from Cabernet Franc grapes, grown on the sandy gravel soils on the left bank of the Vienne. 70% of the grapes are pressed directly, whilst 30% are allowed a short period of skin maceration.

The wine has a pale salmon colour, with intense strawberry aromas and a little spice. On the palate, its attack is intense, with piercing red fruits.

In the warm 2005 vintage, Marc made his rosé using carefully selected grapes with the least potential alcohol, and left a small amount of residual sugar after fermentation to give the wine extra balance and softness.

A good partner for vegetarian and gently spiced dishes.

Touraine Sauvignon 'Les Devants de la Bonnelière' 2005
Sauvignon Blanc is less fashionable than the Chenin grape in this part of the Loire; but this Sauvignon is grown on the clay-limestone slopes above the left bank of the Vienne, giving a wine with more mineral flavours than the floral Sauvignons from further east in Touraine. The wine is made biodynamically.

Fresh lemon and grapefruit flavours make this a delicious summer wine, with good body and a persistent finish.

Drink with river fish and the Loire's delicious goat's cheeses.

Chinon Château de la Bonnelière 'Chapelle' 2003
This is the estate's powerful *vin de garde*. It comes from low yielding vines grown on flinty clay slopes, in the *commune* of Roche Clermault, south of Chinon. It spends a year ageing in oak *barriques* and is then bottled without filtration.

With a dense colour and a concentrated nose, the 2003 still needs time to develop fully. On the palate, the wine's complexity is immediately evident, with rich, concentrated flavours of plums and cherries, cinnamon and spice. The finish is long and exceptionally well balanced.

Drink with red meats or, with bottle age, big game dishes.

ABOVE
The Plouzeau cellars

Domaine Bernard Baudry

9 Coteau du Sonnay
37500 Cravant-les-Côteaux
Chinon

Phone 02 47 93 15 79
Fax 02 47 98 44 44
www.chinon.com/vignoble/
bernard-baudry
bernard-baudry@chinon.com

The Estate

In the village of Cravant-les-Côteaux, Domaine Bernard Baudry makes some of the finest and longest-lived of Chinon's wines. The number of visitors, local and foreign, who arrive here daily to restock their cellars is testimony to the estate's considerable renown.

Bernard Baudry was born into a winemaking family in Cravant. He studied oenology in Beaune, before working in Tours with Jacques Puisais, Touraine's most famous winemaking professor. Bernard began making his own wines in 1982, with only two hectares of vines.

A tasting *chez* Baudry provides a wonderful illustration of the versatility of the Cabernet Franc when grown on different sites. The estate's six principal cuvées are made exclusively from this grape, each from different parcels of vines. The dry Chenin-based Chinon Blanc is a curiosity, available only in tiny quantities direct from the estate.

Today, the Baudry estate includes 30 hectares of vines, which Bernard and his son Matthieu still work mechanically, without using artificial herbicides or insecticides. All grape harvesting is done manually, so that only the best grapes are selected.

Phone in advance to visit and taste at the Baudry cellars. Matthieu speaks good English, and is happy to share his passionate and encyclopaedic knowledge of the wines of Chinon.

UK importers:
Lea & Sandeman
Haynes, Hanson & Clark
Fortnum & Mason
Ballantynes of Cowbridge, Wales

OPPOSITE PAGE
Matthieu Baudry
draws wine from
barrel and tastes in
his cellars

Choice wines:

Chinon Rosé 2005

Cabernet grapes are harvested late in the season, from gravelly clay slopes, and then left to macerate for an hour to gain a little colour before they are pressed. The resulting wine is delicate in both colour and aroma, with crisp red fruit flavours.

This wine is normally for drinking within the year, but the 2005 is unusually full, almost *provençale*, in style. It thus has the structure to improve for two or three years, partnering well with rustic country foods.

Les Granges 2005

From a six-hectare parcel of sandy gravel soils, above a layer of sandy clay, this is an unoaked *cuvée* that can be approached in the years following the harvest.

With a deep purple colour, and earthy blackberry and raspberry aromas, this wine is from a big, ripe vintage, and thus needs until spring 2007 to open up fully. Its unusual concentration is expressed on a rich, peppery palate, with notes of fresh pencil shavings.

Drink with roast pork or veal.

Les Grezeaux 2004

This wine comes from a small parcel of 40 to 60-year-old vines. These are grown on the gravelly soils, and flinty clay sub-soils, at the foot of the slopes of 'Sonnay', above the Baudry estate.

The result is a soft, rounded wine with concentrated aromas of plums and cherries, and leathery hints given by ageing in old oak *barriques*. On the palate, the wine is well structured and intense, but supple, with good length of flavour.

Try with rich meat stews cooked in red wine.

La Croix Boissée 2004

The grapes for this wine are grown on south-facing clay-limestone hillside slopes. The wine is aged for 12-14 months in 1 to 3-year-old oak *barriques*. This is the estate's firmest, longest-lived wine.

Young, concentrated and earthy aromas are most pronounced on the nose, with hints of violet. The palate is yet more intense, with a tannic austerity, but a beautiful balance of power and finesse.

This is a wine that needs time – or rich food!

The 1997 wine from the same vineyard is drinking wonderfully, with complex aromas of cherries, forest floor spice and those hints of pencil shavings that are so characteristic of Chinon's wines.

Au Plaisir Gourmand
2, rue Parmentier
37500 Chinon

Phone 02 47 93 20 48

Au Chapeau Rouge
49, place du Général de Gaulle
37500 Chinon

Phone/Fax 02 47 98 08 08

Restaurant L'Océanic
13, rue Rabelais
37500 Chinon

Phone 02 47 93 44 55
Fax 02 47 93 38 08

Le Café Français
37, place du Général de Gaulle
37500 Chinon

Phone 02 47 93 32 78
www.cafefrancais.fr

BELOW
Chef Jean-Claude Rigollet, with
St. Laurent, patron saint of chefs

Chinon restaurants
For more than 20 years, Chinon's best restaurant has been Au Plaisir Gourmand.

Hidden in an alley off the quay, Au Plaisir is one of Touraine's real gastronomic gems. The seventeenth-century building houses an elegant antique dining room, and on summer evenings, you can eat outside in the intimate terraced garden. The service at Au Plaisir is outstanding, and the restaurant has a uniquely relaxed feel.

Jean-Claude Rigollet has owned Au Plaisir Gourmand for more than 20 years, and gained his Michelin star at the very beginning; but you won't meet a more modest chef anywhere. Jean-Claude's style of cuisine is traditionally French, and fantastically inventive.

Menus are based on the finest seafood dishes. The *Maraîchère de Tourteau* (crab) *Tartare de Tomates au Basilic* is wonderful with a glass of Savennières, from the vineyards of nearby Anjou; a filet of pikeperch roasted in white butter goes perfectly with a simple glass of Mareuil, a little-known wine from south of Nantes.

The wine list features Chinon wines dating from 1947, and includes several vintages of the wine made from Jean-Claude's own two hectares within Chinon's Clos de l'Echo vineyard.

Set menus are between €30 and €65.

Some English is spoken. Book in advance for evenings and weekends. Closed: Sunday evening, Monday and Tuesday lunchtime.

In summer 2006, there was a rumour that Jean-Claude and his wife were considering retirement. The couple denied any such intentions, but if you find the restaurant closed, one-time pupil of Jean-Claude, Christophe Duguin, runs Au Chapeau Rouge, another of Chinon's outstanding restaurants.

Au Chapeau Rouge is a great place to while away a summer evening and watch the people of Chinon go by. Christophe Duguin is proud to buy the ingredients for his dishes from select local suppliers. Wild fish are caught fresh from the River Loire, flavoured with local saffron from the village of Preuilly-sur-Chaise. In the winter, there is an entire menu based around locally snuffled-out truffles.

Menus are between €30 and €60.

Some English is spoken. Book in advance for evenings and weekends. Closed: Sunday evening and all day Monday; and for 2 weeks in February and November.

Present this book to receive a free glass of local sparkling wine with your dessert.

Local wines take pride of place at Restaurant l'Océanic, carefully selected by charming lady patronne Marie-Paule Descombes, and priced from less than €20 a bottle.

Marie-Paule is a member of the *Union des Sommeliers de France*, and offers wines like Charles Joguet's delicious Chinon 'Les Varennes du Grand Clos' 1999, by the glass. She introduced me to a dry white wine called Ampelidae 'Le S', from the 2001 vintage: a Sauvignon-based *Vin de Pays de la Vienne*, with flavours similar to *barrique*-aged dry white Bordeaux. All wines are served in proper Riedel glasses, designed to enhance their aromas.

The wine list changes in harmony with Chef Patrick Descombes' fish-based menus, which cost between €20 and €35. For lunch, you can choose from an even cheaper *Menu Affaire*, which includes a main course, a glass of wine and either a cheese course or a dessert.

L'Aumônière pommes, poires et raisins is the delicious house pudding; the cheese board is based around the products of renowned *fromager* Hervé Mons, with a selection of delicious local goat's cheeses. From time to time, Patrick Descombes also keeps some fine English Stilton, which you can enjoy, à *l'anglaise*, with a glass of aged Port.

Marie-Paule speaks good English; the chef likes to greet his guests, but only in French. Book in advance for evenings. Closed Sunday evening (except in July and August) and all day Monday.

Le Café Français, behind the Mairie, is an atmospheric place to stop for a beer, and regularly hosts an eclectic range of musical events. This is where I watched France beat the Spanish in the 2006 World Cup. I must have looked ambivalent about the result, since when my tab appeared at the end of the evening, it was clearly headed: "L'Espagnol"!

ABOVE
Rigollet's apprentice
Christophe Duguin

BELOW
Lady sommelier:
Marie-Paule Descombes

ABOVE
Bourgueil town centre

Day 5 itinerary (15-30 miles)

Chinon to Montsoreau, via Bourgueil

Leaving Chinon

Follow the D749 west from Chinon along the north bank of the River Vienne towards Avoine. Three miles later, the road bends to the right towards Beaumont-en-Véron. The limestone plateau above Beaumont has south-facing slopes that grow some of Chinon's most powerful and ageworthy wines.

Set back from the bend in the road is Château de Coulaine, one of Chinon's most impressive château-estates and a producer of some of the appellation's most interesting wines.

The Château's owners are Pascale and Etienne de Bonnaventure. Etienne is from one of Chinon's oldest winemaking families, and Château de Coulaine's winemaking history can be traced back to the year 1300. Even until the late 1990s, however, the de Bonnaventures grew grapes as part of a polycultural farm, and Etienne's father's estate comprised only a single hectare of vineyard. This was the Château's clay-limestone Clos Turpenay, which has been planted with vines since the Middle Ages.

The early 1990s saw the expansion of the estate's wine production, and the best terroirs were developed as the farm's other activities waned. By 1997, Château de Coulaine was entirely devoted to winemaking, and in that year, Etienne began converting the estate to organic viticulture.

Pascale and Etienne are happy to welcome visitors, but please contact well in advance to visit the estate and cellars. Within the Château, the de Bonnaventures offer comfortable B&B rooms. ① **02 40 66 44 07**
⌂ **châteaudecoulaine@vinibegood.com**

The Eco-museum and the road to Bourgueil

Immediately after Château de Coulaine, turn left at the sign for Savigny-en-Véron. Follow the vineyard road two and a half miles to the centre of Savigny-en-Véron. Turn left towards the Ecomusée du Véron, and turn left again into the hamlet of Roguinet at the junction with the D118.

The Ecomusée is a state-owned working farm, which presents the area's viticultural heritage within the general context of local peasant life. After visiting the museum, you can wander outside and meet the rare breeds of sheep, goats and horses kept by the Ecomusée, which is set to double in size by 2009.

The museum is open all week, but closed for lunch between 12.30 and 2pm. ① **02 47 58 09 05**
⌂ **www.cc-veron.fr/ecomusee**

Turn right outside the Ecomusée and take the first left towards 'Le Petit Chouzé'. Two miles later, turn left at the small 'bicycle' sign, then turn right onto the D7. Turn left onto the D749 in front of the looming dome of the nuclear power plant and over the bridge, built by the British military during the war. This road leads to the centre of Bourgueil.

Bourgueil

Once a very poor town, Bourgueil's population increased sharply with the building of its power plant in 1957, as did wine production, which had reduced dramatically since the 19th century phylloxera epidemic. The fields to the north and west of Bourgueil that are not planted with grapes are still renowned for the delicious strawberries they produce.

Bourgueil's wines are often compared with those of its near neighbour Chinon, but whilst the latter town

Day 5 at a glance
Itinerary   150 – 155
Wineries   156 – 159
Restaurants   160 – 161

BELOW
Market day in Bourgueil

BOTTOM
Château de Coulaine

has all the relaxed affluence of a genteel tourist destination, Bourgueil is still very much a parochial French market town.

The best time to arrive in Bourgueil is Tuesday morning, when the most characterful of the local markets takes place, and finishes quite abruptly for lunch.

The town's 10th-century Abbey of St. Peter contains an impressive unsupported marble staircase from the 18th century, and a cinema, in the monks' old refectory. The museum is only of mild interest, but if you phone caretaker Mery beforehand, she may let you eat your picnic in the monks' kitchen. Open afternoons only. ① 02 47 97 84 92
⌖ http://abbaye-st-pierre-bourgueil.ifrance.com

The red wines of Bourgueil

Together with Chinon, Bourgueil is a strong contender for the epithet: 'the Loire's finest red wine'. As in Chinon, these wines are made from the Cabernet Franc grape, with up to 25% of Cabernet Sauvignon. The wines can be very similar, and many producers own land in both appellations. Bourgueil is generally deeper in colour, with earthier flavours, than most Chinon. The best vineyards are sited on the limestone-rich slopes beneath the forest north of the town.

The smaller St-Nicholas-de-Bourgueil appellation begins just west of Bourgueil, where the vineyards contain more sand and gravel. The wines are very similar, if generally lighter, and most vignerons in Bourgueil also own land in St-Nicholas.

A great place to begin a discovery of Bourgueil is at the Cave du Pays de Bourgueil, a low-key new underground wine museum, at the point where the vineyards of Bourgueil give way to those of St-Nicholas-de-Bourgueil. The good-natured Anne-Marie Desenne runs the Cave, and organises guided tours and events throughout the year.

Anne-Marie had recently arrived in the area when I visited, and my only gripe was that the wine tasting that followed the excellent visit of the caves could have better represented the town's wines. This may have changed by the time you read this, since I mentioned my concerns to vigneron Yannick Amirault, who looked determined to "have a word". ① 02 47 58 58 40
⌖ www.histoires-en-scene.fr ⌖ www.cavesbourgueil.com

Vines, cellars and restaurants

Domaine Yannick Amirault is the first estate to try in Bourgueil. Follow rue Thiers from place des Halles in the centre of Bourgueil. Join rue Victor Hugo and continue onto rue des Sables, then cross the D10 into rue du Moulin Bleu. The estate is on your left just before the crossroads (see page 156).

This crossroads is a good place to get your bearings. The road west leads into St-Nicholas-de-Bourgueil; straight ahead climbs north into the forest. You will have noticed the blue windmill protruding from the forest beyond the vineyards. This is Le Moulin Bleu, Bourgueil's best restaurant (see page 160).

A right turn at the crossroads leads along route du Vignoble past another excellent estate, Delaunay Père et Fils, towards the village of Benais. ① 02 47 97 80 73

A strange day in Benais

Benais is one of the best-reputed villages of the Bourgueil appellation; its *tuffeau* limestone soils giving wines that can sometimes age for decades. It is also home to the producer of some of my favourite Bourgueils. Many winemakers are gruff, reserved characters, only showing their humorous side several wines into a tasting session. With Pierre-Jacques Druet it would be the other way around.

Pierre-Jacques is a first generation winemaker, and unpopular amongst Loire vignerons for his outspoken dislike of family estates that are passed from father to son over hundreds of years (i.e. most French ones). When I eventually found the Druet estate, Pierre-Jacques was in good humour. He was teaching customers a fascinating technique for predicting how tannins will evolve in a wine that is still young. Put a little salt in your mouth, and then take a swig of the young brew. If it appears soft, the wine will become more rounded with time in bottle. If, however, the wine still feels astringent, it means that the tannins are unripe and will probably never soften.

I expressed my amazement at this technique as the others departed, and Pierre-Jacques offered to drive me to his cellars, about three miles from the winery, for a barrel tasting. And what a superb tasting it was. Barrel samples appeared from the fabulous 2005 vintage, which we compared with fine wines in bottle from the early 1980s. We discussed politics, culture and history for what must have been hours when Pierre-Jacques received a phone call from an impatient customer.

Without warning, Pierre-Jacques flew into a rage, from which he would not recover until after I left. He hung up the phone and racked his brains for the thread of our previous conversation, but his tone had changed.

"Do you know why the world speaks English instead of French?" the vigneron interrogated.

I mumbled something apologetic about the United States.

"One vote!" Pierre-Jacques asserted. "When the United States' Constitution was proposed, a vote was cast as to what the official language would be. English won by only one vote. Otherwise, French would be the world language!"

"Alright," I conceded, then added without thinking: "but in what language were the delegates asked to vote in the first place?"

Pierre-Jacques was by now almost squaring up to me. I was afraid this might turn into one of those Ernest Hemingway moments, so I made my excuses and left to have lunch in a restaurant, instead of chewing on a knuckle sandwich from an unpredictable winemaker.

In conclusion, Pierre-Jacques Druet makes excellent wines, but visits are at the wine lover's own risk.

Softer options

On entering Benais, turn right through the village and down the hill, turning left at the sign for Restigné. Turn left briefly onto the D10, then left again at the sign for Domaine Catherine & Pierre Breton, Bourgueil's finest

BELOW
Unpredictable:
Pierre-Jacques Druet

organic estate (see page 158).

Alternatively, back in the vineyards just north of Bourgueil, try Montlouis vigneron Jacky Blot's new estate, Domaine de la Butte (see page 124). ℗ **02 47 97 81 30** ⌂ **www.jackyblot.com**

Across the River Loire to Montsoreau

Pleasant lodgings are available in Bourgueil (see page 175) for those already tired from the day's tasting, but an extra ten miles takes you to the scenic Loire-side town of Montsoreau, a perfect place to stay the night.

Leave Bourgueil on the vineyard road north of the town, turning left at the crossroads into the St-Nicholas-de-Bourgueil vineyards (see above).

After nearly two miles, turn left at the crossroads towards St-Nicholas-de-Bourgueil. The village of St-Nicholas does not match its wines in interest, so don't plan to spend hours visiting. Turn right into the main street, then left after Restaurant Le Saint Nicholas Gourmand.

I tried this restaurant on my first visit to the town, when the chef told me: "I don't accept cyclists, they only drink water and never spend any money." Didier Marnay is less scary than Pierre-Jacques Druet (see above), so I suggest that any cyclists reading this dismount, hide their helmets, enter the restaurant and order a carafe of water and a bag of crisps. Just for fun.

ABOVE
The village of Candes-Saint-Martin, near Montsoreau

TOP
Montsoreau from across the Loire

OPPOSITE PAGE
Champignonnière

Follow the road to the left of the restaurant to the centre of Chouzé-sur-Loire. In Chouzé, either turn right onto the N152 to the bridge towards Saumur-Champigny, or continue to the quay, where an attractive path runs along the river almost to the bridge. This path is perfect for bicycles and, although small vehicles can drive slowly along here, you wouldn't want to meet too many coming the other way. Turn left when the path obliges you to rejoin the N152 and then, after half a mile, cross the bridge into the Saumur-Champigny appellation.

Just over the bridge, you will see the Champignonnière du Saut aux Loups dug into the *tuffeau* cliff face directly above you. The Loire produces 55% of France's mushrooms, and here you can learn about the different kinds grown in the Champignonnière's 5 kilometres of caves, dug in the 15th century.

The Champignonnière is open from March to mid-November. Rustic (and rather indigestible) lunches are served, based around *galipettes* mushrooms, in the *troglodytique* restaurant. ℗ **02 41 51 70 30** ⌂ **www.troglo-sautauxloups.com**

Over the bridge, turn left at the roundabout. Built against the *tuffeau* rock face, Montsoreau is a wonderful place for an evening stroll, offering panoramic views of the Loire from its high points.

A satisfying way to end a busy day is with a meal at Diane de Méridor, Montsoreau's best restaurant (see page 161).

Domaine Yannick Amirault

5, Pavilion du Grand Clos
37140 Bourgueil

Phone 02 47 97 78 07
Mobile 06 80 68 38 66
Fax 02 47 97 94 78
www.yannickamirault.fr
Info@yannickamirault.fr

The Estate

With its unassuming appearance, the Amirault estate at first looks much like any smallholding anywhere in France. I had time to wander nosily amongst the vines before Yannick appeared on his tractor. He immediately joined me in the vineyard and started explaining his work, the history of his quest for natural winemaking.

Yannick took over only three and a half hectares of vines from his grandfather 30 years ago, and today works 14 hectares in Bourgueil and 6 in Saint-Nicholas-de-Bourgueil. In July, the estate was beginning its 'green harvest'; to remove excess bunches of grapes before they ripen, and to encourage greater ripeness and concentration of flavour in those remaining.

The fermentations take place in a brand new building, designed by Yannick and made from natural materials, or those conducive to the winemaking process. Only natural yeasts are used at the estate, and fermentations are allowed as long as they need. The 2005 harvest was unusually ripe in the middle Loire, and Amirault's wines from that year are sure to be some of the best. A tasting from barrel showed that many of the 2005s were still fermenting, as the yeasts laboured to convert an extraordinary level of natural grape sugar into alcohol.

The estate's wines are bottled without filtration, each one representing the unique personality of a different vineyard terroir.

Phone in advance to arrange a visit. Yannick speaks a little English, his son Benoit a little more. If you're lucky, you might get to visit the Amirault cellars, half a mile from the estate within what is now La Cave du Pays de Bourgueil (see Day 5 itinerary).

UK importers:
Thorman Hunt
Justerini & Brooks
Lea & Sandeman

LEFT
Yannick Amirault begins the 'green harvest'

Choice wines:

Bourgueil 'La Coudraye' 2005 (barrel tasting)

This is the domaine's entry level wine, an assemblage from three terroirs: Les Perrières (sandy clay), Les Sables (confusingly, gravelly) and La Coudraye (sandy soil).

By Yannick's own admission, the 2005 vintage of this wine is like no other he has ever made, with incredibly open natural aromas of young raspberry and cassis. It has great depth of colour, and the palate already shows ripe, silky tannins.

Once bottled, this wine will keep for many years, and can be drunk with red meats. It may all be sold by the time of publication!

Saint-Nicholas-de-Bourgueil 'La Mine' 2004

La Mine is a parcel of 35-year-old vines, grown on gravelly soils. It is unoaked, as Yannick did not want to 'unclothe' it of its naturally pure, fruity aromas.

The palate is classic, supple Saint-Nicholas, with redcurrant and a hint of cassis.

A wonderful wine to drink on its own, or with poultry dishes and rustic salads.

Bourgueil 'Le Grand Clos' 2004

One of Bourgueil's most jealously sought terroirs; Le Grand Clos is a small walled parcel of 50-year-old vines grown on the sandy limestone slopes facing the town.

The wine spends a year in (50% new) oak, and shows deep, intense forest fruit aromas, with sloes and hints of sweet leather. The palate has excellent structure, with redcurrant and spiced blackberry flavours, giving onto a long finish.

This wine needs a couple of years to soften before drinking, and will develop gracefully for another 20.

Bourgueil 'Les Quartiers' 2005 (barrel tasting)

From 50-year-old vines grown on limestone soils at the foot of the Bourgueil *côteaux*, this is typically an intense, mineral, mouth-filling wine.

Having just finished its fermentation, the 2005 vintage of this wine is breathtaking. On the nose, the wine's ripe intense fruits are reminiscent of fine Port, with deep aromas of dark plums; its colour is an almost opaque purple.

The wonder is that this wine is already pleasant to drink, and will certainly keep, and improve, for an age.

ABOVE
Tasting the 2005s
from barrel

Catherine & Pierre Breton

8, rue du Peu Muleau
37140 Restigné
Bourgueil

Phone 02 47 97 30 41
Fax 02 47 97 46 49
Domainebreton@yahoo.fr
www.domainebreton.net

The Estate

It immediately feels like you are somewhere special as you enter the small Breton estate, through the vineyard back roads from Bourgueil; an impression that is reinforced on meeting vignerons Catherine and Pierre.

For the Bretons, winemaking is a natural philosophy, the only ingredients come from the soil, the vine and the air. The wines have uniquely pure flavours, the products of vines that have never known chemical fertilisers, and whose roots dig deep to find nutrients and goodness in the soil. Catherine explains how this gives the wines natural balance, avoiding excessive alcohol and acidity levels.

Since 1991, the couple have worked their 15 hectares of vines in Bourgueil, Chinon and Vouvray following biodynamic principles, hand-harvesting their grapes, and using indigenous yeasts for the juice's fermentation.

In their search for natural ways to make modern, innovative Cabernets, Catherine and Pierre use vinification techniques such as *carbonic maceration*. This is an anaerobic fermentation process, commonly used in the Beaujolais, and useful in softening the often austere Cabernets grown in Bourgueil. The Bretons also make a particularly daring cuvée that issues entirely from ungrafted vines.

The estate's wines keep extremely well, but have very little sulphur added at bottling. Therefore, you must have good, cool conditions of storage to fully benefit from their potential to develop.

Alternatively, you can enjoy a bottle in Bourgueil, with a wonderful meal, at Pierre's brother's restaurant Le Moulin Bleu (see page 160).

Phone in advance to visit the estate. Catherine and Pierre both speak excellent English.

Choice wines:

Bourgueil Cuvée 'Trinch!' 2005

This light, refreshing Cabernet Franc comes from young vines, grown on the clay-limestone soils above the village of Benais. Its name is a Rabelaisian word, meaning 'Cheers, drink!'

Skin maceration at low temperature gives the wine light purple and violet colours, intensifying its primary, fruity aromas of redcurrants and elderberries.

Fruit-driven and moreish on the palate, the wine is relatively light, but has a good tannic bite.

A great partner for cold and grilled meats.

Bourgueil 'La Dilettante' 2005

Cabernet Franc grapes are vinified using *carbonic maceration*, to extract a light ruby colour and very soft tannins. The wine's alcohol content is only 11%, so it is soft, refreshing and easy to drink.

The wine has open, ripe flavours of wild raspberry and strawberry. It is a dry wine, but its fruit flavours are lively and bold, giving a deceptive impression of sweetness.

This wine is best drunk on its own, on a sunny day, with good company.

Bourgueil 'Nuits d'Ivresse' 2004

'Nights of drunkenness' is a common, ignoble translation of something that is closer to 'nights of exuberant pleasure!'

Grapes are grown on clay-limestone soils above the villages of Restigné and Benais; the wine is then fermented and matured in old oak barrels. On the nose, red fruits are mixed with an earthiness reminiscent of leather saddles. The palate is grippy, but with supple tannins.

The wine could be drunk now with poultry or even rich fish dishes, but will improve for fifteen years if kept in a good cellar.

Bourgueil 'Cuvée les Perrières' 2002

From seventy-year-old vines planted on south-exposed flinty clay slopes above Bourgueil, this is a powerful wine, which will keep for decades.

It is aged for two years in (50% new) oak *barriques*, and shows rich, plummy aromas similar to those of a St-Emilion Grand Cru Classé. Spiced dark cherry and mineral flavours appear on a supple, rounded palate. This wine will give pleasure now and for years to come.

Drink with lamb and, with bottle age, rich game dishes.

Restaurant Le Moulin Bleu

7, rue du Moulin Bleu
37140 Bourgueil

Phone 02 47 97 73 13
Fax 02 47 97 79 66
www.lemoulinbleu.com

Restaurant La Rose de Pindare

4, place Hublin
37140 Bourgueil

Phone 02 47 97 70 50
http://la.rose.de.pindare.chez-alice.fr

Eating in Bourgueil

"A restaurant should be the window to a region's wines!" announced a poetic Chantal Breton, when we met. And Le Moulin Bleu's shaded terrace gives unrivalled views of the Bourgueil vineyard. Moreover, Chantal's husband Michel is brother to Pierre Breton, one of the town's most talented winemakers (see page 158).

The restaurant's wine list is predictably superb, with vintages of Bourgueil wines going back to 1964. For €10, you can sample three different wines by the glass with your meal.

Michel's cooking is gastronomic with a firm accent on terroir. Everything is homemade and fresh, and the family works closely with local farmers, including producers of some fantastic goat's cheeses, and *escargots* from the nearby village of St-Michel.

Generous set menus start at €20, and the full gastronomic offering costs €35.

The Bretons speak some English.

Present this book to receive a free apéritif.

Closed Tuesday evening and Wednesday.

La Rose de Pindare sets the best table in Bourgueil centre. The restaurant is wonderfully old-fashioned, with a good selection of local wines.

€10 buy you a filling and delicious *Grande Assiette Bourgueilloise*: a large, rustic salad of hot *rillons* (pork), served with cheese, toast and melon.

Main menus are between €16 and €30.

Closed Tuesday and Wednesday.

LEFT
Le Moulin Blue:
"window to the region's wines"

In one of the Loire Valley's prettiest villages, Diane de Méridor's windows give directly onto the Loire's south bank. The restaurant's interior has an airy, warm feel; the style of the place is 'traditional chic', with the canvasses of local artists decorating the walls.

Stéphanie and Bertrand Dézé took over seven years ago, and Bertrand has developed his own creative style of cooking. All of the ingredients are fresh and the majority are sourced locally, but traditional recipes are infused with a strong influence from the Orient. The chef's own sushi is wonderful as a starter, followed by roasted pikeperch in a light crayfish sauce, served over buttered potato.

The son of a vigneron, Bertrand found the winters too cold for vineyard work, and so decided to become a chef. He travelled the world in search of new recipes, before settling back in the Loire. His brother now runs the family estate, Domaine de la Petite Chapelle, in Saumur-Champigny.

For lunch, the *Menu du Jour* costs less than €15, and the excellent *Menu Saveurs Régionales* is €25. Gastronomic 'formulas' are available for €30, €40 and €50.

Closed Tuesday and Wednesday lunchtimes. Book in advance for weekends.

Present this book to receive a free glass of local bubbly.

Diane de Méridor
12, quai Philippe de Commines
49730 Montsoreau

Phone 02 41 51 71 76
Fax 02 41 51 17 17
Dianedemeridor@wanadoo.fr

BELOW
Bertrand Dézé flambés
a delicious sauce

ABOVE
The town of Saumur

Day 6 itinerary (18 miles)

Saumur-Champigny and
the town of Saumur

A morning in Montsoreau

The turrets of Montsoreau's Château de la Dame give the most impressive views of the town and the Loire. Jean de Chambes, councillor to King Charles VII, built the Château on the south bank of the Loire, in 1455, to control river traffic between Chinon and Saumur. It was the setting for Alexandre Dumas' 19th century romantic novel 'La Dame de Montsoreau'.

The Château visit includes a free tasting, but you can buy the wines for sale more cheaply at the winemakers' cellars. ℃ **02 41 67 12 60**
⌖ **www.chateau-montsoreau.com**

Fontevraud-L'Abbaye

Leave Montsoreau along the D947 and follow the road two miles to the centre of Fontevraud.

The 12th-century Royal Abbey of Fontevraud is one of

Europe's largest and most splendid religious houses. Henry II Plantagenet of England is buried here, with his wife Eleanor of Aquitaine and their son Richard the Lionheart.

The Abbey is unusual in that when it was established, in 1101, it was under an abbess, and this remained so until the French Revolution. At the beginning of the 19th century, the abbey was used as a prison, and was even used after the Second World War to incarcerate those Frenchmen who had collaborated with the German army prior to 1945. The last prisoner left Fontevraud as recently as 1985.

The historical tour of the abbey is excellent, and there are regular exhibitions and musical events throughout the year. ① **02 41 51 73 52** ⤻ **www.abbaye-fontevraud.com**

In front of the entrance to the Abbey, continue across place des Plantagenets, past the Mairie. The fantastic Restaurant La Licorne is 100 yards further on your left (see page 172).

Day 6 at a glance
Itinerary	162 – 167
Wineries	168 – 171
Restaurants	172 – 173

Saumur and Saumur-Champigny

Continue past Restaurant La Licorne, and turn left at the end of rue Robert d'Arbrissel. Follow the road to the right and take the second exit off the mini-roundabout, at the sign for 'Champigny'. Follow the D145 for five slightly hilly miles through the forest into Champigny.

Saumur-Champigny is a small cluster of vineyards within the wider Saumur appellation. Saumur can be red, made from Cabernet Franc and/or Cabernet Sauvignon grapes; white, from the Chenin Blanc, sometimes with small quantities of Chardonnay or Sauvignon Blanc; or sparkling, in which Chenin Blanc can be blended with small amounts of Cabernet, Chardonnay or Grolleau.

Saumur, in all three guises, tends to be a light-bodied wine, and the 'traditional method' sparklers are less interesting than those produced in, for example, Vouvray. Crémant de Loire is the Chenin-based fizz that can come from almost anywhere in the middle Loire. Despite its less specific origins, Crémant de Loire is generally more substantial than sparkling Saumur, as it must be aged on its lees for longer following its second fermentation.

Saumur-Champigny must be a red wine, made from Cabernet Franc and, less often, Cabernet Sauvignon grapes, grown on the soft *tuffeau* near the banks of the Loire, or on the sandier soils further inland. Saumur-Champigny is more robust than plain Saumur Rouge, but its aromas are of delicate red fruits and subtle spices. This is perhaps the most famous red wine of the middle Loire, and it has long been a favourite in the fashionable bistros of Paris.

BOTTOM
The abbey at Fontevraud

A vinous crossroads

Despite its evocative name, the tiny village of Champigny is no longer a big centre of wine production. Woods, rather than vineyards, surround the village, but Champigny is at the centre of the nine *communes* that make up the Saumur-Champigny appellation. So, from Champigny, you have a choice as to which way to head.

If you bear right through the village, the road leads down to the village of Souzay-Champigny and the busy D947 from Montsoreau to Saumur. In Souzay-Champigny, the Chevallier family makes excellent Saumur-Champignys and Saumur Blancs at Château de Villeneuve. The magnificent château dates from the 18th century; built from the same white *tuffeau* rock from which its wine cellars are dug, and from which its wines draw their delicious flavours. ① 02 41 51 14 04 🖰 www.chateau-de-villeneuve.com

In the neighbouring village of Parnay, back towards Montsoreau, the Charruau family has made wines since 1722, at Domaine Val de Brun. This is another star producer whose vineyards are undergoing conversion to organic viticulture. ① 02 41 38 11 85 🖰 www.valbrun.com

The D947 is heavy with traffic throughout the summer, and a little dangerous for cyclists, but the many wine cellars and houses cut into the *tuffeau* rock face are a spectacular site. The most impressive of all are the cellars of Domaine Filliatreau, between Turquant and Montsoreau. The estate's winemaking is based in the hamlet of Chaintré (see below), but these roadside cellars are where the estate prefers to welcome tourists.
① 02 41 52 90 84 🖰 www.filliatreau.com

The route through St-Cyr-en-Bourg

The modern centre of winemaking in Saumur-Champigny is the village of St-Cyr-en-Bourg, west of Champigny.

Follow the road to the left through Champigny at the sign for 'Chacé' and 'Varrains', and continue on the D405 to St-Cyr-en-Bourg.

Turn right in front of the cemetery on entering St-Cyr, and continue straight through the village. The 'Cave des Vignerons de Saumur' is the area's well-reputed co-operative cellar, boasting Saumur-Champigny's most amazing underground cellars (see page 168).

Outside the Cave des Vignerons, turn left onto rue de la Perrière. The next village is Chacé, home to the legendary Foucault brothers of Domaine du Clos Rougeard. This estate's wines are perhaps the most sought-after in the Saumur-Champigny appellation. Visits are strictly by appointment, and demand for the estate's wines frequently leaves the Foucaults short of stock! ① 02 41 52 92 65

Through Chaintré to Saumur

Turn right at the crossroads as you enter Chacé and cross back over the D93. Take the first left into the vineyards, followed by a right towards the hamlet of Chaintré, where English eccentric Krishna Lester makes wine at the beautiful Château de Chaintres (see page 170).

Also in Chaintré are the headquarters of Domaine Filliatreau, a producer whose wines have improved immeasurably in the last ten years. The estate's main tourist cellars are near Montsoreau, on the D947 (see above), but

Filliatreau offers generous tastings from its base in Chaintré. My advice is simply to turn up and give it a try.

Beyond Château de Chaintres, climb the fairly steep hill for half a mile, then turn left onto the D145 towards the centre of Saumur.

The town of Saumur

When I arrived in Saumur, the sun was blazing and the World Cup final between France and Italy was approaching, so emotions were running high. People filled the streets and chants of French pride could be heard from every open window. The match was projected onto an enormous screen in the town centre, where the people of Saumur watched as Zinedine Zidane was provoked, paused, and then headbutted his taunter from the opposing Italian team. Zidane was booked and, shortly afterwards, the Italians won.

The French nation mourned indignantly for the week following the match, which provided me with an excellent opportunity to wander the empty streets, discovering Saumur's many attractions.

Leaving aside its wine industry, Saumur is best known for its 'dressage' displays. The town has an entire equestrian quarter, built in 1763 under Louis XV, to house the royal *Corps des Carabiniers* regiment. Today, Saumur is the headquarters for France's School of Armed Cavalry.

Perched on the hillside above the River Loire, Château de Saumur dominates the town. It dates from the 12th century, when it was part of the royal Plantagenet estate. Philippe Duplessis-Mornay built the Château's fortifications in the 16th century, and it was used as a state prison under Napoléon Bonaparte. It subsequently fell into disrepair, and restoration only began in 1906, when the town of Saumur bought the Château from the state.

But disaster struck Château de Saumur in April 2001 when, in the dead of night, its northwest rampart collapsed onto some of the houses in the town below. Miraculously, nobody was killed, and today the Château is Europe's largest architectural restoration project.

It has not been possible to visit the interior of the Château since 2001, but for a nominal fee you can still walk in the grounds and enjoy the regular art exhibitions that take place. ☎ **02 41 40 24 40** ⌂ **www.saumur-tourisme.net/chateausamur.html**

Another essential visit in Saumur is the Combier distillery. Established in 1834, Combier is the Loire's oldest working spirit and fruit liqueur producer. A delicious range of products, including local Pastis, Chenin Blanc-based brandy and rose petal liqueur are available to taste; the distillery tour is genuinely interesting and informative. ☎ **02 41 40 23 00** ⌂ **www.combier.fr**

Guided boat trips along the river give an insight into river transport history, fishing and navigation techniques, and the history of Saumur, whilst you relax and sip a cool glass of Saumur Brut. Ask at the tourist office for details. ☎ **02 41 40 20 60** ⌂ **www.ot-saumur.fr**

TOP
Domaine Filliatreau

ABOVE
Evening in Saumur

ABOVE
Saumur market

TOP
Combier distillery,
Saumur

BELOW
The view from
Château de Saumur

The wine merchants of Saumur

Saumur is sometimes described as the Loire Valley's own Epernay, and although it is certainly the region's largest centre for sparkling wine production, this is where the similarities end. All of the largest cellars offer guided tours, but these somehow lack the glamorous self-confidence that is such a feature of Champagne. The wines can be good value glugging fizz, but are rarely exciting.

Most of Saumur's *négociants*, or merchant houses, were established in the 19th century in the suburb of St-Hilaire-St-Florent, west of the town. My first experience was at Saumur's largest producer, Gratien & Meyer, whose cellars are cut deep into the cliffs above the D947, as you enter Saumur from Montsoreau.

Gratien & Meyer is the Loire's counterpart to Champagne Alfred Gratien. The German Henkell & Söhnlein group bought the winery in 2001, and has invested heavily in the house's winemaking. The cellars are Saumur's largest, but the winery itself is out of bounds to tourists "because of health and safety legislation", or so I was told! ① **02 41 83 13 32** ⌂ **www.gratienmeyer.com**

Bouvet-Ladubay is an important, dynamic producer with an impressive 8 kilometres of cellars in St-Hilaire-St-Florent. The range of sparkling and still wines is vast. The basic cuvées are very pleasant; the wines become more expensive, and not necessarily better, as more oak is used in their ageing. ① **02 41 83 83 83** ⌂ **www.bouvet-ladubay.fr**

The Maison du Vin de Saumur is adjoined to the town's tourist office. It provides information on the wines of Saumur and the surrounding area, and organises free tastings.Closed Sunday and Monday, and from mid-January to mid-February.

OPPOSITE PAGE
Summer festivities
in Saumur

La Cave des Vignerons de Saumur

49260 Saint-Cyr-en-Bourg
Phone 02 41 53 06 18
Fax 02 41 51 69 13

infos@cavedesaumur.com
www.cavedesaumur.com

The Estate

Established in 1957 by a group of local winegrowers, the Cave des Vignerons de Saumur is one of France's most dynamic co-operative cellars. It includes some 300 growers and produces a third of all Saumur's wines, 20% of which are exported.

Every conceivable style of wine is made here, although dry whites, reds and sparkling wines represent the majority of production. The range is split between blended wines and those produced from single vineyard sites, or *lieux-dits*. They are vibrant, fruity and excellent value for money and, for this reason, you will find them in a large number of local shops and restaurants.

The co-op's 10 kilometres of cellars are Saumur's largest and most impressive. Dating from the Middle Ages, when the Saumurois was an important stone mining area, these cellars are now where the wine's bottling takes place, and are also used to store between six and nine million bottles ready for sale.

There is no museum and little decoration here, but you do get to see how the wine is made, in the guts of a real working winery.

Until the 1980s, this was the largest gravity-based winemaking facility in the region. After pressing, the grape juice would make its way 25 metres below ground, down five subterranean levels, on its vinous journey into being. The winery is now equipped with state-of-the-art computerised technology: space age winemaking that contrasts dramatically with the small-scale operations of most of the Loire's vignerons.

Present the book to Benoit Belda to get a free cellar tour and tasting, which can be in English.

More technical tours are fascinating, but require an advance phone call and a contribution of €5. This is not possible during the harvest.

UK importer:
Tesco

Choice wines:

Saumur Blanc Lieu-dit 'Les Epinats' 2005

This white is made from 100% Chenin Blanc, grown on a 22-hectare parcel of brown limestone near the town of Doué-la-Fontaine.

The nose shows intense aromas of ripe lemon and grapefruit, with an exotic peachiness that follows onto a fresh and intense palate.

Try with light oriental cuisine.

Saumur-Champigny
Lieu-dit "Les Poyeux" 2004

Within the commune of Chacé, Les Poyeux is considered one of the appellation's finest vineyards; the soil is composed of thin clay over *tuffeau*.

Earthy and intense on the nose, with dark cherries and pencil shaving aromas, this is classic Saumur-Champigny: a pure, unoaked expression of Cabernet Franc. The palate is fresh but grippy, allowing further development over the next five years.

Drink with grilled meats or charcuterie.

Crémant de Loire Rosé Brut NV

This 'traditional method' sparkling rosé comes from Cabernet Franc grapes grown exclusively on the *tuffeau* soils within the Saumur appellation. It spends much more than the minimum twelve months ageing on its lees.

The wine's colour is a beautiful pale salmon, with fine persistent bubbles. On the nose, elegant and intense strawberry aromas give onto a pure, refined palate, with excellent length of flavour. This wine is half the price of the cheapest champagne you can buy, and twice as good!

It is a great apéritif, but can be drunk throughout a meal. Perfect for weddings.

Côteaux de Saumur 2003

Only 5000 bottles of this *cuvée* are made in any year, and then only when conditions merit its production.

The Côteaux de Saumur appellation covers a mere 10,000 hectares and is reserved for sweet wines made from the Chenin Blanc.

The grapes from the 2003 harvest ripened to an incredible 19 degrees potential alcohol, and the finished wine contains 80 grammes per litre of residual sugar.

On the nose, the wine is intensely honeyed, but lively and exotic. On the palate it is pleasantly rich, with a fresh zestiness which makes it an excellent apéritif wine.

Try also with *foie gras*.

Château de Chaintres

Chaintres
49400 Dampierry-sur-Loire

Phone 02 41 52 90 54
Fax 02 41 52 99 92
Info@chaintres.com
www.chaintres.com

The Estate

Everyone has heard the story of the British eccentric who went to France, took over an old vineyard, and braved the locals and the adversities of nature to create a new life in rural paradise. And then you taste the wine, reaching deep into your reserves of polite euphemisms for a drink that is, frankly, awful.

Château de Chaintres dates from the 17th century and, with its single 20-hectare vineyard, enclosed within an old monastic stone wall, it is probably Saumur-Champigny's prettiest estate. Owned by the De Tigny family since 1938, the wine has been made by talented English maverick Krishna Lester since the early 1990s. And the wines really are very good.

Once considered the black sheep of Saumur, Krishna has spearheaded a biodiversity project that now includes many of the best vignerons of the Saumur-Champigny appellation. The aim is to reintroduce two bugs into the vineyard ecosystem: *Orius* and *Anagrus Atomus*. The first of these feeds on the dangerous vineyard pest the grape leafhopper, whilst the second eats the leafhopper's eggs. The aim is to eventually eliminate the need for any chemical pesticides in the vineyards of Saumur-Champigny.

Krishna worked variously as a wine buyer for London's Hedges and Butler, a literary agent, theatre lighting designer, hot-air balloon pilot, and in Bordeaux on the chemistry of vinification, before brushing up on his viticulture and taking over the reins at Château de Chaintres.

Krishna humbly claims that winemaking is an easy job, largely doing itself, but that the fruit in the vineyards must be perfect. The estate grows only red Cabernet Franc grapes, from vines with an average age of 40 years, planted on clay-limestone soil. All of the grapes are harvested by hand.

You will probably find Krishna strolling in his vineyard, or deep in the cellars, just listening to the sound of the fermenting wine. Or you may not find him at all, as my two-wheeled visit in June 2006 apparently inspired a new wanderlust in the English wine man.

Look out for Krishna Lester's forthcoming book, about how grape vines and human beings are not all that different!

BELOW
Monastic vineyard

Choice wines:

Château de Chaintres
Saumur-Champigny 2004

This wine is deep purple in colour with an earthy vegetal nose, and fresh mulberry and raspberry fruit aromas. Spiced raspberries show on a palate that still gives a marked tannic bite. This 2004 needed a little time yet to soften.

Drink with grilled meats or stews.

Krishna bottled part of the 2004 vintage with traditional corks, and the rest with artificial closures. The improved fruit intensity in the latter bottles is notable and impressive.

Château de Chaintres
Saumur-Champigny 2003

From the warm 2003 vintage, this wine is deep ruby in colour; the nose shows open, attractive cherry aromas. The palate is soft and ripe, with intense cherry flavours. Acidity levels in the grapes were lower than in 2004, but this wine has good body and an impressive length of flavour.

The 2003 is drinking very well now. Try with poultry or feathered game dishes.

Cuvée des Oratoriens
Saumur-Champigny 2003

Only 3,000 bottles of this wine are made each year, and these are mainly sold at the Château. It is aged in old oak barrels for two years.

The colour is intense, the aromas concentrated and elegant. Spiced sloes and dark cherries show the subtlest evidence of the wine's maturation in wood. The palate is supple, concentrated and complex, with rich berry fruits and a delicious hint of cinnamon spice mid-palate.

This wine could age happily for a decade. It would partner well with red meats or, in a few years, with big game.

TOP
Krishna Lester
enjoys a cigarette
in the vineyard

Restaurant La Licorne

Allée Sainte-Catherine
49590 Fontevraud-l'Abbaye

Phone 02 41 51 72 49
Fax 02 41 51 70 40
www.la-licorne-restaurant.com

La Licorne (The Unicorn) is, as its name suggests, one of the Loire's most fantastic gastronomic establishments. Valérie and Fabrice Bretel took over in 2005, adding their own warmth to the already Michelin-starred restaurant.

Fabrice personally sources all of his ingredients, three quarters of which come from the Loire Valley. If a river fish, for example, cannot be bought fresh, the dish is simply struck off the menu and something new is invented.

Fabrice's style of cooking is creative and refined. An essential starter is the crab profiterole with rocket salad and chives; don't miss the delicious line-caught pikeperch, cooked in a Chinon wine sauce, with fresh garden vegetables.

Menus start at less than €30; the most expensive is a very reasonable €55.

The restaurant is open seven days a week from Easter until the end of September.

Present this book to receive a free apéritif.

Restaurant Les Ménestrels

11-13 rue Raspail
49400 Saumur

Phone 02 41 67 71 10
Fax 02 41 50 89 64
www.hotel-anneanjou.com

Les Ménestrels (The Minstrels) is Saumur's swankiest gastronomic restaurant. The wine list is very fine, and includes many good value bottles, and old vintages.

The service and the food are both excellent, and the renovated 16th-century restaurant building is beautiful. The courtyard terrace is a pleasant place to eat in summer, but try to reserve a table (for two) on the small balcony that overlooks it.

Menus are between €30 and €60, and possibly a touch pricey. The restaurant is attached to Hôtel Anne d'Anjou*** (see page 175)

The restaurant is open seven days a week.

Romauld and Fanny Hardou took over L'Escargot, one of Saumur's oldest restaurants, early in 2006. This is one of the region's best value gastronomic finds, but it is the friendly ambience that the young couple have created that really sets L'Escargot apart.

During the last war, proprietress Madame Lafagne bred the restaurant's snails in the back garden. Today, the *gros gris escargots* that Romauld prepares come from a farm in Cornillé-les-Caves near Angers, and are cooked in sauces including the traditional garlic and parsley, as well as puréed nuts, and Roquefort cheese.

The roasted filet of pikeperch is the house speciality, cooked in a light Saumur Rouge sauce and served on a bed of buttered leeks. The chef's own *Magret de Canard* is also fantastic.

A choice of three courses à la carte is available for only €15 (except at weekends), and the *Menu Dégustation* is €30.

Fanny and Romauld have both worked in London restaurants and speak good English.

Present this book to receive a free apéritif.

Closed Monday and Tuesday in July and August; also Sunday night and Monday throughout the year.

Restaurant L'Escargot
30, rue du Maréchal Leclerc
49400 Saumur

Phone 02 41 51 20 88
Escargot@saumur.com

Sandwiched inauspiciously between a truck stop and a petrol station, on the western outskirts of town, La Promenade is Saumur's finest grill. If you don't mind eating with truckers, or sitting on a (surprisingly atmospheric) neon-lit terrace, this is a fine, friendly place to get a bite.

A butcher by trade, Chef Daniel Jousselin cooks with only the highest quality meats, and otherwise specialises in enormous seafood dishes. Full menus start at less than €15.

The restaurant is open every day from the crack of dawn till the middle of the night.

La Promenade
Boulevard du Maréchal Juin
49400 Saumur

Phone 02 41 50 35 24

Accommodation

Vouvray

Hôtel-Restaurant Le Grand Vatel**
8, allée Brulé
37210 Vouvray
Phone 02 47 52 70 32
Fax 02 47 52 74 52
Ensuite rooms here are available from around €40.

La Rochelière is Anneli Tulkki's elegant manor house B&B. Prices are between €65 and €80.
6, rue Victor Hérault
37210 Vouvray
Phone 02 47 52 61 47
Fax 02 47 40 04 29
www.la-rocheliere.com

Amboise

Hôtel Le Blason**
11, place Richelieu
37400 Amboise
Phone 02 47 23 22 41
Fax 02 47 57 56 18
www.leblason.fr
Excellent value and well equipped.
Prices are between €50 and €60.

Le Choiseul****
36, quai Charles Guinot
37400 Amboise
Phone 02 47 30 45 45
Fax 02 47 30 46 10
www.le-choiseul.com
A lovely period hotel with a great pool.
Prices are upwards of €90.

Montlouis

Montlouis has two **hotels**, at opposite ends of the price scale:
Le Montloire**
Place François-Mitterand
37270 Montlouis-sur-Loire
Phone 02 47 50 84 84
Fax 02 47 45 08 43
In the centre of Montlouis, prices for rooms are around €50.

Château de la Bourdaisière***
25 rue de la Bourdaisière
37270 Montlouis-sur-Loire
Tel 02 47 45 16 31
Fax 02 47 45 09 11
www.chateaulabourdaisiere.com
A mile outside Montlouis on the D140, this 15th-century Château has rooms for €160+.

Le Buisson***
7, rue Madeleine Vernet
37270 Montlouis-sur-Loire
Phone 02 47 50 98 18
www.loire-valley-holidays-jp-chalons.com
Jean-Pierre Chalons runs this **B & B** on the road leading out of Montlouis towards Husseau. Prices are between €60 and €70.

Azay-le-Rideau

Hôtel de Biencourt**
7, rue Balzac
37190 Azay-le-Rideau
Phone 02 47 45 20 75
Fax 02 47 45 91 73
www.hotelbiencourt.com
An attractive, tranquil place to stay the night. Rooms are €50 - €70.

Hôtel-Restaurant*** Le Grand Monarque
3, place de la République
37190 Azay-le-Rideau
Phone 02 47 45 40 08
Fax 02 47 45 46 25
www.legrandmonarque.com
Spacious rooms vary greatly in price between €55 and €190 (for restaurant, see page 137).

Outside Azay on the D751 towards Tours, Marielle Henrion has **B & B** rooms at her wine estate: **Château de l'Aulée**. These cost about €60.
Phone 02 47 45 44 24
Fax 02 47 45 44 34
Chateau-de-laulee@wanadoo.fr

Chinon

Hôtel Diderot**
4, rue de Buffon
37500 Chinon
Phone 02 47 93 18 87
www.hoteldiderot.com
The family Dutheil produces 70 different delicious homemade jams. Prices for rooms are between €45 and €80.

Hostellerie Gargantua
73, rue Voltaire
37500 Chinon
Phone 02 47 93 04 71
Fax 02 47 93 08 02
www.hotel-gargantua.com
Beneath the castle, this hotel has its own brasserie and dining terrace. Prices are €50–€80.

Best Western Hôtel de France***
47- 49, place du Général-de-Gaulle
37500 Chinon
Phone 02 47 98 37 03
Elmachinon@aol.com
A beautifully restored 16th-century house in the heart of Chinon, with all mod cons. High-season prices are between €80 and €180 (for restaurant, see page 148).

Bourgueil

Hôtel le Thouarsais
10, place Hublin
37140 Bourgueil
Phone/Fax 02 47 97 72 05
A cheerful place to stay. Prices are from €30 to €50.

Montsoreau

Hôtel le Bussy**
4, rue Jeanne d'Arc
49730 Montsoreau
Phone 02 41 38 11 11
Fax 02 41 38 18 10
www.hotel-lebussy.fr

Rooms here are exceptional value at between €50 and €70.
Les Visiteurs
21-31, place des Diligences
49730 Montsoreau
Phone 06 16 58 53 09
For something a little more eccentric! Rooms cost €70 to €80.

Saumur

Hôtel Le Volney**
1, rue Volney
49400 Saumur
Phone 02 41 51 25 41
Fax 02 41 38 11 04
www.levolney.com
A small, friendly hotel in the centre of Saumur. Prices are from €40.

Hôtel Anne d'Anjou***
32, quai Mayaud
49400 Saumur
Phone 02 41 67 30 30
Fax 02 41 67 51 00
www.hotel-anneanjou.com
This hotel is attached to Restaurant Les Ménestrels (see Saumur restaurants, page 172). Prices start at €90.

Next door to Hôtel Anne d'Anjou is Jackie and Jean-Marc Aldebert's wonderful **B & B**. Prices start at €65.
31, quai Mayaud
49400 Saumur
Phone 02 41 51 20 22
www.lepatiosaumur.eu

Burgundy

PARIS

FRANCE

Burgundy:
August – September 2006

The Golden Slope

At the heart of Burgundy is its Côte d'Or, or 'Golden Slope', so named for the beautiful complexion of its autumn vineyards. Like all things precious, the soils that form these slopes are in short supply; jealously sought by vignerons the world over. The Côte d'Or is separated into the Côte de Nuits to the north between Dijon and Beaune, and the Côte de Beaune, which begins just north of Beaune and continues south to Chagny. The best wines produced in this small corner of Burgundy are, in my view at least, the finest on the planet.

As you head south from Dijon, the famous village names appear in dizzying succession: Gevrey-Chambertin, Morey-Saint-Denis, Chambolle-Musigny, Vougeot, Vosne-Romanée, and these few before you even break sweat. At first, this can seem intimidating. Ten years ago this part of Burgundy was virtually impenetrable to the casual visitor, but winemakers on the Côte d'Or are becoming more used to welcoming visitors, as they recognise the fierce competition from the global wine market.

Quality control in Burgundy is also undergoing something of a revolution. For many years, the fame of the Côte d'Or was matched only by the infamous variability in the quality of its wines. American wine critic Robert

ABOVE
Pernand-Vergelesses,
Côte de Beaune

Parker famously advised against buying burgundy for less than a tenner a bottle, and although Parker now almost has a price on his head in Burgundy, there was much truth in what he said.

The problem was rooted in something called the *AOC Agrément*, the system by which a wine obtains, or fails to obtain, its 'appellation of origin' status, as a quality wine. This was a real Burgundian backslapping affair: the vignerons got together once a year, tasted each other's wines, and decided that they were all brilliant. Job done.

But the best winemakers argued that up to 25% of wines receiving AOC recognition were of inferior quality and, in reaction to a slump in wine sales following the Millennium, the system is finally receiving a much-needed overhaul. Burgundy's wines will soon be monitored throughout their production, from vine to bottle, and, incredibly, winemakers are being encouraged to go back to school to learn how to taste and spot faults in their own wines!

I wanted to meet Burgundy's iconoclasts, the winemakers who inspired these changes, and who lobbied the authorities for reform. These are vignerons who have always made world-beating wines; their cheaper *cuvées* crafted with the same loving care as their Premiers and Grands Crus.

Early August was, however, a difficult time to set about such a task. This is the beginning of the period of *veraison*, when the small Pinot Noir grapes begin to change colour on the vines, and adopt their eventual purple tint. *Veraison* is the cue for vineyard work to stop. By now, 'green harvesting', or

removing excess grape bunches, is less effective as a way of limiting the vines' yields; and any spraying is done sheepishly, since chemicals are undesirable in the vineyards so close to harvest time. Many vignerons use the opportunity to take their holidays in Provence, from where it is difficult to show Burgundian vineyards to British cyclists. So began a complicated juggling game, as I pedalled to catch winemakers before they left; and then waited until they returned north to prepare for the harvest.

Getting there

Burgundy used to be hard to reach by plane, but by the time of publication, Ryanair will be offering flights from London to Dijon airport, where car rental is available. You can hire bikes from Dijon's tourist office, but Bourgogne Randonées in Beaune is a better bet. ⊠ **7, avenue du Septembre (near the railway station)** ① **03 80 22 06 03**

ABOVE
Red Pinot Noir grapes approaching ripeness

Many Burgundy-loving Brits make the journey each year in their own cars, to stock up at their favourite cellars. From Calais, simply follow the A26 via Reims (see Champagne chapter). This merges onto the A5 south of Reims, and then the A31. Leave the A31 onto the D70 at the Dijon junction. The one-way trip is 350 miles.

The Eurostar is the best way to bring your own bike (for an extra £20), and cars can be hired from Paris Gare du Nord Eurostar terminal.

From Paris, the A6 to Dijon leads past Auxerre and the vineyards of Chablis, on a direct 3-hour drive to the Côte d'Or. From Paris Gare du Nord, follow Boulevard de Magenta east to place de la République. Leave the roundabout south towards the river, and cross over Pont d'Austerlitz. Follow the road south, over place d'Italie, until it joins the A6 to Auxerre and Dijon.

Dijon, capital of Burgundy

Once the capital of the independent province of Burgundy, modern Dijon is an architecturally beautiful, vibrant and cosmopolitan university city. I have always loved Dijon, and it has benefited recently from thoughtful reconstruction work around its ducal palace, on place de la Libération. But there is little tangible evidence – beyond restaurants' wine lists – that Dijon stands at the head of one of the world's most famous wine regions.

Burgundy's Valois dukes may have played a crucial role in the development of Burgundy's wine trade, but you have to head south towards Chenôve to begin to see how (Day 1 itinerary). The *Fête de la Vigne* takes place in Dijon on the first weekend of September, but this is more a traditional French folk festival than a jamboree for wine lovers.

Home of mustard

The link with wine appears in the city's world-famous product, Dijon mustard. This was traditionally made using a mixture of mustard seed and the sour juice of green, unripe grapes (called the *verjus*), in the days before viticultural techniques, clonal selection and global warming allowed the fruit to ripen more or less fully every year. It wasn't until the mid-eighteenth century that

verjus was replaced by vinegar.

Unlike, for example, wine from Gevrey-Chambertin, or cheese from Epoisses, Dijon mustard can legally be made anywhere in the world. The Dijonnais are unlikely ever to insist on a protected appellation, since the city's producers depend almost entirely on Canadian mustard seed imports. On the other hand, if you buy *moutarde de Bourgogne*, it must come from Burgundy.

If in doubt, just do everything

Museums, galleries and public attractions in Dijon are all free. The mustard museum will be closed by the time you read this; the logical thing would be its incorporation into the Musée de la vie Bourguignonne, the museum of Burgundian life, but I suspect that this is unlikely. ⊠ **15-17, rue Sainte-Anne** ☎ **03 80 44 12 69**

However, if you only see one thing in Dijon, let it be the Musée des Beaux Arts, housed in the Palais des Etats within Dijon's grand old ducal palace. ⊠ **Place de la Libération** ☎ **03 80 74 52 09**

The main Dijon tourist office near the train station is not very good, although it is the only place in Dijon where you can hire bikes. They also have

Segways, those NASA-designed motorised two-wheel contraptions that were alleged to be foolproof, until George W. Bush fell off one. I asked if I could take one into the vineyards, and was greeted with deadpan disdain:

"You 'ave to follow *ze guide*!"

If you want more information on the city's history and attractions, there is a good information bureau within the ducal palace, between rue des Forges and the Cour d'Honneur.

Dijon Hotels

Dijon's best hotel – and restaurant – is Hostellerie du Chapeau Rouge****. You get the feeling that the €130+ bill for a room is more often paid by the company than by the individual. ① **03 80 50 88 88** 🖰 **www.chapeau-rouge.fr**

Just off place Darcy, Hôtel du Nord*** has good rooms for about €90 and a nice wine bar, but cyclists need to negotiate bike storage before booking a room. ① **03 80 50 80 50** 🖰 **www.choicehotels.fr**

The more I live in French hotels, the more convinced I am by large hotel chains. You could do a lot worse than the Campanile near the train station, particularly at weekends when the high-season tariff of €70 drops to nearer €55. ① **03 80 43 40 01** 🖰 **www.campanile.fr**

Weather, climate and when to visit

The wider region that is viticultural Burgundy begins to the north around Auxerre, close to the vineyards of the eastern Loire. This is Chablis country. About a hundred miles to the southeast begins the Côte d'Or. Situated at a latitude of around 47 degrees north, the Côte d'Or's continental climate gives cold, harsh winters and often hot summers. Rain is a constant worry, especially around harvest time when it can cause rot to take hold in the vineyards, or swell the grapes, diluting their flavours.

Continuing south through the Côte Chalonnaise, another hundred miles leads through the Maconnais and into the Beaujolais, not far north of Lyon. The climate here is more Mediterranean, and the wines very different from those further north.

The Côte d'Or had apparently suffered as much as the Loire Valley from the *canicule*, or blazing heat, of July 2006, but this ended abruptly as I arrived in Burgundy. The weather turned from scorchingly hot to breath-condensing cold within a week, and the rains came with depressing regularity throughout a chilly August.

Winemakers are worriers. A few days' relief brought

by the long-awaited rain turned to anxiety when the clouds failed to clear. As the grapes ripen, they become increasingly vulnerable to various kinds of rot. And this close to the harvest, there is no question of jeopardising wine quality by spraying the vines with chemicals. Winemakers in the Côte de Nuits also had to contend with hail in early August, which caused considerable damage to many Grand Cru vineyards.

Back in August 2004, rain was also a problem, but the harvest was helped by a dry September. This is the month that is traditionally said to either make or break a vintage. But the rain showed little mercy to the Côte d'Or in 2006, and the vintage was a difficult one.

The best time to visit the Côte d'Or is in the spring and early summer. From mid-August, winemakers take their holidays, and when they return, there is the frantic job of bottling the previous year's wines to make room in the winery for the new vintage. The small-scale nature of most growers' operations means they will have little time to spare during the harvest in September, so October is the ideal time to buy wine. Driving wine home is also most advisable during this cool month.

ABOVE
A moment's rest during a busy harvest!

OPPOSITE PAGE TOP
Château de la Rochepot, Hautes-Côtes de Beaune

The Côte d'Or, ancient centre of an independent province

Burgundy reminds me in some ways of my home in southwest England. The region is within easy reach of the country's capital, and its villages mix the civilising, sometimes deadening, effects of money with a unique parochial authenticity. The winemakers here are very definitely farmers, and even the best renowned amongst them rarely live in ostentatious splendour.

"Je suis fier d'être Bourguignon" (I am proud to be Burgundian) is a staple sing-along at every Burgundian folk event, and this pride is easily understood in the context of Burgundy's powerful independent history.

Viticulture was practised in Burgundy from Roman times, and the Côte d'Or's vineyards can be traced to the 4th century AD. It became a Frankish kingdom in 534, and as early as 587, King Gontran of Burgundy donated vines to Dijon's St-Bénigne Abbey. The region's powerful religious houses began isolating the plots of land, or *climats*, best suited to viticulture, forming the basis of today's complex *appellation contrôlée* system on the Côte d'Or.

Emperor Charles II created the duchy of Burgundy in 877, but the region's golden age really began in 1364, when John II of France handed the fief to his son Philippe the Bold, first of Burgundy's Valois dukes. Philippe and his dynastic successors gained vast territories, as far afield as Luxembourg and Alsace, and by the beginning of the 15th century, the duchy played a dominant role in French politics. Burgundy's agriculture, trade and industry were then the most important anywhere in Europe, and Dijon was one of its biggest cultural centres.

As the power of the abbeys grew alongside that of Burgundy's rulers, wine became a luxury product and a strong symbol of prosperity. The holdings of the abbeys had grown unchecked as their riches had increased, and by the 18th century, they owned nearly all of the Côte d'Or's best vineyards. With little financial pressure to sell their wines, the abbeys were able to produce smaller quantities of a better product, which they offered as gifts to visiting princes and popes.

At the dawn of the Renaissance, the dukes of Burgundy presided over the finest winemaking region in Christendom. Wines were served at their famous banquets, and became the forerunners of today's diplomatic, or 'corporate', gift. But the decadent luxury in which Burgundy's dukes lived, and the enormous land acquisitions of its religious houses, meant that when the French Revolution came in 1789, it was well supported by Burgundy's ordinary folk.

Modern Burgundy

The Revolution defined the viticultural landscape of modern Burgundy. Royal and ecclesiastical estates were broken up and the land was redistributed. A year after the Revolution, in 1790, Napoléon established his law of inheritance, whereby all children inherited equal portions of their parents' land. The next 200 years saw the repeated division of estates' holdings, resulting in today's patchwork of tiny vineyard parcels, particularly on the Côte d'Or.

As individual land holdings shrank, it became increasingly difficult for growers to make a living producing and selling such tiny quantities of wine.

BELOW
Beaune market

Marriages between winemaking families stalled the process, creating today's

double-barrelled surnames: the Coche-Bizouards, Rossignol-Févriers, and a thousand others. But the important development came in the early 18th century, when merchants began buying and blending wines from many small growers, and marketing them under their own labels. By the end of the 19th century, merchant families like the Patriarchs and the Bouchards of Beaune controlled most of Burgundy's winemaking, and this would remain so until the late 20th century.

The 1980s saw the reputations of certain larger *négociant* houses tarnished by the overproduction of lesser quality wines. Small 'boutique' wineries became increasingly fashionable, and the growers of Burgundy saw their chance to tip the balance of power.

The average vineyard holding in Burgundy is increasing, but it is still only around 6 hectares. Such small-scale viticulture in a notoriously unpredictable climate presents the region's growers with one of the winemaking world's biggest challenges. Those who have risen to it have bottled some of the finest wines ever made, and the most famous among them can effectively name the prices their wines fetch.

Burgundy's 'other' estates have suffered from the slump in the region's wine sales since the Millennium. This was a much-needed kick up the behind for those who had profited from their association with Burgundy's finest domaines, and it injected a new urgency into the fight for wine quality.

Terroir and the appellation system: scratching the surface

The terroir of the Côte d'Or was first studied in the middle ages, by those zealous monks who quite literally tasted the soil in their quest to understand its properties. Scientific investigations into the Côte began in the 17th century, and continued through the Enlightenment. Even today, this part of Burgundy attracts more geologists, meteorologists and viticulturists than any other wine region.

The Côte d'Or is sited along a complex geological fault line; its calcium-rich clay-limestone soils form a forty-mile ridge, a graveyard of prehistoric marine life. The slopes face mainly east, towards the morning sun, and south, particularly in the more southerly Côte de Beaune. The best vineyards are planted on the lower slopes, at an altitude of around 250 metres. Here the soil is more nourishing than it is in the hills, but less fertile than in the plains, where more ordinary wines are grown. The slopes protect the vines from the westerly winds and the worst of the rain, and the vineyards are high enough to avoid frost pockets.

BELOW
Château du Clos de Vougeot

TOP
Walking in the vineyards, Savigny-lès-Beaune

But this is where simple explanations break down. The minute variations in soil and aspect have been endlessly scrutinised, together with differences in climate both between and within individual vineyards, as scientists struggle to explain how one vineyard can create wondrous nectars, whilst its neighbour makes only ordinary wines. I have highlighted specific examples throughout this chapter, but mine are the simple explanations. At the limits of human understanding, magic and religion reappear, and soil chewing starts to look like a not-so-silly way to understand the Côte d'Or's terroir.

In contrast to the 'how' and the 'why', the 'which' at least has been thoroughly explained. The Côte d'Or's vineyards are the world's most rigorously delimited, with a well-established hierarchy from the most ordinary to the best reputed. The *appellation contrôlée* system in the Côte d'Or is the most complex in France, but its basics can be easily understood as a 'pyramid of quality'.

At the top of the pyramid are 30 Grands Crus. These are the finest single vineyards, whose names stand alone on bottle labels. Just to confuse, however, many of the best Grand Cru vineyards' names have been suffixed to those of nearby villages, whose vignerons seized the opportunity to gain glory by association. Thus the village of Gevrey became Gevrey-Chambertin, Chambolle became Chambolle-Musigny, and so on. It is rare to find a Côte d'Or village that was not swept up by this trend.

Next come the Premiers Crus, of which there are 561. The quality of these vineyards varies considerably, but Premier Crus such as Les Perrières in Meursault or Les Amoureuses in Chambolle-Musigny, make wines that can, at their best, rival the Grands Crus. The names of Premier Cru vineyards must appear alongside the name of their commune on bottles.

The third classification is that of commune, or 'village', wines. These are the Gevrey-Chambertins, Meursaults, Puligny-Montrachets etc. that do not come from vineyards with a superior classification. The name of a single *lieu-dit* vineyard may be added, in smaller type.

Lastly, at the bottom of the pyramid, is generic 'Bourgogne'. This is generally made from grapes grown in the fertile plains, but I have tasted wines at this level, from good producers, that knock spots off badly made (and over-priced) Premier Crus! Indeed, the best producers will de-classify village appellation, or even Cru, wines to generic 'Bourgogne' in difficult vintages, to protect their reputations. These are some of the Côte d'Or's best value wines; they can be drunk soon after bottling, and are increasingly labelled with the names of the region's principal two grape varieties: the white Chardonnay and the red Pinot Noir.

The Chardonnay grape is grown the world over, but its home is in Burgundy, where it produces white wines with a unique combination of weight and mineral complexity. It is also the main ingredient in Burgundy's sparkling *Crémants de Bourgogne*. Burgundy is at the northernmost limit for the production of fine red wine. The dark-skinned Pinot Noir grape is, like Chardonnay, native to Burgundy. It is notoriously capricious: over-ripe grapes make jammy wines, and insufficient ripeness gives unpleasant stalky flavours. But in the best sites on the Côte d'Or, the Pinot Noir makes wines with bewitching perfumes and indescribably delicious flavours.

Chardonnay and Pinot Noir are the only grapes that are widely used for the production of quality wines on the Côte d'Or. The Côte de Nuits to the north is planted almost exclusively with Pinot vines; the Côte de Beaune grows both grapes, but is perhaps more famous for its whites from villages such as Meursault and Puligny-Montrachet.

The white Aligoté grape is grown in small quantities by many vignerons, and can make good value, fresh light wines. A white relative of the Pinot Noir is the white Pinot Beurot. This is the same grape as Alsace's Pinot Gris, making similarly 'fat' wines, but in Burgundy it is always dry, and its authorisation for quality wine production is very limited. Pinot Noir's country cousin, the red Gamay grape of the Beaujolais, was once grown extensively on the Côte d'Or, but today it is extremely rare.

And no French wine region would be complete without its own fearsome grape spirit! *Marc de Bourgogne* is the Burgundian *digestif*, distilled from grape skins after their final pressing.

Wine & food

Burgundy spent most of its history as an independent province within France, but its culinary traditions have emerged as the very quintessence of provincial French cooking. Think of your favourite French dish, and the chances are that it comes from Burgundy. *Coq au Vin*, *Boeuf Bourguignon* and, of course, *Escargots à la Bourguignonne*, are all specialities of the Burgundian table. This is the region of long lunches, where rustic overlaps with refined in the hands of some of France's best chefs.

Burgundy has its powerful dukes to thank for the richness and variety of its cuisine. The dukes' over-indulgence found expression in the extravagant banquets and gastronomic festivities that are still a big part of the Burgundian calendar.

Burgundy is also extremely rich in natural ingredients. The area of Bresse in the region's south is prized for the quality of its poultry, whilst the Charolais, to the west, is where some of the world's finest beef cattle are reared. The River Loire's tributaries to the west of Dijon provide fresh river fish; the large Burgundian *gros gris* snails live wild in vineyards and lush grazing pastures across the region. As elsewhere in France, a variety of game beasts are hunted in Burgundy's forests, and these are served as staples of autumn restaurant menus.

The red and white wines of Burgundy are important ingredients in its cooking. The most famous example is the hearty *Boeuf Bourguignon*, a beef stew cooked slowly in red wine, to which onions, bacon and mushrooms are added. Similar ingredients are used with chicken in Burgundy's other signature dish, *Coq au Vin*. The sauce was traditionally thickened with the blood of the cockerel itself. White wine and cream are also used to make sauces for lighter meats, such as chicken, duck and feathered game.

Fresh vegetables abound in Burgundy. Parsley and garlic are used with butter to cook Burgundy's fat, succulent *escargots*. These two ingredients also appear in savoury jelly pressed with ham, to make *jambon persillé*. Some of France's most varied charcuterie, such as *saucisson* and pâté, are specialities in a region where pig farming is widespread.

Blackcurrant bushes thrive in the wild scrubland that surrounds the vineyards in the cool upper slopes, or Hautes-Côtes, above the Côte d'Or. These are used to make Burgundy's famous liqueur *Crème de Cassis*, but they also feature in a range of delicious desserts, with other locally grown soft fruits.

Burgundy produces some of France's richest, creamiest cheeses, which are excellent partners for the region's fuller bodied wines of both colours. The most famous is the *Epoisses*. Since 1991, *Epoisses* has, like Burgundy's quality wines, benefited from its own appellation-controlled status, and can therefore only be produced in certain parts of the Côte d'Or, and at the fringes of some bordering *départements*. *Epoisses* is a pungent, full-flavoured cheese, the rind of which is washed in the local grape spirit, *Marc de Bourgogne*.

Driving, cycling or walking

Cycle tourism is less developed on the Côte d'Or than it is, for example, in the Loire Valley, but the area is nonetheless perfectly suited to it. Don't be fooled by the word 'Côte': the best roads run parallel to the hillside vineyards, and rarely force you to climb too far into them – unless you want to. The one exception is the Hautes-Côtes de Nuits between Nuits-Saint-Georges and Pernand-Vergelesses (Day 3 itinerary), but even here the distances are relatively short, and the hills very approachable. The short optional foray into the Hautes-Côtes de Beaune is a little more challenging (Day 5 itinerary).

The Côte d'Or is probably the best region to attempt a mix of all three methods of getting around. Each section of the itinerary is an easy, self-contained cycle trip, and each includes suggested extra walks or cycle routes following from the main day's itinerary. This is a particularly popular area for hill walkers, and every tourist office is well stocked with maps outlining the area's footpaths.

This is also the region in which the argument is strongest for bringing your own car. Wine tourism is in its infancy in much of Burgundy, particularly in the more prestigious villages of the Côte d'Or. Many of the vignerons own small, scattered parcels of land and employ surprisingly few pairs of hands to work them. Their time is therefore short and tourists are more likely to be welcomed as potential, immediate, customers.

Bringing your own transport is an excellent opportunity to buy those less expensive, but well made, burgundies that are inexplicably hard to find in the UK. Burgundy is the most seductive of wines, so when tasting the more expensive bottles, it is wise to have worked out your budget in advance. Also remember that the pricier wines may need five to ten years ageing to show their true, extraordinary, potential.

OPPOSITE PAGE
TOP LEFT
Pinot Noir grapes at *veraison*

OPPOSITE PAGE BOTTOM
Château de
Savigny-lès-Beaune

THIS PAGE
BELOW
Local characters

Summary itinerary

Days 1 & 2
The Côte de Nuits

Dijon is only a stone's throw from this northern part of the Côte d'Or, and the famous villages of Gevrey-Chambertin, Chambolle-Musigny and Vosne-Romanée, not to mention the famous Clos de Vougeot vineyard and its monastic Château. The Côte de Nuits is famous for its powerful, long-lived red wines, made from the Pinot Noir grape. It includes many of Burgundy's most prestigious Grand Cru vineyards.

On the map, this area looks almost too small to occupy two days of holiday, but this is really a minimum requirement to discover these extraordinary vineyards.

Tips for cyclists
At less than 20 very flat miles, these two days could not be easier for the cyclist. The vineyard road hugs the foot of the Côte and leads straight through its famous villages. This is an easy self-contained two-day trip, from Dijon to Nuits-Saint-Georges.

Days 3 & 4
The Hautes-Côtes de Nuits and Beaune's northern neighbours

The Hautes-Côtes de Nuits, or 'Upper Slopes', seem to belong to a different region from the lower-lying Côte de Nuits. The fresh mountain air gives lighter wines of both colours, and the high-trained vines are grown amongst other field crops. The views from these hills are spectacular, and on sunny days you can see as far as the snow-capped Alps.

Descending towards the village of Pernand-Vergelesses, you enter the Côte de Beaune north of the city of Beaune. The villages here are amongst the most friendly in the region.

Don't miss the collection of fighter jets at the

Château in Savigny-lès-Beaune.

Tips for cyclists
The Hautes-Côtes is a ride of moderate difficulty, which requires some fitness to be enjoyable. The third day's itinerary is not more than 20 miles.

Day 4 is much easier: a maximum of 12 flat miles leaves time to explore the villages of Savigny-lès-Beaune and Aloxe-Corton before you make your way to Beaune.
It is worth planning an extra day to discover Beaune, capital of Burgundy's wines.

Days 5 & 6
The Côte-de-Beaune

Pommard and Volnay are the most prestigious red wine villages south of Beaune. The latter is famous for its 'feminine' wines, whilst the former produces a powerful, muscular style.

Day 5 finishes in Meursault, possibly the most famous white wine village in Burgundy; the following day begins in Puligny-Montrachet, the other contender. It is fascinating to compare the rich, buttery Meursault style with Puligny's concentrated apples and honeysuckle flavours.

Before continuing though Chassagne-Montrachet to Santenay, climb beyond the Côte de Beaune through the villages of Auxey-Duresses, Saint-Romain and Saint-Aubin. Many great bargains are to be found here, and this extra trip is a chance to visit the stunning hillside Château de la Rochepot.

Tips for cyclists
There is a well-signposted cycle route through the vineyards all the way from Beaune to Santenay. Little more than 12 miles separate these two towns, but the 'extra trip' into the hills is a fairly tough 9-mile ride.

This section is a flexible two-day trip, and bikes can be hired in either Beaune or Santenay.

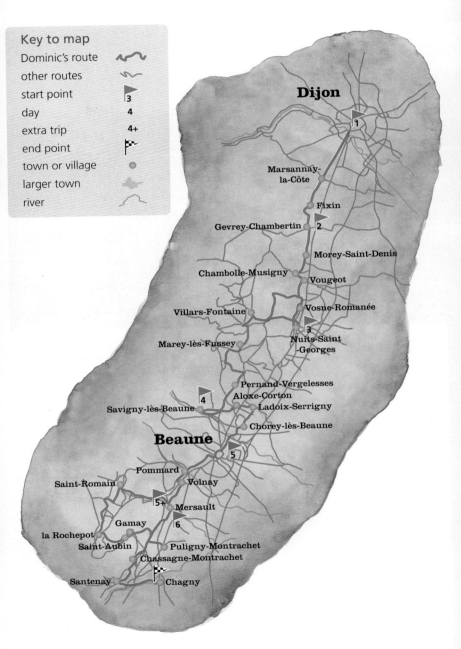

Key to map

Dominic's route

other routes

start point   3

day   4

extra trip   4+

end point

town or village   ●

larger town

river

Dijon

Marsannay-
la-Côte

Fixin

Gevrey-Chambertin   2

Morey-Saint-Denis

Chambolle-Musigny

Vougeot

Vosne-Romanée

Villars-Fontaine

3

Marey-lès-Fussey

Nuits-Saint
-Georges

Pernand-Vergelesses

Aloxe-Corton

Savigny-lès-Beaune   4

Ladoix-Serrigny

Chorey-lès-Beaune

Beaune

5

Pommard

Volnay

Saint-Romain

5+

Mersault

Gamay

6

la Rochepot

Saint-Aubin

Puligny-Montrachet

Chassagne-Montrachet

Santenay

Chagny

Day 1 itinerary (10-15 miles)
The Northern Côte de Nuits

Dijon to Marsannay-la-Côte

Leave Dijon along rue Docteur Albert Rémy in front of
the train station, and follow signs to Beaune. Pass the
canal port on your right and then fork right off the
emerging N74 into rue de Chenôve.

The first village is Chenôve, an ancient centre of wine
production, with a once important vineyard that extended
to 450 hectares. The village's Clos du Roy and Clos du
Chapître were famous medieval vineyard names, but
Chenôve has largely been swallowed up as a Dijon suburb,
and is somewhat reminiscent of an outsized ski resort
without the snow.

Clos du Roy is the township's only remaining vineyard
(see Domaine René Bouvier, page 200), now part of the
Marsannay appellation. But a right turn into rue Roger
Salengro leads to the village's gigantic 15th century
Pressoirs des Ducs de Bourgogne, the last remnants of
the village's medieval ducal estate. These wooden
winepresses are an awesome monument to medieval

engineering, and operated commercially until 1926. Once a year, in the third weekend of September, they are brought back to life in the *Réveil des Pressoirs*, part of the fête which celebrates the village's winemaking heritage. You can visit the Pressoirs free of charge from the beginning of July to the end of September.
① **03 80 51 55 00**

Before leaving the village and entering Marsannay, turn left at the roundabout to eat at the village's fine restaurant Le Clos du Roy. ✉ **35, avenue du 14 Juillet** ① **03 80 51 33 66** Note that it is closed in August.

Marsannay-la-Côte

Marsannay itself is virtually contiguous with Chenôve, but the heart of the village is a pleasant foretaste of rural Burgundy. Having observed the fate of neighbouring Chenôve, there is a strong local movement in Marsannay to prevent Dijon's further encroachment on the village: *Halte à l'urbanisation – trop, c'est trop!*

Marsannay's battle to keep its rural identity has been reflected in its struggle to promote its wines, which in turn has given rise to a dynamic spirit amongst the village's winemakers. It has only been entitled to its own appellation since 1987, and can now apply this to its red, white and rosé wines. Marsannay is unique in the Côte d'Or for producing a Pinot Noir rosé with a village *appellation*. Marsannay rosé was the invention of three of the village's vignerons, led by Joseph Clair, following the First World War; the aim was to have a wine that could be sold soon after the vintage, to help the financial plight of the poor vignerons.

Today, Joseph Clair's grandson runs Domaine Bruno Clair, Marsannay's best-known estate. Turn left on entering the village into rue du Vieux College to visit the cellars, by appointment only. ① **03 80 52 28 95** ✆ **www.bruno-clair.com** An easier grower to visit is Domaine Fougeray de Beauclair in the centre of town; the wines are great and the visit requires no advance phone call (see page 198). Otherwise, make an appointment at Domaine Huguenot. ① **03 80 52 11 56** Take the second right after the tourist office to visit the estate.

A good place to start in Marsannay is at the village's charming tourist office, which also houses it's small museum, La Maison du Patrimoine. Additionally, it arranges guided vineyard tours and wine tastings between July and September.

Marsannay boasts one of the region's very best restaurants, in Les Gourmets (see page 202).

Day 1 at a glance

Itinerary	192 – 197
Wineries	198 – 201
Restaurants	202 – 203

BOTTOM
Marsannay's resistance to urbanisation

BELOW
Ancient wine presses at Chenôve

ABOVE
Tasting with Vincent
Berthaut

BELOW
Gutsy: Benigne Joliet
and his wife

**OPPOSITE PAGE
TOP LEFT**
The church of St
Antoine, Fixey

**OPPOSITE PAGE
TOP RIGHT**
Manoir de la Perrière

**OPPOSITE PAGE
BOTTOM**
Fixin

Marsannay to Fixin

From Marsannay, continue along the D122 through the village of Couchey and, before entering Fixin, turn left into the hamlet of Fixey to visit the Côte d'Or's oldest Romanesque church, built in the 10th century and dedicated to Saint-Antoine. To reach the centre of Fixin, turn right before descending back to the D122 and follow rue des Hervelets through the vineyards.

Between Marsannay and Fixin, the soft and pretty wines of the former village undergo a dramatic gender change. Domaine Berthaut is an excellent grower to visit in Fixin, although the wines can be slightly unforgiving in youth. Vincent and Denis have a generous open-door policy, but you will have to exercise charm – and your best Burgundian French – if you want to taste slightly older wines. ☎ **03 80 52 45 48**
🖰 www.domaine-berthaut.com

The best known grower in Fixin is Domaine Pierre Gelin who owns the Premier Cru vineyard Clos Napoléon in its entirety (*en monopole*). ☎ **03 80 52 45 24** At the time of writing, however, a fascinating scenario was unravelling at Manoir de la Perrière, chez Joliet Père & Fils. For the 2005 vintage, Benigne Joliet recruited the great Philippe Charlopin, of Gevrey-Chambertin, as his 'consultant winemaker'. Joliet is the exclusive owner of Fixin's Premier Cru Clos de la Perrière vineyard, a site with a long history of fine wine production, but his recruitment of Charlopin is extraordinary for two reasons. The first is that, whilst the hiring of celebrity consultants is commonplace in Bordeaux, it is much rarer in Burgundy; the second is that Joliet used to charge about 20 euros a bottle for his wines, but in August 2006, the 2005 was already on the market at €80. That's the price that collectors pay for Grand Cru Gevrey-Chambertin!

Some call Joliet gutsy, others think he is insane; what is certain is that the wine is very fine. I had come anticipating the sort of modern 'garagiste' wines you find in Saint-Emilion and Pomerol, over-extracted, super-concentrated and only drinkable after long cellaring. But even before its bottling, the wine I tasted in barrel showed elegant, mineral flavours, with concentrated fruit, firm, ripe tannins and a silky mouth feel: a powerful expression of Premier Cru Fixin terroir. But don't take my word for it, Benigne and his wife are charming types, and you can visit their beautiful estate and vineyards without appointment. ☎ **03 80 52 47 85**

Past the Manoir above Fixin is Parc Noisot, within which is François Rude's sculpture of 'Napoléon awakening to immortality', commissioned in 1895 by

ABOVE
Château Stéphen
Liégeard, Brochon

TOP
Napoléon awakening
from the dead

Captain Claude Noisot of Napoléon's Imperial Guard. The small museum is, I discovered, only open in the afternoon at weekends between mid-April and mid-October.

On to Gevrey

Continue past the small road that leads to the park, over the hill into the village of Brochon. The vineyards here are entitled only to the Côte de Nuits-Villages appellation, but both Domaine Berthaut in Fixin and Fougeray de Beauclair in Marsannay own land here. The main attraction is the neo-Renaissance Château Stéphen-Liégeard, built in 1900 and now the local *lycée* (college). Guided visits take place in July and August, in the afternoons from Thursday to Sunday. ① **03 80 52 93 01**

The road past the entrance to the Château leads towards the N74, where you will find the large cheese producer Fromagerie Gaugry. The dairy produces seven different soft Burgundian cheeses, including the powerful, appellation-controlled *Epoisses*. Through glass panes you can follow the cheese on its journey into being. There is no pressure to buy, but this is the most temptingly brilliant sales technique I have ever seen. Remember: hot cars, days on the road and strong cheese do not mix! ① **03 80 34 00 05** ⑦ **www.gaugryfromager.com**

Gevrey-Chambertin

The next village is the first of the Côte's legendary names. As you approach from Brochon, the vineyards of the Gevrey-Chambertin appellation extend to your left beyond the N74 road. This is unusual in the Côte d'Or, where the eastern – 'wrong' – side of the main road is generally reserved for vines producing generic Bourgogne Rouge wines. The aberration is explained in Gevrey by the predominance of pebbly soils washed down from the Combe Lavaux valley, instead of the more fertile clay on the flatlands in other communes. The limestone soils in Gevrey-Chambertin generally contain a high proportion of clay, making them ideally suited to the Pinot Noir, the only grape planted in the commune.

Every lover of red burgundy comes to Gevrey-Chambertin with a name in mind, a personal *coup de coeur*, someone you absolutely must visit. If yours happens to be the legendary Armand Rousseau or the cult-inspiring Denis Mortet, be prepared for disappointment, as neither welcomes visitors. The same is increasingly true of the high-profile Philippe Charlopin, who is involved in making wine at so many of the Côte d'Or's estates that he is rarely to be found at his own, in Gevrey-Chambertin.

I had pre-arranged an appointment at my favourite

estate, Domaine Sylvie Esmonin, perched in between the church and the picturesque vineyards above the village. The estate's wines show that superb balance of elegance and spicy power that defines great Gevrey-Chambertin. Sylvie apparently receives visitors by appointment…but she forgot mine!

Phone ☎ **03 80 34 36 44**, and I wish you better luck than I had.

Otherwise, contact the talented young Bernard at Domaine René Bouvier, another star of Gevrey-Chambertin (see page 200).

The centre of Gevrey is quiet and civilised, if a little lacking in lustre. If arriving towards the end of the week, it is worth visiting the medieval Château de Gevrey-Chambertin, which looms large above the town. It is now owned by the *négociant* house Labouré-Roi. Visits are from Friday to Sunday. ☎ **03 80 34 36 12**

ABOVE
Château de
Gevrey-Chambertin

Scaling the valley

The Combe Lavaux Valley, in which Gevrey-Chambertin nestles, is a popular spot for hikers. For a brisk clamber to the top of its beautiful gorge, follow the D31 up through Gevrey until you reach the Combe Lavaux car park on your left. Continue on foot, following the blue signs indicating the *Sentier des Crêtes*. This well-signposted path is around 5 miles, and the highest point gives superb panoramic views of the Côte d'Or. On fine, clear days you can apparently see as far as the Alps. I didn't.

Domaine Fougeray de Beauclair

44, rue de Mazy
21160 Marsannay-la-Côte

Phone 03 80 52 21 12
or 03 80 51 25 75
Fax 03 80 58 73 83
www.fougeraydebeauclair.fr
fougeraydebeauclair@wanadoo.fr

The Estate

Jean-Louis and Evelyne Fougeray created Domaine Fougeray de Beauclair as recently as 1978, with less than 1 hectare of vines. Today, the family owns 20 hectares on the Côte d'Or, producing mainly red wines from the Pinot Noir, but also a Marsannay rosé, a sparkling rosé, and a rare white Marsannay made entirely from the Pinot Blanc grape.

Jean-Louis' son-in-law Patrice Ollivier now manages the estate. Patrice comes from a winemaking family in the Languedoc, and met Laurence Fougeray, his future wife, whilst working as an oenology professor. At the time, Laurence was his student.

When I arrived in Marsannay in midsummer, most of the village's winemakers were on holiday, but not Patrice. "I never leave in August," Patrice explained. "If disaster strikes before the harvest, I want to be there to deal with it myself."

The estate's wines are subtle and fruity, characterised by their purity of flavour and a thoughtful use of oak. Patrice ensures that the domaine's vines yield only small quantities of top quality grapes, which are then subjected to a rigorous process of selection. 20% of the estate's production is sold in the Côte d'Or's restaurants, where they enjoy considerable prestige.

The estate also owns vineyards in the Languedoc, so this is the place to buy rare southern specialities such as the white Picpoul de Pinet.

Patrice and Laurence speak English, and are happy to receive visitors throughout the week.

UK importer:
Oxford Wine Company

Choice wines:

Rosé de Marsannay 2005

Made from Pinot Noir grapes that have been macerated on their skins for at least a day, this rosé is deeper in colour than most from Marsannay, as the majority of estates press the grapes directly after picking.

On the nose, the red fruit aromas are intense, with strong mineral hints. The palate is beautifully rounded, showing peachy, almost exotic, flavours.

This wine partners as well with spicy Asian cuisine as it does with rustic Burgundian dishes.

Marsannay Rouge 'Les Saint-Jacques' 2004

It took the Fougeray family 20 years to acquire and plant what is now perhaps regarded as Marsannay's best vineyard. It is called Les Saint-Jacques (shellfish) after its stony, fossil-rich soil, high on the slopes overlooking the village.

The wine's aromas are classic 'pretty' Marsannay: roses and redcurrants, but with the underlying minerality of its terroir. The palate shows red fruits with a slight mineral austerity, hinting at a few years' ageing potential.

A great partner for *Boeuf Bourguignon* or *Coq au Vin*.

Fixin 'Clos Marion' Monopole 2001

From one of Fixin's most historic vineyard sites, this wine is made from sixty-year old vines, yielding less than 30 hectolitres per hectare.

Fairly light in colour, but showing only slight signs of ageing, the wine's nose is rather feminine for a Fixin, with aromas of cherries and nail varnish (in a good way). The palate is full of concentrated, supple cherry fruits.

This wine could be enjoyed on its own, with feathered game or roast lamb.

Bonnes-Mares Grand Cru 2003

The family works the part of the Bonnes-Mares vineyard that is inside the commune of Morey-Saint-Denis, producing one of Burgundy's most cherished red wines.

The wine is deep, rich and complex. Its lively spiced cherry and plum aromas are in perfect balance with the influence of oak. The palate is rich and mouth filling, and shows, in the words of Patrice, "perfect harmony".

In its youth, drink this wine with red meats and mild cheeses, but Patrice recommends keeping it even "until the wedding of a child born in its year of production", when it will partner wonderfully with game dishes.

RIGHT
Patrice Ollivier with
baby son Justin

Domaine René Bouvier

29 B, route de Dijon
21220 Gevrey-Chambertin

Phone 03 80 34 36 12
Fax 03 80 34 16 00
René-bouvier@wanadoo.fr

The Estate

The 17-hectare Bouvier estate is concentrated principally in the appellations of Gevrey-Chambertin and Marsannay, and is today run by 'young talent' Bernard Bouvier. Three times winner of Burgundy's *Jeunes Talents* award, Bernard's manner is taciturn, as he prefers his wines to speak for themselves. And this they do in volumes. To be a *Jeune Talent*, your wines not only have to beat those of young stars in your own village, but all of those in the area: in Bernard's case, the entire Côte de Nuits.

Bernard believes that his wines must be the finest possible expression of their terroirs, and of the vintages in which the grapes are grown. In a difficult year, no quarter is given to lesser bunches on the sorting table. The 2004 harvest saw 20% of the (already careful, manual) harvest simply thrown away. No herbicides, pesticides or chemical fertilisers are used in the vineyard, where healthy old vines have dug deep roots to find nutrients in the soil.

The style of the estate's Gevrey-Chambertins is less robust and spicy than many, but the wines have an elegant power all of their own. The family's original base was Marsannay, and their wines from this village are soft in the mouth, but fairly deep in colour. The Bouviers are proud owners of the Marsannay's *Montre-Cul* vineyard, which translates evocatively as something like "Show yer backside!"

Visits are by appointment; the more notice given, the better.

UK importer:
Thorman Hunt

LEFT
Young Talent:
Bernard Bouvier

Choice wines:
Marsannay Rouge 'Clos du Roy' 2004
Clos du Roy is the only vineyard within the township of Chenôve (see page 192), now part of the wider Marsannay appellation. The sandy-clay soils here give wines with more structure than the 'pretty' Pinots from the vineyards around Marsannay.

Characteristic red fruits mix with earthy spices on the nose. On the palate, the spices attack first, followed by flavours of soft fruits and an attractive firm acidity.

This will be drinking well in a year or so, with a nice rare-cooked tuna steak.

Gevrey-Chambertin 'Racines du Temps' 2004
The wine's name, 'the roots of time', is a hint at the 80-year-old vines from which it hails. Less coded are the words on the label: *très vieilles vignes*! This is one in the eye for growers whose 'old vines' have barely lived two decades.

The grapes from these vines are small and concentrated, giving an intensely flavoured juice. The aromas combine violets and red fruits, with a hint of oak that has yet to soften. The flavours are explosive and give onto a silky, graceful finish.

I could happily drink this wine now with roast lamb, but it will gain in complexity for ten to fifteen years.

Gevrey-Chambertin
Premier Cru 'Petite Chapelle' 2004
Bordering the Grand Cru Chapelle-Chambertin, this is one of Gevrey's best-reputed Premier Cru vineyards. The nose is ripe and perfumed, with concentrated aromas of cassis, redcurrant and eucalypt.

Savoury cassis and strawberry flavours develop onto a silky, incredibly persistent finish. The wine is already drinking remarkably well, but will need a few years to marry with poultry and feathered game, as its perfect partners.

ABOVE
Bizarre-looking:
the vine-straddling
tracteur-enjambeur

Grand Cru Charmes-Chambertin 2004
This is a powerful Grand Cru wine that needs time to open. Its colour is dark; its aromas are complex, showing black cherries and intense minerals. Even early in its life, the wine has a remarkable ripe softness on the palate, and there are already strong hints of the developed black fruits and pungent flowers that will characterise its flavours in the years to come.

Twenty years will see the wine constantly developing new wonders, as a partner for hare, rabbit and other kinds of game.

Restaurant Les Gourmets
8, rue du Puits-de-Têt
21160 Marsannay-le-Côte

Phone 03 80 52 16 32
Fax 03 80 52 03 01
http://les-gourmets.com

This small restaurant is one of the Côte d'Or's most highly esteemed, and you barely need cross the threshold to understand why. Chef Joël Perreaut and his wife Nicole have owned the place since 1979, and what they offer today are the fruits of their considerable experience. There is something intangible and priceless about the experience at Les Gourmets: an all-pervasive feeling of relaxed self-confidence that reaches beyond Joël's culinary brilliance.

The restaurant has kept its Michelin star for over twenty years, thanks in part to a dedicated and long-serving restaurant team. And many eat at Les Gourmets simply to paw the list of over 600 extraordinary wines. It is hard to believe that they all exist, until you are led downstairs into a cellar itself worthy of an award – imagine an entire wall devoted to the famous Domaine de la Romanée-Conti!

Joël's cooking is based firmly on Burgundian traditions, but the recipes evolve constantly, in harmony with the seasons and with changes in the wine list. There is always a good choice of wines by the glass, and the sommelier's advice is gospel. Set menus are available from between €30 and €60. Nicole believes that every customer deserves "a fête" when they eat out, and here you will get nothing less.

Closed from Sunday evening to midday Tuesday, the first half of August and from mid-December to mid-February.

Present this book for a free house apéritif.

TOP
Relaxed self-confidence:
Joël Perreaut

LEFT
Impressive: an entire
wall for Domaine de la
Romanée-Conti!

Eating in Gevrey-Chambertin

The Gevrey restaurant scene has changed somewhat in the last five years. French presidents and their chums once made the journey to eat at Les Millésimes: highly exclusive, irreproachably suave and…closed. Around the time of its closure, Gevrey's other refined establishment, La Sommelerie, changed hands, and its ambience is now somewhat faded.

My advice in Gevrey is to keep it simple, and in this way you will eat well.

Chez Guy and Family is neither modern nor traditional; more than a bistrot but entirely unpretentious, the restaurant's style is best called 'contemporary' and seems to appeal to everyone. It is open 7 days a week. Menus are between €25 and €32. (The hotel no longer exists.)

Otherwise, pay a visit to Le Bonbistrot. Attached to the more expensive Rôtisserie du Chambertin, this Parisian-style bistrot serves rustic Burgundian dishes in a pleasant, relaxed environment.

Closed Sunday evening and Monday and Tuesday lunchtimes, and annually for two weeks in August and one week in March.

Unusually for a French village, you can wheel into Gevrey-Chambertin mid-afternoon and catch a bite to eat. One of the town's finest growers, Philippe Charlopin, owns the wine bar Chez Gaston, where a few euros buys you a plate of *escargots*, or a selection of cheeses, with interesting wines by the glass. The attached wine shop is one of the village's best.

Closed Tuesday.

Chez Guy and Family
Phone 03 80 58 51 51
www.hotel-bourgogne.com

Le Bonbistrot
Rue du Chambertin

Phone 03 80 34 33 20
www.rotisserie-bonbistrot.com

Chez Gaston
33 & 35, rue des Baraques

Phone 03 80 58 50 46

RIGHT
Chez Guy and Family

Day 2 itinerary (10-15 miles)

The famous vineyards of the Côte-de-Nuits

Leaving Gevrey via Le Chambertin

As you leave Gevrey-Chambertin along the D122, the village's second most famous Grand Cru vineyard, Chambertin-Clos-de-Bèze, appears on your right; followed by the one you will have been waiting to see, Le Chambertin. Unlike Clos-de-Bèze, Le Chambertin was never a monastic vineyard, but rather a field, or *champ*, owned by a peasant named Bertin. By the mid-19th century it was sufficiently esteemed to prompt the enterprising winemakers to suffix it to their village's name. But the vineyard's appearance is as ordinary as its wines are extraordinary, which, if anything, adds to their mystery.

Morey-Saint-Denis

Little more than a mile further on, the Morey-Saint-Denis Grand Cru Clos de la Roche is on your right before you enter that village. The equally celebrated Grand Crus

Clos des Lambrays, Bonnes Mares (see Domaine Fougeray de Beauclair, page 198), Clos Saint-Denis and Clos de Tart all climb the hillside from the village centre. Clos de Tart is wholly owned by the Mommesin house. Clos des Lambrays became a Grand Cru as recently as 1981 and belongs to its eponymous estate, which welcomes visitors by appointment. ① **03 80 51 84 33** ⤷ **www.lambrays.com**

Opposite the church is the Caveau des Vignerons de Morey-Saint-Denis, the recently opened retail outlet for twelve of the town's winemakers, including Domaine des Lambrays. You won't get to meet the winemakers here, but you will be able to taste and compare wines from the town's different producers. ① **03 80 51 86 79** ⤷ **caveau-des-vignerons@wanadoo.fr**

Day 1 at a glance
Itinerary 204 – 209
Wineries 210 – 213
Restaurants 214 – 215

Chambolle-Musigny

Half a mile along the road, Chambolle-Musigny boasts its own larger, more dynamic shop, the Caveau de l'Escargot de la Côte, which represents over 40 growers from all over the Côte d'Or. Here you can taste wines from the likes of Laurent or Georges Roumier, otherwise inaccessible to tourists, or take the educational train ride through the vineyards. ① **03 80 62 84 01**

The village of Chambolle is somehow more charming than neighbouring Morey, and its church houses some impressive 16th century frescoes. Like Gevrey-Chambertin, it nestles beneath its own imposing valley, Combe Ambin. The town's vineyards include the larger part of Grand Cru Les Bonnes Mares, which it shares with Morey-Saint-Denis to the north, and Grand Cru Le Musigny, which nudges against Clos de Vougeot south of the village. Chambolle-Musigny only produces red wines, which show a perfumed delicacy and velvety structure that earn them their reputation as 'feminine'. Les Amoureuses and Les Charmes, in Chambolle-Musigny, are two of the Côte d'Or's finest Premier Cru vineyards.

As you enter Chambolle-Musigny, the excellent restaurant Le Chambolle is on your left (see page 214). The estate to visit, Domaine Hudelot-Baillet, is directly opposite (see page 210).

The Côte's most beautiful vineyard

Leave Chambolle-Musigny along rue du Tilleul, and then turn right into the vineyards instead of descending into the village of Vougeot. The Côte d'Or's most picturesque Grand Cru vineyard, the Clos de Vougeot, appears through the trees, surrounded by its famous monastic Château du Clos de Vougeot.

Cistercian monks at the nearby abbey of Cîteaux erected the vineyard's walls in 1336, and built the press-house and wine cellar in the same century. In 1551, abbot Dom Losier commissioned the building of the present-day château, as a centre for welcoming visitors and preparing feasts, and it remains thus to this day.

Following the French Revolution and the dissolution of the monasteries, the 50-hectare Clos de Vougeot was sold into private ownership. It was sold off in pieces in the 19th century, and now belongs to eighty different estates. Many argue that the wise monks' intentions were for wines to be produced from Clos de Vougeot as a whole, the perfect blend of subtly different microclimates. Its division has certainly led to differences in quality between growers' wines, and here more than anywhere, the name of the producer is crucial.

Château du Clos de Vougeot witnessed much of the French Revolution's destructive mayhem. In the 20th century, two World Wars wreaked further havoc, and it wasn't until after the second of these that the Château was restored to its former glory by its current owners, the *Confrérie des Chevaliers du Tastevin*.

So who are the *Chevaliers*?

With their ostentatious robes and gold medallions, the *Chevaliers de Tastevin* practically define French folkloric 'bling'. Their more serious purpose is to promote and protect the reputation of Burgundy's wines.

Established in 1934, the *Confrérie* organises two tastings, or *tastevinages*, per year: one in the spring for red burgundy, and one on the 1st September for white wines and for the wines of Beaujolais. Their objective is to recognise and reward the wines that best represent their respective Burgundian appellations. 250 representatives of all areas of the wine trade blind taste around 700 wines, and those wines that are selected, the *tastevinés*, go to market bearing the crest of the *Confrérie*. Vincent Rapet (see page 224) explained to me that very little discussion takes place between the tasters, lest the dominant personalities around the table have a disproportionate influence on the others' judgements.

You can visit the Château every day without appointment. ☎ 03 80 62 86 09
🖰 www.tastevin-bourgogne.com

Where to taste in Vougeot

Continue past the entrance to the Château du Clos de Vougeot, then turn left towards Domaine Bertagna. The wines here have improved immeasurably since 1982,

ABOVE
Château du
Clos de Vougeot

TOP
Chambolle-Musigny:
a charming village

OPPOSITE PAGE
TOP
The *Chevaliers de
Tastevin* preside over
the *Tastevinage*

when a German winemaking family bought and renovated the winery. The estate produces a rare white Vougeot Premier Cru. You can taste here without appointment, although cellar tours are not encouraged.

The estate also owns an incredibly good value hotel with stunning views of the Château and the Clos de Vougeot vineyard. ☎ **03 80 62 86 04** ⌐ **www.domainebertagna.com**

Vosne-Romanée

Rejoin the road above the Château, then fork left in front of the sign announcing the Grand Cru vineyards of Flagey-Echézeaux (curiously peppered with bullet holes and covered in anti-fascist posters when I visited!) A further mile leads to the village of Vosne-Romanée, home of Grand Crus La Tâche, Le Richebourg and the most famous of them all, La Romanée-Conti. The last of these is wholly owned by the domaine of the same name. Even the rich and the famous join a waiting list to taste at Domaine de la Romanée-Conti, but it is worth peering through the painted gates just to marvel at the enigmatic banality of what is probably the world's most prestigious wine estate (Rue Derrière le Four).

It is not immediately obvious where to start in Vosne-Romanée. The easiest place is the shop in the tiny village

centre, owned by François Gerbet. The Gerbet estate's wines are very good; but if you're searching for fine Grands Crus, plan a rendezvous with local character François Lamarche, although you may well find him short of wine to sell. ℡ **03 80 61 07 94** ✆ **www.domaine-lamarche.com**

I also visited Domaine Gros Frère & Soeur, part of Vosne's extended Gros winemaking clan. It was mid-August and no one was around except for Colette Gros, the retired Soeur, who showed me the cellars. The wines are perfect examples of that silky elegance that makes the red wines of Vosne-Romanée so magical. Arrange a tasting here if you possibly can. ✉ **6, rue des Grands Crus** ℡ **03 80 61 12 43**

Perhaps the best advice is to continue through the village and fork left towards the main road, the N74. Here you will find the unmissable restaurant La Toute Petite Auberge (see page 214) on one side of the road, and leading biodynamic winemaker Bruno Clavelier on the other (see page 212).

Through the Vineyards to Nuits-Saint-Georges

Continue a further few miles along the N74 into Nuits-Saint-Georges, or climb back into Vosne-Romanée, past the Mairie on your right. Then turn left into rue des Chaumes, and left again along the vineyard road. This road is pretty rough in places, but gives excellent views of the patchwork of steeply sloping vineyards above Nuits-Saint-Georges as you approach the town.

The other option is to leave Vosne the way you came and, instead of turning right to Vougeot, carry straight on up the hill into the villages of Corboin and Concoeur. In the second of these is the farm shop Fruirouge, which produces a range of delicious products made from locally grown fruits. ℡ **03 80 62 36 25** ✆ **www.fruirouge.fr**

Continue through the village until you meet the D25, then turn left towards Nuits-Saint-Georges.

Nuits-Saint-Georges

On the map, Nuits-Saint-Georges looks similar in size to Gevrey-Chambertin, but whilst Gevrey is a wine village, Nuits is definitely a town – and one in which the winemakers seem almost to fade into the stonework. In many cases, the only indication of a house's vinous credentials is a small plaque on the front gate, humbly sporting a great name.

Nuits-Saint-Georges is surprising in having no Grand Cru vineyards, although its Premier Cru vineyards make interesting, often good value, red wines. Nuits is home to many of the Côte d'Or's merchant houses; the most famous of which is Faiveley, although this is not one for tourists.

There is plenty to do in Nuits-Saint-Georges, so I would save wine estate visits for the following morning. An interesting grower to visit is Gilles Remoriquet (see page 222); another is Domaine Chauvenet-Chopin. ① 03 80 61 00 72

Otherwise, call on innovative *négociant* Nicholas Potel, at 44, rue des Blés. ① 03 80 62 15 45.

Nuits-Saint-Georges' other attractions: Burgundy's 'other drinks'

Nuits-Saint-Georges' Cassissium claims to be "the largest venue in Europe devoted to the blackcurrant"! Owned by Védrenne, the Côte d'Or's biggest producer of *crème de cassis*, the Cassissium museum and factory visits are interesting, without being obvious sales pitches.

Open every day between 10am and 1pm, then 2pm to 7pm. ① 03 80 62 49 70 ⊕ www.cassissium.com

The Imaginarium is an ambitious, hands-on attraction devoted to bubbles in wine, run by Louis Bouillot, the region's largest producer of sparkling *Crémant de Bourgogne*. The Imaginarium was in its infancy when I visited…so I reserve judgement. ① 03 80 62 49 70. Opening times as for the Cassissium.

Both are to be found outside the town in the direction of the *autoroute*.

A vineyard walk in Nuits

There is a well-conceived and usefully signposted route through the vineyards of Nuits-Saint-Georges, called Sentier Félix Tisserand, which allows you to climb the Côte at your own pace, offering excellent panoramic views of the town and the Jurassic mountains beyond.

From place de la République, pass the ivy-leafed *Beffroi* (belfry) into rue du Grenier à Sel. Take rue Notre Dame past the main church, Eglise St Denis, to quai Fleury. On the opposite side of the road, follow rue de Chaux into the vineyards and from here follow the white arrows.

Allow around two hours for a leisurely bimble.

Domaine Hudelot-Baillet

21, rue Basse
21220 Chambolle-Musigny

Phone 03 80 62 85 88
Fax 03 80 62 49 83
Hudelot-baillet@club-internet.fr
www.domaine-hudelot-
baillet.com

The Estate

When Dominique Leguin first arrived in the Côte d'Or in 1992, it was as a soldier, not a winemaker. He had been posted to the military barracks in Nuits-Saint-Georges, and it was whilst playing rugby locally that he met his future wife Valerie Hudelot-Baillet, an enthusiastic supporter. Dominique's love for Burgundy's wines led him to study viticulture in Beaune and, ten years later, he was in charge of all vinifications at the Chambolle-Musigny estate. A father of two and researcher for the BIVB (Bureau Interprofessionel des Vins de Bourgogne), Dominique somehow still manages to offer the warmest welcome in Chambolle.

Dominique's philosophy of viticulture is simple: the soil is alive! Exchanges between the roots of the vines and the earth are effected indirectly, by the micro-organisms living deep beneath the vineyards' surface. Without these benign bugs, Dominique believes the concept of 'terroir' makes little sense. The encouragement of insects' natural predators allows the soil to sustain itself organically, and butterflies are prevented from reproducing in the vineyards by the use of harmless 'sexual confusion' pheromones.

For anyone who believes that ultra-modern wineries are essential for wine quality, Domaine Hudelot-Baillet is food for thought. Here things are very traditional, and as in so many village centre wineries, space is in short supply. The wines show all the perfumed refinement that defines Chambolle-Musigny, and this is a great place to learn about differences in the village's terroirs. The estate also produces very good less expensive Passetoutgrain, Bourgogne Pinot Noir and Hautes-Côtes de Nuits, all made from grapes grown around Chambolle.

Tastings are possible for most of the year. Phone in advance to meet Dominique, who speaks some English.

UK importer:
Christopher Piper Wines, Devon

OPPOSITE PAGE
Military man turned vigneron:
Dominique Leguin

Choice wines:

Chambolle-Musigny Vieilles Vignes 2004

From a single parcel of seventy-year-old vines, yielding tiny quantities of grapes, this wine is deep in colour, with an intense nose. Aromas of cherries and nail varnish (good) are complemented by complex vegetal hints as the wine begins to develop.

On the palate, the tannins are soft and ripe, and the flavours have an exuberant velvetiness that is unmistakably Chambolle.

I would drink this wine on its own or with fish cooked in red wine sauce.

Chambolle-Musigny Premier Cru 'Les Charmes' 2004

One of Burgundy's finest Premiers Crus, Les Charmes lives up to its name, making wines of fantastic freshness and elegance.

Cherry and raspberry aromas follow onto a supple, but weighty palate. The finish is extremely long and delicate, with a mineral complexity that has yet to develop fully.

A few years will see the wine showing its best side, and it will continue to evolve for ten further years.

Chambolle-Musigny Premier Cru 'Les Cras' 2004

This Premier Cru is a very different beast. Situated on higher, stonier ground just behind the Hudelot-Baillet estate, its proximity to Les Bonnes Mares Grand Cru makes itself felt.

The nose is savoury and earthy, almost smoky, with cocoa hints. On the palate, its attack is intense and fruity, with a brooding spicy finish.

This wine will develop wonderfully with time in bottle; five to ten years will see it partner well with big game and red meats.

Grand Cru Bonnes Mares 2004

Typically a more rugged wine than Chambolle's better known Grand Cru Le Musigny, this 2004 has developed surprisingly intense cassis and redcurrant aromas whilst in bottle.

Its palate combines all the spicy power of Les Cras with the elegant fresh fruits of Les Charmes. A wine of this intensity needs time to soften, and will develop happily for twenty years.

Drink with full-flavoured game dishes, or simply on its own, after a few years' ageing.

Domaine Bruno Clavelier

6, route nationale
21700 Vosne-Romanée

Phone 03 80 61 10 81
Fax 03 80 61 04 25
Domaine-
clavelier@reseauconcept.net

The Estate

This estate was discovered back in 1992 by one Clive Coates, and in the same year, began bottling all of its own wines. Foreign markets quickly took heed and today the estate exports 60% of its production. The young Bruno Clavelier took over the estate's six hectares in 1987. His grandfather had resisted the 1970s fashion for chemical warfare against vineyard pests, and so left Bruno some of the "cleanest" soils in the Côte d'Or. The estate received organic certification from ECOCERT in 1999.

But Bruno's philosophy reaches beyond the organic, and is founded on stricter, biodynamic principles. Above the estate's 18th century vaulted cellar, long fermentations take place in large open wooden vats, many of which are more than a century old. For Bruno, stainless steel creates a sterile, "empty" environment that is alien to the natural world. He explains that, just as superbugs mutate and wreak havoc in disinfected hospital wards, similar aberrations take place in the vineyard and winery if all germ life is eradicated.

The estate's Premier Cru vineyards reach from Gevrey-Chambertin to Nuits-Saint-Georges and include a wide variety of terroirs, most of them planted in the years following the Second World War. The wines' flavours are extremely natural, showing an uncommon mineral purity; all benefit from time in bottle.

Phone in advance to arrange a tasting.

UK importers:
Decorum
Laytons
Howard Ripley

LEFT
Bruno Clavelier beside
large old oak vats

Choice wines:
Vosne-Romanée
Premier Cru 'Les Beaux Monts' 2004
High above the famous Grands Crus of Vosne-Romanée, the poor limestone soil of Les Beaux Monts gives its wines a masculine, flinty character, but with refined red fruit on the nose.

The wine shows flavours of dark cherry, blackberry and strawberry, with spiced bread on the rear palate.

A few years ageing will soften this wine. Drink with red meats.

Chambolle-Musigny
Premier Cru 'Combe d'Orveaux' 2004
Perched on the steep hillside above Le Musigny, Chambolle's finest Grand Cru, the wines from the Combe d'Orveaux vineyard have all the strawberry, raspberry and spice aromas of the village's best, but with a firm, almost rustic, power on the palate.

"If Chambolle-Musigny is feminine," says Bruno, "then this is a difficult woman."

The wine could afford to soften with age. It will become a very versatile partner for either white or red meats.

Nuits-Saint-Georges
Premier Cru 'Au Cras' 2004
Just beneath the Premier Cru vineyard Les Damodes (see Gilles Remoriquet, page 222), Au Cras benefits from porous fissured soils and an eastern exposure to the sun's rays. The soils thus reflect the heat that builds up during the morning, throughout the day.

The vineyard's proximity to Vosne-Romanée shows in its elegant aromas of blackberry, liquorice and cherry, but the power and spice on the palate are all Nuits-Saint-Georges'.

This is the perfect partner for that most Burgundian of dishes, *Coq au Vin*. It will go equally well with feathered game or hare.

Grand Cru Corton 'Le Rognet' 2004
On the eastern slopes of the hill of Corton above the town of Ladoix-Serrigny, Le Rognet shares its eastern exposure and porous limestone soil with the larger Bressandes vineyard (see Domaine Comte-Senard, page 234).

The wine shows well in its youth, but has a good twenty years ageing potential. Smoked meat, quince and damson jam aromas dominate the nose; the palate is a wonderful balance of power and finesse.

Bruno describes this as a "suave" wine, best drunk with game birds.

Restaurant Le Chambolle
Route des Grands Crus
21220 Chambolle-Musigny

Phone/Fax 03 80 62 86 26

In the heart of the Côte de Nuits' smallest wine village, Le Chambolle represents the finest in traditional Burgundian cuisine, in a cosy familial environment. Eric Claudel's cooking is simple, fresh and delicious; the *Clafoutis d'escargots* in a creamy parsley sauce is an essential starter, followed by the chef's rich, flavoursome *Boeuf Bourguignon*.

Eric and his wife Martine know all of the local winemakers, and their restaurant wine list is selected from extensive tastings. Martine speaks English, and is as generous with smiles as she is with advice about the best winemakers to visit. Eric also likes to leave the kitchen during calm moments to chat with diners.

It is a bizarre and impressive sight to watch Eric alone at work in the kitchen without even the help of a dishwasher! But this makes reservation at weekends essential. The maximum number of diners is capped at fifteen, so that neither service nor food preparation is compromised.

A full four-course meal at Le Chambolle is only €25. Closed Wednesday and Thursday.

La Toute Petite Auberge
R.N. 74
21700 Vosne-Romanée

Phone 03 80 61 02 03
Fax 03 80 61 34 31

BELOW
Innovative: Chef Franck Boyer

When Franck and Florence Boyer arrived in Vosne-Romanée in 1993, *la Toute Petite Auberge* was just that: a small country inn. The original stone building dates from the end of the 18th century, and was apparently always painted its current vivid pillar-box red.

The restaurant's enormous popularity has forced an inevitable expansion, so that today Franck presides over a dedicated team of ten. The restaurant's ambience is, however, undiminished. Franck is very much his own boss, and has so far spurned the advances of the restaurant classification crews, to keep his own agenda intact.

The Auberge's menu changes regularly, the product of brainstorming sessions that include the entire kitchen staff. An interesting starter is the house *foie gras*, freeze-cooked at -190 degrees to give it a unique buttery texture. Another Boyer speciality is a version of the traditional harvest time meat-and-veg stew, the *potée*, incorporating poached *foie gras* and pikeperch.

Menus are from €35 to €50.
Closed Tuesday evening and Wednesday.

Eating in Nuits-Saint-Georges

Months before arriving in Burgundy, I had been recommended **Restaurant L'Alambic** by vigneron Philippe Brun, in Aÿ-Champagne.

L'Alambic is where the vignerons of Nuits-Saint-Georges come to eat, and nationally acclaimed sommelier Michel Philippon in turn sells all of their wines, with good simple Burgundian food.

A mere €26 buys you a full meal with a different glass of wine to match each course.

Made a *Confrère* of the *Chevaliers de Tastevin* in 2004, Michel is proud to be the son of humble vineyard workers. Like its owner, Restaurant L'Alambic has few pretensions, and thus many friends.

Closed Monday lunchtime, and Sunday night in winter.

Present this book to receive a free kir apéritif.

Restaurant "Le Chef Coq" is the gastronomic restaurant attached to the luxurious Hôtel la Gentilhommière. Set menus are upwards of €45, which is a little expensive.

During the week, however, lunchtime menus are served from about €20, and in summer, you can enjoy your meal on the terrace beside the hotel pool.

Restaurant L'Alambic
Rue du Général de Gaulle
21700 Nuits-Saint-Georges

Phone 03 80 61 35 00
Fax 03 80 61 24 65
www.lalambic.com

Restaurant "Le Chef Coq"
Tel 03 80 61 12 06
Fax 03 80 61 30 33
www.lagentilhommiere.fr

RIGHT
Restaurant l'Alambic

TOP
Nationally acclaimed sommelier,
Michel Philippon

Day 3 itinerary (15-20 miles)

The Hautes-Côtes de Nuits into the Côte de Beaune

Climbing the Upper Slopes

After a wine tasting in Nuits-Saint-Georges (see Day 2 itinerary, and page 222), leave the town along the D25, passing the Romanesque 13th century church of St-Symphorien on your left. Continue past Hôtel-Restaurant La Gentilhommière just outside of town (see page 264) and follow the road until the right turning onto the D35 to Villars-Fontaine.

The ascent into the Hautes-Côtes de Nuits (the Upper Slopes) is short, but the change in landscape is sudden and remarkable. One of the greatest things about France is that impression of unlimited space each time you reach the summit of a new hill.

Villars-Fontaine and the Hudelot family

As you approach Villars-Fontaine, the vines of the village's largest producer, Patrick Hudelot, rise towards the forest to your right. These vines are very different to those on the lower slopes of the Côte de Nuits. They are trained high on their wires, in widely spaced rows. This allows essential exposure to the sun's rays in these higher, cooler Hautes-Côtes vineyards, where grapes ripen a full week later than those on the Côte d'Or. It also allows better air circulation and the use of proper tractors, instead of the unsteady vine-straddling *tracteurs-enjambeurs* more common on the lower slopes. The vineyard you pass before entering the village is Les Genevrières. With a slope of 27%, only a suicidal vigneron would risk using an *enjambeur* here.

Despite the vineyards' suitability to mechanised viticulture, Patrick Hudelot insists on hand-harvesting his grapes, and the estate has been fully organic since the year 2000. Patrick is a real force for reform in the quality of the region's wines; his reds, particularly, are excellent value traditional light-coloured burgundies. Les Roncières and Les Genevrières are the finest expressions of Patrick's art. Visitors are welcome all year, although Patrick speaks no English. ① **03 80 61 50 37** ⑁ **www.domaine-patrick-hudelot.com**

The brothers Henri and Bernard Hudelot created the original Hudelot estate in 1973, twelve years after the creation of the Hautes-Côtes appellation. Before the 1960s, this area was polycultural farmland, mainly devoted to soft fruits, grain growing and grazing pasture. The brothers Hudelot eventually created two separate estates. Henri's son Patrick took over his father's domaine; Bernard's daughter Armele now makes the wine at Château de Villars-Fontaine. The wines made at the latter estate couldn't be more different from Patrick's: deeply coloured, tannic and aged in new oak barrels, they are made for the long haul.
① **03 80 62 31 94** ⑁ **www.domainedemontmain.fr**

The road to Marey-lès-Fussey

Opposite Villars-Fontaine's wonderful inn, the Auberge du Côteau (see page 226), take the small road leading down the hill towards Meuilly. On entering Meuilly, bear left through the village and turn left briefly onto the D25, then right onto D115 towards Marey-lès-Fussey.

A steady climb leads you through a mix of vines and assorted other field crops. Two miles later, turn right onto the D8 past the once great restaurant La Maison des Hautes-Côtes. Years ago this was owned by Bernard Hudelot, but when I visited it seemed to have become home to squatters.

Marey-lès-Fussey's main wine producer is Domaine Thevenot Lebrun. The brothers Daniel and Jean Thevenot

Day 3 at a glance
Itinerary   216 – 221
Wineries   222 – 225
Restaurants   226 – 227

BELOW
Domaine Patrick Hudelot

BOTTOM
Patrick Hudelot amongst his vines

ABOVE
The Hautes-Côtes
de Nuits: open
spaces and
high-trellised vines

are good-natured and well worth visiting. They produce a rare Pinot Beurot (Pinot Gris) which is tolerated if not strictly permitted by appellation regulations. They also make a wonderful *crème de cassis* and a very fine slightly sparkling Aligoté, so this is the place to stock up on *Kir* ingredients. ① 03 80 62 91 64
⌂ www.thevenot-le-brun.com

On to Pernand-Vergelesses, and into the Côte de Beaune

Climb the steep track just past Domaine Thevenot Lebrun on your left, or take the next, more forgiving, left on leaving the village. The view from the top of the hill is a spectacular 360-degree panorama, and from here you really can see the Alps.

The next village is Echevronne, where Jean-Michel Jacob makes excellent wines at Domaine Lucien Jacob. Apart from his 7 hectares of vines in the Hautes-Côtes-de-Beaune, Jean-Michel has acquired important Premier Cru holdings in Beaune and Savigny-lès-Beaune, making extraordinary wines from Premier Cru vineyard Les Vergelesses in the latter appellation. ① 03 80 21 52 15

Continue through Echevronne and turn left onto the D18 straight to Pernand-Vergelesses; or double back through Echevronne and turn right into the hillside vineyards, then fork right towards Magny-les-Villers. Ahead of you as you enter that village is its big name, Domaine Jayer-Gilles. Its owners are relations of the famous Henri Jayer in Vosne-Romanée, and the Magny estate is more likely to welcome visitors than the one in Vosne. ① 03 80 62 91 79

Follow the sign right towards Pernand-Vergelesses, and then make sure you turn right again opposite the public phone box. This small hill takes you briefly into the Hautes-Côtes de Beaune, before descending into the Côte de Beaune and the pretty village of Pernand-Vergelesses.

Pernand-Vergelesses

After the right fork into the village, you pass under Sous Frétille; the village's largest Premier Cru vineyard devoted to white Chardonnay grapes. In the village itself, a right turn leads uphill to the peaceful park, Plateau de Frétille, from where you get wonderful views of the village below, and of the famous vine-covered hill of Corton to the south.

The village's small 12th century church is its showpiece, surrounded by the stone houses and cellars that descend the hillside opposite the vineyards of Corton. No one knows exactly when the church was built, but it mixes Byzantine Roman, Cistercian and even Gothic architectural styles, its roof decorated with the unmistakably Burgundian multi-coloured tiled roof.

The village's white and red wines are real favourites of mine, showing an intense fruity minerality. They tend to cost less than those of neighbouring Aloxe-Corton, although nowadays often not much, and most of the village's vignerons own land in both appellations. A small side street above and to the left of the church leads to Domaine Rapet Père & Fils (see page 224), but there are many growers worth visiting here. Domaine Denis Père & Fils ☎ **03 80 21 50 91** and Laleure-Piot ☎ **03 80 21 52 37** are both good bets, but it would be a shame to pass through the village without stopping in at Domaine Jaffelin Père & Fils. ☎ **03 80 21 52 43**

ABOVE
Pernand-Vergelesses

BELOW
The church in
Pernand-Vergelesses

Save Corton, and continue to Savigny-les-Beaune

Descend the hill and turn left at the roundabout towards the hill of Corton. As you pass the famous Grand Cru vineyard Le Charlemagne on your left, Laurent Peugeot's excellent fusion restaurant Le Charlemagne greets you directly opposite (see page 227).

As you approach the Premier Cru vineyard L'Ile des Vergelesses on the right, cyclists can take the vineyard path to the right, which leads to Savigny-lès-Beaune; motorists take the next right turn. Either way, you pass over Les Lavières, one of Savigny's best-reputed Premier Cru vineyards.

Arriving in Savigny-lès-Beaune

Savigny is my favourite of the Côte d'Or villages. With around 1000 inhabitants, it is the largest of Beaune's neighbours, and its proximity to the region's wine capital gives it a refreshingly civilised air. The village is just large enough to get lost in, although never for long, with a good number of friendly vignerons, two trendy (-ish) bars and, of course, a beautiful château.

As a boy, I'm sure I said to myself, "When I grow up, I want to live in a castle with a huge collection of motorbikes, touring cars and fighter jets." As an adult, I have often dreamed of owning a beautiful wine estate. But Volnay vigneron Michel Pont has achieved both of

these ambitions since buying Château de Savigny in 1979.

The present-day Château dates from the 17th century; its estate includes 40 hectares of vineyard, mainly in the Côte de Beaune, with 4 hectares of vines surrounding Pont's collection of fighter planes within the Château's own grounds. This is much more than a museum, it is all the museums you will ever need rolled into one. My advice is to plan a visit, tomorrow. Bring your kids, their friends and yours. Allow at least an hour and a half to take everything in. Under these circumstances, you could be forgiven for overlooking the estate's wines.

The château is open every day throughout the summer from 9am to 6.30pm. ➀ **03 80 21 55 03** ⌂ **www.chateau-savigny.com**

Savigny's church of St-Cassien is also worth a peep, with its 12th century belfry and 15th century fresco paintings.

The village used to have a very good restaurant in La Cuverie. This was changing hands when I visited, but I would give it a try. ➀ **03 80 21 50 03**

TOP
Madame Maurice of
Domaine du Prieuré,
Savigny-lès-Beaune

LEFT & BELOW
Vineyard festivities:
Savigny en tous sens

OPPOSITE PAGE
Spectacular:
Château de Savigny

Domaine Remoriquet

25, rue de Charmois
21700 Nuits-Saint-Georges

Phone 03 80 61 08 17
or 03 80 61 24 84
Fax 03 80 61 36 63
Domaine.remoriquet@wanadoo.fr

The Estate

In a way typical of Nuits-Saint-Georges, you almost don't notice as you pass the small entrance to the Remoriquet estate; little to suggest that you are standing above some of the town's most interesting wines.

And there are few people from whom you will learn more about the Côte de Nuits than Gilles Remoriquet. As president of the BIVB's (Bureau Interprofessionel des Vins de Bourgogne) technical commission, Gilles represents the vanguard of Burgundy's winemaking wizardry. An advocate of natural 'reasoned' viticulture, Gilles uses fungus-based potions that work to avoid rot in the vineyard, a sort of penicillin for vines which has no adverse effects on wine quality. He was the town's first to install a new 'gentle' de-stemming machine, now also used by progressive négociant Nicholas Potel.

Gilles is the 4th generation to work the Remoriquet wine estate, with just under 11 hectares of vines, mainly in Nuits-Saint-Georges and the Hautes-Côtes de Nuits. The range starts at less than 5 euros per bottle for a white Aligoté, but even the formidable Premier Crus are surprisingly affordable.

Gilles Remoriquet is above all a man of excellent humour with a warmly infectious personality. He organises occasional group weekends for those who want to discover the Côte de Nuits from the perspective of one of its most meticulous winemakers. Contact the estate for details.

LEFT
Giles Remoriquet finishes
his 'green harvest'

Choice wines:

These notes are from a comparative tasting of the 2003s. The wines are extraordinarily rich and ripe, and this is a vintage of which the estate is justifiably proud. All will develop for at least ten years.

Nuits-Saint-Georges
Premier Cru 'Rue de Chaux' 2003

Rising north-west of Nuits-Saint-Georges, rue de Chaux has deep brown limestone soils, and so its deep-rooted vines suffered less from the 2003 drought than other vineyards.

The wine has a good deep colour and, although still a little closed on the nose, this is clearly a powerful wine, with satisfyingly earthy flavours and firm tannins.

Rue de Chaux needs a few years' bottle age to show its best, but with some development it will be an excellent accompaniment for rich game dishes.

Nuits-Saint-Georges
Premier Cru 'Les-Saint-Georges' 2003

The Premier Cru that added its illustrious name to the town in the 19th century is composed of light fossil-rich soils; its wines show power and finesse in equal measure.

On the nose, pure aromas of red fruits are echoed on an intense, concentrated palate: here the attack is strong, followed by an elegant, supple mid-palate and a very long, spicy finish.

Drink with red meats in red wine sauces, or with cheese.

Nuits-Saint-Georges
Premier Cru 'Les Damodes' 2003

The south-east-facing Damodes vineyard is actually closer to the town of Vosne-Romanée than it is to Nuits-Saint-Georges, and its elegant style is in many ways more similar to the wines from the former village. The soil is brown limestone and fine gravel, concealing complex layers of clay and limestone.

Les Damodes caught the 2003 sun face-on, and sugar levels rose faster than the tannins matured. The grapes stayed on the vines until these had softened, and the resulting wine had nearly 15% potential alcohol! The wine is massively rich, soft and plummy, with spices that evoke almost Mediterranean flavours. It retains the elegance of its terroir and, incredibly, you don't even notice its alcoholic strength…until the third glass.

The wine partners well with red meats, game and medium-strength cheeses.

Domaine Rapet
Père & Fils

21420 Pernand-Vergelesses

Phone 03 80 21 50 05
Fax 03 80 21 53 87

The Estate

The Rapets are one of the Côte d'Or's oldest winemaking families, the proud owners of a *tastevin* bearing the family name and the date 1792. Their wines embody all of the fruity charm, minerality and elegance that is Pernand-Vergelesses, the sometimes-overlooked little brother of Aloxe-Corton.

The family owns 18 hectares of vines in Pernand-Vergelesses, Aloxe-Corton, Savigny-les-Beaune and Beaune. Vinifications take place in a new *cuverie*, in traditional Burgundian open vats. The grapes are hand-harvested in small plastic trays, then subjected to a rigorous selection process. They are fed into fermentation vessels by a conveyor belt; nature and gravity do the rest. The use of pipes and hoses is kept to a minimum to avoid any rough handling of the precious liquid. Vincent Rapet believes that the winery should act only as a vehicle for the expression of *terroir*, and work in the vineyard is carried out with utmost respect for soil and vine.

In many estates you only get to taste the young wines just bottled: the ones that are for sale, but which are often not ready to drink. With Vincent Rapet it is the other way around. You might well get to taste a superb old vintage wine only to find that the estate has none left to sell! For Vincent, this is the only way to show people how Burgundy's best wines can develop – with a little patience.

On my visit I met an English couple who had made a special trip to this estate from Geneva. Once they had filled up their car, they were off home back to Switzerland. Enough said.

UK importers:
Daniel Lambert Wines Ltd.
Avery's of Bristol

LEFT
Vincent Rapet describes
the terroirs of
Pernand-Vergelesses

Choice wines:

Pernand-Vergelesses Blanc
Premier Cru Sous-Frétille 2004

The hill of Frétille rises above the town of Pernand-Vergelesses, just north of the more famous Corton. This Premier Cru vineyard shares its illustrious neighbour's brittle chalky soil, and faces directly south.

The young wine is pale lemon in colour with flashes of green. On the nose, it shows classic Pernand stony minerality, with ripe lemons and a suggestion of gunflint. Its flavours too are fresh and mineral, with hints of almond.

This is a wine with good length and a firm structure, making it a great partner for fish dishes in sauce, or even light poultry.

Pernand-Vergelesses Rouge
Premier Cru Ile des Vergelesses 2004

Perfectly located beneath the steeper Premier Cru vineyard Les Vergelesses, the wine grown on Ile des Vergelesses combines the finesse typical of the vineyard above with the fullness of body characteristic of Les Basses Vergelesses, on the lower slopes.

Its nose shows well-defined cherry aromas and satisfying savoury spices. The palate in its turn is delicate yet earthy. This wine gives pleasure early in its life but will also age well.

The same wine from 2002 is more open and rounded, with developed cherry aromas. Its finish is long, elegant and intense.

Try with light game dishes.

Grand Cru Corton-Pougets 2003

Between Le Corton and Le Charlemagne on the hill's south-western slopes, Pougets shares the former's iron-rich stony soils. The wine's deep colour reflects the richness of the 2003 vintage, as does the use of 50% new oak in the wine's ageing.

Typically for the vintage, the aromas are open and intense, reminiscent of dark plum fruits with overtones of cinnamon spice. But an early harvest and careful vinification have given this wine a freshness to match its power, and it will therefore keep well.

This is a wine to drink towards the end of a meal, with red meats or game, and to accompany the cheese plate.

Grand Cru Corton 1996

A blend from two Corton *clos*, Les Chaumes and Les Perrières, this is how Corton should be tasted: ten years old. The wine's beautiful brick red colour announces the lively complexity it shows on the nose: ripe mushrooms and damp undergrowth. Its flavours dance on the palate, with a velvety structure and harmonious finish.

A perfect partner for game birds and medium-strength cheeses; otherwise drink this wine on its own to appreciate the full breadth of its flavours.

L'Auberge du Côteau
Villars-Fontaine
21700 Nuits-Saint-Georges

Phone 03 80 61 10 50

As you stroll into the Auberge du Côteau, its warmth greets you immediately, almost as a pleasant smell. The odour itself is of the wonderful grills for which the place is so popular, cooked to perfection over one of the house's log fires. In the winter, the atmosphere is apparently cosier still, when game beasts and rustic broths are prepared for the ravenous hunters.

Perched on lower slopes of the Hautes-Côtes de Nuits, the Auberge appears to have been run for a lifetime by Chef Bernard Baudry (no relation of the Chinon vigneron of the same name). But Bernard had in fact bought the restaurant a mere three months before my visit on the 18th August, which also happened to be his birthday. Bernard admits that he struggled to understand the village's wines when he first arrived, but quickly became a passionate supporter of its seven vignerons.

You can enjoy any of the wines of Villars-Fontaine with menus that start at less than €12 at lunchtimes. You are guaranteed to leave this restaurant with a full belly and a big smile on your chops, possibly asking yourself the same question I was: "Why isn't there a place like this where I live?"

Closed Monday and Tuesday.

Good fusion cuisine is something of a rarity in Burgundy, a region already rich in its own culinary traditions, and suspicious of the unnecessarily complicated. But fusion for Laurent Peugeot means anything but a confusing sprinkle of the exotic. Le Charlemagne marries what is great about both Japanese and Burgundian cuisine: simple, delicious flavours.

It was whilst working in Beaune's finest restaurants, including Le Jardin des Remparts and L'Ecusson, that Laurent met his future Japanese wife-to-be. When she returned to Tokyo, the enamoured chef followed, plunging himself into an alien culture, without speaking a word of the language. With four subsequent years of total immersion, Laurent became fluent in both the language and gastronomy of Japan.

The couple returned to Burgundy and took over Le Charlemagne in 2001. Overlooking the historic vineyard of the same name, you can drink its finest wines alongside sushi based on Burgundian *escargots* and fresh *langoustines*, and a host of other creations. The wine list is comprehensive and includes many keenly priced bottles. Laurent believes in the potential of Japanese wines, but has not yet found an importer who shares his enthusiasm!

The menus start at the almost-never-served €22 ensemble, but you can expect to pay at least forty or fifty (not including wines) if you want to let your hair down. The restaurant received a well-deserved Michelin star in 2005.

Closed Tuesday and Wednesday. Advance booking is advised for evenings.

Restaurant le Charlemagne
**Route des Vergelesses
21420 Pernand-Vergelesses**

Phone 03 80 21 51 45
Fax 03 80 21 58 52
www.lecharlemagne.fr

Day 4 itinerary (10 miles)
From Savigny to Beaune

The Wines of Savigny-lès-Beaune

According to one of Savigny's wall inscriptions – reproduced at the entrance to its Château – the village's wines are "nourrissants, théologiques et morbifuges" (nourishing, doctrinally correct and curative).

Possibly as a consequence of the village's dynamism, the wines are often not cheap. They are most often red and typically have a smooth texture and a full body, but can range from the coarse to the extremely refined. The village's best-known Premier Crus are Les Lavières and Les Vergelesses, both on the Pernand-Vergelesses side of Savigny, the wines sharing much of Pernand's breeding. The wines made from the vineyards closer to Beaune are generally earthier. Savigny is also an important centre for sparkling wine production.

The best grower to visit is Domaine Chandon de Briailles (see page 234), for its superb wines and a great welcome in a stunning situation.

The best time to visit Savigny is the first Sunday of

September, when the wonderfully named *Savigny en tous sens* takes place. 'Savigny in every way, sense and direction' is an organised vineyard walk in which you gradually discover the village's wines, accompanied by rustic snacks (including the only French pork scratchings I have ever tasted!). The whole thing culminates in a meal with music and festivities. This festival has only existed since 2003, the brainchild of Madame Maurice, wife of Jean-Michel Maurice, of Domaine du Prieuré, who was also the village mayor at the time of writing. Contact the estate for details; the wines are also some of the village's best value. ✉ **23, route de Beaune** ① **03 80 21 54 27**

On the first weekend of May, all of Savigny's vignerons open their doors, and you can simply stroll in and taste their wines. This is a good chance to try the wines of the great, but otherwise inaccessible, Domaine Simon Bize. ✉ **23, rue Chanoine Donin** ① **03 80 21 50 57**

Coming round the mountain

From the centre of Savigny-lès-Beaune, follow the road past Château de Savigny, over the crossroads and out of the village. Fork left at the sign for Pernand-Vergelesses and Aloxe-Corton, then follow the next sign for Aloxe. Continue over the crossroads, then turn right towards the village.

Aloxe-Corton

As you enter Aloxe-Corton and turn left towards its centre, you pass through an area given over to large *négociant* houses such as La Reine Pédauque. Aloxe is also home to the original estate of *négociant* Louis Latour, which centres on the 18th century Château Grancey at the foot of the hill of Corton. The house produces some very good white – and less interesting red – wines. ① **03 80 24 81 10** 🖑 **www.louislatour.com**

Aloxe-Corton's finest estate, Domaine Comte Senard, is in the village centre (see page 236).

As you approached Aloxe, the tiled roof of Château de Corton André will have caught your eye, so why not pop in for a tasting. The Château was built in the 15th century, but reconstructed in the 17th following the Wars of Religion. The cellars are older, forming the crypt of the church that once stood on the site. Merchant house La Reine Pédauque now owns the Château. The white wines especially are very well made. ① **03 80 26 44 25** 🖑 **www.pierre-andre.com**

Day 4 at a glance
Itinerary   228 – 233
Wineries   234 – 237
Restaurants   238 – 239

BELOW
Château de Corton André

BOTTOM
The village of Aloxe-Corton

The famous hill

Photographs of Corton tend to portray it as a neatly rounded large mound, topped with tightly cropped afro-hair-styled trees. This is the impression it gives when you approach from Beaune, but Corton is actually almost a ridge, with its Grand Cru vineyards facing west, south and especially east. Corton is notable in being celebrated for producing both white and red Grand Cru wines, although its whites tend to fetch higher prices.

Close to the town of Pernand-Vergelesses, on the hill's western flank, is the Corton-Charlemagne Grand Cru vineyard. Red vines are grown here, but it is more famous for its whites, which thrive in the limestone-rich soils. The vineyard was apparently so named because Charlemagne's wife preferred her husband to drink the white wines from the hill, as those least likely to stain his beard (almost certainly nonsense, since beards were highly unfashionable at the time).

Firmly structured reds are grown all around the hill. The best come from the east-facing clay-rich Grand Cru vineyards, particularly Les Bressandes, Le Clos du Roi, Renardes and the vineyard Le Corton itself. These wines can rival some of the finest, most powerful Grand Crus from the Côte de Nuits.

The road to Beaune: Ladoix-Serrigny and Chorey-lès-Beaune

From Aloxe-Corton, you have a choice. To head for Beaune directly via Chorey-lès-Beaune, leave the village the same way you arrived (down rue Plonchot), but instead of turning right towards Savigny, carry on across the N74, then follow the road where it bends right into the village of Chorey-lès-Beaune. Alternatively, to visit the village of Ladoix-Serrigny, carry on past Château de Corton André and cross the N74 slightly to the north.

Savigny-lès-Beaune and Aloxe-Corton are tough acts to follow, so you may find these two villages underwhelming. Chorey produces light, fruity reds. If you're interested in trying the wines, make an appointment at Domaine Tollot-Beaut, on rue Alexandre Tollot. ② 03 80 22 16 54

The wines of Ladoix are more distinguished, and can be excellent value red and white country cousins of the area's more famous names. The village's *Balade Gourmande,* which takes place on the first Sunday in July, predates *Savigny en tous sens* (see Day 3 itinerary) by a number of years, but is otherwise a very similar – if considerably larger – affair. Ask at the Mairie for details.

Two fine Ladoix estates are Domaine Edmund Cornu & Fils ② 03 80 26 40 79 and Domaine Nudant.② 03 80 26 40 48 The latter of these is on the main road, the N74.

Chorey-lès-Beaune is a short hop from Ladoix, and from Chorey you can pick up the D20F and then turn left onto the D20, which leads into the centre of Beaune.

BELOW
Nearing the harvest: ripening Pinot Noir grapes

Beaune

As the centre of Burgundy's wine trade, Beaune attracts almost twenty times its own population of 23,000 in visitors each year. It is a great place to plan a brief visit

as a tourist or wine lover, but I know young people who have spent long, cold winters in Beaune, and ended up climbing the ancient city walls in frustration. Money buys large houses and the vitality of towns like Beaune retreats into their living rooms.

Beaune was the capital of the Duchy of Burgundy until the 15th century, and its wealth grew during the Renaissance with its flourishing wool trade. In the 19th century, its central position on the fledgling rail network made the town a strategic point for blending wines from all over France before their journey north to market.

Where to start

After an initial wander in and out of Beaune's narrow medieval streets, the obvious place to begin a discovery of the town is at the Hotel-Dieu opposite the tourist office, on place des Halles. The medieval town square is also where Beaune's market is held every Saturday morning.

The Hotel-Dieu is the building which houses the famous Hospices de Beaune, founded in 1443 by Nicholas Rollin and his wife Guignone de Salins, to provide care for the town's poor and sick. As recently as 1973, the Hospices' medical function was transferred to a modern unit. So visitors can now walk in the *Salle des Pôvres*, the beautifully decorated pauper's ward leading into the Hospices' Gothic chapel, which allowed the weak patients to make their prayers without having to move too far. Don't miss the multi-coloured demonic dragons in the ward, whose gaping jaws spit out the ceiling's crossbeams; or the comical faces of Beaune's medieval bourgeoisie, each one associated with a different animal to symbolise their respective vices.

ABOVE
The famous hill
of Corton

BELOW
Beaune

The highlight of the Hospices' museum is Rogier van der Weyden's polyptych painting, commissioned by Chancellor Rollin in the 15th century. Placed above the altar in the chapel, patients were only allowed to admire the object's divine beauty on Sundays and on feast days. But for most, the central attraction of the Hotel-Dieu is its multi-coloured tiled roof, the most flamboyantly striking example of this most Burgundian phenomenon.

The Hospices today owns 63 hectares of important vineyards in the region, bequeathed to it over the centuries by philanthropic local landowners. Every year, on the first Sunday of November, Beaune comes alive for the world's most famous charity wine auction, *la Vente des Vins des Hospices de Beaune*.

Visits are possible throughout the year.
ⓘ 03 80 24 45 00 ⌂ www.hospices-de-beaune.tm.fr

BELOW
The famous roof:
Beaune's Hôtel-Dieu

Beaune, wine capital of Burgundy

Most people are surprised to learn that Beaune's own vineyards represent the most extensive of any Côte d'Or appellation, at over 650 hectares. The majority of these vineyards are classed as Premier Cru, and a good proportion belongs to Beaune's large *négociant* houses. The wines are red and white; the best are soft and intensely fruity in their youth, but capable of ageing for ten years or more in bottle.

The best Beaune *négociant* to visit is Patriarch Père et fils. The house owns Burgundy's largest and most impressive underground cellars, and the tour is friendly and interesting. Once you have explored part of the cellars on your own, you are met by a sommelier, and you are then free to taste various wines at your leisure. You almost don't notice as the cellar becomes a shop, but there's a note of urgency in the intern's voice as she reminds you that this is your last chance to buy the wines you have tasted "under cellar conditions". But remember that there are plenty of better wines elsewhere. ✉ **5-7, rue du Collège** ✆ **03 80 24 53 79**

Patriarch also owns L'Athenaeum in place des Halles: a 'cultural centre' where you can buy wine, books, decanters, glasses and other paraphernalia, arrange a wine tasting or just plonk your children in the kiddie section for a few quiet minutes.

A better large *négociant* from whom to buy wine is Bouchard Aîné et Fils. Founded in 1731, the house is now owned by the large Boisset group. The "five senses" cellar tour is crass and confusing, but this is the *négociant* house best represented on Burgundy's restaurant wine lists. ✆ **03 80 24 06 66** ⌂ **www.bouchard-aine.fr**

I was surprised to learn that Beaune's leading biodynamic *négociant,* Jean-Claude Rateau, also allows visits by appointment. ✉ **26, route de Bouze** ✆ **03 80 22 98 91**

A thirst for knowledge

If you would like to learn more about the wines of Burgundy, Beaune is the place to do it. Contact L'Ecole des Vins de Bourgogne for their list of tasting courses. ✆ **03 80 26 35 10**
⌂ **www.ecoledesvins-bourgogne.com**

The other option is to pay a visit to Beaune's famous winemaking college, the *Lycée Viticole*. Make an appointment to tour the cellars and taste the students' wines, which are very good, albeit with a degree of youthful exuberance in their oak ageing. ✉ **16, avenue Charles Jaffelin** ✆ **03 80 26 35 81**

Do not be tempted by Vin Sensation, at the bottom of rue d'Enfer (Hell's Road). Damien Delattre runs the show here, an extremely bad-tempered Burgundian who all but punched me for arriving without having done my homework on his shop. I explained that I wouldn't have come if I already knew everything, and he chased me out!

Just browsing

Beaune is full of wine shops, and these are generally only worth visiting if you have no time to drop in on the winemakers themselves. La Cave des Vieilles Vignes, on avenue de la République, is one of the most reasonable, and also has shops in Meursault and Santenay in the Côte de Beaune; the wines are mainly from producers in these two villages. Prices may well be the same as they are at the wineries, and are unlikely to be more than 10% higher. ☏ **03 80 24 19 44**

Other attractions

Beaune's own wine museum was in serious need of modernisation when I visited. The 16th century ducal palace in which it is housed is more interesting than the exhibition itself. ✉ **23, rue d'Enfer** ☏ **03 80 22 08 19**

It would be a shame to leave Burgundy without learning anything about mustard. So in the absence of a museum in Dijon, why not book a guided tour at La Moutarderie Fallot, which claims to be "the last great independent mustard mill in Burgundy". The tour is interactive-ish and a bit expensive at 10 euros, but you do get to make your own mustard, and you are given a free pot of theirs as you leave. ☝ **www.fallot.com**

Contact the tourist office for details of the visit. ☏ **03 80 26 21 30**

TOP & OPPOSITE PAGE TOP
The Beaune jazz and wine festival

RIGHT & OPPOSITE PAGE MIDDLE
Beaune market

Domaine Chandon de Briailles

1, rue Soeur Goby
21420 Savigny-lès-Beaune

Phone 03 80 21 52 31
Fax 03 80 21 59 15
Contact@chandondebriailles.com
www.chandondebriailles.com

The Estate

"Owned by the same family since 1834, Domaine Chandon de Briailles belongs to the Count and Countess Aymard-Claude de Nicolay and their children. Count de Nicolay inherited the estate from his grandmother, Countess Chandon de Briailles, herself related to the well known Champagne estate Moët et Chandon."

So reads the estate's small promotional leaflet, and it all sounds very grand. The winery is, moreover, adjoined to the magnificent 17th and 18th century Manoir de Nicolay and its beautiful garden, visited by the Queen Mother Elizabeth of England in 1976. But it is the smiling warmth of the estate's owners, rather than any pomp or splendour, which is immediately striking.

The "children" referred to are cellarmaster François and his sister Claude, who are involved at all levels of the winemaking process. A charmingly unassuming pair, their impeccable command of English is the only obvious suggestion of a distinguished family heritage.

The estate is unusual in owning very few vines on basic village appellation soil. The majority of the vineyards are Premier Cru Savigny-lès-Beaune and Pernand-Vergelesses, but the estate also has important holdings in Grand Cru Corton. The wines are certified organic, and have been made following biodynamic principles since 2005. The vinifications are very traditional, taking place in open vats; colour and soft, ripe tannins are extracted from whole bunches of handpicked red grapes by the old-fashioned method of grape treading. The estate uses only a tiny proportion of new oak, preferring instead to age the wines in older wood for longer, in the perfect conditions of the estate's 13th century monastic cellars.

Visits are by appointment, any day but Sunday.

UK Importers:
Lay & Wheeler
Tanners
Charles Taylor Wines

Choice wines:
Savigny-lès-Beaune Premier Cru
'Les Lavières' 2005 (barrel tasting)
On the border with the Pernand-Vergelesses appellation, this Premier Cru vineyard is made of hard, stony subsoils, forcing the vine roots to dig deep channels between the rocks.

The wine's nose shows intense raspberry aromas. On the palate, fresh red fruit and mineral flavours are balanced by a firm, ripe tannic structure. The finish is particularly impressive, defying anyone to suggest that the wines of Savigny lack length.

An extremely versatile food partner, this will match with anything from salmon to delicate red meat dishes.

Pernand-Vergelesses
Premier Cru 'Ile des Vergelesses' Blanc 2004
From a small parcel that has only been planted with white Chardonnay vines since 1988, this wine is possibly my favourite from the estate.

Fresh, mineral aromas of melon and white peach anticipate a palate full of rich, ripe and faintly exotic flavours. The wine's excellent acidity appears on a long, well-balanced finish, a hallmark of the estate's white wines.

A fantastic partner for lobster and other shellfish.

Grand Cru Corton Blanc 2004
This wine is a blend from three Corton Grand Cru vineyards: Les Bressandes, Les Chaumes and Les Renards, giving the wine extraordinary balance and complexity.

Very different from the previous wine, this Corton was aged on its lees for 8 months, and shows creamy aromas reminiscent of a patisserie shop. The palate is rich and creamy, but shows the citrus notes of a wine that is still obviously young. A lovely hit of cinnamon mid-palate lets you know you're definitely drinking Grand Cru Corton; the finish reveals a perfect balance of fatness and acidity.

With five years ageing, this wine will develop a richness to match with even *foie gras* and feathered game dishes.

TOP
Winemaking siblings:
Claude and François

RIGHT
Manoir de Nicolay

Domaine Comte Senard

Clos des Meix
21420 Aloxe-Corton

Phone 03 80 26 41 65
Fax 03 80 26 45 99
www.domainesenard.com
Table@domainesenard.com

OPPOSITE PAGE
Philippe in the estate's
Grand Cru *monopole*
vineyard Corton Clos
des Meix

THIS PAGE
BELOW
A hearty meal with
Philippe Senard and
daughter Lorraine

The Estate

It is not always that a Côte d'Or village's most prestigious estate also offers its warmest welcome. Throw an excellent meal into the bargain and you have an essential visit for Corton freaks and gastronomes alike.

Domaine Comte Senard's winemaking now takes place in Beaune, but you can visit the family estate in Aloxe-Corton and drink a range of wines to Grand Cru level alongside regional dishes, themselves conceived to best complement the wines. The 'formulas' cost between €30 and €50, far less than any equivalent restaurant experience.

The domaine is run by Daniel and Philippe Senard; Daniel is the great grandson of Jules Senard, creator of the family's *monopole* Grand Cru vineyard Corton Clos des Meix. Philippe is possibly Burgundy's friendliest, most erudite winemaker, full of stories of his sailing adventures with fellow vigneron François Faiveley, of Nuits-Saint-Georges, and their crew of like-minded eccentrics. He works closely with his daughter Lorraine, who is the seventh generation of winemaking Senards, and now completely in charge of the estate's white winemaking.

The estate's 9 hectares of vineyards are scattered around the famous hill of Corton, and were supplemented in 1989 by the purchase of Domaine des Terregelesses. The wines from both estates are elegant, bold and thoroughly individual; Philippe Senard has introduced the practice of cold pre-fermentation macerations for the estate's red wines, believing that the absence of alcohol during skin maceration helps preserve purity of fruit flavours in the wine, whilst extracting good colour. Nothing pleases Philippe more than re-tasting a wine from a difficult past vintage only to find that, with time in bottle, it has developed into something marvellous.

Open from April until the end of November: 10am till 6pm, Monday to Saturday.

Phone in advance to eat at the domaine. Everyone here speaks good English.

UK importer:
Fine & Rare Wines, London

Choice wines:

Aloxe-Corton Blanc 2001
100% Pinot Beurot

This is the only wine from the village of Aloxe-Corton to be made from the Pinot Beurot (Pinot Gris) grape, and with a production of less than 1000 bottles a year, you'll be lucky to get a taste.

Its nose is expressive, almost exotic, with strong hints of butterscotch. The wine has a characteristic fatness on the palate, and is low in acidity. Ageing in 50% new oak barrels gives a long, broad finish.

Great when drunk on its own or with seafood in creamy sauce.

Grand Cru Corton-Bressandes Rouge 2000

With a colour that is just turning garnet at the edge of the glass, and open aromas of red fruit and intense minerals, Philippe Senard announces "The beginning of the wine's adulthood!"

Traditionally a rounded, supple wine, this nonetheless has a rich, unctuous structure and ripe cherry flavours, reminiscent of a wine from the Côte de Nuits to the north.

2000 was not hailed as a great vintage, but this is a fine wine that will keep for a good five years. Drink with roast meats or poultry in rich sauce.

Grand Cru Corton Clos des Meix Rouge 1999

Bordering Grand Cru Le Charlemagne, the south-west-exposed Clos des Meix is fully owned by the Senards, and is situated just behind the estate.

The wine's colour is deep ruby, and its red fruit aromas are mixed with an earthy smokiness. On the palate it is predictably powerful, with firm tannins and a long finish.

This is a match for game or richly flavoured cheeses.

Grand Cru Corton en Charlemagne Rouge 1998

The estate rented part of 'En Charlemagne' from Aloxe-based *négociant* house Louis Latour with the intention of planting white Chardonnay vines. But the first harvest of Pinot Noir grapes, in 1998, impressed Philippe so much that he decided instead to devote the parcel to the production of red Corton.

The soil's high limestone content gives the wine its mineral, smoky aromas. On the palate, there is an explosion of red fruit flavours, followed by a slightly bitter finish.

With a smile, Philippe says that this 1998 reminds him of the best 1988s, which started out awkwardly, but went on to show rare brilliance.

Le Jardin des Remparts
10, rue de l'Hôtel-Dieu
21200 Beaune

Phone 03 80 24 79 41
Fax 03 80 24 92 79
www.le-jardin-des-remparts.com

BELOW
Chef Roland Chanliaud

Beaune's best restaurant

There are so many good restaurants in Beaune that it is tough to pick one as a first among equals, but here it is nonetheless: Le Jardin des Remparts.

Roland Chanliaud created Le Jardin in 1990, in a splendid townhouse just inside Beaune's ancient city walls; yet pomp and tradition were the furthest things from the young chef's mind. The son of a local delicatessen, Roland believes in studying the basics of flavour, the building blocks of his trade.

For Roland, cooking has no rules, and this openness of spirit has led to inventions such as his notorious *Tartare de charolais aux huîtres Gillardeau, écume de mer*. Oysters with beef tartare might sound unlikely, but it works brilliantly: the flavour of the oysters dominates, whilst the beef provides a firm texture, adding its own rich complexity of flavour.

The wine list is impressive, if a little pricey. Bottles start at around €30, and at the top end you can enjoy your meal with a bottle of Grand Cru Le Richebourg from Domaine de la Romanée-Conti, for €1390. That's not a price, it's a date! Fortunately there is always an interesting selection of wines by the glass for between €6 and €15.

The menus are €55 and €65, supplemented by a simpler lunchtime offering for €30. Anything you eat here is guaranteed to be wonderful. The 'coffee menu' is the best I've ever seen.

Closed Sunday and Monday, and for a couple of weeks in February and March.

The chefs' choices

There are two restaurants in Beaune that are big favourites of the region's chefs. The first is Le Sushi Kai, a Japanese restaurant run by chef Laurent Peugeot, of Le Charlemagne in Pernand-Vergelesses (see page 227). Many actually prefer Le Sushi Kai to its Michelin-starred big brother.

The second is L'Ecusson. It had been disrobed of its Michelin star at the time of writing, but Chef Jean-Pierre Senelet is widely acknowledged as a star of his trade.

Good value gastronomy

Another of the town's great chefs, Jean-Marie Daloz, learned his craft at L'Ecusson, and now owns Le P'tit Paradis near place de la Halle. Menus are available from about €20, and the chef only cooks with fresh, seasonal ingredients.

Don't bother reserving a table. The restaurant is smaller than a posh bathroom and the management's attempts to cram in more than 20 diners are ridiculous. Turn up, walk in, and if you can move, sit down.

And then there's Ma Cuisine. Reservations here are imperative: if the restaurant isn't closed, it is likely to be fully booked. The style of cooking is more Burgundian than at Le P'tit Paradis, and the wine list is more impressive. Menus start at €20. Bono from U2 apparently eats here, so it is bound to be ethical too.

If you feel like a quick midday bite in the centre of town, try Le Bistrot Bourguignon in rue Monge, just off place de la Halle. Self-styled "flying sommelier" Jean-Jacques Hegner offers some great wines by the glass, with or without food; he is also the man behind Beaune's September jazz festival.

If you order a meal here, show the book for a free kir apéritif.

Le Sushi Kai
50, rue du Fb Saint Nicolas

Phone 03 80 24 02 87

L'Ecusson
Square Malmédy
(off place Madelaine)

Phone 03 80 24 03 82
www.ecusson.fr

Le P'tit Paradis
25, rue du Paradis

Phone 03 80 24 91 00

Ma Cuisine
Passage Saint-Hélène

Phone 03 80 22 30 22

Le Bistrot Bourguignon
Phone 03 80 22 23 24
www.restaurant-
lebistrotbourguignon.com

www.jazzabeaunefestival.com

LEFT
Le P'tit Paradis

BELOW
"Flying sommelier" Jean-Jacques Hegner

ABOVE
Leaving Meursault

Day 5 itinerary (6-14 miles)

Beaune to Meursault

Leaving Beaune

Leave the centre of Beaune along Avenue de la
République, and turn left onto the city's small ring road.
Cyclists take the first right at the sign for Auxerre and
the *véloroute* (cycle path). Motorists take the next right,
signposted Chalon-sur-Saone; this road is the
continuation of the D974 south of Beaune.

The cycle route, and how motorists can join the party

After the turning to Auxerre, cyclists turn left at the first
small crossroads into the vineyards of Beaune. After
taking the next right, the cycle route to Pommard is well
signposted, beginning by skirting the foot of the
extensive Beaune Premier Cru vineyards.

Once on the D974, motorists turn right off the
roundabout opposite the Cave des Vignerons des
Hautes Côtes, onto the D973. As the Côte d'Or's only
co-operative cellar, the Cave des Vignerons is worth

popping into for a tasting. There are sure to be plenty of bottles open. ① **03 80 25 01 00**

The second turning to the right takes you through Pommard Premier Cru Les Petits Epenots, the lower part of one of the village's finest vineyard sites. Turn left at the next crossroads to join the vineyard road to Pommard.

Day 5 at a glance

Itinerary	240 – 243
Extra Itinerary	244 – 245
Wineries	246 – 247
Restaurants	248 – 249

Pommard & Volnay

Both Pommard and Volnay are highly reputed for their red wines; the village of Volnay is the smaller and more charming of the pair. Volnay's 'feminine' wines have long been more fashionable than the more muscular wines of Pommard, showing softer and more elegant red fruits even in their youth. The village also boasts a better restaurant.

Pommard's wines can be equally fine, but the village's iron-rich soils give them a firmer structure and more earthy flavours than those of its neighbour. These are wines that need time in bottle to soften and develop.

Pommard

The best place to plan an appointment in Pommard is at Domaine A-F Gros – François Parent. This estate was created in the late eighties, and combined the inheritance of Anne-Françoise, of the extensive Gros family in Vosne-Romanée, with that of François Parent in Pommard.

The couple's estate now includes some of the best land in both Côtes, including Grand Crus Le Richebourg and Les Echezeaux in the Côte de Nuits and the two best Premier Crus in Pommard: Les Epenots and Les Rugiens. They also have vineyards in less expensive appellations.

The estate is on your left as you enter the village, on Grande Rue. ① **03 80 22 61 85 www.af-gros.com www.parent-pommard.com** Give at least a week's notice to visit; but avoid the harvest period, from mid-September to mid-October.

The good, the bad and the expensive

Pommard is one of Burgundy's most famous wine villages, so you wouldn't expect its wines to be cheap. It is worth visiting Château de Pommard to admire its 21-hectare vineyard, the largest in the Côte de Beaune, and its beautifully restored 19th century buildings. But the Château is the first in a series of grandiose estates on the Côte de Beaune whose wines are, quite simply, far too expensive.

Ask any of Pommard's winemakers what they think of "the Château", and you will be greeted with shrugs of super-Gallic proportions…because the wines never were very good. That is until 2003, when Maurice

Giraud, one of France's richest businessmen, bought the dilapidated Château and restored it to its former splendour. Giraud employed Gevrey-Chambertin's famous Philippe Charlopin as chief winemaker, so 2004 will be the first vintage at the Château made entirely by the great man.

After visiting the Château, I was led to one of a series of small tasting rooms, and as I entered, I noticed an employee furtively making off with a bottle of what I noticed was the 1993. My curiosity was raised, so I asked for the bottle to be returned and presented in its elusive glory. So it was uncorked and samples were poured. At this point, the distinguished figure of Giraud himself entered the room. He had heard there was "a journalist" about, and had come to shake hands. He explained to the small group that we were lucky to be tasting an old vintage of which so few bottles remained. He bade us enjoy, then left.

My own feelings were reflected in the faces of the other confused tasters: everyone was underwhelmed. How much, I asked, for an average wine in such a sexy bottle? €100.

This kind of price exaggeration is not good news for those trying to persuade the world that Burgundy is value for money. When Charlopin's legendary expertise does prevail in the Château's wines, one can only imagine the new price tags the wines will carry! ① **03 80 22 12 59**
⌂ **www.chateaudepommard.com**

And on into Volnay

If all that tasting has given you an appetite, I would hold on for a mile until you reach Volnay. Don't eat at the overpriced Restaurant "Le Pommard"; the simple bistrot attached to Hôtel du Pont opposite is pretty good.

Continue through Place de l'Eglise in Pommard, the headquarters of Domaine Courcel, one of the village's finest and longest-established wineries (visits by appointment). ① **03 80 22 10 64** Join rue de la Métairie, which leads back into the vineyards to Volnay. This is suitable for cars, but be prepared to use the passing places.

It is fortunate that 'Rossignol' is such a pretty name, because that's what most of Volnay's vignerons are called, in some form or other. On entering Volnay, turn right past the ivy-covered Restaurant Le Volnaysien (see page 250). This restaurant is cheaper than it looks, and a fine place to stop for a bite. Carry on past the church and through the village, on rue du Mont, to visit my favourite of the village's Rossignols, Domaine Rossignol-Février (see page 246). Otherwise, try Rossignol-Jeanniard on the same street. ① **03 80 21 64 23**

Through Volnay's Premier Cru vineyards to Meursault

Most of Volnay's Premier Cru vineyards descend the slope beneath the village, and you have a wonderful view of these from beside the village's Mairie.

From the church, follow rue de la Combe, and then bear left towards the D973. Cross the main road and continue towards Meursault, passing under celebrated Volnay Premiers Crus Les Caillerets and Clos des Chênes, before these vineyards give way to those of Meursault.

Meursault

This is the first of the three great whites of the Côte de Beaune, and of that Meursault-Puligny-Chassagne trio, this first is perhaps the most famous internationally. Deliciously rich flavours of "butter", "toast" and "hazelnuts" are often associated with Meursault, and the wines generally show their charm earlier in life than do those of neighbouring Puligny-Montrachet. The appeal to an American market is easily understood, and Meursault is said to have been a favourite at the table of Thomas Jefferson in the late 18th century.

But Meursault's 20th century cult status has arrived more recently than Puligny's, and living memory still recalls winemakers carting their wares down to the N74 in an attempt to trap the passing trade. Perhaps for this reason, the village feels livelier and more open. It is, of course, also bigger than Puligny and Chassagne combined, with more vineyards and vignerons, and therefore more wine to sell.

Meursault's bustling town square incorporates its Hôtel de Ville, a reconstructed medieval château complete with Burgundian tiled roof; the church of St-Nicholas, the château's ancient chapel, and a massage parlour. This is Nathalie Mounier's Spa Bourgogne, where therapeutic anti-oxidising potions, based on vineyard products, are used to promote calm and relaxation. A 40-minute Grand Cru Massage, for example, will set you back €40. Pampering sessions here are by appointment only. ① 03 80 21 19 91

TOP
Meursault centre

If you manage to re-invigorate yourself, there is plenty to taste in Meursault, and many of the village's vignerons also have holdings in the less expensive nearby villages of St-Romain, St-Aubin and Auxey-Duresses (see extra trip).

A good place to start is the very reasonable Cave des Vieilles Vignes, in place de l'Hôtel de Ville, one of a small Côte de Beaune chain of shops (see Beaune, page 233). ① 03 80 21 29 07 But you are in Meursault, so why not make an appointment at the brilliant Domaine Coche-Bizouard, on rue de Mazeray (see page 248). Further along this road is Patrick Javillier's new boutique and tasting cellar. The estate's winemaking has moved to a modern facility on the outskirts of town, but here you can taste and buy in a pleasant environment. ① 03 80 21 65 50

Another local character who is making a name for himself in Meursault is Hubert Chavy-Chouet, brother of Philippe Chavy in Puligny-Montrachet. Find him in rue de Mazeray. ① 03 80 21 61 74

Take a stroll in the grounds of the largely 19th century Château de Meursault, but avoid the expensive cellar tour and tasting, the purpose of which is a hard sell. The wines are made by the Château's owner, Beaune *négociant* Patriarch Père & Fils (see page 232). ① 03 80 26 22 75 www.chateau-meursault.com

If you happen to be in Meursault at ten o'clock on a Thursday or a Saturday morning, the small tourist office offers guided tours of the village. ① 03 80 21 25 90 ⌂ www.ot-meursault.fr

ABOVE & BELOW
The Hautes-Côtes
de Beaune

OPPOSITE PAGE
Château de la
Rochepot

Day 5 extra trip

A whistle-stop tour of the 'value villages' via Château de la Rochepot

From Meursault, this 8-mile round trip takes you through the villages of Auxey-Duresses, St-Romain and St-Aubin. These are all part of the Côte de Beaune appellation, although this extra trip leads into the Hautes-Côtes de Beaune. The villages are less well known than many on the Côte, and the wines are often real bargains.

Cyclists leave what you don't need in Meursault: this is a challenging ride.

Meursault to Saint-Romain

Leave the centre of Meursault along rue de Lattre de Taffigny, and turn left onto the D17E. Then turn left again onto the D973 into Auxey-Duresses.

Many Meursault growers own land in Auxey-Duresses, and the wines can be great value Meursault alternatives. The best grower to visit in Auxey is Domaine Michel Prunier & Fille. ① **03 80 21 21 05**

Continue through Auxey-Duresses and turn right onto the D117E into the tiny hamlet of Auxey-le-Petit. The road leads up towards St-Romain, and gives fantastic views of the wooded cliff face of the Hautes-Côtes de Beaune.

Saint-Romain is the last of the pretty Côte de Beaune villages before the vineyards of the Hautes-Côtes begin. It is an important centre for barrel production, as the cooler climate here is perfect for the slow weathering of staves needed for making the finest *barriques*. Red grapes grown at this altitude generally make lighter wines than those from the lower-lying vineyards. The village produces some excellent whites, and a good place to buy these is at the fine biodynamic estate Domaine Thierry Guyot. ① **03 80 21 27 52**

Through the Hautes-Côtes-de-Beaune to Château de la Rochepot

Follow the road to the left through St-Romain at place du Pont, and then up the teeth-grittingly steep hill into the Hautes-Côtes. When the vines reappear, it is in the Hautes-Côtes de Beaune. The views of the landscape here are some of the region's most spectacular, almost reminiscent of the mountains of the Jura to the east. Turn right and continue up the hill towards the village of Orches. Turn left inside the village and follow the road through Baubigny a mile or so later. You are greeted over the brow of the next hill by the glistening tiled

rooftop of Château de la Rochepot.

The original Château was a 12th century construction, and most of what stands today was built by Alexandre de Bourgogne a hundred years later. Following the Revolution, the Montmorency family bought and restored the Château to its impressive former glory. Guided tours are daily – except on Tuesday – between April and October. Visits are in French and English.
① **03 80 21 71 37**  **www.larochepot.com**

Back through Saint-Aubin and Gamay

Continue through the village of la Rochepot and turn right at the junction with the D973. Le Relais du Château is immediately on your left: a decent hotel with a good, traditional restaurant. ① **03 80 21 71 32** **www.relais-du-chateau.com**

Take the next left turn onto the D33, which begins a long, satisfying descent into the village of Saint-Aubin. Time seems almost to have stood still in the small, stone-built Saint-Aubin, a traditional winemaking village wearing little make-up. Try dropping in on Isabel and Bernard Prudhon for a tasting near the village's Romanesque church. ✉ **15, rue du Jeu de Quilles** ① **03 80 21 35 66**

From the village centre, take rue des Perrières, on which you will find the excellent Domaine Gérard Thomas. ① **03 80 21 32 57** Follow the road (still the D33) until it forks left onto the old Roman road towards the village of Gamay.

One-time resident of the village château, the Seigneur du May, is supposed to have brought back the Gamay grape from the crusades, and it is thus that the village acquired its name. Today, Gamay is better known as the red grape of the Beaujolais; the village of Gamay is part of the St-Aubin appellation, and its extensive Premier Cru vineyards are too valuable to be planted with Gamay vines. The star of the village is Jean-Claude Bachelet who, in addition to his Saint-Aubins, also makes excellent white Premier Cru Chassagne-Montrachet and a rare red Puligny-Montrachet! ① **03 80 21 31 01**

Take rue du Château through the village of Gamay, and over the small crossroads at the sign for Blagny. This steep final climb takes you far above the famous vineyard Le Montrachet, and you barely notice the tiny hamlet of Blagny as you pass through it before descending the hill. Blagny, in fact, straddles the appellations of Meursault and Puligny-Montrachet, and its stony soil produces some very fine Premier Cru wines.

In front of you at the foot of the hill is the village of Puligny-Montrachet. A left turn leads back along the vineyard road/cycle route to Meursault.

Domaine Rossignol-Février Père & Fils

**Rue du Mont
21190 Volnay**

**Phone 03 80 21 62 69
or 03 80 21 64 23
Fax 03 80 21 67 74
Rossignol-fevrier@wanadoo.fr**

The Estate

Frederick Rossignol-Février is one of Burgundy's quietest revolutionaries, a militant force for quality in the region's wines.

After bottling his 2004 vintage, Frederick noticed to his horror that all wines above the level of generic 'Bourgogne Rouge' had been tainted by a faulty batch of corks. So he immediately withdrew the entire vintage from the market. But the wine was far from undrinkable. In fact, the taint was so slight that it would have been imperceptible to the average taster!

The estate bottles the entire production from its 8 hectares of vines in Volnay, Pommard, Meursault and Beaune, and sells a full 60% to private customers. Frederick is therefore used to welcoming visitors at his estate, but you will need to be brave to scale the steep ladder into the small fermentation room, and either small or flexible to squeeze through the low opening into the cellar-tasting room.

With a simple honesty, Frederick explains that he follows biodynamic principles of vinification 'as far as he understands them'. The bottling of the estate's red wines, for example, only takes place when the moon is in its 'fruit phase' of the biodynamic calendar, whilst whites are handled when it is 'in flower'.

Domaine Rossignol-Février is particularly notable for the quality of its entry level Bourgogne Rouge Pinot Noir. Frederick frequently offers this wine in blind tastings to those who are suspicious of burgundies below village level, and they are always impressed – even before they learn that it costs less than 6 euros a bottle.

Phone in advance to visit the cellars throughout the year except, of course, during the harvest. I did not ask whether Frederick speaks English, but it would surprise me…

LEFT
Frederick
Rossignol-Février

Choice wines:

Bourgogne Pinot Noir 2004

On the nose, this wine is pure, exuberant Burgundian Pinot Noir, with young redcurrant aromas. In the mouth, it is rounded and fruity, but with enough structure to benefit from some ageing.

Drink with summer barbecues or grilled fish.

Volnay 2002

This wine generally shows its best after three to five years in bottle. 2002 produced a wine for longer ageing.

On the nose, the wine is still tight and would benefit from decanting, but it is already showing the delicate red fruit aromas so characteristic of Volnay. On the palate, it has an uncommonly firm structure, with tannins and acidity that still need to soften. A long, complex aftertaste hints at the wine's great potential.

Drink with roast meats or *Magret de Canard*.

Volnay Premier Cru 2003

This wine is blended from the two Premiers Crus vineyards Carelle-sous-la-Chapelle and Les Angles, the former on the slopes beneath the more famous Premier Cru Bousse d'Or.

In 2003, the grapes were picked early and transferred to their fermentation vessels as soon as possible, to preserve the freshness of the fruit. The result is a wine with aromas of strawberries and raspberries, and a hint of 'Rhônish' herbs. Acidity and alcohol levels are in good balance on the palate; the flavours are intense but not jammy.

A very fine partner for Burgundy's signature dish, *Boeuf Bourguignon*.

ABOVE
Rossignol-Février,
father & son

Pommard 2003

This is a big, deeply coloured wine, typical of the village's style. The aromas are of spiced plums and dark cherries, but again despite the hot vintage, the wine does not seem 'cooked'.

The wine's beefy tannic structure is inevitable, and it needs to age for this to soften. The flavours show a pleasing dark intensity, with cinnamon hints on a long finish.

Two or three years will see this wine marry well with pheasant and hard cheeses.

Domaine Coche-Bizouard

5, rue de Mazeray
21190 Meursault

Phone 03 80 21 28 41
Mobile 06 09 84 23 45
Fax 03 80 21 22 38
Coche-bizouard@wanadoo.fr
www.coche-bizouard.com

The Estate

A grower of considerable local renown, Alain Coche has for years exported much of his estate's production, but still insists on pricing his wines fairly. His success has allowed him to ignore the fashions for early-drinking and heavily oaked wines, so what you get here is that unique combination of power and finesse that is great Burgundy.

Alain prefers the terroir to give the wines their character, and so he never ages them in more than 20% of new oak barrels. But don't be deceived, these are big, concentrated wines that require ageing to show their true colours; wines for wine lovers, and worth waiting for. Alain offers generous tastings, and evidently loves to share his customers' pleasure. I tasted the range of about twenty wines the morning after *Savigny en tous sens*: a real treat, but very hard work!

The estate includes about ten hectares of vines in Meursault, Puligny-Montrachet and Pommard, as well as in 'good value' appellations, most notably Auxey-Duresses. Alain's son Fabien has largely taken over the vinifications, and also runs a small négociant business, Coche-Bouillot (note that it might not be obvious which estate's wine you have in your glass).

Tasting at the estate is possible for most of the year, although it is best to phone in advance. Fabien speaks some English, Alain very little, but you're bound to receive a warm welcome.

UK importers:
Richards Walford
The Wine Society

LEFT
Hard work, but a real treat:
tasting with Alain Coche

Choice wines:

Whites

Meursault 'Les Luchets' 2004

Situated near the top of the slopes above Meursault, Les Luchets is a parcel of poor, stony soil, giving wines with mineral and gunflint aromas. On the palate, the wine is rounded with good concentration, already showing signs of the rich butteriness that is characteristic of Meursault.

This is a wine that will develop for ten years or longer, but will be ready to drink within the next year or two. An excellent partner for fish, but also (according to Alain) *foie gras*!

Puligny-Montrachet Premier Cru 'Les Folatières' 2004 (Domaine Coche-Bouillot)

This is my favourite of the range: pure Premier Cru Puligny on the nose, with aromas of stones, honeysuckle and almonds. Sheer elegance, with power in reserve! The palate has a lovely minerality and a finish that goes on forever.

The wine will probably reach its peak within five to ten years. Subtly flavoured fish would make a good partner, but I think it is wonderful simply drunk on its own.

Reds

Monthelie Premier Cru 'Les Duresses' 2004

The village of Monthelie shares the rocky slopes of this Premier Cru vineyard with Auxey-Duresses to the south-west. Yet this wine reminds me more of Volnay, with its mix of red fruit and violet aromas. On the palate, it is earthier, with firm but already well integrated tannins. Five years should see the wine showing its best.

Red meats and mild cheeses make good partners; game dishes might drown the wine's more subtle flavours.

Pommard Premier Cru 'La Platière' 2004

Just above the better known hillside Premier Cru Les Arvelets, La Platière is situated closer to the vineyards of Beaune than Volnay. The wine's style is elegant and mineral, with an intense nose of red fruits. The flavours are of pungent roses, with a well-balanced spicy, tannic finish to remind you that you're still in Pommard.

Enjoy this gentle giant, after four or five years' ageing, with hearty game dishes.

RIGHT
Alain Coche with
grandchildren

Restaurant Le Cellier Volnaysien

Place de l'Église
21190 Volnay

Phone 03 80 21 61 04
Fax 03 80 21 21 95

Nathalie Gente-Pont runs this traditional, atmospheric restaurant in her family's 200-year-old wine cellars in the centre of Volnay. Here I found local winemakers eating in an old wood-beamed fermentation room, young couples flirting on the outdoor terrace, and a Canadian film crew noisily dining in the vaulted cellar where the wines once matured.

Nathalie's father Michel owns the spectacular Château de Savigny, in Savigny-lès-Beaune (see page 220). Unlike at the Château, there are no jet aircraft or racing cars here, but the Château's own bottlings duly fill the restaurant's wine list. This is also a good place to try wines from Volnay, Pommard and their smaller sibling Monthelie, at very fair prices.

The menus are between €13 and €27, and include good value, simple regional dishes such as *coq au vin, oeufs en meurette* and, of course, snails.

Open for lunch only during the week, and on Saturday evening. Closed Wednesday.

Present this book for a free *kir* apéritif.

Having run more fashionable gastronomic establishments in Beaune, Chef Philippe Devilard bought and transformed La Goutte d'Or (The Drop of Gold), a one-time truckers' inn on the outskirts of Meursault, into the town's finest eatery. But the beauty of La Goutte today is that it has kept its old-fashioned, unpretentious simplicity.

Philippe serves freshly prepared traditional Burgundian dishes, in which flavours are bold and garlic is an important ingredient. Philippe grows his own vegetables, and buys meat directly from the local abattoirs, butchering it himself. The simple wine list is overwhelmingly local, with a reassuring number of wines from Meursault Domaine Coche Bizouard, and therefore very reasonably priced.

Set menus are available at around €20. In summer 2006, there was an ensemble based entirely around snails and frogs' legs – "especially for the Brits"! An adjoined bistrot feeds the hungry local vineyard workers with an even cheaper, more rustic menu.

Closed Thursday evening and Sunday.

Present this book for a free apéritif.

Auberge la Goutte d'Or
37 rue Charles Giraud
21190 Meursault

Phone 03 80 21 60 56
Fax 03 80 21 68 05
www.lagouttdor.fr.st

Day 6 itinerary (10 miles)

The world's greatest white wines & the southern tip of the Côte d'Or

Meursault to Puligny-Montrachet

Leave place de l'Hôtel de Ville in Meursault on rue des Ecoles, crossing the bridge over the village's tiny stream, the *Ruisseau des Cloux* (Burgundian patois for *clos*). Join rue du Clos de Mazeray and follow the road past the walled vineyard of the same name.

About a mile beyond Meursault, the cycle path takes a sharp right and then a turn left. At this point, larger vehicles are advised to continue and take the next right. Before the road enters the vineyards of Puligny-Montrachet, it passes between Les Genevrières, Les Charmes and Les Perrières, the three finest of Meursault's Premier Cru vineyards, unsurprisingly within a stone's throw of Puligny-Montrachet.

Follow the cycle path left after a small copse, down into the village of Puligny-Montrachet.

Uncovering Puligny-Montrachet

At first, Puligny feels very closed. The number of vignerons here is smaller than in Meursault, the general standard of winemaking is very high and so, therefore, are prices. But this is what you would expect in what must be the world's most prestigious white-winemaking village. The wines are less exuberant in their youth than those from Meursault, but have a nervy, sometimes exotic, freshness and complexity that are rarely matched by its neighbours. Puligny is a typical Burgundian paradox in being at once bourgeois, over-civilised and extremely parochial. But on a second glance, there is plenty to do in a village with its fair share of young, dynamic vignerons.

The best-of-the-best here are Domaines Carillon, Etienne Sauzet and Leflaive. Needless to say, none of these does visits or direct sales. Don't confuse the last of these with Olivier Leflaive Frères, Puligny's most important *négociant* house (although Olivier's almost identical labels seem designed to do just that). By now, you may be tired of making appointments, so why not grab a meal with a tutored tasting at Olivier Leflaive's *table d'hôte* in the village centre (see page 258).

A name to look out for in Puligny is Chavy. On entering the village, you pass Domaine Gérard Chavy, and you may well find his wines in Puligny's excellent restaurant Le Montrachet (see page 262). But the domaine is now split between his two sons, Jean-Louis Chavy ① **03 80 21 38 85** and Alain Chavy. ① **03 80 21 39 27** Both estates make excellent wines, and receive visitors by appointment. Their cousin Philippe, brother of Meursault's Hubert Chavy, also makes extremely good wines. ① **03 80 21 92 41**

I can't resist also mentioning Domaine Bzikot. Sylvain Bzikot took over from his father in the late 1990s, and only then started bottling the estate's wines rather than selling them to the Beaune *négociants*. The results have been very fine, and have raised appreciative eyebrows in local blind tastings. ① **03 80 21 33 39**

Young aficionado Julien Wallerand runs the boutique Caveau de Puligny-Montrachet, and from him you will learn much about Puligny's wines and winemakers, and where to find them. ⊠ **1, rue de Poiseul** ① **03 80 21 96 78.**

The vineyards of Puligny-Montrachet

The cycle route leads back out of Puligny in a direct line towards the world's most expensive soil. The first crossroads is where Olivier Leflaive's brother Patrick likes to bring his customers, as the best place to view the village's

Day 6 at a glance
Itinerary	252 – 257
Wineries	258 – 261
Restaurants	262 – 263

BELOW & BOTTOM
The harvest in
Puligny-Montrachet

Grand Cru vineyards. From here to your left are the Grand Crus Bienvenue-Batard-Montrachet and Batard-Montrachet. Beyond the next crossroads on your left is the most famous of them all, Le Montrachet, with the more steeply sloping stony Chevalier-Montrachet above.

Domaine Leflaive was harvesting its extensive portion of the Chevalier-Montrachet when I cycled by in late September. My own vivid memories of harvesting grapes are of vineyard horseplay, of splattering whole bunches of grapes in the faces and down the backs of other *vendangeurs*. These games are fun, but I've seen them also end in tears and even punch-ups. "Not in Grand Cru vineyards," Leflaive's foreman told me. Grape throwing here is at best an "instantly dismissable offence".

From Puligny to Chassagne-Montrachet

Turn left at the crossroads to skirt the foot of Le Montrachet as you head towards Chassagne. Just over half of the Le Montrachet lies within the Puligny-Montrachet appellation, but Chassagne is where most of those who own it live. As you cross the N6 into the village of Chassagne-Montrachet, the number of arrows bearing wine estates' names is testimony to its concentration of winemakers. The winery doors somehow seem to re-open in Chassagne, and it is far easier simply to drop in on winemakers here than it is in Puligny.

A generation ago, Chassagne was known for its red rather than its white wines. These can still represent excellent value, although Pinot Noir vines are constantly being replaced by the more fashionable Chardonnay, simply because white Chassagne sells for double the price of its reds. This is a shame, since many terroirs are clearly better suited to making the earthy characterful Pinot Noir wines that are Chassagne-Montrachet Rouge. The whites tend to be more floral than those in Puligny, but in the hands of the best winemakers, they can achieve excellent concentration and depth of flavour.

The famous name in Chassagne-Montrachet is Domaine Ramonet. You can visit by appointment, but the more famous wines will already have been hoovered up through trade channels. ✉ **15, rue de Puits** ☎ **03 80 21 30 88**

The two biggest winemaking families in Chassagne are the Gagnards and the Moreys, and the latter of these is by far the more approachable. My advice is to contact Jean-Marc Morey in the village centre (see page 260). He may forget your appointment, but if he's around, Jean-Marc is a real character and his wines are the best value in Chassagne. If Jean-Marc has gone home (he now lives in Meursault), try his brother Bernard Morey on the outskirts of Chassagne in the direction of Santenay. ✉ **3, rue de Morgeot** ☏ **03 80 21 32 13**

Another one not to miss is Domaine Guy Amiot & Fils. ✉ **13, rue du Grand Puits** ☏ **03 80 21 38 62**

Familiar rules of thumb apply vis-à-vis Château de Chassagne-Montrachet: look, but don't touch. The wines are expensive; the (admittedly beautiful) *chambre d'hôte* rooms are extraordinarily pricey. ☏ **03 80 21 98 57** ⌂ www.michelpicard.com

From Chassagne to Santenay, the southern tip of the Côte d'Or

Leave Chassagne-Montrachet along the D113a towards Santenay, following signs for the cycle route. After passing Domaine Bernard Morey on your left, the Chassagne-Montrachet Premier Cru vineyards La Boudriotte and then Morgeot are below the road to your left. These clay-rich vineyards are the village's best suited to growing red grapes, making firm, age-worthy wines.

As you cross the appellation boundary into the vineyards of Santenay, the road skirts the foot of one of its finest Premier Cru vineyards, Les Gravières, above which is the village's picturesque windmill.

Santenay

Santenay is in two parts. The first, larger area of the village is Bas-Santenay. This is home to most of the shops, best winemakers and the village's best restaurant, Le Terroir (see page 263). When I arrived in 2006, the village centre was a building site, but the extensive work should be finished by the time of publication.

When the slump in Burgundy's wine sales came following the Millennium, it first hit the Maconnais in the south of the region. It spread north through the Côte Chalonnaise like a vineyard disease, and landed squarely on the doorstep of Santenay as it arrived in the Côte d'Or. The result is a new dynamism amongst its winemakers, and less complacency than can be found in the more famous villages. Plenty of doors are open in Santenay, with signs in the streets inviting you into cellars for *dégustations*.

As in most of the region, the best estates prefer visits by appointment. I would make one with Françoise & Denis Clair. Denis is an exuberant Burgundian vigneron of the old school, and very keen to speak English. The estate makes great Premier Cru Santenay whites and reds, whilst the Saint-Aubin Premier Cru whites can rival good Chassagne-Montrachet village wines.

✉ **14, rue de La Chapelle** ☏ **03 80 20 61 96**

TOP
Harvesting red grapes in Chassagne-Montrachet

BELOW
The windmill above the vineyards of Santenay

Two other vignerons to consider are Domaine Jessiaume Père et Fils ✉ **10, rue de la Gare** ☎ **03 80 20 60 03** and Lucien Muzard. ☎ **03 80 20 61 85** 🕸 **www.domainemuzard.com**

Château de Santenay once belonged to Philippe-le-Hardi, the first of Burgundy's Valois dukes. The (more recently added) multi-coloured roof tiles are a temptation to tourists, but the Château is not open for visits. You can, however, taste the products of the Château's large wine estate, with vineyards mainly to the south in the Côte Chalonnaise. Unannounced tastings are possible. I was not greeted well here, but the management assured me that "the problem would be rectified!" ☎ **03 80 20 61 87** 🕸 **www.chateau-de-santenay.com**

It is worth popping into the small, helpful tourist office by the train station for information on the area. ☎ **03 80 20 63 15** They also rent bikes more cheaply than in Dijon if you feel like following the itinerary in reverse.

Santenay by numbers

Follow the D113 through Santenay and either turn right towards the higher part of the town, Haut-Santenay, or continue and turn left towards the Casino de Santenay on avenue des Sources. This vineyard casino features all of the usual gambling games, has its own restaurant, and organises various themed *soirées*. ☎ **03 80 26 22 44**

Haut-Santenay is a pretty, well-restored little village. It is dominated by Château de la Crée, which had just changed hands when I visited, and may allow visits in the future. So watch this space.

Beyond Haut-Santenay is the tiny hamlet of St-Jean. You can visit its small Gothic church on weekend afternoons, but the walk up the hill otherwise offers wonderful views of Haut-Santenay and the last of the Côte d'Or's vineyards to the south.

Staying in and around Santenay

For a village – or town – the size of Santenay, there is a surprising lack of accommodation, and this therefore fills up quickly.

The hotel is called L'Ouillette, and has only four rooms, which cost less than €50. ✉ **Place du Jet d'eau** ☎ **03 80 20 62 34** Otherwise try Madame Moniot's B&B at 44, Grande rue. ☎ **03 80 20 60 52**

The alternative is to take the D113 past the tourist office two and a half miles to Chagny. Chagny is actually in the Côte Chalonnaise viticultural area, in the Saone-et-Loire *département*, rather than the Côte d'Or. It is an industrial town that has worked hard to benefit from its fortuitous location between the two Côtes. You will therefore find plenty of decent hotels and restaurants in Chagny, as well as the region's finest of both, Lameloise. There was local outcry when the restaurant lost its third Michelin star; but at this level, who is really counting? Menus start at €90, and rooms are nearly €200. ✉ **36, Place d'Armes** ☎ **03 85 87 65 65**

ABOVE & TOP
Château de Santenay

OPPOSITE PAGE
TOP LEFT
Exuberant Burgundian:
Denis Clair

OPPOSITE PAGE
TOP RIGHT
The first signs of Autumn

OPPOSITE PAGE
BOTTOM
Haut-Santenay

Olivier Leflaive Frères

Place du Monument
21190 Puligny-Montrachet

Phone 03 80 21 37 65
Fax 03 80 21 33 94
www.olivier-leflaive.com
contact@olivier-leflaive.com

The Estate

Olivier Leflaive created his own *négociant* business in 1984, handing the reins of the older family estate, Domaine Leflaive, to his cousin Anne-Claude, a leading light for Burgundy's biodynamic movement. The fruits of Olivier's own 15 hectares of vines are supplemented by the grapes he buys from other quality-conscious growers on the Côte d'Or. Olivier and his brother Patrick dislike the term '*négociant*', with its connotations of size and compromise, as most of the grapes the estate buys are grown along organic lines.

The Leflaive brothers pioneered the concept of 'eating chez the vigneron' on the Côte d'Or, with La Table d'Olivier. The meals are fairly simple, but the wines are very good, and Pascal Wagner's dynamic tutored tasting while you eat is alone worth the visit. For €40, you can try seven wines with your meal; and €50 buys you fifteen, including Premiers Crus from Puligny-Montrachet, Chassagne, and Meursault.

Book in advance to take the interesting guided tour of the state-of-the-art Leflaive winery; but being only 50 cm above sea level, this is no place for cavernous cellars! More recently, Olivier Leflaive has added vineyard workshops and a hotel to the estate's portfolio of attractions. Book well in advance, especially for weekends, as the opening of the hotel will have added to La Table d'Olivier's already keen following.

Open from March to November.

UK importers:
Corney & Barrow
Lay & Wheeler

TOP
La Table d'Olivier

LEFT
Stainless steel fermentation
vessels of different sizes,
each one corresponding to
a different parcel of vines

Choice wines:

Chassagne-Montrachet Premier Cru Blanchots 2001

The wine's reserved nose confirms that it still needs time to open. But a swig reveals great power and finesse, filling the mouth with an extraordinary complexity of flavour.

The Blanchots vineyard is directly opposite the Grand Cru Criots-Batard-Montrachet, and the wines share their neighbour's ability to develop for years in bottle.

Drink with fish in creamy sauce, poultry in wine-based sauces, or with medium-flavoured cheeses.

Meursault Premier Cru Poruzots 2002

The limestone soils of this Premier Cru vineyard give a wine with a classically rich Meursault nose of hazelnuts-and-butter. On the palate, it has excellent weight and acidity, with concentrated fruit and an extremely long, nutty finish.

This wine could happily age for five to ten years, but is already giving much pleasure. Drink with poultry in rich sauce, or with Burgundy's full-flavoured soft cheeses.

Puligny-Montrachet Premier Cru Champ Gain 2002

This is perhaps the house's best-known Premier Cru vineyard, situated on the slopes high above the village. 'Champ Gain' means a field reclaimed, in this case from the forests above the vineyards of Puligny-Montrachet.

The wine shows classic Puligny finesse, although it is still slightly awkward on the nose. On the palate, its character shines through, with kiwi fruit flavours and a rich, well-structured mouth feel.

This is a fine wine from a great vintage, and will continue to develop for many years.

Pommard Premier Cru Epenots 2001

Olivier Leflaive's reds represent only a tiny proportion of the house's production, but are made with extreme care, using techniques such as cold maceration and cool fermentation, for the maximum extraction of colour and aroma.

Epenots is one of Pommard's finest Premier Cru sites, incorporating Les Petits Epenots and the (confusingly, smaller) vineyard Les Grands Epenots. Both are sited on south-south-east-facing slopes, on stony red clay and limestone soils.

The wine reveals concentrated aromas of plums and spiced cherries, with a rich, tannic structure on the palate. It will develop and soften over the coming years, but is already drinking extremely well.

A great partner for fine red meats, cooked rare or in rich stews.

ABOVE
Patrick Leflaive in front of Le Montrachet: the Côte de Beaune's most famous vineyard

BELOW
Pascal Wagner's tutored tasting

Domaine Jean-Marc Morey

3 rue Principal
21190 Chassagne-Montrachet

Phone 03 80 21 32 62
Fax 03 80 21 90 60

The Estate

In the heart of the peaceful village of Chassagne-Montrachet, Jean-Marc Morey's estate is a hive of activity. Hemmed in on all sides by his neighbours' wineries, the courtyard is likely to be filled with an assortment of barrels, *tracteurs-enjambeurs* and other vineyard machinery. The estate was preparing for the harvest when I visited; the appointment of a British cyclist had been forgotten in the rush to make way for the new vintage.

In the midst of the chaos, Jean-Marc emerges from his cellars in good humour. He has keenly observed the changing fashions in wine, but insists on making his Burgundies in the traditional way. The flavours of the wines are overwhelmingly natural; they have that rare ability to show well in their youth yet develop gracefully for years in bottle. Restaurant wines *par excellence*.

The estate has existed for many generations, and today includes nine hectares of vines in Chassagne-Montrachet, Santenay, Saint-Aubin, Beaune and Pommard. All grapes are hand-harvested and no yeast is added to get the fermentations going. White wines represent roughly half of the production, and are fermented then matured for a year in *barriques*, of which a maximum of 20% are new. The estate's excellent red wines mature in up to 25% new oak for a longer period of 18 months.

I was fascinated to learn that Jean-Marc does not publish the 'cellar door' prices of his wines. It upsets some of his foreign importers when their customers learn they can buy fine Chassagne-Montrachet Rouge directly from the estate for as little as eight and a half euros. That's about a fiver!

It is strangely puzzling that Jean-Marc Morey had no UK importer at the time of writing…

LEFT
Method in the madness:
Jean-Marc Morey's front yard

Choice wines:

Chassagne-Montrachet Blanc
Premier Cru 'Les Chaumées' 2004

Situated on the higher, steeper slopes above Chassagne, Les Chaumées gives wines with floral aromas of wild grass and white peach. The flavours are rounded and slightly exotic, balancing the wine's good acidity and full mouth-feel.

This wine will keep for ten years, but is already a good accompaniment for white meats, fish in rich sauces, or veal.

Chassagne-Montrachet Blanc
Premier Cru 'Caillerets' 2004

The Caillerets vineyard is situated on the lower slopes nearer the village, bearing wines of considerable substance, which need five to fifteen years ageing to show their best.

Already, the wine is displaying characteristic aromas of grilled almonds and nuts, with tight aromatic notes reminiscent of Condrieu in the Rhône Valley. On the palate, firm acidity and concentrated flavours hint at the wine's great potential to develop, as a partner for shellfish and creamy poultry dishes.

Chassagne-Montrachet Rouge
Premier Cru 'Champs-Gains' 2004

This wine shows all the earthy aromas of wild raspberries and minerals that typify red Chassagne-Montrachet. The palate reveals the power and intensity of a fine Premier Cru.

This wine will develop nicely for more than ten years, but its velvety tannins and soft red fruit flavours will give pleasure much sooner.

Drink with poultry or red meats in red wine sauces.

Beaune Rouge Premier Cru 'Les Grèves' 2004

In contrast with the earthiness of Chassagne-Montrachet, this Beaune 1er Cru hits you with intensely ripe aromas of strawberry, cherry and violets. On the palate, the attack is explosive; the flavours developing into something supple, dark and velvety.

The openness of this wine makes it enjoyable early in life with grilled oily fish or rich game casseroles. It might, however, age well for two decades.

ABOVE
The good-natured
Jean-Marc

Hôtel-Restaurant Le Montrachet
**Place des Marronniers
21190 Puligny-Montrachet**

**Phone 03 80 21 30 06
Fax 03 80 21 39 06
www.le-montrachet.com**

BELOW
Chef Thierry Berger
(tallest) with kitchen staff

Le Montrachet was highly regarded until 2003. But there's nothing like the loss of a Michelin star and the employment of a new chef to inject new life into a restaurant.

Since taking over, young Chef Thierry Berger has introduced a delicious new lunchtime menu, *Le Climat du Mois*, which costs only €30. Other menus are served for €55 and €75.

Every dish here is made from the finest, freshest ingredients. The chef's meticulously prepared Burgundian escargots, for example, are some of the best I have ever tasted.

But the real reason for eating at Le Montrachet in summer is to sit on its tranquil terrace and watch the sleepy village of Puligny go by. At harvest time, you can laugh with the grape pickers as they loll or play acrobatics on the village green opposite the restaurant. This was one of the highlights of my trip.

The wine list is also surprisingly good value, boasting almost a thousand different wines.

The restaurant is never closed, except during November and December.

Restaurant Le Chassagne
**4, impasse des Chevenottes
21190 Chassagne-Montrachet**

**Phone 03 80 21 94 94
Fax 03 80 21 97 77
www.restaulechassagne.com**

Le Chassagne serves food worthy of a Michelin star, in one of the Côte d'Or's most famous wine villages, at amazingly fair prices.

The seven-strong restaurant team clearly enjoys an excellent relationship with both regulars and tourists, constantly developing new skills under the paternal guidance of Chef Stéphane Léger.

Stéphane's cooking is "traditional Burgundian revisited", with a strong leaning towards his obvious delight, seafood. Burgundy's fashionable marriage of *escargots* with *langoustines* finds particularly great expression in Stéphane's kitchen.

The menus change twice each season. Full four-course meals cost between €30 and €50.

Don't be frightened by the wine list's initial concentration on the Chassagne-Montrachet Premier Crus. These are keenly priced, but inevitably not cheap. Have a look for the wines made by Chassagne's vignerons in the less expensive Côte d'Or appellations. Or choose from the six excellent wines available by the glass.

Closed Sunday evening, Monday, and Wednesday evening.

Present this book to receive a free glass of Michel Colin's excellent Crémant de Bourgogne.

BELOW
Chef Stéphane Léger (head of table), with the Restaurant Le Chassagne "family"

Everything about Le Terroir suggests rusticity, from its name and traditional country décor, to the incredibly reasonable prices of its menus.

Fabrice Germain's cooking is, however, extremely refined. Even the *Menu du Marché* (€20) is lovingly prepared with fresh ingredients, and with meticulous attention to cooking times. Fabrice believes that these should be as short as possible so that none of the ingredients' flavours are lost.

Corinne Germain is as dynamic a host as her husband is talented with a saucepan. A Sommelier de Bourgogne, she also writes wine-related articles for the magazine Bourgogne Aujourd'hui.

The restaurant's wine list is correspondingly fabulous. It features many star winemakers of Santenay, and includes their cheaper wines from the recently created 'Maranges' appellation south of the town.

Closed Thursday and Sunday evenings; also Wednesday evenings between November and March.

Present this book for a free *Kir* apéritif.

Restaurant Le Terroir
**19, place du jet d'eau
21590 Santenay**

**Phone 03 80 20 63 47
Fax 03 80 20 66 45
www.restaurantleterroir.com**

RIGHT
Fabrice and
Corinne Germaine

Accommodation

Gevrey-Chambertin

Gevrey has two very fine and reasonably priced 3* hotels. Both have a warm, unpretentious atmosphere; the first is better located near the village centre.

Hôtel les Grands Crus***
Rue de Lavaux
21220 Gevrey-Chambertin
Phone 03 80 34 34 15
Fax 03 80 51 89 07
www.hoteldesgrandscrus.com
Room prices are €70 and €80.

Hôtel Arts et Terroirs
28, route de Dijon (N74)
21220 Gevrey-Chambertin
Phone 03 80 34 30 76
Fax 03 80 34 11 79
www.arts-et-terroirs.com
Rooms are between €60 and €100.
Bike hire is available.
Present the book for a free glass of wine.

There are three B & Bs in Gevrey, and all require advance booking. The one to try is attached to Jean-Philippe Marchand's wine estate, in the centre of the village.
4 rue Souvert
21220 Gevrey-Chambertin
Phone 03 80 34 38 13
Fax 03 80 34 39 65
www.marchand-jph.com
Prices start at €40 for ensuite rooms, including breakfast.

Nuits-Saint-Georges

If you manage to book far enough in advance to get a room, then try
La Gentilhommière*** just outside Nuits-Saint-Georges on the road to Villars-Fontaine (see day 3 itinerary).
Rooms are available from €85. This former hunting lodge boasts an outdoor pool, a good restaurant, and a wonderfully tranquil setting at the foot of the Hautes-Côtes de Nuits.
13, Vallée de la Serrée
Phone 03 80 61 12 06
www.lagentilhommiere.fr

Another good place is the **Hostellerie Saint Vincent***** near the centre of town, attached to Restaurant l'Alambic. Prices start at around €70.
Rue du Général de Gaulle
Phone 03 80 61 14 91
www.hostellerie-st-vincent.com

For something simpler in the heart of the town, try **Hôtel-Bar l'Etoile**. The bar downstairs is propped up by ageing locals nursing *demi-pressions*, but the rooms are clean and should cost around €50.
5, place de la Libération
Phone 03 80 61 04 68

Savigny-lès-Beaune

The first place I would try in Savigny is **Marie-Christine Leclercq's** *chambre d'hôte*. Situated between the Château and Domaine Chandon de Briailles (see page 234), Marie-Christine is a schoolteacher recently turned winemaker. She owns tiny parcels of vines from Nuits-Saint-Georges to Volnay.

16, rue du Général Leclerc
Phone 03 80 26 14 71
www.domaine-leclercq.fr

Otherwise, there are two decent two-star hotels in the village, both of which have rooms for under €60.
Lud' Hôtel
31, Rue de Citeaux
Phone 03 80 21 53 24
www.lud-hotel.com

Hôtel-Restaurant L'Ouvrée
Route de Bouilland
Phone 03 80 21 51 52

Beaune

You can pay a lot to stay in Beaune, but as in most places this size, there are choices and therefore bargains. I would avoid the four-star places. Whatever your means, anything that costs over €100 per night should give more pleasure than these hotels do.

Make for place Madeleine, where you will find three good value places. The best of these is the 3-star **Hôtel de la Paix**, where prices start at about €75.
45, rue du Faubourg Madeleine.
Phone 03 80 24 78 08
www.hotelpaix.com

Otherwise try the 3-starred **Hôtel de la Cloche**, which is around €10 cheaper.
40-42 rue Faubourg Madeleine.
Phone 03 80 24 66 33
www.hotel-cloche-beaune.com

Or there is **L'Auberge Bourguignonne** (not to be confused with Le Bistrot Bourguignon in the town centre), where rooms are available for less than €60.
4, place Madeleine
Phone 03 80 22 23 53

Meursault

If you can get a room at **Domaine du Moulin aux Moines** between Meursault and Auxey-Duresses, then this is the place to stay. A monastic wine estate in the 10th century, the wine is now pretty awful (a fact which cannot have gone unnoticed by Monsieur Hanique), but with a chambre d'hôte this good, who cares? A room costs €80. Breakfast, strangely, is an extra €7.
Phone 03 80 21 60 79
www.laterrasse.fr

Another great bet is Pascal Molinot's *chambre d'hôte* **Les Ecureuils** near the crossroads in Meursault that leads towards the D974. Rooms start at about €50, and you get breakfast and the use of a small kitchenette.
20, rue Pierre Joigneaux
Phone 03 80 21 27 82
www.lesecureuils-meursault.com

Meursault's best value hotel is Hôtel du Centre, in the heart of the village. Prices start at €60.
4, rue de Lattre de Tassigny
Phone 03 80 21 20 75

Puligny-Montrachet

If you decide to stay in Puligny-Montrachet, and find Hôtel-Restaurant Le Montrachet (see page 262) a bit steep, try instead Madame Ravaut's nearby *chambre d'hôte* and wine estate. Rooms start at €60.
14, rue de Poiseul
Phone 03 80 22 65 49

Alsace

PARIS

FRANCE

Alsace: October & November 2006

A magical land

In the famous words of Harry Lime in the film The Third Man: "In Switzerland they had brotherly love; they had 500 years of democracy and peace, and what did that produce? The cuckoo clock."

Just over the border from Switzerland, in Alsace, centuries of Franco-Germanic fighting, stark religious and political divides, and an insatiable love of good food and wine, gave birth to something rather more inspiring.

And Alsace is more than just a producer of great wines. It is a fairytale land of medieval-Gothic towns and villages, of mountains and castles, chic restaurants and cosy country inns. The Alsatians are totally unique. "Reserved at first, but warm and genuine when you get to know them" is said of many peoples, but nowhere is this truer than in Alsace. There is a real spirituality about the Alsatian character, and this is a tangible force in the region's winemaking. Whilst an earthy Burgundian vigneron might talk about power, balance and structure in his wines, the Alsatian will tell fantastic stories about how they make him feel.

Alsace is the French region best adapted to wine tourism, which overlaps seamlessly with its many other attractions. The tourist trade in Alsace is an important factor in its wine sales, and even the most prestigious estates are happy to receive visitors.

Alsace is a young wine appellation that many foreign markets still find confusing. The trade bodies supposed to promote Alsace are seemingly oblivious to the irony in the promotional slogan "Alsace, France's best-kept secret". But the result is that Alsace wines are still largely to be discovered.

The wine route begins north of my proposed itinerary in Marlenheim, in the *Bas-Rhin*, or Lower Rhine, *département*. It continues south to the vertiginous vineyards above Thann in the south of the *Haut-Rhin*, or Upper Rhine. I have concentrated on the heart of Alsace, that stretch where the highest concentration of great winemakers and terroirs are to be found.

What's that funny language?

Most young Alsatians speak French, with a charming singsong local accent. "It's chic to speak French," is what schools have taught since the War ("and if you don't, you may be punished!"). But the older generation still widely speaks Alsatian, a dialect of German.

In the 1940s, many Alsatians would have struggled to form a sentence in French, but understood perfectly the orders barked by their Nazi occupiers. Nothing could surprise a population that changed nationalities five times between 1871 and 1945!

Getting there

My advice is to begin a tour of Alsace in the Bas-Rhin, before making the journey south to the more famous villages around Colmar. The place to start

is the town of Obernai, close to Strasbourg. If flying to Bâle-Mulhouse airport to the south, take the train directly north to the region's capital.

Rail links are very good, and Strasbourg will have a high-speed TGV link from Paris by the time of publication. If arriving by ferry, simply pick up the A26 from Calais to Reims (see Champagne chapter), then the A4 to Strasbourg.

Strasbourg

The region's capital is only loosely linked with its wine production, although it is a great centre of gastronomy. Emile Jung's double-Michelin-starred Restaurant Au Crocodile is one of the most famous in France, and the one all Alsatian chefs want on their CVs. ✉ **10, rue de l'Outre** ✆ **03 88 32 13 02** ✆ www.au-crocodile.com But Strasbourg has a good selection of less expensive restaurants and *winstubs*. Try La Maison des Tanneurs "the home of choucroute" on the rue du Bain-aux-Plantes, in the pretty Petite France district. ✆ **03 88 32 79 70** ✆ www.maison-des-tanneurs.com And for an uncompromisingly rustic introduction to Alsace, book a place at S'Muensterstuewel on Place du Marché aux Cochons de Lait. ✆ **03 88 32 17 63** This restaurant is named after and within a stone's throw of Strasbourg's must-visit attraction, the Cathedral.

Strasbourg's vinous wonder is the *Hospices Universitaires de Strasbourg*. Founded in 1395, the Hospices was until the War an important vineyard owner and merchant house. After 1945, the Hospices continued to provide aid for the sick, but was gradually forced to sell off its vineyards; its viticultural activities ceasing completely in the early nineteen nineties.

In the last years of the same decade, a handful of vignerons and wine lovers revived the Hospices' neglected treasures, and the public can now visit its extensive vaulted cellars, and marvel at ancient wine presses and vintages in cask dating from 1472. ✉ **1, place de l'Hôpital (Near quai St-Nicholas)** ✆ **03 88 11 64 50**

Strasbourg has no winemakers, but Le Vinophile, just around the corner from the Modern and Contemporary Arts Museum (see below), is one of Alsace's best wine shops. Its owner, Michel Le Gris, only sells the finest of the region's organic wines. ✉ **10, rue d'Obernai** ✆ **03 88 22 74 06**

Strasbourg is an important brewing city, and you can visit the old Kronenbourg brewery in route d'Oberhausbergen, although production has now moved to nearby Obernai (see below). ✆ **03 88 27 41 59** ✆ www.kronenbourg.fr Otherwise, microbrewery La Lanterne makes its own beer in the old city centre. ✉ **5, rue de la Lanterne** ✆ **03 88 32 10 10**

Staying in Strasbourg

Strasbourg's most beautiful and luxurious hotel, Château de l'Ile****, is on the way out of the city towards Obernai, in Ostwald (see below). Rooms cost at least €180. ✉ **4, quai Heydt, Ostwald** ✆ **03 88 66 85 00** ✆ www.chateau-ile.com

For mere mortals, Maison Rouge*** is a comfortable place, perfectly situated off Place Kléber in the city centre. Expect to pay upwards of €80. ✉ **4, rue des Francs-Bourgeois** ✆ **03 88 32 08 60** ✆ www.maison-rouge.com

Close to the *Hospices Universities de Strasbourg* is the charming and well-priced (€45-100) Hôtel Au Cerf d'Or**. ✉ **6, place de l'Hôpital** ✆ **03 88 36 20 05**

ABOVE
Strasbourg by night

TOP
Strasbourg
Cathedral

Weather, climate and when to visit

Alsace's climate is one of the most unusual and extreme in France. At between 47.5 and 49° North, these latitudes should be the outer limits of quality wine production, but Alsace benefits instead from a unique microclimate, creating perfect conditions for the vine.

The Vosges mountains exert the biggest influence on Alsace's weather. Rising to an altitude of 1424 metres, they dramatically reduce the Atlantic's moderating influence, giving a harsh continental climate. Summers in Alsace are hot, with cool nights, allowing ripeness to be achieved whilst preserving fresh flavours and acidity in the grapes.

Long, mild autumns ensure slow ripening, adding complexity to the grapes' flavours. Cold nighttime mists spill down from the Vosges, and are burned off by the sun's rays the following morning, allowing the development of *botrytis*, or 'noble rot', that concentrates flavour, acidity and sugar in the late harvest wines. But when winter comes it hits hard, and temperatures are frequently the lowest in France.

A significant feature of Alsace's climate is its extremely low rainfall. The Vosges create a barrier for the eastbound rain clouds, which drench their summits with 2000 mm of precipitation per year, leaving Colmar with only 550 mm. This makes the city France's driest after Perpignan.

But 2006 surprised everyone. Alsace had suffered the heat of July followed by cold in August. September had been warm but humid, and when the torrential late September and early October rains came, less noble forms of rot took hold in the vineyards. This was when I arrived in Alsace, and I found winemakers with a lot on their minds. The harvest in Alsace often lasts into December, but this was a risk no one would take in 2006. The grapes were sufficiently ripe for early picking, and even for the production of 'late harvest' wines, but this would be a very early late harvest.

The harvest is a great time to be in Alsace, when villages are hives of activity. Summer is the time for village festivities, and spring is when to beat the tourist coaches. In the last 10 years, the Alsace tourist board has plugged the final hole in the region's perennial popularity, by creating the *Marchés de Noël*, or Christmas Markets, which animate many towns and villages from the end of November. 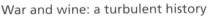 **www.marche-de-noel-alsace.com**

War and wine: a turbulent history

The history of winemaking in Alsace predates the Romans. Viticulture was practised throughout the Middle Ages, but Alsace's real period of prosperity began in the 16th century. However, although France emerged victorious from her Thirty Years War with Germany in 1648, this period had witnessed the near total destruction of the Alsatian vineyard.

Very little changed until after the French Revolution. Then with the onset

Obernai Tourist Office

ABOVE
Obernai,
Ville de départ

ABOVE
The end of an early
grape harvest

of the 19th century, an uncontrolled frenzy of replanting began. Inferior vine varieties such as the productive Kniperlé were grown on easily cultivated soils in the fertile plains; the best hillside vineyards at the foot of the Vosges were left abandoned. Wines were watered down and sugar was added to boost alcohol levels, as the vineyards' owners tried to maximise quantity at the expense of quality.

More disastrous still was the introduction of foreign, notably American, vines towards the end of the 19th century. These plants brought with them diseases such as Oïdium (powdery mildew) and the Phylloxera louse, which would devastate Europe's vineyards. When Germany re-annexed Alsace in 1871, the situation worsened as the invading power relegated Alsace to the production of reliable bulk wine for the domestic market, to protect Germany's own fine winemakers from undesirable competition!

Alsace became French again in 1919, and the consequences of the German policy became starkly apparent. Starved of the markets along the Rhine River, for which its vineyards had been planted, Alsace was suddenly forced to compete with the wine regions of France, at a considerable disadvantage.

Rags to recovery

After the ravages of the Second World War, Alsace began to re-emerge as a producer of world-class wines. The region lacked the famous names of the Bordeaux châteaux, and its ancient monastic vineyard sites were saddled with obscure Germanic names. The solution was the birth of the single 'varietal' wine; a marketing initiative that has since been copied the world over.

Instrumental in the development of Alsace wines was a handful of enterprising growers who, towards the end of the 19th century and the beginning of the 20th, began bottling and branding their own wines and those of neighbouring farmers. Families such as the Trimbachs, the Beyers and the Hugels emerged at the vanguard of a developing wine appellation. In 1895, the Cave de Ribeauvillé became France's first co-operative wine cellar, followed by others who today count among Alsace's most respected winemakers.

1945 saw the creation of the official blueprint for Alsace's accession to *appellation contrôlée* status, which it finally received in 1962.

Alsace today

Alsace is a wine appellation still in its infancy, and one that is fast evolving to meet its enormous potential. Two thirds of Alsace's production is sold in France, where it accounts for an incredible 40% of quality white wine sales. The region's often family-run merchant houses bottle more than 40% of Alsace wines and 18 strong co-operative cellars count for almost as much again. The remainder is produced and sold by the independent growers.

As the system bends under opposing pressures from influential growers and powerful merchant houses, the next ten years is likely to see radical changes in the rules. This could bring, for example, a new list of Premier Cru as well as Grand Cru vineyards, which would make *appellation Alsace* more like that in Burgundy's Côte d'Or.

Grape varieties, terroir and styles of wine

The majority of Alsace wines are white and either dry or off-dry in style, but beyond this, the variety is enormous. A typical winemaker has three fairly distinct ranges of wines, breaking down roughly as follows:

1. The fruit-driven wines

These are the entry-level blends, made from single grape varieties and vinified with no wood contact to preserve the grape's character. Alsace is unique in France in its focus on grape varieties in the production of *appellation contrôlée* wines.

There are 11 grape varieties, or *cépages*, permitted in Alsace. The first is the Chasselas, a fairly bland grape often used as a base for the region's basic blends. Called Edelzwickers, or "noble blends", these rarely live up to their namesake.

Next is the much-maligned Sylvaner, capable of producing wines with great freshness and finesse if grown on the right soils and with controlled yields. You could be forgiven for some confusion over the Pinot Blanc. Also known as the Klevner or Clevner, this is a non-aromatic, full-bodied variety with its origins in Burgundy. It is often blended with the flavoursome Auxerrois, although this is not always mentioned on the label.

Also of Burgundian origin is the Pinot Gris, known as Pinot Beurot in the Côte d'Or. This grape was traditionally called the "Tokay d'Alsace" since, according to legend, it was brought to the region by Marshall Lazare de Schwendi in 1565, following his defeat of the Turks in Hungary. Modern studies have disproved the Magyar link, and European law now forbids the use of the word "Tokay" on Alsatian bottles. The wines are full-bodied and mineral, developing savoury aromas and an opulent mouth-feel.

Muscat is the first of the aromatic varieties, and generally makes a light dry, grape-scented wine. In Alsace there are two distinct but related varieties. The Muscat d'Alsace is identical to the Muscat à Petits Grains found in the south of France, and of Oriental origins. The Muscat Ottonel is an earlier-ripening more recent crossbreed.

Most people remember their first taste of the floral, exotic and sometimes spicy Gewurztraminer. Alsace's most famous and unusual grape, the "Gewurz" (meaning "spice") was imported from Italy's South Tyrol at the end of the 19th century, and gradually supplanted its less aromatic cousin the Traminer. This latter is now known as the Klevener de Heiligenstein, now only grown around the commune of Heiligenstein in the Bas-Rhin. The pressed skins of Gewurztraminer grapes are distilled into Alsace's most

popular spirit, the aromatic but fiery *Marc de Gewurztraminer*.

The king of Alsace grapes is the Riesling, which now covers more vineyard area than any other variety. Imported from Germany during the Middle Ages, the Riesling benefits from the long Alsatian autumns, achieving incredible levels of ripeness and aromatic complexity, whilst maintaining its fresh, steely acidity. Most Rieslings have at least some ageing potential, and the best examples are amongst the world's longest-lived white wines.

Often overlooked by Alsace's marketing campaigns is the 9% of its vineyard planted with the red Pinot Noir. This was traditionally used to make rosés and light red wines, but in warm vintages many producers make serious, ageworthy red Pinot Noirs that compare well with good burgundies.

The last grape is the ubiquitous Chardonnay. Generally blended with Pinot Blanc and other grapes, this is an increasingly important ingredient in the region's excellent traditional method sparkling wines, or Crémants d'Alsace.

2. The terroir wines

Just as Alsace has been torn politically between warring nations, its geology has been formed by subterranean clashes, resulting in France's most complex terroir. The stony lower slopes of the Vosges are where the finest wines are grown, at an altitude of between 150 and 350 metres. But here it is impossible to generalise about soil type. Granite, sandstone, limestone, clay, volcanic schist and dozens of subdivisions of each can exist within a single commune. Add to which an appellation system in its infancy, and the rebelliousness of the Alsatian spirit, and you are left with... arguments.

As in Burgundy, Alsace's best vineyard sites have been recognised since the Middle Ages, when many of them belonged to powerful religious houses. But it was only in 1975 that the Institut National des Appellations d'Origine (I.N.A.O.) confirmed a list of vineyards that could be called Grand Cru. These are the terroirs that transcend and even overpower the character of grape variety, producing wines with uniquely complex and individual flavours that often need at least five years to show their potential.

There are 50 Grand Cru vineyards, but their exact boundaries are the subject of many disputes. Three of the biggest merchant houses, Trimbach, Hugel and Léon Beyer, have boycotted the Grand Cru appellation, arguing that their own parcels or "clos" within larger Grand Cru are superior to the rest of the vineyard.

A Grand Cru wine must be made from one of the four "noble" grape varieties of Alsace: Riesling, Gewurztraminer, Pinot Gris and Muscat. Unsurprisingly, not all winemakers are happy with this, but the saga doesn't end there. Vineyards have particular affinities for certain grape varieties, but if a site favours more than one of these, then why not create a Grand Cru blend? This is forbidden by regulations, but hasn't stopped iconoclasts like Jean-Michel Deiss from creating field blends in all of his Grands Crus vineyards; never mind the rules.

3. Late-harvested and super-sweet wines

Sweet wines are made from many grape varieties, but to be called either *Vendanges Tardives* or *Sélection des Grains Nobles*, they must be made from one of the four "noble varieties" (see above), and this has caused inevitable fuss.

Vendanges Tardives are late-harvested wines, made from overripe and shrivelled grapes, or ones that have benefited from 'noble rot'. The authorities impose strict controls on the picking of these grapes, which must contain a minimum level of natural sugar, or potential alcohol. In practice, winemakers produce *Vendanges Tardives* in most years when disaster does not strike. It is forbidden to enrich the must with added sugar (chaptalization) prior to fermentation.

Much rarer is *Sélection des Grains Nobles*, made from individually selected 'nobly rotten' grapes. The same strict controls are applied as for *Vendanges Tardives*, but the grapes' sugar content must be higher still. The production of this style requires perfect conditions, and waiting for these involves risk, so a producer might only make *Sélection des Grains Nobles* once in a decade.

Wine & food

Alsace has a rich, hearty culinary tradition in which country recipes merge effortlessly with modern haute cuisine. Even the best-respected chefs are not afraid to add a *touche de terroir* to their cooking. Alsace has a higher concentration of Michelin-starred restaurants than any other French region, but more numerous still are the cosy *winstubs* (or *wistubs* in the Haut-Rhin), created by Alsace's winemakers following the War as a way of selling their wines with simple country food.

The Alsatian table has undergone something of a revolution in the last ten years. Young cooks are keen to experiment with international flavours, using exotic herbs and spices which have a natural affinity for the region's aromatic wines. The presentation of traditional Alsatian cuisine is also being reinvented. Chef Olivier Nasti in Kaysersberg, for example, has created a sushi-bar-cum-night-club based around the Alsatian *tarte flammée*.

The *tarte flammée*, or *flammekueche* in Alsatian dialect, is like a thin crust pizza, topped with *crème fraîche* and flamed in a wood-burning stove. Bakers traditionally made these with their spare dough, throwing on onions and bacon, or whatever else there might be to hand.

The pig is an important animal in the Alsatian kitchen, and it is with ham, pig's knuckle, and pork sausages that its most famous speciality, *choucroute*, is made. Here there is no escaping the Alsatian translation: this is *sauerkraut*, although in Alsace it is somehow infused with enough French gastronomic brilliance to make it delicious. *Choucroute* was born of the need to preserve cabbage through the long, cold Alsatian winter. It is chopped, soaked and then cooked in white wine, juniper berries, black pepper, salt, cloves, crushed garlic and sometimes cumin seed. *Choucroute* is also used as a bed on which to serve pikeperch and other river fish in creamy sauces. These dishes are wonderful when served with a glass of dry Sylvaner or Riesling.

Every part of the pig is used in rustic recipes such as *presskopf*, or pressed pork brawn, and *baeckaoffa*, the Alsatian hotpot made from alternate layers of meat seasoned in wine, and potato mixed with onion.

Alsace has a large Jewish population, using poultry as an alternative to pork meat. The goose, and later the duck, have been essential for the production of *foie gras*, which only became common in its now more famous home, the Périgord, during the Second World War, when many of Alsace's Jews fled south to escape the German army. *Foie gras* is homemade in the best restaurants, and goes very well with Pinot Gris or Gewurztraminer in their sweeter incarnations.

Despite arcane hunting laws in Alsace, game is abundant in its forests, so you will find delicious wild venison, pheasant, hare and boar on autumn menus. These marry well with more powerful red Pinot Noirs.

An abundance of fruit trees grow the apples and plums (*quetsch*) that go into making delicious tarts and cheesecakes. Alsace's most famous dessert is *kougelhopf*. Translating as "rising dough", this is mixed with sultanas and a glass of *quetsch* spirit, before being topped with almonds and put in the oven. Often served partly as an ice cream, this marries well with either Gewurztraminer or crémant d'Alsace. *Kougelhopf* is also made as a delicious savoury snack, with bacon and nuts.

Soft, pungent cheeses are made on the farms west of the wine route. The best known of these is the appellation-controlled Munster, originally produced in the town's Benedictine abbey. Here again, Gewurztraminer is the vinous accompaniment. The farms that produce these cheeses often double up as country inns, or *fermes auberges*.

Driving, cycling or walking

Each estate in Alsace produces a very large selection of wines. Even those vignerons with UK importers are unlikely to export more than a few of their labels, so arriving in your own car is the ideal way to take home your favourites.

However, with its excellent air and rail connections, Alsace is the perfect place to plan a cycle tour. Most of the wine route offers a choice between the flat land beneath the vineyards, the gently rolling slopes through the villages, and the more challenging routes into the Vosges. If cycle tourism is most developed in the Loire, then it is best organised in Alsace. The existing cycle paths are generally well signposted, although they haven't all been planned with wine travel in mind. Furthermore, the railway line runs the entire length of the wine route and all trains carry bikes.

Created in the 18th century, the Club *Vosgien* is Europe's oldest hiking club. It was formed at the same time as the Alsatian plain was linked to the Vosges by a rural rail network, allowing the region's manufacturing workers to take short breaks in the mountains. The *fermes auberges* sprung up around the same time to satisfy their appetites (see above).

Less challenging are the vineyard walks in many Alsatian wine villages. Although explanations tend to be in French and German, the paths are well indicated, and further information is always available in local tourist offices, which themselves organise guided vineyard walks at set times in July and August.

ABOVE & OPPOSITE PAGE LEFT
Cooks at Flammé & Co. restaurant in Kaysersberg

TOP
The Alsatian speciality *kougelhopf*, or 'rising dough'

Getting to Obernai from Strasbourg

Strasbourg International airport is almost as close to Obernai to the west as it is to Strasbourg to its east, so if you are flying, you may want to proceed directly to stage one of the tour.

Obernai is around sixteen miles from Strasbourg, and my advice to all but complete cycle-heads is to take the train. They all carry bikes free of charge, and the ride to Obernai is less interesting than what follows. Obernai is just nine miles from the airport via Geispolsheim (see below), but the place to hire bikes is Strasbourg.

By car, leave Strasbourg west from Boulevard de Lyon along the D392 (route de Schirmeck). After the airport, take the N422 directly to Obernai.

Cyclists follow signs to "Lingolsheim" from the centre of Strasbourg, past place Hans-Jean Ark and the Museum of Modern and Contemporary Arts. Continue along the cycle path, which is signposted "Lingolsheim" and "Montagne Verte", taking quai du Brulig where the path briefly peters out. At the next fork, carry on left, and follow signs for "Eckbolsheim" and "Molsheim". When you reach route de Schirmeck (D392), turn left onto this road and follow it for two miles until the turning left onto the D484 for "Ostwald" and "Montagne Verte".

In Ostwald, turn right in front of the church towards Geispolsheim. Follow signs onto the D84, which leads through the village of Geispolsheim and into Blaesheim. After Blaesheim, the cycle path diverges from the main road, and from these cereal fields you get the first views of the Vosges mountains ahead.

Pass a small group of warehouses on rue du Tramway, turn right and follow the cycle signs to the village of Innenheim; then turn left to Krautergersheim. Turn right onto the D207 towards Obernai, then left immediately onto the cycle path that leads into the town.

Summary itinerary

Days 1 & 2
The Bas-Rhin

The wine villages that separate Obernai and Sélestat in the Lower Rhine are more rustic, and attract fewer tourists, than the more famous ones near Colmar.

The summits of the Vosges mountains to the west of the wine route are lower in this northern part of Alsace, giving the vineyards less protection from the elements than the ones further south. The wines are less headily intense than those from the Upper Rhine, but the best can show unparalleled elegance. You will find some of Alsace's most exciting winemakers in villages like Andlau, Mittelbergheim and Dambach-la-Ville, and the wines they produce are amongst the region's most keenly priced.

Tips for cyclists

Most of this 30-40 mile section follows the D35, setting the tone for the gentle climbs and short descents of the Alsace wine route. The exception is the climb to Mont-Sainte-Odile (763 metres altitude) from Ottrott. This is an essential detour for cyclists with a reasonable level of fitness, as the views from the Mount's summit are spectacular.

Days 3 & 4
The northern Haut-Rhin

Just north of the villages of the Upper Rhine, the hills above Kintzheim boast many of Alsace's most fascinating tourist attractions. The route passes France's oldest falconry and 'Monkey Mountain', on its way to Alsace's only fully restored hillside castle, the Château de Haut-Koenigsbourg.

The wine villages that follow are the most famous in Alsace. Ribeauvillé and Riquewihr are home to the region's most important wine merchant houses and, together with

Kaysersberg, form that trio of architectural beauty that most visitors to Alsace come to behold. Tourist numbers diminish in villages such as Bergheim and Kientzheim, where some of Alsace's most inventive winegrowers live.

Tips for cyclists

This section is less than 30 miles, leaving time for a full exploration of its various attractions, beginning with another optional climb, to the Château de Haut-Koenigsbourg (755m altitude). The remainder of the route is only slightly hillier than days 1 & 2. A picturesque cycle path begins in Kintzheim and follows an old Roman road across the flatlands all the way to Bennwihr, but passes beneath – not through – the wine villages.

Days 5 & 6
Colmar and its neighbours

The string of famous wine village names continues with Turckheim, Wettolsheim and Eguisheim on the outskirts of Colmar, capital of Alsace wines. Supposedly the most Alsatian of Alsace's cities, Colmar was spared the destruction of successive wars, its picturesque Little Venice district offering unparalleled photo opportunities and an excellent selection of restaurants. Colmar's biggest attraction is its spectacular Unterlinden Museum, France's most visited provincial museum.

South of Eguisheim, the main tourist trail ends as you scale the hill to Husseren-les-Châteaux, traversing the stonewalled vineyards south to Rouffach, the ancient religious capital of the Upper Rhine, and site of Alsace's School of Viticulture.

Tips for cyclists

At only 12 miles, day 5 is designed to leave time for a visit of Colmar. Day 6 is 15-20 rather hillier miles. The climb is a steep one from Eguisheim to Husseren-les-Châteaux, but there is also a cycle path that passes instead beneath the vineyards directly to Pfaffenheim, and then Rouffach.

Key to map

Dominic's route
other routes
start point
day
extra trip
end point
town or village
larger town
river

Obernai
Ottrott
Mont-Sainte-Odile
Heiligenstein
Barr
Mittelbergheim
Andlau
Itterswiller
Epfig
Dambach-la-Ville
Scherwiller
Châtenois
Sélestat
Haut-Koenigsbourg
Kintzheim
St-Hippolyte
Orschwiller
Rodern
Rorschwihr
Bergheim
Ribeauvillé
Hunawihr
Riquewihr
Beblenheim
Kaysersberg
Kientzheim
Ammerschwihr
Katzenthal
Ingersheim
Turckheim
Colmar
Wintzenheim
Wettolsheim
Eguisheim
Husseren-les-Châteaux
Voegtlinshofen
Gueberschwihr
Pfaffenheim
Westhalten
Soultzmatt
Rouffach

ABOVE
Obernai town square

Day 1 itinerary (12-24 miles)
From Obernai to Andlau

Obernai, *Ville de Départ*

Obernai is a little way north of where Alsace's famous Grand Cru vineyards begin, but I fell in love with the town and resolved to make it my starting point, only to find that others had had the same idea. 189 others to be exact. The conspiratorial winks from passing cyclists and the yellow jerseys hung from every shop front said it all. I was aware that the preamble to the Tour de France had circled Strasbourg, but I had ignored any possibility of the race crossing my own path. The world's biggest cycle event began in Obernai on the 3rd July 2006, and I had been in Tours.

The extremely good literature provided by the tourist office insists that Obernai is "a city". All it lacks is a cathedral, although the neo-Gothic Catholic Church of St Peter and St Paul is said to be the "greatest sanctuary in Alsace after Strasbourg Cathedral". Obernai was largely spared the ravages of two World Wars, and its mixture of medieval and Renaissance architecture is beautifully preserved.

Since the fifties, Obernai has become an important centre for tourism and industry, and its population has more than doubled in the same period. If you approach on the train from Strasbourg, you pass the massive headquarters of Kronenbourg, France's largest brewer. Kronenbourg moved its operations here from Strasbourg in 1969. Tourist visits still take place at the original brewery in Strasbourg (see page 270).

Obernai is hardly world-famous for its wines, but it has at least one fine producer in Domaine Seilly.
✉ **18, rue de Général Gouraud** ☎ **03 88 95 55 80**

Outside the very helpful tourist office, you will find directions for the first of the region's many hillside vineyard walks.

Obernai is an essential gastronomic stopover. Nicholas Stamm's La Fourchette des Ducs ☎ **03 88 48 33 38**, opposite the railway station, belongs to that elite club of double-Michelin-starred restaurants, and the more affordable Bistro des Saveurs is one of my favourites in the region (see page 290). For something simpler, try Winstub O'baerenheim "Chez Gerard". ✉ **46, rue du Général Gouraud** ☎ **03 88 95 53 77**

Obernai to Ottrott

From the Hôtel de Ville in the centre of Obernai, follow rue Chanoine Gyss past the Church of Sts Peter and Paul. Turn left at the sign for Ottrott and follow signs for a further two miles.

The Pinot Noir grape thrives on Ottrott's iron-rich soils, and the village produces firm, long-lived red wines. *Rouge d'Ottrott* plantings cover a mere 25 hectares, but the wine is protected by its own confrérie, 'The Brotherhood of the Horn'! A good place to taste the village speciality is at Jean-Charles Vonville's cellars in Place des Tilleuls, as you enter the village. ☎ **03 88 95 80 25**

The climb through Ottrott past the church reveals a couple of decent restaurants. L'Hostellerie des Châteaux is the most gastronomic – and a little expensive. Four-star rooms cost more than €100. ☎ **03 88 48 14 14** ⌂ **www.hostellerie-chateaux.fr** A good value alternative is A l'Ami Fritz, where menus are served from €22. ☎ **03 88 95 80 81** ⌂ **www.amifritz.com** The 3-star hotel is very reasonable; the wine estate opposite (Fritz-Schmidt) is less interesting. Keep these places in mind if visiting Mont Saint Odile, where the restaurant is somewhat simpler.

Day 1 at a glance
Itinerary   280 – 285
Wineries   286 – 289
Restaurants   290 – 291

BOTTOM
The Tour de France lives on

The climb to Mont-Sainte-Odile

Continue through the higher part of Ottrott to Saint-Nabor, and in that village turn left onto the D103. At the junction with the D109, a left turn leads back down the hill to Heiligenstein, the next village on the wine route. The other choice is to begin the climb to Mont-Sainte-Odile, Alsace's second most visited tourist attraction.

I was surprised by the relative painlessness of this six-mile climb, but it was a very cool day, I had no baggage, and I had by this stage spent around five months on the road. All of these things make a difference, so remember that an altitude of 763 metres is about half that of an alpine ski resort, and you will have to scale the greater part of this. Cyclists can shave two miles off the climb by turning right at the "no entry" sign after the St-Jacques holiday residence (but yes, shorter does mean steeper). Otherwise, continue and turn onto the D854 towards the summit.

The history of the Mount dates back much further than Sainte Odile's legacy, as proved by the six-mile Pagan Wall that surrounds it, the longest continuous stonework construction in northern Europe. Sainte Odile arrived in the 7th century after her father Etichon, third duke of Alsace, moved to Obernai. Odile was born blind and grew up in a monastery, but recovered her eyesight when she was christened at the age of twelve. Her father built a religious house on the Mount in acknowledgement of his daughter's religious vocation.

From the top of the Mount, the views into the forested lower reaches of the Vosges mountains are spectacular. On autumn mornings, the wine villages far below are shrouded in a ghostly cloud of fog, through which you might see the occasional church steeple or the ruins of a hillside castle.

OPPOSITE PAGE
Mont-Sainte-Odile: Alsace's most visited religious monument

BELOW
The forest below Mont-Sainte-Odile

Through Heiligenstein

Retrace your steps to Saint-Nabor, then continue to the small roundabout and turn right onto the D35 towards Heiligenstein; otherwise follow signs from Mont-Sainte-Odile straight to Barr. This more direct route to Barr leads past the ruins of the 13th century Château de Spesbourg.

Heiligenstein is another village with a speciality, the Klevener grape. Also known as the Traminer, this is the once more common ancestor of today's Gewurztraminer. With the same fat structure as its modern descendent, the white wines produced from the Klevener are less aromatic but age well, generally needing time to show their best.

Many vignerons from Barr own land or buy grapes here, but if you're keen to taste the Klevener de Heiligenstein on its home soil, drop into Domaine Heywang ☏ **03 88 08 91 41** or Domaine Daniel Ruff ☏ **03 88 08 10 81**, both on rue Principale.

Heiligenstein has its fair share of vineyard paths, most leading back up towards Mont-Sainte-Odile. Don't miss the statue of Ehrhard Wantz in the village centre, the man credited with introducing the Klevener grape to the village in the 18th century.

Behind the Mairie, the village's well-reputed restaurant is Au Raisin d'Or. ☏ **03 88 08 95 23**

Barr

With more than 6,000 inhabitants and a good number of négociant houses and co-operative cellars, Barr is one of the Bas-Rhin's biggest winemaking towns. As you enter the village, the famous Grand Cru vineyard Kirchberg de Barr rises on the hillside to your right (not to be confused with the Kirchberg de Ribeauvillé in the Haut-Rhin). Perhaps the vineyard's finest expression is négociant Domaine Klipfel's spicy Gewurztraminer from the tiny Clos Zisser, a superior enclave within the larger Grand Cru vineyard. Klipfel's cellars are among Alsace's most impressive; the domaine owns its own museum, and there are sure to be plenty of wines open to taste. ☏ **03 88 58 59 00** ☝ **www.klipfel.com**

Before you reach the main place de l'Hôtel de Ville, the Musée de La Folie Marco is on your right in rue du Docteur Sultzer. This museum of Alsatian bourgeois furniture is housed within the mansion built by the bailiff of Barr, Louis-Félix Marco in the 18th century, and is set within its own beautiful gardens. ☏ **03 88 08 66 65**

On the same road, drop into Domaine Hering, if for no other reason than to try the fabulous Riesling Grand Cru Kirchberg Cuvée Emile Gustave. ☏ **03 88 08 90 07** ☝ **www.vins-hering.com**

ABOVE
Place de l'Hôtel de Ville in Barr, with winstub S'barrer Stubbel on the right

TOP
Vincent Stoeffler tastes wine in his cellars in Barr

The Hôtel de Ville (town hall) is Barr's most impressive building. It stands on the site of the town's 13th century castle, which was apparently destroyed several times by the devil, before finally being wiped out by fire in a later incident. The town hall itself has suffered various attacks, beginning with the Armagnacs in the 15th century, and finally in 1944 during the battle for *Libération*.

Beside the town hall is Jacky Schmitter's cosy winstub S'barrer Stubbel, which serves superb choucroute at absurdly low prices. ① **03 88 08 57 44** Another good dining option is Au Potin, a Lyonnais-style bistro at the other end of town. ✉ **11, rue de Général Vandenberg** ① **03 88 08 88 84**

If you're not already tired of vineyard walks, you can climb from outside the Hôtel de Ville past the Protestant Church of St. Martin, and follow the signposted route (in French) around the Kirchberg vineyard. And if you're still short of something to taste, Domaine Stoeffler makes fine organic wines, including an excellent Klevener de Heiligenstein. ✉ **1, rue des Lièvres** ① **03 88 08 52 50** ⌂ **www.vins-stoeffler.com**

Before continuing to Mittelbergheim, cross the railway line towards the small village of Gertwiller, Alsace's capital of *pain d'épices*, or spiced bread. Here you can visit the museum and shop devoted to the village speciality, which is open all year round. ① **03 88 08 93 52** ⌂ **www.paindepices-lips.com**

Growers with attitude

Past Domaine Klipfel's tasting cellars, follow signs for Mittelbergheim up the hill onto the D362. This road takes you through the centre of a curious Grand Cru vineyard, the Zotzenberg.

With the ever more zealous enforcement of Alsace's appellation regulations came a protracted wrangle between growers and authorities regarding the Zotzenberg vineyard. The rule is that a Grand Cru wine must be made from Riesling, Gewurztraminer, Muscat or Pinot Gris grapes. But the Mittelbergheimers complained that Sylvaner was best suited to the Zotzenberg terroir, and that its Grand Cru appellation should therefore be applied to wines made from this grape. In 2005 the growers finally won their battle, making the Zotzenberg the first official exception to the rules governing Grand Cru grape varieties.

Mittelbergheim

Officially one of France's prettiest villages, Mittelbergheim's sloping streets house an incredible concentration of

winemaking energy. Lucas Rieffel is the village's brightest young talent (see page 286), but négociant Albert Selz also makes excellent wines.
① **03 88 08 91 77**

Three fine restaurants in Mittelbergheim ensure that you will never be short of a place to eat, and all have excellent wine lists. The first to try is Restaurant Gilg, the most 'classic' of the three (see page 290).

Last stop, Andlau

By car, take rue de la Montagne past Mittelbergheim's hôtel de ville, then turn right onto the D62 to Andlau. Cyclists instead turn right past Restaurant Gilg, and then left onto the cycle path. Both routes lead through the lower reaches of the Wiebelsberg Grand Cru vineyard before entering Andlau.

Andlau is another town with a good selection of restaurants. For sheer rustic charm, I recommend Pierre Zinck's La Relais de la Poste (see page 291); but Au Val d'Eleon is perhaps equally good, and serves Marcel Kreydenweiss's basic wines by the pitcher. ① **03 88 08 93 23**

The Kreydenweiss estate is the one you must visit in Andlau (see page 288), but André & Remy Gresser grow superb Rieslings on the Grand Cru Wiebelsberg, and wonderful Rieslings and Gewurztraminers on the Grand Cru Moenchberg between Andlau and Eichoffen. ✉ **2, rue de l'Ecole** ① **03 88 08 95 88** ⌂ **www.gresser.com**

Another Andlau producer who has made a name for himself, particularly for his Riesling Grand Cru Wiebelsberg, is Guy Wach. ✉ **5, rue de la Commanderie** ① **03 88 08 93 20**

Domaine Rieffel

11, rue Principale
67140 Mittelbergheim

Phone 03 88 08 95 48
Fax 03 88 08 28 94
Andre.rieffel@wanadoo.fr

The Estate

I was eating at Le Bistro des Saveurs in Obernai when I was bowled over by this estate's Grand Cru Wiebelsberg Riesling. I had been discussing the wines of one of the Lower Rhine's famous merchant houses with Chef Thierry Schwartz, when he uncorked Rieffel's Riesling as a comparison.

"So you see the difference," remarked the chef, seeing the pleasure in my face.

Lucas is the third generation of Rieffels to bottle his estate's wines, and a passionate exponent of the area's terroirs. The young winemaker led me on a tour of the vineyards of Mittelbergheim and Andlau, to see at first hand the dramatic differences in soil from one vineyard to the next. Lucas harvests all grapes from these individual sites manually, placing them into small 30-kilo boxes, before carefully transporting them to the winery, so as to preserve the freshness and character of the wines.

As the speciality of Mittelbergheim, Lucas believes that the Sylvaner grape has a handsome future, particularly since its authorisation for the production of Grand Cru Zotzenberg in 2005. The grape's combination of freshness and body make it wonderful to drink either on its own or with food, and even Rieffel's simplest Sylvaner resembles a fine, full-bodied *sur lie* Muscadet.

The wines spend up to two years ageing on their lees, giving them an intense mineral complexity and length of flavour. Lucas ages some of the less aromatic varieties in old oak *barriques*, not to impart oak flavour, but to give the wines fuller aromas and a rounded fatness in the mouth.

UK importer:
Berry Brothers & Rudd

LEFT
Lucas Rieffel amongst his vines in the Grand Cru Zotzenberg

OPPOSITE PAGE
TOP
Lucas serves his wines at the autumn Grand Cru tasting in Kientzheim

Choice wines:

Pinot Blanc 'Gebreit' 2004
Grown on the granitic soils of nearby Andlau, this Pinot Blanc is from a parcel originally destined for Crémant d'Alsace, but one of such high quality that Lucas vinified it separately and aged it for 11 months in oak.

The result is a wine with an intense creamy nose, showing hints of fresh vanilla. In the mouth, the wine is firm but rounded, with ripe lemon flavours, good acidity and a long dry finish.

Wonderful drunk on its own or with richly flavoured fish.

Sylvaner Grand Cru Zotzenberg 2005
The estate resisted the temptation to plant 'authorised' Grand Cru grape varieties in the Zotzenberg prior to 2005, so this wine comes from Sylvaner vines with between 25 and 45 years age.

Concentrated mineral and ripe lemon aromas are given an attractive creaminess by the wine's secondary, 'malolactic' fermentation. On the palate, it has freshness and weight in equal measure, with a mouth-filling minerality.

An extremely versatile food wine, try it with cooked fish, charcuterie, light vegetarian dishes or even white meat.

Riesling Wiebelsberg Grand Cru 2001
After tasting the same wine from the 2004 vintage, it is clear that a few years bottle age improve this wine immeasurably.

Grown on the sandy soils of the Wiebelsberg Grand Cru in Andlau, the wine is made from grapes with a high level of maturity. On the nose, it is spicy and mineral, with elegant quince aromas and a hint of honey. Spicy orange peel and quince flavours give onto a long, stony finish, where the wine's residual sugar is perfectly balanced by a firm thread of acidity.

Drink with rich, spicy food; something light cooked in an orange and cardamom sauce would be the perfect partner. Already showing well, this is a wine that could age happily for a further ten years.

Gewurztraminer Grand Cru Zotzenberg Vendanges Tardives 2003
Picked in mid-October, this wine's aromas are pure late-harvested Gewurztraminer: lychees, honey and an intense spice that is characteristic of the variety when grown in the Zotzenberg.

The spices explode on the palate. The wine is both elegant and exotic, with surprisingly crisp acidity, well-integrated sweetness and an incredibly long finish.

Drink with exotic fruit desserts, as an apéritif or with *foie gras*.

Domaine Marc Kreydenweiss

12, rue Deharbe
67140 Andlau

Phone 03 88 08 95 83
Fax 03 88 08 41 16
Marc@kreydenweiss.com
www.kreydenweiss.com

The Estate

There is something very poetic about Marc Kreydenweiss's Andlau estate. In 1989, Marc pioneered biodynamic viticulture in the Bas-Rhin, with the intention of re-establishing balance and harmony in the vineyard. Marc's wife Emmanuelle and their children Antoine and Manfred now also work on the 12-hectare estate, and share Marc's happy philosophy.

Emmanuelle is an enthusiastic exponent of wine-and-health, believing that wine should help rather than hinder digestion. She talks of the natural trace elements on which the flavour and goodness of wine depend; the concentration of these elements (called dry extract) in the estate's wines is certainly helped by average vine yields of less than 40 hl per hectare, about half the authorised limit in Alsace.

The family's winemaking heritage dates back three centuries, to the time when their existing underground wine cellars were built. Most of the estate then belonged to the monks in the abbey opposite. Don't miss the 12th century subterranean support pillar, a vestige of the now dismantled chapel above the Grand Cru Kastelberg vineyard.

The Kreydenweiss wines are unusual in Alsace in that they all undergo 'malolactic' fermentation. They show creamy minerality in their youth, and all age extremely well. Outside of the late picked range, the wines tend to be drier than many in the region, and are therefore very versatile food partners.

In 1999 Marc Kreydenweiss bought Domaine des Perrières in the Costières de Nîmes appellation in the Rhône valley. This estate is also farmed biodynamically and the wines are, as you would expect, very good.

Phone in advance for an excellent tutored tasting overlooking the sheer slopes of Grand Cru Kastelberg vineyard.

UK importer:
Champagnes & Chateaux
Adnams (for Domaine des Perrières)

ABOVE
Emmanuelle Kreydenweiss welcomes tasters from five different countries

OPPOSITE PAGE
Emmanuelle with grape pickers at the end of the harvest

Choice wines:

Clos Rebberg Riesling 2003

Translating as 'Wine Mountain', Clos Rebberg is an ancient site, replanted by Marc Kreydenweiss in 1995. The vineyard needs to be terraced, as the slopes would otherwise be too steep for vineyard work.

Grey schist soils are perfect for the Riesling, giving the wines a characteristic stony smokiness and honeyed lime on the nose. The youth of the vines helps the wine to develop early, and the 2003 is already showing some maturity, with aromas of petrol (good) and spiced apples.

The palate is full and ripe, yet dry and savoury, making it a great match for delicately flavoured white fish.

Grand Cru 'Wiebelsberg' *La Dame* Riesling 2003

Further down the valley but contiguous with Grand Cru Kastelberg, the Wiebelsberg vineyard shares its illustrious neighbour's steep southeast-exposed slopes. But the soil couldn't be more different and so neither could the wines.

Pink sandstone allows excellent drainage and heat reflection, big advantages in rainy years. The wine's aromas are ripe and floral, with the confident citrus of the Riesling developing hints of cinnamon. The palate is soft and mineral, with an impressively long finish.

The wine shows its best after about five years in bottle. Drink with creamy fish dishes.

Grand Cru 'Kastelberg' *Le Château* Riesling 2003

First mentioned as a vineyard site in 1064, Kastelberg's soil is a unique form of schist called 'de Steige', only found in Andlau.

This is a wine that needs more than five years to begin its development, and is therefore a little shy on the nose. Its extraordinary complexity and concentration is better expressed on the palate, where ripe grapefruits and savoury lemons mix with a creamy minerality.

10-20 years in bottle will reveal cinnamon and gunflint aromas. This is a dry wine that will partner wonderfully with grilled fish or sushi.

Grand Cru 'Moenchberg' *La Moine* Pinot Gris 2003

Situated between Andlau and Eichoffen to the east, Benedictine monks planted their vines on these south-facing slopes as early as 1097. *Moenchberg* means 'Monk's Mountain'.

The soils are rich in the glacial deposits on which the Pinot Gris grape thrives, giving the wine elegant aromas of honey, dried fruits and quince. On the palate, it is rich and spicy, with a well-balanced sweetness and incredible length.

The wine is made in a Vendange Tardive style, with around 30 grammes per litre of residual sugar; a good partner for spicy food, Stilton cheese or *foie gras*.

Restaurant Le Bistro des Saveurs

35, rue de Sélestat
67210 Obernai

Phone 03 88 49 90 41
Fax 03 88 49 90 51

It is hard to know where to begin praising this restaurant. The décor simply breathes country chic, and the entire place is filled with the warm smiles of proprietress Hélène Schwartz. The man himself, Thierry Schwartz, is a young chef whose talent and ambition seemingly know no bounds.

Having worked alongside the great Joël Robuchon in Paris, Thierry opened Le Bistro des Saveurs in 2002 and had a Michelin star within a year. Thierry's philosophy is simple: it is the primary ingredient in any dish that should be allowed to shine. "There is more complexity of flavour in a single carrot from a good grower than can be found in the most elaborate recipe," the chef explains.

Thierry is good friends with most of his suppliers, and is often to be found in their fields early in the morning, pulling carrots or cutting coriander leaves himself. At the time of writing, Thierry was preparing his own "book of passion", introducing his favourite producers, their products and his own select recipes.

The restaurant wine list fully represents Alsace's most interesting vignerons; sommelier Stephane Menard's advice is impeccable, and in good English. Menus are extraordinary value at €32 and €44. I hope they remain so with the inevitable increase in Le Bistro's profile.

Closed Monday and Tuesday; and towards the end of October, for the February school holidays, and the end of July to the beginning of August.

Restaurant Gilg

1, route du Vin
67140 Mittelbergheim

Phone 03 88 08 91 37
Fax 03 88 08 45 17
www.hotel-gilg.com

Serving as the village bakery until the 1950s, today's restaurant started life as one of the region's first *winstubs*, then considered sufficiently innovative to earn it a Michelin star. The menu today is more refined, but the restaurant has kept its old-fashioned slippers-and-pipe feel, and there are still a few dishes to remind diners of the place's rustic roots.

The house *foie gras* is delicious, cooked traditionally *en brioche* with truffles. During the hunting season, game dishes are clearly one of Chef Vincent Reuschle's specialities. Try also the classic pan-fried scallops, cooked in a celery and saffron sauce, alongside a glass of the village's famous Sylvaner. Set menus range from €27 to €70.

Despite its name, Restaurant Gilg is completely independent of the eponymous wine estate opposite, although as you might expect, the owners are cousins. Georges Gilg's wine list represents the finest of the village's vignerons, many of whose wines are available by the *carafe*. Have a look at the sections of the list that cover Bordeaux and Burgundy. Here you might find wines from Chateau Lafite-Rothschild or Domaine de la Romanée Conti, respectively, at lower prices than collectors pay through the trade – although still rather outside of my budget.

Closed Tuesday and Wednesday, and for three weeks in January and two at the end of July-beginning of August. **Present this book for a free apéritif.**

The attached hotel is extremely good value; particularly the luxury rooms (€85). These require advance booking.

At first glance a simple country watering hole, Le Relais de la Poste offers a real surprise with some truly delicious dishes. The restaurant's rustic wooden interior is interspersed with artifacts from Pierre Zinck's collection of primitive art, each one with its own fascinating story to tell. And Pierre is a storyteller *par excellence*.

The Zinck family has lived in Andlau for generations, and Pierre is proud to prepare the most traditional Alsatian recipes. Wild mushrooms are a particular passion of the chef; his *Salade Forestière* incorporates girolles, ceps and three other delicious kinds of fungi. The 'suggestions board' is the place to look for the week's new flavours, and this is where I found the most delicious, and enormous, stuffed pig's trotter, served with shredded cabbage and *gratin dauphinois* potatoes.

But Pierre is a gastronomic chef by training, having worked at Le Chambard in Kaysersberg long before the Nasti brothers took over (see page 327). The homemade *foie gras*, served with Gewurztraminer jelly, is a delicious testimony to this aspect of Pierre's talent.

Prices for main courses are between €10 and €20 and any one of these will satisfy even the most ravenous appetite.

Present this book for a free apéritif.

Restaurant-Winstub Le Relais de la Poste

**1, rue des Forgerons
67140 Andlau**

Phone 03 88 08 95 91

The view of Dambach-la-Ville
from St. Sebastien's Chapel

Day 2 itinerary (15 miles)

Andlau to Sélestat

A morning stroll around Andlau

Surrounded by forests on three sides, Andlau nestles in
the valley of its eponymous fast-flowing river, which
drove the town's mills during the Middle Ages. Andlau's
timber-framed houses belonged to the ordinary
townspeople, whilst the powerful elite lived in the more
grand stonework buildings built during the Renaissance.

Andlau grew around its Royal Abbey, founded in 880
by Richarde, wife of the Carolingian Charles the Fat,
great grandson of the Emperor Charlemagne. The
abbey was closed in 1791, and was used as a prison and
then as a factory before developing its modern vocation
as a hospice. Andlau has been a place of pilgrimage
since pre-Roman times, and its connections with fertility
rituals are depicted in the surprisingly erotic 12th
century stonework carvings above the bell tower
entrance to the church.

The small tourist office provides an itinerary for a
walking tour of Andlau. The highlight is the small path

that runs between the town's northern ramparts and the Kastelberg Grand Cru vineyard.

Day 2 at a glance
Itinerary 292 – 297
Wineries 298 – 301
Restaurants 302 – 303

Andlau to Dambach-la-Ville

From outside the tourist office in Andlau, follow the D253 towards Epfig and Dambach-la-Ville. This road climbs southeast from Andlau, giving remarkable views of the Alsatian plain on one side and the Andlau Valley on the other. Turn right onto the D35 after a mile, then left into Itterswiller.

Itterswiller is another beautiful 'village in bloom', showing its best aspect from beneath the Emmebuckel (Bee Hill), over which it looks. Called *Itineris Villa* in Roman times, Itterswiller certainly is a good place to stop for a meal and plan the rest of your day. The village's architectural and gastronomic centrepiece is Winstub Arnold ➀ **03 88 85 50 58**, a fine place to discover the village's often good value wines with the best Alsatian cooking. Otherwise, drop into Domaine Léon Faller for a tasting. ➀ **03 88 85 50 49**

A diversion via Epfig

There are two good reasons for continuing the extra mile to Itterswiller's sibling village Epfig. The first is that it is home to André Ostertag, one of Alsace's most gifted and iconoclastic organic winemakers. André's Riesling and Pinot Gris from the Grand Cru Muenchberg above Nothalten are wines of extraordinary individual character; but the domaine also produces formidable wines from the local hillside vineyards of less wide renown. ✉ **87, rue Finkwiller** ➀ **03 88 85 51 34**

The other reason for visiting Epfig is the remarkable 11th-12th century Chapel of Saint Marguerite. Situated about a mile beyond the N422 on the east side of Epfig, this is one of the oldest Romanesque edifices in Alsace. The Chapel's architecture is characteristically simple, and its interior is decorated with the remains of 15th and 16th century wall paintings. Quite surprisingly, an audio introduction to the Chapel's history is available at the push of a button – in English.

On to Dambach

The D35 leads directly down from Itterswiller into tiny Nothalten, the next village on the route. The D703 from Epfig jumps straight across to Blienschwiller, beyond Nothalten.

Nothalten's Grand Cru Muenchberg vineyard is a perfect south-facing crescent of poor, sandy soils that drain easily and retain the sun's heat. Don't confuse this

BELOW
The Lower Rhine villages: blissfully free of tourist hordes

vineyard with the Moenchberg in Eichoffen, although both names are Alsatian dialect translations of "Monk's Mountain". Apart from André Ostertag's creations from this site, try Domaine Armand Landmann's Riesling from the same, in the village of Nothalten. ① **03 88 92 41 12**

Nothalten is also home to the rebellious and brilliant Patrick Meyer of Domaine Julien Meyer. Often passed over by the press for his unorthodox style, Patrick makes biodynamic wines with delicious natural flavours, and sells them at very honest prices. ① **03 88 92 60 15**

Blienschwiller is the next village, and is dominated by its own less well-known Grand Cru, the granitic Winzenberg. Excellent Rieslings and Gewurztraminers are grown here, and the village itself has a good number of talented winemakers. Call on Domaine Hubert Metz ① **03 88 92 43 06** for a tasting, or stop for a bite in the village restaurant Le Pressoir de Bacchus (see page 302).

Sanctuary and skulls

The D35 leads through the upper entrance to Dambach-la-Ville, and then straight out through its eastern tower, La Porte de Dieffenthal. Before you enter the town, turn right at the signpost to St Sebastian's Chapel.

The Chapel is intimately connected with the history of Dambach. Originally the parish church of the now non-existent village of Oberkirch, it remained a place of pilgrimage after Dambach's ramparts were erected in the 14th century, and the surrounding villagers sought refuge within its walls. The Chapel was also a sanctuary for the healthy when the Black Death entered Dambach in the 14th century. Today, visitors come to admire the Chapel's 17th century wood-carved high altar, a thing of incredible beauty. But behind the Chapel, in its ossuary, make sure you peer through the iron bars at the pile of human skulls and bones, the remains of the peasants of Scherwiller who unsuccessfully revolted against their lords in 1525. Above the door reads the macabre inscription:

"That which you are, we were;
that which we are, you will be"

Dambach-la-Ville shows its best aspect from the Chapel above its vineyards, and this is the starting point for walks to the ruins of Château de Bernstein (following the blue discs).

Wine capital of the Bas-Rhin

In the 18th century, Dambach-la-Ville became an important centre of wine production, and is now home to some of the Bas-Rhin's most important merchant

houses. Just beyond the Porte de Dieffenthal are the two best reputed, Willy Gisselbrecht (see page 298) and Louis & Claude Hauller. ① **03 88 92 40 00** ⌂ **www.louishauller.com** Both have extensive holdings in Dambach's 450 ha of vineyards; 56 hectares of these are planted within the large – many believe too large – Frankstein Grand Cru.

Interesting smaller growers to visit are Yvette and Michel Beck-Hartweg, on rue Clemenceau that bisects the old town. ① **03 88 92 40 20** ⌂ **www.vins-beck-hartweg.chez-alice.fr**

In Dambach-la-Ville, you will also find some of the Bas-Rhin's most delicious *tartes flammées* at Hôtel-Restaurant A la Couronne. But Yves Kientz only fires up his ovens for the evening service, so for lunch you may have to settle for choucroute. ① **03 88 92 40 85** ⌂ **www.couronne-dambach.com**

Dambach-la-Ville to Sélestat

About 3 miles south of Dambach-la-Ville along the D35 is the village of Scherwiller. It is tempting to continue straight along the road towards Châtenois, but have a look first at the pretty centre of Scherwiller. A good winemaker to visit here is André Dussourt. ① **03 88 92 10 27** ⌂ **www.domainedussourt.com**

André's son Paul is active in promoting the region's wines, and is involved in Scherwiller's annual *balade gourmand*, a vineyard walk that takes place every July. Contact the estate for details. Dussourt makes a good barrique-aged red Pinot Noir from his holdings in Blienschwiller, as well as an unusual sparkler made only from Riesling.

Like Scherwiller, Châtenois has no Grand Cru vineyards, but Domaine Bernhard-Reibel is a must-visit estate, producing fabulous wines from some exciting local vineyards (see page 300). The large Church of St George otherwise dominates Châtenois; the multi-coloured roof tiles of its medieval tower are reminiscent of those in Burgundy, offering a wink at Alsace's Habsburg past. The *gîte d'étape* below the church is used by hillwalkers and hunters and occasionally as a centre for political refugees.

Another mile finds you in Kintzheim (not to be confused with Kientzheim further south), the last village of the Bas-Rhin. Against the silhouette of Château de Haut-Koenigsbourg, Kintzheim is a pretty place to stop for a quick meal. The Auberge St-Martin claims to be "the emperor of *tartes flammées*", and these are served noon and night. ① **03 88 82 04 78**

Praelatenberg is Kintzheim's Grand Cru vineyard, on whose granitic slopes excellent Rieslings and a range of

ABOVE
That which you are…

OPPOSITE PAGE BOTTOM
The high altar in St Sebastian's Chapel, Dambach-la-Ville

BELOW
The skulls of revolted peasants

other grape varieties are grown. The vineyard's name translates as "Prelate's Mountain," and derives from the days when the powerful abbey at Ebermunster owned it. Most of the vineyards now belong to growers in nearby Orschwiller.

A break in Sélestat

The 3-mile journey from Kintzheim along the D159 to Sélestat takes you away from the wine route, but it is worth the diversion. Before doing this, consider visiting the Volerie des Aigles, the falconry just above Kintzheim in the direction of Haut-Koenigsbourg, since air displays only take place in the afternoon (see also beginning of Day 3 itinerary). Along the road into Sélestat is another big tourist attraction, Cigoland, the region's theme park based around storks, and designed to help with their reintroduction to the region. ① **03 88 92 05 94** 🖰 **www.cigoland.fr**

On approaching Sélestat, continue over two roundabouts, after which cyclists can turn right onto a bike path over the railway lines into the centre of town.

Sélestat is famous for its Humanist Library, bequeathed to the town by scholar Jean de Westhus on his death in 1452. The library now contains works by Martin Bucer, Erasmus and other humanist scholars. It also houses Matthias Ringmann's Cosmographiae Introductio; printed in nearby Saint-Dié in 1507, this is the first document in which the world's westernmost continent was referred to as "America", and is thus considered to be the continent's christening.

Amongst Sélestat's other attractions are its 13th-16th century Church of St George with its flamboyant Gothic western tower, and the beautiful 2000-hectare nature reserve to the east of the town, Le Ried de l'Ill. Ask for details at the tourist office, which also rents bicycles. ① **03 88 58 87 20** 🖰 **www.selestat-tourisme.com**

There are no winemakers in Sélestat, but you can find the region's best wines, and some of its most delicious cuisine, in L'Hostellerie Abbaye la Pommeraie (see page 303). Also drop into Benoît Wach's award-winning patisserie in rue des Chevaliers in the centre of town. ① **03 88 92 12 80**

OPPOSITE PAGE RIGHT
Sélestat's Church of St George

OPPOSITE PAGE LEFT TOP & MIDDLE
Châtenois

OPPOSITE PAGE LEFT BOTTOM
Kintzheim (not Kientzeim!)

Willy Gisselbrecht

5, route du Vin
67650 Dambach-la-Ville

Phone 03 88 92 41 02
Fax 03 88 92 45 50
Info@vins-gisselbrecht.com
www.vins-gisselbrecht.com

The Estate

Following World War II, Willy Gisselbrecht was one of the first farmers in Dambach-la-Ville to convert the whole of his estate to wine production. The family has grown grapes in the village since the 17th century, but prior to Willy's tenure, vines were but a part of a larger polycultural farm.

The vineyard holdings have been expanded slowly, as the family has only bought land when the finest plots have become available. Following from the work of the grandfather, Léon Gisselbrecht has steered the estate towards uncompromising quality, leaving his sons Philippe and Claude with 17 hectares of the finest vineyards in Dambach-la-Ville and nearby Epfig, Scherwiller, Châtenois and Nothalten.

This is quite a large estate that also buys grapes from other quality-conscious growers in the Bas-Rhin. Claude explains that these growers are paid above the market rate for their efforts, as an incentive to good viticulture. But where there is a carrot, there is also a stick. In 2006, many of the grapes that have arrived at the winery have been turned away. "This is a terrible thing for a grower," admits Claude, "but we cannot jeopardise the quality of our wines."

Claude believes that the success of the 2006 vintage will be decided very much in the winery. The quality of the juice is potentially high, but will need careful clarification to eliminate off-flavours in the eventual wine.

Tasting is without appointment from Monday to Saturday. Winery tours are possible, but require advance booking.

If you spend more than €100 here, present this book for a free extra bottle.

UK importers:
Stokes Fine Wines, London
Peter Osbourne, Oxford

LEFT
Claude Gisselbrecht
takes time out from
a difficult harvest

Choice wines:

Riesling 'Schiefferberg' 2004

This is a truly individual single vineyard Riesling, from south-south-east exposed slopes situated just over the first mountain to the west of Dambach-la-Ville.

The schistose soil here is quite different to the granite around Dambach, and the wine has intense, unusual rhubarb aromas. On the palate, it is fresh, intense, ripe and elegant. The style is just off-dry.

This wine drinks very well young, on its own, with lightly spiced Thai food, or even apparently with rhubarb tart!

Pinot Gris Grand Cru 'Frankstein' 2002

Dambach's sprawling Frankstein Grand Cru vineyard is best known for its intense Rieslings, but this Pinot Gris shares the same nervy mineral aromas of the Riesling when grown on the vineyard's granite soils. These soils drain well, which helps prevent rot in wet years.

On the palate, the wine is rich, full and honeyed, with an intense mineral attack, followed by a long passion fruit finish. The wine's concentration is a feature of the vines' low yields, and although its style is medium-dry, it partners well with fish in rich sauces, or even light curries.

Gewurztraminer Grand Cru 'Frankstein' 2002

The beautiful pale golden colour of this wine immediately sets the mouth watering. Its aromas are exotic and include apple compote, honey, ripe melon, peach and mango.

Flavours are of exotic honeyed compote. The wine has a fat, full mouth-feel, with complex mineral notes appearing on a long finish.

An exuberant medium-sweet style makes this Gewurztraminer a good match for exotic fruit desserts, but also sweet and sour Chinese dishes. It will develop for a further ten years in bottle.

Gewurztraminer Vendanges Tardives 2000

Super-ripe 'nobly rotten' grapes give this Gewurz a deep gold, almost amber colour. The aromas are typical of the grape variety: pungently spicy, with hints of orange peel, cloves and other dried fruits, nuts and spices. These are as distinct on the nose as they are on the palate, where the wine's elegance and concentration is reflected in a great length of flavour.

This is a wine to drink on its own, perhaps as an *apéritif*, or with *foie gras*. It could age happily for a further five years.

RIGHT
A wooden grape
picker, carved into an
enormous oak barrel

Domaine Bernhard & Reibel

20, rue de Lorraine
67730 Châtenois

Phone 03 88 82 04 21
Fax 03 88 82 59 65
www.domaine-bernhard-reibel.fr
Bernhard-reibel@wanadoo.fr

The Estate

This estate's story is at once tragic and captivating, owing much to the strength and resolve of Madame Cécile Bernhard-Reibel. The family had been producing its own fine wines for years when, following WWII, Cécile's father was killed in the vineyard by an unexploded landmine. At that time Cécile was only two years old, and the estate reverted to selling its grapes to the local co-operative cellar.

"I bottled my first vintage in 1981," says Cécile with a beaming smile, and since that time the estate has become one of the Bas-Rhin's best reputed. A good friend of the Zind-Humbrechts in Turckheim, Cécile learned much about natural viticulture and, with the help of her son Pierre, the twenty-hectare estate has been farmed organically since 2002.

Pierre Bernhard is an exciting character, a winemaker of rare passion. When I arrived (very late) at the winery, one of the presses had broken down, but Pierre was all grins and solutions. Once the problem had been fixed, Pierre drove me to his own pet vineyard, the Weingarten (wine garden), where he is experimenting with biodynamics. Before entering the Weingarten, we walked through the nearby Meisenberg vineyard, in which you can feel the stillness, the quiet and the warmth. A few paces further, and the Weingarten is a full degree cooler, with a fresh breeze and is noticeably nosier. This, Pierre confirmed, is the magic of terroir. By standing in the vineyards, you have a faint understanding of why their wines taste so radically different.

Phone in advance to visit. Pierre speaks excellent English, and will do so mischievously when you make your first blunder in French! The family should have some slightly older vintages for sale.

UK importers:
Stone, Vine & Sun

LEFT
Pierre Bernhard with broken wine press

OPPOSITE PAGE
Pierre with daughter Félice and son Stanislas, and grandparents

Choice wines:

Riesling 'Rittersberg' 2000
From the hard granitic and crystalline black mica soils above the neighbouring village of Scherwiller, this is a typically nervy Alsace Riesling, with piercing aromas of lime and minerals.

Steely, firm and dry on the palate, this is a powerful wine with the potential to age for another ten years. A versatile food partner, try with cooked fish or spicy Thai dishes.

Riesling 'Weingarten' 1999
Previously the property of the Archbishop of Strasbourg, the 'Wine Garden' is protected from the elements by its surrounding forest. Wholly owned by Bernhard & Reibel and with no neighbours, this is an ideal place for vineyard experiments.

The wine's colour is a brilliant gold, and the nose is sheer honeyed elegance, with fine dried fruits. The palate is rich, with a superb length of flavour. The impression is one of dryness despite the wine's residual sugar, which is perfectly balanced by its body and acidity.

Drinking perfectly now, this is a great partner for lobster bisque.

The two wines that follow are named after Pierre Bernhard's children. Both are wines of incredible character, made in a style that is just drier than Vendanges Tardives. They are harvested from the Rittersberg vineyard on the granitic hillside above Scherwiller.

Gewurztraminer 'Cuvée Félice' 2004
The nose shows delicate, exotic flowers and minerals. The palate is exuberant but wonderfully elegant, with mango flavours and a good concentrated finish.

Drink with exotic fruits and sorbets, or on its own as an *apéritif*.

Pinot Gris 'Cuvée Stanislas' 2002
With a dark gold colour, this wine has complex spicy, almost animal aromas. Its palate shows surprisingly powerful flavours of savoury spice and dried fruits. The finish is long, revealing delicious hints of Amontillado Sherry, with a satisfying thread of acidity.

A great *apéritif*.

Restaurant Le Pressoir de Bacchus

**50, route du Vin
67650 Blienschwiller**

**Phone 03 88 92 43 01
Fax 03 88 92 43 01**

BELOW
'Lady chef' Sylvie Grucker,
with husband Gilles

"Wow, a female chef in France, that's a rarity," were the first, clumsy words I spoke to Sylvie Grucker.

Silence.

"In French, *female* is a term we only apply to animals," she replied, and then started to laugh. "I am a *femme* chef!"

But how did Sylvie come to run a restaurant in a small no-frills wine village in the middle of Alsace? From a family of restaurateurs, she had toyed with the idea of leaving the trade until she saw this place for sale, and fell in love with it.

Sylvie talks much of love when she explains her way of cooking. "I don't like the term *gastronomic,*" she says, "because it implies that the food is expensive. I want to cook something that is refined, but affordable to young people and those with families." The food at Le Pressoir is stylish; the atmosphere is blissfully unpretentious. Locals might pop in for a light bite and a beer, whilst tourists stop to taste the local wines and eat a ludicrously cheap 3-course meal, from €25.

Sylvie's husband Gilles takes care of the service, offering a wine list with a difference: the wines only come from the village of Blienschwiller. Every one of the village's 24 winemakers is represented, making a unique window into its vigneron community. The most expensive wine for sale is a Riesling Grand Cru Winzenberg from Domaine Hubert Metz, at €25. Plenty of wine lists start at that price! The restaurant does sell wines from further afield, but you will have to ask for them specially.

Closed Tuesdays, and Wednesday lunchtimes (and possibly Mondays from 2007); also Wednesday evenings low season.

Present this book for a free apéritif.

It can be difficult to know what to expect from luxury hotel-restaurants, particularly if you wheel up on a bike in a ski-suit on a cold November's day. Under these conditions, "Hello sir, may I help you?" can have a sinister dispatching air about it. But La Pommeraie is a rare example of the great French unpretentious, with an Italian owner. Pasquale Funaro and his wife Christiane offer the kind of friendly welcome you might expect at a rural B&B, and this is felt in the hotel's two restaurants, the "Gastronomic" and the *Apfelstuebel*.

The Gastro is simply one of the finest of its kind, and I'll wager that with Chef Daniel Stein at the stove, one Michelin star might in time become two. Daniel's recipes are classic French with a nod towards the Italian border, combining creative flavours with a wonderful simplicity of presentation. A goose *foie gras* entrée, for example, comes in two parts: one is prepared the traditional way as a *terrine*, the other comes as a creamy mousse served like a *crème brûlée*!

The Apfelstuebel might be rustically Alsatian in décor, but its menus are decidedly refined. The full menu here, including wine, is around €50, and there is one for less than €30 at lunchtimes. The important thing is that the food is prepared in the same kitchen and with the same fresh ingredients and by the same cooks as for the Gastro. The difference is in the style of cuisine, which is more Alsatian, and not in its quality. The extraordinary restaurant team also offers the same impeccable service, with wines chosen by the house's very own lady sommelier, Audrey Meyer.

A *Relais & Château* hotel based in a 12th century Cistercian monastery is going to cost money, and at between €150 and €320, Hôtel La Pommeraie is outside of most sensible budgets. If you can afford it, however, the rooms are enormous, and this really is one of France's classiest hotels.

L'Hostellerie Abbaye la Pommeraie

8, avenue du Maréchal Foch
67600 Sélestat

Phone 03 88 92 07 84
Fax 03 88 92 08 71
www.relaischateaux.com
/pommeraie

RIGHT
Palatial elegance at
L'Hostellerie

TOP
Pommeraie Chef
Daniel Stein

ABOVE
The misty mountains
below Château de
Haut-Koenigsbourg

Day 3 itinerary (17 miles)

Sélestat to Ribeauvillé

Alsace's greatest attractions

As well as including at least two of my favourite winemakers, Day 3 takes you past some of Alsace's most popular tourist sites. My advice is simply to get up early and do as much as possible.

From Sélestat, double back to Kintzheim and follow rue du Général de Gaulle past Jean-Marie Koehly's brightly-coloured cellars. As you leave the village, turn right towards the ruins of Château de Kintzheim, site of the Volerie des Aigles, France's first falconry. Spectacular air displays take place here between April and October at 3 pm and 4 pm, and also at 5 pm in the summer months on weekends and bank holidays. ☽ **03 88 92 84 33** ⏚ **www.voleriedesaigles.com**

A further mile and a half's climb takes you to the Montagne des Singes, "Monkey Mountain", a walk-through nature reserve where over 300 endangered Barbary Macaques from the Atlas Mountains live. These monkeys seem totally unfazed by tourists or by the late

autumn cold, and everyone is provided with a free handful of popcorn with which to feed them. One escaped during my visit, and did a Yogi Bear with a family's picnic before returning self-consciously to the enclosure.
① 03 88 92 11 09 ☝ www.montagnedessinges.com

Beyond the Montagne des Singes is Alsace's most visited tourist attraction and the region's only fully restored castle, Château de Haut-Koenigsbourg. On the map, this might look like a horrific five-mile climb for any cyclist, but it really is surprisingly benign.

Standing at an altitude of 755m, the Château is bisected by the ancient wine and grain trade route (from north to south) and by the salt and silver road (from east to west); its strategic importance has been well understood since the 12th century. Originally a pair of châteaux, extensive rebuilding and reinforcement took place in the 1500s to help withstand the new weapon of the age, that which led to the abandonment and ruin of almost all of the region's castles: the cannon.

The Château's exceptional restoration dates from the first years of the 20th century, a time when Alsace was under German control. German Emperor Wilhelm II had a personal interest in the project, considering himself the natural successor of the Habsburg and Hohenstaufen dynasties to whom the Château once belonged. He entrusted the restoration to architect Bodo Ebhardt, with the aim of creating a museum of medieval life.
① 03 88 82 50 60 ☝ www.monum.fr

Back on the wine road

From the Château de Haut-Koenigsbourg, either follow the road back down to Kintzheim and take the D35 through Orschwiller to St-Hippolyte; or turn right at the sign for St-Hippolyte shortly after beginning the descent.

St-Hippolyte is another beautiful village with a red vinous speciality, Rouge de St-Hippolyte. The address to head for is the wonderfully named Domaine du Windmuehl on the route du Vin. ① 03 89 73 00 21
☝ www.vins-bleger.com

If the climb to Haut-Koenigsbourg has left you tired or peckish, why not plan a break at St-Hippolyte's Hôtel-Restaurant du Parc (see page 314).

Rodern and Rorschwihr

An unassuming little village, Rodern's hidden magic lies in its unusual blue sandstone and granite soils, making its vineyards perfect for growing the Pinot Noir, the village's most planted grape. The winemaker to call on is Charles Koehly, on the aptly named rue du Pinot Noir

Day 3 at a glance
Itinerary	304 – 309
Wineries	310 – 313
Restaurants	314 – 315

BELOW
Château de Kintzheim

BOTTOM
Cheeky monkey

that runs through the village. ① 03 88 73 00 61

The next village is Rorschwihr, and beneath the imposing belfry of its church, awaits a surprise in Maison Rolly-Gassman. I knew that this estate made good wines, but I had not previously understood just *how* good they are. Having worked at estates such as Zind-Humbrecht in Turckheim (see page 336) and Domaine Huet in Vouvray (see page 114), Pierre R-G took over from his parents Marie-Thérèse and Louis in 1997. He explains that Rorschwihr is sited at the beginning of the geological fault line of Ribeauvillé, and that the village consequently has an incomparable variety of different soil types, 21 to be exact. This partly explains the massive range of wines available at the estate: there were 58 on the list when I visited, plus others available on request!

Pierre is passionate about the winemaking history of his village, which grew rich under a partnership of religious and secular authorities. Before the Revolution, the wines of Rorschwihr were so well renowned for their ageing potential, that they were never drunk before they had matured in bottle for at least 25 years.

Maison Rolly-Gassman is unusual for the high proportion of *Vendanges Tardives* and *Sélection des Grains Nobles* wines it produces. Amazingly, in 2006 all of the estate's Riesling, Pinot Gris and Gewurztraminer grapes produced these styles of wine (did they harvest too late?). A further surprise is the red Pinot Noirs the estate makes from its holdings in Rodern. The lightest of these is similar to very fine Sancerre Rouge, but the most concentrated are enough to give plenty of great burgundies a run for their money. ① 03 89 73 63 28

Before leaving Rorschwihr, climb the hill through the village to its small nature reserve, from where you get the best views of the town and its vineyards.

Before arriving in Bergheim, you should have made an appointment at Alsace's finest wine estate, Domaine Marcel Deiss (see page 310). Otherwise, Domaine Gustave Lorenz next door makes excellent wines ① 03 89 73 22 22, as do Domaines Freyburger ① 03 89 73 63 78 ⏚ www.freyburger-gc.fr and Emile Halbeisen ① 03 89 73 63 81 ⏚ www.halbeisen-vins.com

Seeking refuge in Bergheim

Known to locals as "little Riquewihr without the tourists", take time to stroll around Bergheim's 14th century city walls, onto which many of its houses are built. Then as you enter through the imposing Gothic *Porte Haute*, "Upper Gate", don't miss the stone carved "Lack'mi", the portrait of a pursued criminal dropping his drawers and showing his backside before disappearing inside the

ABOVE
Château de Haut-Koenigsbourg

**OPPOSITE PAGE
TOP**
Bergheim: a haven for criminals...

**OPPOSITE PAGE
BOTTOM**
Entering Bergheim

city's boundaries. Bergheim was a haven for the perpetrators of "excusable and non-premeditated crimes" from the year 1361.

But the town's tolerant attitude was not extended to witches, and in the Maison des Sorcières opposite the church you can learn about the witch-hunts that took place between 1582 and 1683. Open from Wednesday to Sunday in July and August, then on Sundays in September and October – and only in the afternoons.
℗ 03 89 73 31 98

For an excellent meal and even better wines, book a table at Bergheim's best restaurant, Wistub du Sommelier (see page 315).

Getting to, and tasting in, Ribeauvillé

From Bergheim's *Porte Haute*, take the last exit off the mini-roundabout and follow signs onto the D1b to Ribeauvillé. Cyclists can turn left before Domaine Marcel Deiss, and then immediately right onto the vineyard path. Head right at the small sign for Ribeauvillé, and this path leads into the centre of town. Cyclists will therefore need to double back onto the D1b to visit Ribeauvillé's most exciting grower, André Kientzler (see page 312).

Ribeauvillé is home to some of Alsace's finest *négociant* houses; the most prestigious of which is Trimbach. Trimbach is most famous for its Clos Saint-Hune, a small parcel of vines within the larger Rosacker Grand Cru vineyard above the village of Hunawihr. The Trimbachs' refusal to mention the name Rosacker on the wine's label is a defiant protest that the rest of the vineyard does not match Clos Saint-Hune in quality; a typically Alsatian two-fingers at the appellation authorities. Make an appointment to visit and taste at the Trimbach cellars. ✉ **15, route de Bergheim**
℗ 03 89 73 60 30

As you enter Ribeauvillé's old town through the eastern gate, it is worth also visiting the Louis Sipp estate. The Sipps claim to be growers first and merchants second, as most of their production comes from their own organic vineyards. The Rieslings grown on Ribeauvillé's Grand Cru Kirchberg and the Gewurztraminer from the Grand Cru Osterberg are particularly delicious. One of the real benefits of tasting here is that you are likely to find wines with a few years bottle age. ✉ **5, Grand Rue** ℗ **03 89 73 60 01**

Established in 1895, the Cave Vinicole de Ribeauvillé claims to be the oldest French winemaking co-op... although Alsace was German at the time of its creation! It is certainly one of the region's best reputed and most stylish, making particularly good Rieslings and

Gewurztraminers from Grand Crus Altenberg de Bergheim and the Osterberg above Ribeauvillé.
✉ **2, route de Colmar** ✆ **03 89 73 61 80**

Ribeauvillé for the curious

Ribeauvillé is the first of the Haut-Rhin's great tourist spots, although it is large enough to feel like a real working town. In the Middle Ages, this was the seat of the powerful lords of Ribeaupierre, who imposed order on the town in the 11th century after the anarchy following the collapse of Charlemagne's empire. Their three ruined castles still dominate the forested hills above Ribeauvillé.

Ribeauvillé has a good tourist office ✆ **03 89 49 08 40**, which provides details of the town's historical buildings and the highlights along its medieval main street and surrounding secluded alleys. Behind the church on place de la Mairie is the Convent of the Sisters of the Divine Providence. You can visit and taste the nuns' own wines although, to be honest, divine providence has yet to shine on these. ✆ **03 89 73 60 71**

Turn left off this side road onto rue du Lutzelbach to find the pedestrian pathways that lead towards the three castles. From the car park, you can either walk

BELOW
The village of Rodern

straight through the forest, or turn left up Passage Jeanelle to climb through the vineyards.

Ribeauvillé for the hungry

Long Ribeauvillé's finest restaurant, the Michelin-starred Haut-Ribeaupierre was for sale when I visited, but it is bound to stay one of Alsace's best addresses: 1, route de Bergheim. ① **03 89 73 87 63**

The other flawless gastronomic option is Au Valet de Coeur, which is a little way out of town. Continue through the centre of Ribeauvillé onto the D416, and then climb the hill for two miles. Menus here are €35 to €80; room prices are surprisingly reasonable.
① **03 89 73 64 14** ⌖ **www.valetdecoeur.fr**

For something more rustic back in Ribeauvillé, try Wistub Pfifferhuss. Hiding behind one of the many splendid facades along Ribeauvillé's main street, Grand'rue, this is where to look for fresh authentic Alsatian cooking and a great wine list. Pfifferhuss is as popular with locals as it is with tourists, so be prepared to reserve a table in advance. ✉ **14, Grand Rue**
① **03 89 73 62 28**

Domaine Marcel Deiss

15, route du Vin
68750 Bergheim

Phone 03 89 73 63 37
Fax 03 89 73 32 67
Marceldeiss@marceldeiss.fr
www.marceldeiss.fr

BELOW & OPPOSITE
Jean-Michel Deiss,
Alsace's most fearsome
winemaker!

The Estate

It is almost unfair to begin a day's tasting at Domaine Marcel Deiss, since a visit here requires at least a day's subsequent quiet reflection. These are some of the world's greatest wines, and in Alsace they are, for me at least, the first among illustrious equals.

Jean-Michel Deiss is one of the great polymaths of winemaking: a geologist, historian, philosopher, and a total nutcase. He has run the estate since 1975, and admits that for the first ten years he was unhappy with the wines he was making. These were highly acclaimed varietal wines, but Jean-Michel hankered after a purer expression of his vineyards' terroirs. One day, he had a complaint that one of his Rieslings was very nice but "didn't taste much like a Riesling", and this was the straw that broke the camel's back.

Henceforward, Jean-Michel created 'field blends' in his best vineyard sites, in the way familiar to his grandfather in the 1940s. He began to replant different vine varieties alongside one another, harvesting the grapes together. Since then, these 'terroir wines' have been labelled only by vineyard name, and each is the expression of a single plot of land by different grape varieties.

For Jean-Michel, vines need to live like monks in the vineyard, without luxuries such as fertiliser, and so transcend their suffering to bear divine fruit. The grapes, on the other hand, need the most loving tenderness in the winery. Many speak of Riesling's propensity to develop intense petrol aromas with age, but Jean-Michel believes this is too often the result of rough treatment: aromas such as these come from the fruit crying out in pain, its self-expression distorted by the violence of mankind! It seems almost trivial to point out that the estate is biodynamic.

You are as likely to meet the charming Marie-Hélène, who speaks good English, as you are to taste with her fearsome spouse.

UK importers:
Graham Garner, Folly Wines (Agent)
Lea & Sandeman

Choice wines:

The first three wines are 'Premiers Crus in waiting' (for changes in appellation rules). All have an ageing potential of between 10 and 15 years.

Rotenberg 2002

The iron-rich limestone soils of the Rotenberg are the most ancient in Bergheim. From Riesling and Pinot Gris vines, the wine's nose is of mandarin, ripe lemons and even peach. The palate shows a complex exotic intensity, with a firm citrus acidity, which lingers on a powerful spicy finish.

A very versatile food wine, its freshness and finesse make a good accompaniment to fish, but it has sufficient body to suit white meats and enough energy for exotic, Korean dishes.

Schoffweg 2003

The 'Ewe's Way' vineyard is a breezy, west-facing parcel of friable limestone soil, perfect for growing Riesling and Pinot vines without the risk of rot.

The wine is characterised by its intense vanilla aromas, with hints of cloves and iodine. The vanilla notes were present even before Jean-Michel started ageing the wine in *barriques*, prompting his own study into wines grown on similar soils in other regions. He found that these aromas were common to all, and that the wines did tend to benefit from oak ageing.

The wine comes alive on the palate, where it shows a huge unctuous intensity, giving the impression of sweetness even in the absence of any residual sugar.

Burg 2003

Jean-Michel describes the marl soils of the Bergheim Burg as "a cemetery", the remains of the creatures killed by the cold following the Jurassic age. And the wine's nose is a sombre mystical one, with notes of incense, cloves and nutmeg.

Again on the palate, the wine is more open, with an almost exotic attack and a rich, smoky finish. Almost fifty grammes per litre of residual sugar become hidden in the general balance of the wine with a few years' bottle age.

A great partner for saffron rice and Indian cuisine.

Schoenenbourg 2002

This wine comes from a field blend in the Grand Cru Schoenenbourg. The vineyard's slopes face south towards Riquewihr, and are composed of gypsum marl soils covered by sandstone.

With aromas more mystical even than the Burg, hints of incense smoke and resin dominate a still very young wine. Jean-Michel describes this as an "austere wine from the Protestant town of Riquewihr", with a richness and colour that is hidden from a first glance.

The palate is far richer, with explosively spicy flavours. A less pronounced acidity is further softened by the wine's richness and fullness of body.

This is a wine that could improve over twenty years.

André Kientzler

**50, route de Bergheim
68150 Ribeauvillé**

Phone 03 89 73 67 10
Fax 03 89 73 35 81
domaine@vinskientzler.com

The Estate

From Château les Crayères in Reims to the cosiest Alsatian winstub, André Kientzler has for years captivated the restaurant trade with his vinous creations. People order the wines in restaurants; the following day, they're knocking on André's door. And meeting with the man himself is every bit as exciting as the wines he makes.

A tasting with André begins with a discussion of the terroirs of Ribeauvillé, followed by a comfortable silence as you dig in. André doesn't want to influence your judgement, as he believes that tasting is a purely subjective matter. But your own pleasure will be reflected in the vigneron's face as the conversation starts back up.

André is honest about the problems with the 2006 harvest and admits he has had to rack each vat of juice twice in order to separate the particles of rot and maintain finesse in the wines. He believes that the Riesling particularly could be of a high quality, but is ready to de-classify his Grand Cru wines to simple *appellation Alsace* if the wines fall short of brilliance.

In 1972, the Kientzler winery moved from the centre of Ribeauvillé (now André's sister's hotel) to a new vineyard site on the main road towards Bergheim. From the windows of the tasting room, you get a wonderful view of the family's vines in the Osterberg Grand Cru; part of an impressive 12-hectare estate that also includes parcels in Grand Crus Geisberg and Kirchberg de Ribeauvillé.

André Kientzler is a keen cyclist, who's empathetic dislike for rain inspired a much-appreciated lift back to Kaysersberg on a wet late October afternoon, with my bike in the boot of his car.

UK importers:
H & H Bancroft
Stone, Vine & Sun
Vine Trail, Bristol

LEFT
André Kientzler stands opposite Grand Cru vineyard Kirchberg de Ribeauvillé

Choice wines:

Auxerrois "K" 2004

The Auxerrois grape is not allowed into the Grand Cru wines of Alsace, but the grapes that go into this wine are nonetheless planted in the Grand Cru Kirchberg vineyard. Hence the "K".

Fifty year-old vines, low yields, and grapes picked at full maturity make this an Auxerrois of Grand Cru intensity. Many of these grapes were attacked by noble rot in 2004, but a good proportion was not, giving the wine a good balance of freshness and concentration. Aromas of pink grapefruits and honey give way to an intense, fruity palate with good minerality.

Just drier than the *Vendanges Tardives* style, enjoy as an apéritif or with salads and terrines.

Muscat de Kirchberg Grand Cru 2003

The Muscat Ottonel thrives on the sunny sandstone and marl slopes of the Kirchberg. This wine is a delicate lemon-green in colour, with fresh floral and grapey aromas, infused with wild herbs.

In the hot sun of 2003, these grapes were harvested at the end of August to maintain their freshness of flavour and acidity. The wine is fermented fully dry, showing delicacy and a great length of flavour.

Drink as an apéritif or with fresh asparagus.

Riesling de Geisberg Grand Cru 2002

Doesn't five years change everything! This 2002 is drinking perfectly, showing beautiful honeyed aromas of passion fruit and intense minerals. On the palate, the wine's freshness confirms that it could mature for a further ten years without much trouble.

The south facing Geisberg is contiguous with the Kirchberg to its east, but the sandy marl slopes here are steeper, planted in terraces to make vineyard work possible.

This wine would be perfect with a nice big lobster.

Gewurztraminer Vendanges Tardives 2002

From small parcels of vines reserved for the growing of late harvest wines, this Gewurz shows intense, sweet aromas of grapes, fresh lychee and even sweat (your own, when you actually like the smell!).

On the palate, the concentration of the wine is formidable, with a well-balanced sweetness and great length. This is a difficult wine not to swallow, even in a professional tasting.

A perfect match for *foie gras* or exotic fruit desserts.

If you get the chance, try also the super-concentrated and luscious *Sélection des Grains Nobles* from the Grand Cru Geysberg vineyard. The estate only makes this wine once every ten years, when conditions are perfect.

ABOVE
The Kientzler family at work in the winery

Hotel-Restaurant Le Parc
6, rue du Parc
68590 Saint-Hippolyte

Phone 03 89 73 00 06
Fax 03 89 73 04 30
www.le-parc.com

BELOW
The family Kientzel on
their restaurant terrace

When Joseph Kientzel and his wife Carmen took over Le Parc in 1982, the restaurant served simple *plats du jour*, with a small selection of local wines. With Joseph as chef, the cuisine evolved and an excellent wine list developed. The Kientzels are friends with Alsace's most famous vignerons, but Joseph likes also to represent young winemaking talent in Saint-Hippolyte, such as the dynamic Marc Bléger of Domaine Hubert & Bléger.

In 2005, the gears shifted again when Joseph employed Emmanuel Perrin as *chef de cuisine*. Having worked exclusively in Michelin-starred establishments, Emmanuel has brought with him an impeccable attention to detail and a hunger for recognition in the gastronomic world. When not at the stove, Emmanuel combs the vineyards and forests for wild herbs and fruits, and his menus change according to what he finds.

The style of cuisine is traditional but with taste combinations intended to challenge the conservative palate. Menus in the gastronomic restaurant are not 'set'; prices depend rather on how many courses you eat. These start at just over €30 for two courses, rising to €65 for the *menu de dégustation*. The hotel's simpler *winstub* serves a *menu de terroir* for €20.

If booking a room in the hotel, cyclists can phone ahead to have their luggage picked up – a big advantage for those anticipating the climb to Château de Haut-Koenigsbourg! Rooms are €72-160.

Closed midday Monday and Tuesday; also for the second half of January and at the end of June.

The Wistub was created in 1984 by "France's best sommelier" Jean-Marie Stoeckel, giving young chef Patrick Schneider a lot to live up to when he and his wife Antje took over in 2000. But an ever-improving wine list has kept pace with Patrick's deliciously rustic brand of cuisine, and the Wistub du Sommelier now enjoys greater popularity than ever amongst locals.

Patrick likes to cook with simple, country ingredients, each one of his recipes telling its own story. "You don't need to buy lobsters and truffles to serve something great," he says. "When I make my *presskopf*, I don't mess around: heads, trotters etc…it all goes in." Conversely, however, Patrick only serves the best goose *foie gras*, since he finds its flavour more refined than that of duck.

Patrick tells how he got the secret recipe for his wonderful Mediterranean-inspired *tartare de boeuf* from a Spaniard whilst he worked part time in a pizzeria years earlier. He tried once to remove this *entrée* from the Wistub menu, and was almost lynched by local diners. Try it with a glass of Vincent Stoeffler's Klevener de Heiligenstein and you will see why.

Menus start at €16, and à la carte prices are extremely reasonable, allowing an exciting and varied choice of different courses.

Leave this book where Antje can see it, and you might get (even) more generous portions!

Closed Tuesday evening and Wednesday.

Wistub du Sommelier
51, Grand' Rue
68750 Bergheim

Phone 03 89 73 69 99
Fax 03 89 73 36 58
www.wistub-du-sommelier.com

RIGHT
Proud chef:
Patrick Schneider

ABOVE
Lunch at a
ferme auberge in
the mountains

Day 4 itinerary (10 miles +)
Alsace's most famous wine villages

Ribeauvillé to Riquewihr

From Ribeauvillé, you are heading south to the village of
Hunawihr, and there are at least two ways of getting
there. Simplest is to follow the D1b from Ribeauvillé,
turning right into Hunawihr a mile later.

The direct vineyard road is more picturesque, but the
climb is a steep one. From place de l'Hôtel de Ville in
Ribeauvillé, follow rue Klott up towards the town's
southern bypass, then cross over into rue du Vignoble.
On the steepest stretch just before you enter the forest,
the stone wall to your right supports Zind-Humbrecht's
Clos Windsbuhl vineyard, entirely planted with Pinot Gris.
The vines are cultivated biodynamically, and you may well
see sheep grazing on the grass between their rows. The
descent into Hunawihr passes through the village's
Grand Cru Rosacker vineyard. Here Riesling and
Gewurztraminer vines are planted on marl-limestone soils;
a helpful roadside map of the vineyard provides detail.

Hunawihr is another village whose beauty has received

official recognition. The winemakers to visit are the Mittnacht Frères, in the lower part of the village. The estate has important holdings in the Grand Cru vineyards of Rosacker, Osterberg, Muehlforst and Mandelberg. The wines are made biodynamically and are extremely good value. The family also has bed & breakfast rooms available, and owns the village winstub Suzel. ✉ **27, route de Ribeauvillé** ✆ **03 89 73 30 85**

Back down on the main road (D1b) between Ribeauvillé and Riquewihr is the Reintroduction Centre for Storks and Otters. Here you can learn how sea mammals catch their prey, watch the otters through a glass tunnel and, in the spring, listen to the chatter of the newborn baby storks. ✆ **03 89 73 72 62** 🖱 **www.cigogne-loutre.com**

From Hunawihr, rue de Riquewihr is the continuation of the cycle path, and perfectly suitable for cars. The road descends into Riquewihr just to the west of the Grand Cru Schoenenbourg that overlooks the town.

Riquewihr

Riquewihr has more to offer the casual tourist than any other town in Alsace. Many of its medieval buildings remain intact, as do the town's ancient ramparts and the towers that surround it. Most impressive is the Tower of Dolder, at the top of rue du Général de Gaulle. The tower was built in 1291 as a watchtower and belfry. The bell could be used to warn of impending attack, of which there was such a constant danger that the tower was reinforced by a second fortress wall in 1500.

Of the town's several museums, the Thieves' Tower and Winegrower's House is the most fun, situated near the Tower of Dolder in rue des Juifs. Apart from learning how criminals were tortured during the Middle Ages, there are regular exhibitions, like the fascinating one of the town's occupation by the Nazis in the 1940s. ✆ **03 89 47 92 15** Among Riquewihr's other unmissable visits is the Féerie de Noël, Kathe Wohlfahrt's perennial Christmas shop, which draws you into a childhood dream of handmade toys, gifts and decorations. ✉ **27, rue du Cerf** 🖱 **www.feeriedenoel.com**

Wine, food and beer in Riquewihr

The wines of Riquewihr have enjoyed renown since the Middle Ages, when their firm structure allowed them to be exported across the Rhine into Germany and further north to the Low Countries, Scandinavia and Britain. This is also where many of Alsace's big négociants are based, the most important of which is Hugel & Fils.

Hugel does not actively encourage cellar visits, but

Day 4 at a glance

Itinerary	316 – 321
Wineries	322 – 325
Restaurants	326 – 327

BELOW
A rustic bite

BOTTOM
The town and vineyards of Riquewihr

you can taste some of Alsace's most famous wines in the house's boutique on rue de la 1ère Armée.
① 03 89 47 92 15 ⌁ www.hugel.com

Better geared-up for tourists is Dopff au Moulin, on the roundabout just east of the old town. The speciality here is sparkling wine, which represents about half of the house's production. Tastings are free for individuals; phone in advance to join a cellar tour. ① 03 89 49 09 69 ⌁ www.dopff-au-moulin.fr

I was looking for the young dynamic winemaker making waves and ruffling feathers in Riquewihr. The closest thing is Franck Mittnacht, at Domaine Mittnacht-Klack, on rue des Tuileries just outside the old town to the south-west. The estate's name may sound like an unpleasant nocturnal experience, but the wines are very good, requiring time to show their best. Franck Mittnacht may be short with you on the subject of cellar tours, but tastings are free and without appointment. ① 03 89 47 92 54

If you're looking for somewhere to eat in Riquewihr, you will be spoiled for choice. Top of the pile is La Table du Gourmet (see page 326), but there are numerous excellent *winstubs*, including La Table's fashionable new sister establishment d'Brendelstub. Try also Au Tire Bouchon, the winstub attached to the cellars of Maison Zimmer on the main street. Hearty menus begin at €16, and this one kicks off with a deliciously creamy choucroute soup, followed by very fine...choucroute, and a dessert you almost certainly won't have room to finish.
① 03 89 47 91 61 ⌁ www.riquewihr-zimmer.com

And why not indulge the beer monster by making an appointment with Gilbert Holl, who makes strong, delicious country brews at the Brasserie Artisanale de Riquewihr. The brewery is near the Dopff au Moulin cellars, at 8, avenue Jacques Preiss. ① 03 89 73 70 34 ⌁ www.gilbertholl.com

The road to Beblenheim, or through the mountains

The vineyard road (and cycle path) follows the geological fault line south from Riquewihr, passing between the Grand Cru vineyards Furstentum (to the east) and Schlossberg (to the west) before descending into the village of Kientzheim. This is known as "the three milligram road" as, in local myth, *gendarmes* don't patrol it after hours with their breathalysers! This route is extremely pretty, but it cuts out the first part of the itinerary that follows. Another far more energetic, and less vinous, option is to climb the hill west from Riquewihr into the *Pays Welsch* via Fréland and a group of other ancient Celtic settlements in the

Vosges. This road rejoins the N415 and a cycle path back down the valley into Kaysersberg. Plan at least half a day by bike for this energetic detour into the forest.

To continue along the wine road, leave Riquewihr to the east past the cellars of Dopff au Moulin, and briefly join the D1b back towards Ribeauvillé, turning right into the small hillside village of Zellenberg. The big name here is Jean Becker, but I would advise against visiting. The inviting signs are for Bentley drivers, not cyclists.

If everything about Zellenberg's Michelin-starred Restaurant Le Maximilien ① 03 89 47 99 69 was as good as Chef Jean-Michel Eblin's cooking, this might be Alsace's best restaurant, but the wine list is uninspired and the atmosphere is a little chilly, so I would try the more rustic Auberge du Froehn near the village centre. ① 03 89 47 81 57

Beblenheim to Kientzheim

The descent towards Beblenheim takes you through the Grand Cru Froehn to the north of Beblenheim's more famous vineyard, the Sonnenglanz. At the D3, turn right into Beblenheim and then left into rue Jean Macé to visit the village's star producer, Domaine Bott-Geyl (see page 322). Beblenheim is a fairly unassuming village, only notable for being the birthplace of Jean Macé, founder of the Society of Public Libraries in the Upper Rhine. The village co-operative cellar "Au Château" also makes very good wines. ① 03 89 47 90 02  www.cave-beblenheim.com

Beblenheim is the last of the pretty villages before Kientzheim, so advice to cyclists is to follow rue du Petit Château past Domaine Bott-Geyl, and then fork right into the vineyards towards Sigolsheim and then Kientzheim. Motorists continue on the main road through Beblenheim, and then turn left onto the D10 through Mittelwihr and Bennwihr. The cycle path briefly rejoins the D10, but cyclists can then turn right onto the path that skirts the foot of the Mambourg Grand Cru vineyard. Motorists continue to the roundabout and turn right at the sign for Kientzheim.

Kientzheim

You won't need much persuading to visit Kientzheim as you approach its medieval city walls with their beautifully preserved cylindrical turrets. Kientzheim's Château de la Confrérie Saint-Etienne is home to Alsace's own robed brotherhood, whose role it has been to protect and promote the wines of Alsace since the 14th century. The Confréres' history is therefore much longer than that of the more famous Chevaliers de Tastevin in Burgundy. Like the Chevaliers, the Confréres organise annual tastings to recognise and reward the region's finest wines, which go to market bearing their "Sigillé", or seal of quality.  www.confrerie-st-etienne.com

Towards the end of November, the Château also plays host to the annual

ABOVE
The Tower of Dolder

OPPOSITE PAGE
TOP
The vineyards of
Riquewihr in autumn

OPPOSITE PAGE
BOTTOM
The narrow streets
of Riquewihr

presentation of Alsace's Grands Crus, when growers uncork their recently bottled Grand Cru wines for the public and the trade. The Château houses the excellent Alsace Wine and Vineyards Museum, which acts as a small village tourist office during the summer.
ⓒ **03 89 78 21 36**

A tasting in Kientzheim, then on to Kaysersberg

Whilst strolling through Kientzheim's cobbled streets, have a look at the waterway that was diverted through the village to provide for the town's hygiene in the 12th century. Imagine how it looked when this small canal was the town's bustling main street. The essential estate visit is Domaine Paul Blanck (see page 324), but the Kientzheim & Kaysersberg co-operative cellar also makes very good, and rather cheaper, wines. ✉ **10, rue des Vieux Moulins**
ⓒ **03 89 47 13 19**

Kaysersberg is another mile along the D28, or by the cycle path that runs along the lower reaches of the Schlossberg Grand Cru vineyard. On the left-hand side of the road before entering Kaysersberg is one of the region's most prestigious wine estates, Domaine Weinbach. Set behind its own vineyard enclosure, the Clos des Capucins, this beautiful estate is unusual in being run by three ladies, Colette Faller and her two daughters Catherine and Laurence. Visiting Domaine Weinbach is a little tricky by Alsatian standards, but certainly worth a try, since the wines are absolutely brilliant. Avoid Mondays, Fridays and weekends. ⓒ **03 89 47 13 21**
⌂ **www.domaineweinbach.com**

Kaysersberg

From its eastern ramparts, Kaysersberg follows the River Weiss upstream into its eponymous valley, Alsace's historical link with its sister region Lorraine. Kaysersberg is equal to Riquewihr in architectural beauty, but its lack of any large wine merchant houses gives it a more relaxed, rural feel.

Kaysersberg was an important trading post from the 13th century when King Adolphe of Nassau made it an Imperial town. Protected by its imposing castle high above the River's north bank, many of Kaysersberg's medieval ramparts remain, although the town needed extensive reconstruction following the devastation of 1944. From behind Place de la Mairie outside the tourist office, take rue du Château up the footpath to explore the castle's ruins. The view from the Château's turret makes it worth climbing its spiralled staircase, but be prepared to take a few steps in pitch-darkness!

ABOVE & TOP
The vineyards of Bergheim

**OPPOSITE PAGE
TOP LEFT**
Flammé & Co.

**OPPOSITE PAGE
TOP RIGHT**
Kaysersberg Castle behind Grand Cru vineyard, the Schlossberg

**OPPOSITE PAGE
MIDDLE**
Winstub du Chambard

OPPOSITE PAGE BOTTOM
Fairytale streets in Kaysersberg

Domaine Bott-Geyl

**1, rue du Petit Château
68980 Beblenheim**

Phone 03 89 47 90 04
Fax 03 89 47 97 33
www.bott-geyl.com
info@bott-geyl.com

The Estate

I forget the vineyard name, the vintage and the grape variety, but I am sure the first Alsace wine I ever tasted came from Domaine Bott-Geyl. I remember then being seduced by the pure opulence of the wine's flavours and, for the pleasure they give, these are still amongst my favourites from the Haut-Rhin.

One rarely meets a more meticulous winemaker than Jean-Christophe Bott. Whatever you may ask of Jean-Christophe, you will never get less than a full answer. The estate has been organic since the year 2000 and entirely biodynamic since 2002, but Jean-Christophe's is not the quasi-religious fervour of some of the movement's proponents. His goal is quite simply "to give birth to a natural, healthy product of high quality." And what more could you ask?

The family's winemaking history dates from the 18th century, but it was Jean-Christophe's father Edouard Bott who established today's estate in 1953. Within forty years, plantings had increased from 4 to 13 hectares, and by 1960 the estate was bottling all of its own wines.

Jean-Christophe brings to his winemaking the experience he gained from working in various French and New World wine regions. On a visit to the Beblenheim estate today, you are as likely to meet a Japanese intern as an apprentice winemaker from New Zealand, such is the openness of Bott-Geyl and the prestige the domaine's wines enjoy.

UK importer:
Majestic Wine Warehouse

Choice wines:

Muscat de Riquewihr "Grains Passerillés" 2003

From the unnamed soils of Riquewihr, the hot sun of 2003 did something extraordinary with these grapes. "Grains Passerillés" means that the grapes were shrivelled when picked, concentrating their flavours. Yields were incredibly low at 25 hl per hectare.

The aromas are complex and unusual, of menthol and aniseed spice; its mouth-feel is similarly spicy, but with surprisingly good acidity, helped, according to Jean-Christophe, by a long period of lees contact before the wine was bottled.

With 25 grammes per litre residual sugar, the wine nevertheless feels quite dry. Ideal as an apéritif, or with fresh melon.

Pinot Gris Grand Cru Furstentum 2002

The pebbly limestone-marl soils of the Furstentum overlook the village of Kientzheim. A direct southern exposure allows the growth of a semi-Mediterranean vegetation around the vines.

A warm nose of intense, spiced pears and apple *confit* is typical of the vineyard site. On the palate, the attack is an explosion of candied pears, developing onto a long spicy finish.

The wine's firm acidity gives the impression of dry ripeness. Try with strong cheeses or white meats in creamy sauces.

Pinot Gris Grand Cru Sonnenglanz 2002

Beblenheim's own Grand Cru vineyard, this is the site on which this estate produces its finest wines. The soils are of stony limestone, giving generous wines that age well.

Elegant mineral aromas dominate the nose, but the palate is fierier, showing pears and grapefruit, with a sweet, exuberant and spicy mid-palate. The Sonnenglanz generally produces more restrained wines than the Furstentum, but the former site gave wines with a marked exoticism in 2002.

Sonnenglanz is an excellent site for the development of 'botrytis', and this shows on the wine's long, honeyed finish. This is an excellent partner for pan-fried *foie gras* or cheese.

Gewurztraminer Grand Cru Sonnenglanz Vendanges Tardives 2002

With a very bright golden colour, this Gewurz is already showing open exotic aromas of spiced mandarins and cinnamon. On the palate, intense peach and mandarin flavours are followed by a deliciously toasty finish. Jean-Christophe explains that this final flavour comes from a slight oxidation of the grapes on the vine during the 'botrytisation' process. He admits that this worried him at first, but that the resulting flavours are more wonderful than he had ever hoped.

With well over 100 grammes per litre residual sugar, this wine resembles a *Sélection des Grains Nobles*. Try with sweet and spicy desserts.

ABOVE
Jean-Christophe
Bott pours wine for
Japanese sommeliers

Domaine Paul Blanck

32, Grand' Rue
68240 Kientzheim

Phone 03 89 78 23 56
Fax 03 89 47 16 45
www.blanck.com
info@blanck.com

The Estate

This estate's name is intimately connected with that of the Schlossberg vineyard that rises above the villages of Kientzheim and Kaysersberg. As early as 1927, Paul Blanck successfully lobbied to make the Schlossberg a pilot for the then conceptual Alsace Grand Cru appellation. In 1975, with Paul's sons Marcel and Bernard at the helm, the Schlossberg became Alsace's first Grand Cru vineyard.

A generation later and a new dynamism has taken shape in the cousins Philippe and Frédéric Blanck, who have increased the estate from 24 to 36 hectares of vines, more than a third of which are planted on Grand Cru soil. Frédéric is "the artist", and according to Philippe, this explains his sometimes taciturn nature. With a respect for people as strong as his passion for wine, the huge bear-like Philippe Blanck is the very epitome of Alsatian hospitality – and Jeremy Clarkson's most affable doppelgänger. My simple tasting with Philippe turned into a day's exploration of Alsatian gastronomy and the hidden wonders of the Vosges mountains. Philippe is currently one of the Alsace's most active forces in the promotion of the region's wines abroad.

Philippe's father Marcel might now be in his seventies, but he still cycles more than fifty kilometres a day, and regularly sets off for other wine regions with nothing but bike, panniers and a Michelin Locale. Phone in advance and you might be lucky enough to join Marcel for an afternoon's spin in the vineyards.

UK importers:
Adnams, Waitrose
John Armitt, London

OPPOSITE PAGE TOP
Philippe Blanck chats with his cousin, manager of the village co-operative cellar

OPPOSITE PAGE BOTTOM
Philippe talks with the Beautiful Books team!

Choice wines:

Gewurztraminer Altenbourg 2004

Just below Grand Cru Furstentum, this is one of Alsace's 'potential' Premier Cru vineyards. Its rich soils are perfect for growing Gewurztraminer grapes, their chalk content giving the wine elegant peachy aromas, with the clay lending an intense earthy character.

Exotic fruits fill the mouth, and continue onto a soft, creamy mid-palate. The finish reveals a warm, long spiciness that also shows on the nose with a second sniff.

A real gastronomic wine! Try with prawns or white meats in sweet Chinese sauces.

Riesling Grand Cru Furstentum 2002

These Riesling vines are planted on a steep, stony patch of ground in the upper reaches of the Furstentum, a vineyard with a uniquely sheltered, almost Mediterranean microclimate.

The varietal character of the Riesling is almost overpowered by the powerful influence of the vineyard's terroir. The nose is fat and expressive, with a richness almost akin to that of a Meursault, although the wine has undergone no oak ageing. But then the palate has a surprise in store, with intensely direct, menthol-infused mineral flavours, a bracing acidic structure, and a long, concentrated dry finish.

This is a wine from a great vintage that still requires time to open fully. It could age well for over 20 years.

Riesling Grand Cru Schlossberg 2003

The complex granitised sandstone soils of the Schlossberg rise to an altitude of 350 metres. The wines often show a delicate florality on the nose, developing into more mineral flavours with a few years' age.

But the hot weather in 2003 gave a wine with powerful cinnamon spice aromas, more typical of Condrieu in the Rhône Valley than an Alsace Riesling. On the palate, these spices are yet more pronounced, and different flavours are perceptible with every sip. The wine's style is medium-dry, but with a surprisingly healthy thread of acidity.

Although this wine could age well, it is already showing well as a partner for a range of powerful, exotic dishes.

Riesling Grand Cru Wineck-Schlossberg 2002

With granitic mica soils similar to those in Turckheim's Grand Cru Brand vineyard, the Wineck-Schlossberg in Katzenthal has a uniquely brilliant microclimate for the Riesling.

In 2002, the site produced a wine with exceptionally elegant aromas of flowers, smoke and honeyed minerals. The palate is at first uncompromisingly citrus, but the intensity of its flavour then hits you like a train, developing a great length of flavour on a dry finish.

This is a wine with a great potential to age. Drink with sushi, or vegetarian dishes.

It is interesting to compare Paul Blanck's Riesling from this site with that of Domaine Meyer-Fonné (see page 334), the grapes for which were picked at a more advanced level of ripeness.

La Table du Gourmet
5, rue de la 1ère Armée
68340 Riquewihr

Phone 03 89 49 09 09
Fax 03 89 49 04 56
www.jlbrendel.com

D'Brendelstub
48, rue du Général de Gaulle

Phone 03 89 86 54 54
Fax 03 89 47 87 30

BELOW
Chef Jean-Luc Brendel
with winemaking chum
Philippe Blanck

"One of the best restaurants in France," was Philippe Blanck's recommendation of La Table du Gourmet, so I was unlikely to turn down an invitation to join him there for a bite to eat.

In the heart of a town that Philippe describes as Alsace's Mont-Saint-Michel, La Table is an ancient wine cellar, its wooden-beamed interior dating from the year 1539. The décor is at once bright, modern, warm and traditional, reflecting the innovative cuisine of Chef Jean-Luc Brendel.

Entrées are served in a tapas style, with delicious flavour combinations such as smoked mussels in a creamy masala sauce, or battered prawns with rice cooked in coconut milk, served with homemade mango chutney. Autumn is the season for traditional game dishes, like the pigeon in a truffle and cocoa sauce, with wild mushrooms and mashed potato. This is a wonderful partner for Domaine Paul Blanck's full-bodied Pinot Noir "F" (for 'Furstentum') from the big 2003 vintage.

Jean-Luc's sister Fabienne is the sommelière, offering excellent advice on wine and food partnerships. A keen sports cyclist (the kind that really enjoys suffering), she will probably have done fifty miles in the Vosges mountains before beginning the evening's service.

La Table du Gourmet is closed Tuesday, Wednesday and Thursday lunchtimes and from the beginning of January to mid-February.

Summer 2006 saw the opening of d'Brendelstub, Jean-Luc Brendel's ultra-modern take on the traditional Alsatian *winstub*. Meats can be seen turning on spits, and *tartes flamées* are flamed in an open wood-burning stove.

The shortened but inspired wine list at d'Brendelstub will be supplemented by another "more confidential one" that you may have to ask for specially.

Prices for menus at La Table du Gourmet start at under €40, and you will pay about twice that à la Carte. D'Brendelstub is very much cheaper.

Dining with the Nasti Brothers in Kaysersberg

In the year 2000, Olivier and Emmanuel Nasti bought hotel-restaurant Le Chambard, and have since established an almost total monopoly on the Kaysersberg restaurant scene.

The gastronomic restaurant keeps the Michelin guide starry-eyed each year, with its fine food and Emmanuel's exemplary wine list. But I somehow preferred the brothers' cheaper Winstub du Chambard, in the adjoining dining room. Only the freshest ingredients are used in all of Olivier's recipes, and the chef clearly has a great talent for this traditional style of cooking. The two-course *Menu Stub* is only €17, and the enormous €21 Menu de Terroir might include a wonderful onion tart, followed by homemade *choucroute*, and then a lemon sorbet served with *Marc de Gewurztraminer*.

The real flash of brilliance, however, came in 2006, when Olivier opened Flammé & Co. in the building opposite. Inspired by the fashionable Sushi bars on a visit to Japan, the chef returned to Kaysersberg determined to create something similar based around the traditional Alsatian *tarte flammée*. Emmanuel's brother-in-law Olivier Lammert joined the brothers Nasti as manager of Flammé & Co, and has left no stone unturned in developing Olivier's dream.

You can pop in for a meal (evenings only) anytime until midnight, and choose from a range of savoury or sweet *tartes flammées*, with a small selection of "antiflammées" for those with flammée fatigue. A well-selected wine list concentrates on the cheaper wines from Alsace's great producers, and fashionable ratafia-like cocktails are served by the test tube. The diner can move seamlessly from the restaurant to a table in the dark, intimate upstairs room, where a DJ might be putting down some mellow vibes; and your tab follows you electronically.

The average per-head spend is around €25, and the young are already travelling from Colmar and even Strasbourg to spend evenings here. Flammé & Co. has all the ingredients of a brilliant international restaurant chain waiting to take off.

The Chambard hotel is comfortable, kitsch and very expensive.

Le Chambard & Winstub du Chambard
9-13, rue du Général de Gaulle
68240 Kaysersberg

Phone 03 89 47 10 17
Fax 03 89 47 35 03
www.lechambard.com

Flammé & Co.
Phone 03 89 47 16 16
Fax 03 89 47 18 23
www.flammeandco.fr

BELOW
Olivier and
Emmanuel Nasti

BOTTOM
Wood burning stove
at Flammé & Co.

Day 5 itinerary (12 miles)

The road to Colmar, Capital of Alsace wines

Kaysersberg to Ammerschwihr

Double back through, or around, Kientzheim, and then turn right onto the D111 towards Ammerschwihr.

Ammerschwihr saw its golden age in the 1500s, when its Bourgeois Tower and the greater part of its Church of St Martin were built. But the 1944 bombardments destroyed most of this once beautiful village, to which the remains of the Hôtel de Ville in its centre pay tribute. The village's recently created Grand Cru is the Kaefferkopf, which grows excellent Rieslings and Gewurztraminers. In Ammerschwihr, Domaine Jean-Baptiste Adam makes an excellent Riesling-Gewurztraminer blend from this site, called Cuvée Traditionnelle. ✉ **5, rue de l'Aigle** ✆ **03 89 78 23 21**

A great place to discover the village's other winemakers, such as the lesser known but excellent Domaine Binner ✆ **03 89 78 23 20** 🖑 **www.alsace-binner.com**, is

Philippe and Simone Gaertner's chic country hotel-restaurant Aux Armes de France. ✉ **1, Grand' rue** ✆ **03 89 47 10 12**

Through the Kaefferkopf to Katzenthal

Briefly rejoin the N415 that skirts Ammerschwihr in the direction of Colmar, and then take the road immediately to the right that leads through the Kaefferkopf vineyard into Katzenthal.

The ruins of the 13th century Château de Wineck dominate the little wine village of Katzenthal, as the only castle in Alsace that is completely surrounded by vines. But these are not just any vines; they belong to the prestigious Grand Cru Wineck-Schlossberg. The village's unmissable winery is Domaine Meyer-Fonné (see page 334), but it would be a pity not to visit Domaine Clément Klur, on rue des Trois Epis. This estate produces fine biodynamic wines, and is well used to welcoming visitors. Clément is one of Alsace's most charming vignerons, describing the consumption of wine as "a daily priority of life" – in moderation, of course. ✆ **03 89 80 94 29** ✏ **www.klur.net**

Getting to Turckheim via Niedermorschwihr

The simplest way to Niedermorschwihr is along route de Niedermorschwihr, from opposite the church in Katzenthal. Follow this road to the crossroads and turn right into the village.

Alternatively, to the left of Domaine Clément Klur in Katzenthal, there is a small path leading towards Niedermorschwihr. This is no place for cars, but I would advise cyclists to give it a try: if you can manage the beginning, you will have no trouble with the rest. The path traverses the sheer terraced granite slopes of the Grand Cru Sommerberg, "Summer Mountain," and gives fantastic views of Niedermorschwihr below and Colmar to the east. Slightly to the north of Colmar, you will also see a hillock topped with woodland, looking rather like a little Alsatian version of Burgundy's famous Corton hill. This is the Grand Cru Florimont.

Domaine Justin Boxler is now run by Justin's son Pierre and his sister Anne, who grow very fine Rieslings and Gewurztraminers on the Florimont, its limestone soils ensuring that the wines need time to show their best. The estate's Sommerberg Riesling shows its characteristic flavours of ripe lemons and minerals earlier in life. These are wines of exceptional value. ✆ **03 89 27 11 07** ✉ **15-16, rue des Trois Epis**

BELOW
The remains of Ammerschwihr's pre-war
Hôtel de Ville

ABOVE
Katzenthal, as seen from Grand Cru
vineyard Wineck-Schlossberg

BELOW
Katzenthal's best-natured vigneron:
Clément Klur

Niedermorschwihr is otherwise another pretty village with a wonderful gastronomic highlight. This is Christine Ferber's boutique Au Relais des Trois Epis, on rue des Trois Epis. Christine's delicious homemade jams have won her international acclaim. She sells these alongside little marzipan animals, magazines, charcuterie and general supplies…and of course the many books she herself has written. ① **03 89 27 05 69**

A good rustic restaurant to try in the village is Caveau Morakopf, also on rue des Trois Epis. ① **03 89 27 05 10** ⌂ **www.caveaumorakopf.fr**

Turckheim

From the centre of Niedermorschwihr, follow rue de l'Eglise down the hill towards Turckheim. A vineyard plaque indicates that you have entered Turckheim's famous Grand Cru Brand vineyard, and tells the story of the Battle of Turckheim, when French forces defeated the German imperial army on the vineyard site in 1674.

Turckheim is the last of Alsace's beautifully restored walled towns before Colmar. The town's upper entrance, the Porte de Munster, is also known as "the gate of torture", where witches and others condemned to death would pass before being executed.

The town's first reconstruction came in the 18th century, following the Thirty Years War from 1618 to 1648. Turckheim's more recent traumas in the 1940s are represented in the Musée Mémorial des Combats de la Poche de Colmar, within the 18th century cellar where the town's residents sought refuge in the dark days of 1944 and '45. Open between July and September.

✉ **25, rue du Conseil** ① **03 89 80 86 66**

But Turckheim's biggest contribution to the world since the 8th century has been in its wines. Outside of the old town, over the railway line on Route de Colmar is Turckheim's essential visit: Domaine Zind-Humbrecht (see page 336). Beyond the Gate of Torture, it is also worth checking out one of the region's best-respected co-operative cellars, the Cave Vinicole de Turckheim. ① **03 89 30 23 60** ⌂ **www.cave-turckheim.com**

A good place to learn about Turckheim's lesser-known winemakers is in its finest restaurant, L'Homme Sauvage (see page 338). Indeed, the family that owns the restaurant bottles and sells its own very pleasant wines.

The approach to Colmar

I would enter Colmar via Ingersheim, possibly stopping for a bite at the winemakers' favourite Taverne Alsacienne (see page 339). From the centre of

Turckheim, turn left before crossing the railway lines, and follow Route d'Ingersheim into the village.

This close to Colmar, very few villages remained standing following the War. The outskirts of Colmar were where American intelligence believed that the remaining German battalions were based in 1945, and so this is where they dropped the bombs of their final assault.

Ingersheim is home to another good co-operative cellar, Cave Vinicole Jean Geiler. ⊠ **45, rue de la République** ① **03 89 27 90 32** Otherwise, continue past the co-op, over the roundabout and then right into the vineyards to visit René & Vincent Fleith-Eschard. The family makes wines of impressive purity from the hillside *lieux-dits* vineyards to the west of Ingersheim.
① **03 89 27 24 19**

From Ingersheim, cross back over the bridge and follow signs onto the D11b to Colmar. Continue straight over the roundabout, where cyclists can take the underpass. From here, the D418 leads straight into the centre of Colmar. This is also the best cycle route into the city.

Colmar

The most Alsatian of Alsatian cities, Colmar is almost a caricature of the region's colourful medieval-Gothic beauty. A single flying visit is not enough for a full exploration of Colmar's many flower-bedecked streets, its grand courtyards and bustling squares. Prettiest and most photogenic is the Little Venice district, which straddles the canal in the southern part of the old town. This is where many of Colmar's best restaurants are to be found (see page 340).

First on any tourist agenda is the Unterlinden Museum. Housed within Colmar's 13th century Dominican convent, the museum is an enormous collection of archaeological treasures, sculpture and painting, and an exhibition of Alsatian history and culture. Its most important artefact is the breathtaking *Retable d'Issenheim*. Sculpted by Nicolas de Haguenau and painted by Matthias Grünewald in the 16th century, this is one of the world's finest examples of medieval religious art. ① **03 89 20 15 50**
⌐ **www.musee-unterlinden.com**

Colmar's most famous son is Auguste Bartholdi, creator of New York's Statue of Liberty. His birthplace is now the Bartholdi Museum, and in front of the city's ancient *Douane*, or customs office, stands his statue of the imperial general Lazare de Schwendi. Legend tells that Schwendi brought back the 'Tokay' Pinot Gris grape variety in 1565 after fighting the Turks on Hungarian soil. Although the grape's supposed Hungarian roots have

ABOVE
Interesting characters at Colmar's Christmas markets

TOP
Colmar's Little Venice district

been disproved, the recent legal ban of the word "Tokay" on bottles of Alsatian Pinot Gris is a sore point amongst many vignerons. ✉ **30, rue des Marchands** ☎ **03 89 41 90 60**

Colmar and wine

As wine capital of Alsace, Colmar plays rather a subdued role compared with that of Beaune in Burgundy or Bordeaux in…Bordeaux. The major merchant houses are not here, but in the smaller wine villages, and many people are surprised even by the existence of winemakers in the city, and by the extensive vineyards on the plain beyond its northwestern suburbs.

There are two wineries well worth visiting, at different ends of town. As you enter Colmar, Domaine Viticole de la Ville de Colmar is on rue de Stauffen, just off the N415 (see above). Famous ampelographer Chrétian Oberlin created this small *négociant* house in 1895, which owns land in Colmar's Harth *lieu-dit* vineyard near the estate, as well as Grands Crus in Eguisheim, Wintzenheim, Ingersheim and Sigolsheim. ☎ **03 89 79 11 87** 🖱 **www.domaineviticolecolmar.fr**

On Colmar's south-eastern flank near the motorway, is perhaps its most interesting winery, Domaine Schoffit. One of the region's only winemakers to battle for the recognition of the Chasselas grape, Bernard Schoffit's vineyards around Colmar include old Chasselas vines, producing excellent wines in tiny quantities. The estate also owns Clos Théobald in Grand Cru Rangen de Thann further south, as well as part of the Sommerberg Grand Cru in Katzenthal. ✉ **66-68, Nonnenholzweg (off rue des Aubepines)** ☎ **03 89 24 41 14**

Colmar stages the annual Foire aux Vins d'Alsace, an entire week of festivities and wine-tasting that takes place in the city in August. 🖱 **www.foire-colmar.com** It is also the base for the CIVA (Conseil Interprofessionel des Vins d'Alsace). One of France's worst wine trade bodies, the CIVA nonetheless produces fine glossy things and has a website that is more helpful than its employees. 🖱 **www.vinsalsace.com**

OPPOSITE PAGE TOP
Little Venice

OPPOSITE PAGE BOTTOM LEFT
The Unterlinden Museum

OPPOSITE PAGE BOTTOM RIGHT
The incredible Retable d'Issenheim

Meyer-Fonné

24, Grande-Rue
68230 Katzenthal

Phone 03 89 27 16 50
Fax 03 89 27 34 17
Felix.meyer-fonne@libertysurf.fr
www.chez.com/meyerfonne

The Estate

When I arrived, Félix Meyer had finished harvesting his grapes, and the juice was busy bubbling away in fermentation vats. Félix was checking the water valves that emerge from the top of each vessel, that typically Alsatian device for visually surveying the fermentation's progress as carbon dioxide is expelled. I asked if I could visit the rest of the winery, and if showing me a tractor and a plough was meant as a joke, then I admit I was tickled.

The estate's 11 hectares is shared between the communes of Katzenthal, Ingersheim, Ammerschwihr, Colmar and Bennwihr, and with certain exceptions, the wines share a characteristic elegance and lightness of touch. They drink relatively early, but have the potential to age well. The "terroir wines", those from specific parcels, are vinified and aged in oak *foudres* to help them develop more open, complex aromas. Félix eloquently decries the use of selected yeasts to enhance aromas in wine: "There's no point in vinifying separate parcels in different vessels," he says, " if they're all going to come out tasting the same".

Like so many Alsatian vignerons, Félix has a thoroughly individual approach to winemaking, pushing appellation regulations to their limits. I knew that a wine labelled Pinot Blanc might as easily come from the Auxerrois grape, but Félix quickly dashed my naïve delusions that the blending experiments end there. His Pinot Blanc contains, amongst other things, Pinot Gris, and there are apparently those who "de-classify" 100% Pinot Gris wines under this guise!

Unusually for a winemaker, Félix is refreshingly keen to offer his wealth of advice on other great estates and winemakers in the surrounding villages.

Phone in advance to visit.

Present this book for a 5% discount on wines bought.

UK importer:
Lay & Wheeler

Choice wines:

Riesling Grand Cru Wineck-Schlossberg 2004

Not to be confused with the Grand Cru Schlossberg vineyard in Kientzheim, this wine comes from old Riesling vines planted on the south-facing granite and mica soils of the Wineck-Schlossberg to the north of Katzenthal.

The wine is made from over-ripe, partially 'botrytised' grapes, and the first hint of this is in its beautiful pale golden colour. The nose is delicate and feminine, showing ripe lemon and ginger notes, underpinned by a firm minerality. On the palate, it is intense and concentrated, with great acidity and length of flavour.

Already drinking well, the wine has the potential to age for fifteen years. Try with grilled fish or sushi.

Riesling Kaefferkopf 2004

The Kaefferkopf was made a Grand Cru vineyard in 2005, and the wine will be labelled as such from 2006. Its east-facing sandy marl soils should have been classified as such years before, according to local growers, and give more masculine wines than the Wineck-Schlossberg with which it is contiguous.

A restrained nose of minerals and white flowers has yet to develop the intense petrol notes of its maturity. It is a wine that needs seven or eight years to open fully. The fatness of the wine on the palate is reminiscent of Pinot Gris, combining a full body with bracing acidity.

The vigneron's advice is not to be scared of the 18 grammes per litre of residual sugar. The wine is an excellent partner for white meats in rich sauces.

Gewurztraminer Grand Cru Wineck-Schlossberg 2004

From super-ripe but healthy grapes, the granitic soils of the Wineck-Schlossberg lend this Gewurz a trademark elegance and femininity.

The honeyed floral aromas of the grape are joined on the palate by complex flavours of fresh herbs and cloves, quite reminiscent of Chartreuse. Try with spicy Mexican food.

Pinot Gris Hinterburg de Katzenthal Sélection des Grains Nobles 2001

These east-facing granite and mica slopes are so steep that the vineyards are planted in terraces. A cool, fertile decomposed subsoil is a perfect bed for the Pinot Gris, allowing it to produce excellent sweet wines.

The wine shows rich aromas of pears, passion fruit and honey. Ripe and exotic flavours on the palate develop into a smoky, spicy finish, the defining characteristic of wine grown on this terroir.

With about 100 grammes per litre of residual sugar, this is a perfect partner for *foie gras*.

ABOVE & OPPOSITE PAGE
Felix Meyer

BELOW
Typically Alsatian: large valves to release carbon dioxide during the wine's fermentation

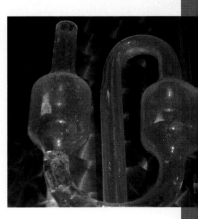

Domaine Zind-Humbrecht

4, route de Colmar
68230 Turckheim

Phone 03 89 27 02 05
Fax 03 89 27 22 58

The Estate

Tell any wine lover that you are visiting the vignerons of Alsace, and the response is a familiar one: "Zind-Humbrecht, and then who?" The powerfully erudite Olivier Humbrecht became France's first ever Master of Wine in 1988, passing both gruelling papers in English, and at an age when most young men are still wondering where to begin. Olivier's command of English is indeed astonishing, spoken with the slight accent acquired from his Scottish wife Margaret.

Today's estate was created in 1959 when the Humbrecht family's vineyard at Gueberschwihr was added to that of the Zind family at Wintzenheim. 40 hectares of vines are spread between these two villages as well as Hunawihr, Turckheim, and Thann to the south. The entire estate has been certified biodynamic since 2002.

The current cellars were built on the outskirts of Turckheim in 1991, and despite their modern appearance, they have been constructed as the best means of promoting traditional vinifications. Everything is done by gravity, and slow fermentations are carried out in old oak vats of a hundred different sizes, each one corresponding to an individual parcel of vines.

The fermentation of the 2005 vintage was still in full swing when I asked Olivier Humbrecht about the prospects for 2006. This was the estate's shortest and earliest harvest in twenty years, as the grapes were picked hurriedly to beat the elements. "The vineyard year is in many ways like the academic one," he told me. "If you study hard for six months, a week's flu before the exams shouldn't ruin your chances." Similarly, rain at vintage time will not destroy a crop from vines that have been well looked after throughout the year. If fertiliser is not thrown at the vines, their vigour is controlled; the skins of the grapes should be tough and healthy, and in this case rot won't cause too much damage.

Phone in advance to visit. Ask after any bin ends and older vintages that might be available.

UK importers:
The estate exports up to 85% of its annual production. The wines are available from Gauntleys of Nottingham (the agent), Berry Bros, Waitrose, the Wine Society, Lay & Wheeler, and so on.

Choice wines:

Each wine is marked with an *indice* from 1 to 5, usefully indicating ascending levels of sweetness.

Riesling Grand Cru Rangen de Thann Clos-Saint-Urbain 2004

Clos-Saint-Urbain is a 2-hectare parcel of vines situated within the Rangen vineyard, Alsace's southernmost Grand Cru. The Rangen's high altitude makes it a cool site, but its steep south-facing slopes give perfect conditions for ripening.

The vineyard's volcanic soils give a wine with flinty, mineral aromas, reminiscent of the fine Rieslings of Austria's Wachau region. The palate is rich and powerful, combining a piercing steeliness with a spicy, white pepper finish.

This is a full, dry wine (*indice 1*) from old vines, that needs further ageing to express itself fully, and could easily keep for 15 years.

Pinot Gris Rotenberg 2004

The Rotenberg is a north-west-facing parcel of stony limestone, overlaid with a thin layer of iron-rich soil. Situated at high altitude in the village of Wintzenheim near the Hengst Grand Cru, yields here are naturally very low, as the vine roots struggle to penetrate the tough terrain.

Typical of young Pinot Gris grown on limestone soils, the wine is slow to develop its characteristic aromas of white flowers. On the palate, the wine is already explosive, with exotic toasty flavours, good acidity and a lingering finish. *Indice 2*.

The wine is beginning to show well, and will age gracefully for a further ten years. Drink with roast pork and apple sauce.

Riesling Clos Windsbuhl Vendange Tardive 2004

The gods smiled on Clos Windsbuhl in 2004. On the opposite side of Riquewihr from Grand Cru Schoenenbourg, a cool summer followed by a warm vintage period ripened the Riesling to perfection but kept a firm thread of acidity in the wine.

The nose is still very tight, showing the lime-scented minerality associated with the vineyard's limestone soil. On the palate, the wine is rich, intense and sweet, as all of its grapes were attacked by 'noble rot' – the only one of the estate's vineyards where this happened in 2004.

The wine's high concentration of sugar and acidity only allowed the wine to ferment to 9% alcohol, at which point the yeast could do no more. It will need a good ten years to begin to show its extraordinary potential. *Indice 5*.

ABOVE &
OPPOSITE PAGE
Powerfully erudite:
Olivier Humbrecht

A L'Homme Sauvage
19, Grand'rue
68230 Turckheim

Phone 03 89 27 56 15
Fax 03 89 80 82 03

The Wild Man is very much my kind of restaurant: refined but not too posh, jazzy without being trendy. It dates from the 17th century, and is thus the oldest restaurant in Turckheim, but its history goes back further than that. The wild man in question was apparently an African slave who was held captive on the site for show purposes, during a less noble period of Alsatian history.

The building was originally constructed as a winery, and its courtyard terrace is still surrounded by the ancient cellars, now used to house Chef John Oed's chickens. John took over the restaurant in 2002, having worked at Au Fer Rouge in Colmar, Le Chambard in Kaysersberg and for a year in the United States. His cooking is strongly influenced by oriental flavours, and the East would have been his next port of call had a wife and family not intervened.

Once a year, John participates in the nation-wide *journée de goût*, a "day of taste" for local children, in which he teaches them the simplicity of delicious cooking and challenges them with new flavours such as oysters. A free spirit with few culinary prejudices, John nevertheless draws the line at "French fries". "I want people to taste something different when they come to my restaurant," he says. "You can eat fries anywhere in France."

The best time to dine at L'Homme Sauvage is during the summer months, when tables are set on the courtyard terrace, so you can eat under a canopy of vines with clucking chickens running free range underfoot.

Menus start at less than €20; a three-course meal à la carte costs €45. **Show this book for a free coffee or apéritif.**

Closed Sunday evening and Wednesday.

LEFT
The wild man, John Oed, and his wife

I can still hear the repetition of this restaurant's name in the mouths of Alsatian winemakers. This is where most of them come to eat, and all of their best wines are represented on Joëlle Guggenbuhl's extraordinary *Carte des vins*, at prices that make an example of most other restaurants.

Joëlle is as keen to promote young lesser-known Alsatian winemakers as he is to offer the region's classics, and the selection of wines from elsewhere in France is equally impressive. The menu is eclectic, with regional specialities such as *choucroute* and *Kougelhopf glacé* taking their place alongside veal kidneys cooked in Guinness, and a fish dish prepared *à l'orientale* in sweet and sour sauce. Full menus range from €15 to €50+.

If a simple look at Joëlle's wine list isn't education enough, he has formed a partnership with Thierry Meyer, one of Alsace's leading wine specialists, and the two of them organise themed meals with wine tastings once a month. This might, for example, be a comparative tasting with the region's three big merchant houses that conspicuously defy the Grand Cru appellation: Léon Beyer, Hugel and Trimbach. All three houses are present at the tasting, and each one of four courses is served with three different wines.

Visit ⑦ www.oenoalsace.com for more information, or to book a place on one of the monthly tastings.

Present this book at the restaurant for a free apéritif.

Closed Sunday evening, all day Monday and Thursday evening.

La Taverne Alsacienne
99, rue de la République
68040 Ingersheim

Phone 03 89 27 08 41
Fax 03 89 80 89 75
Tavernealsacien@aol.com

RIGHT
Joëlle Guggenbuhl,
chef and wine lover

JY'S
19, rue de la Poissonnerie

Phone 03 89 21 53 60
www.jean-yves-schillinger.com

Rendezvous de Chasse
7, place de la Gare

Phone 03 89 23 59 59
www.grand-hotel-bristol.fr/
fr_restaurant.htm

Colmar's top tables

As the wine centre of a region so rich in gastronomy, there is a predictable concentration of Michelin-starred and other impeccable restaurants in Colmar. The most stylish of these is JY'S, although Alsace is the very last thing on the menu here. Chef Jean-Yves Schillinger's cooking leads you through France, Italy and Spain en route to Japan, whilst you sip a glass of Alsace's finest Riesling on the restaurant's idyllic riverside terrace in Little Venice. Menus are fantastic value at €28 to €63.

Closed Sunday and Monday lunchtime.

The other great gastronomic table in Colmar is Rendezvous de Chasse, in the less likely location of place de la Gare. Attached to but independent of Grand Hôtel Bristol, here you will find that classic Alsatian duo of chic-gastro-joint-with-winstub-attached. The gastronomic restaurant is a pearl of classic French cuisine, and a favourite amongst Alsace's vignerons. At the stove, Michaela Peters is the only *femme chef* in Alsace with a Michelin star.

Open seven days a week.

BELOW
Gilbert Brenner tastes
wine in Colmar's best
winstub

Keeping it real in Colmar

Colmar is a bourgeois city and a big holiday destination, and the hardest thing to find amongst the tourist traps is that fine authentic ye olde *winstub* on the one hand, and the young energetic bistro-wine bar on the other.

The *winstub* – or *wistub* (this is the Haut-Rhin) – to visit is Gilbert Brenner's, in Little Venice. Despite its touristy location, it is local bums that hog the seats in Brenner's, and no evening goes by without a steady stream of *habitués* popping in to try a new wine, share holiday snaps or just to enjoy the good humour of Colmar's favourite patissier-turned-restaurateur.

Gilbert is good friends with many of the Haut-Rhin's vignerons, and serves a fine selection of their wines by the carafe. The staple Alsatian menu includes homemade *foie gras* and a delicious pikeperch served on a bed of choucroute. But for a choice of dishes that changes almost weekly, have a look at "mon plaisir", Gilbert's own suggestions board.

Closed Tuesday and Wednesday.

At the other end of the scale, but just down the road, is the recently opened Le Verre de Terres, a restaurant-wine bar described by vigneron Jean-Pierre Frick as "a breath of fresh air in Colmar".

Owner Elliott Bihler is a fanatical wine lover with a special passion for natural flavours. He doesn't subscribe to the "organic bandwagon", but most of the wines he sells are broadly from this family. You can choose from about twenty wines by the glass, from Alsace to the Auvergne, but I would ask for Elliott's own recommendation.

When he opened Le Verre de Terres, Elliott employed Chef Laurent Marlot to prepare stylish lunchtime menus, but demand became so great that this quickly extended to evenings too. Laurent claims that he doesn't have a "style of cuisine"; he cooks whatever takes his fancy, and the following day, he makes something else.

So menus change daily and prices follow the deals Laurent can squeeze from his suppliers. "And I'm a devilish haggler," says Laurent. A three-course meal at lunchtime is typically €12 or €24, and around €30 in the evening.

Closed Saturday midday, Sunday, and Monday evening.
If dining, show this book for a free apéritif.

Wistub Brenner
Phone 03 89 41 42 33
www.wistub-brenner.fr

Le Verre de Terres
11, rue de Wickram

Phone 03 89 23 61 10

BELOW
School man turned
sommelier Elliott Bihler

ABOVE
Eguisheim as
the sun sets

Day 6 itinerary (15-20 miles)
Continuing south of Colmar

Leaving Colmar

The quickest way for motorists to reach the next village, Wintzenheim, is by the D417 from the centre of Colmar. I would advise cyclists to double back to Turckheim through Ingersheim (see Day 5 itinerary), then cross the railway lines and take the first turning right, a one-way street that leads straight to Wintzenheim.

Through Wintzenheim to Wettolsheim

Wintzenheim is home to Maison Josmeyer, one of Alsace's best wine estates (see page 348). The town is also the gateway to the Munster Valley, and a short drive along the D417 leads past the 13th century Château de Pflixbourg on its way to the town of Munster, where the region's strongest and most famous cheese is made.

As the D417 enters Wintzenheim from Munster, it bisects the town and becomes rue Clemenceau. Follow the 'cycle' signs to Wettolsheim off this road onto rue du Général Castelnau. Turn left into rue du Maréchal

Joffre, and then cyclists can take the third right into rue du Vignoble; motorists continue and bear right onto rue Feldkirch towards Wettolsheim.

Rue du Vignoble cuts through the famous Grand Cru Hengst vineyard. Translating as "the Stallion", the superb Gewurztraminers grown on the Hengst's limestone soils have an untamed character in youth, but develop gracefully in bottle. The site also grows some fine Rieslings and Pinot Gris.

Day 6 at a glance

Itinerary	342 – 347
Wineries	348 – 351

Winemaking Wettolsheim

Much smaller than its neighbour, Wettolsheim is also more charming, with its attractive 18th century church of Saint Remi and a rather unexpected early 20th century replica of the grotto at Lourdes. The village's winemaking dates from the 13th century when the abbey at Munster had extensive vineyard holdings here.

Domaine Barmes-Bucher makes extremely good biodynamic wines in the village; the cellars are on rue Saint Gertrude. ① **03 89 80 62 92** But my favourite Wettolsheim producer is Domaine Albert Mann. Brothers Maurice and Jacky Barthelmé make the wines, and their respective spouses Marie-Claire and Marie-Thérèse oversee the day-to-day running of the estate. "Nothing is added or removed from our wines," Jacky explains. "If you achieve balance in the vineyard, you don't need to tamper with the juice in winery."

The wines at Domaine Albert Mann have a characteristic softness and, as a rule, a degree of residual sugar. The Pinot Gris and Gewurztraminers from the Hengst Grand Cru are particularly fine, and the Gewurztraminers grown on the calcareous Steingrubler Grand Cru above Wettolsheim show a racy, intense exoticism. But the estate is perhaps most famous for its Pinot Noirs, fantastic big reds that develop an almost Mediterranean spiciness. Demand for these is so high that they tend to be sold "as a favour" to faithful customers. ① **03 89 80 62 00** ✉ **13, rue du Château**

BOTTOM
Jean Meyer, winemaker
at Domaine Josmeyer

Chewing tobacco

If eating at La Palette in Wettolsheim, it pays to be a little wary of the chef's creativity. I was recommended a *foie gras* that had been cooked in coarse tobacco, served with the empty tube of an expensive cigar. *Nuit gravement à la santé*, the writing told me. A minute after tucking in I began to sweat and tremble. As a non-smoker, the nicotine hit was too intense, and I was forced outside into the fresh air to recuperate. "There's nothing else in there," the chef assured me, as I stumbled back to the table.

ABOVE
Michel Ginglinger,
with wines maturing
in his cellar

Next stop, Eguisheim

Eguisheim is one of Alsace's most beautiful villages, a Mecca for wine lovers. The village was lucky to survive two World Wars, and many people simply come to wander around the storybook streets that run the length of Eguisheim's ramparts in perfect concentric circles. The town spreads outwards from its restored 8th century castle, the birthplace of Pope Saint Leo IX, one of the Catholic Church's great reformers.

Eguisheim boldly claims to be "the cradle of Alsace wines", and the town can trace its winemaking back to the 4th century Roman occupation. It boasts two famous Grand Cru vineyards, the Pfersigberg and the Eichberg. The pebbly limestone soils of the former produce elegant, ripe Gewurztraminers, as well as fine Rieslings, Muscats and Pinot Gris. The Eichberg is composed of marls and Vosges sandstone, and grows rich and opulent Rieslings, Pinot Gris and Gewurztraminers.

On and off the beaten track in Eguisheim

The most famous *négociant* house in Eguisheim is Léon Beyer. The Beyer family began making wine in the village in 1580; the wines are characteristically dry, elegant and ageworthy. With Trimbach and Hugel, Léon Beyer completes the trio of famous houses who have upset authorities and growers by eschewing the use of Grand Cru vineyard names on their bottles. The tourist boutique is in Place du Château; cellar visits are by appointment only. ① 03 89 21 62 30 ⑪ www.leonbeyer.fr

Léon Beyer is the obvious choice, so why not visit a grower like Paul Ginglinger instead. The family has made wines in the village since 1636, and today the young Michel Ginglinger runs the show. Michel has worked at fine wine estates in Alsace and Burgundy, and as far afield as Chile and South Africa in his quest for winemaking greatness. Michel employs the most natural viticultural methods to achieve the purest flavours in his wines, which are the very epitome of Alsatian elegance. ① 03 89 41 44 25 ✉ **Place Charles de Gaulle**

Eguisheim's Cave Vinicole Wolfberger is another great co-op to look out for ① 03 89 22 20 20 ⑪ www.wolfberger.com; or take Gilbert Brenner's advice (from Wistub Brenner in Colmar) and visit vigneron and magician Jean-Luc Freudenreich, at 32 Grand'rue. ① 03 89 41 44 25

With over twenty restaurants, Eguisheim is better equipped to feed tourists than almost any place on earth. The village's best renowned is the Michelin-starred Caveau de Eguisheim in place du Château. ① 03 89 41 08 89 But I enjoyed a wonderful, traditional and relaxed meal at the lesser-known La Grangelière, and I'm tempted to recommend this slightly cheaper place first. ✉ **59, rue du Rempart Sud** ① 03 89 23 00 30

Taking the high road

The road south of Eguisheim leads two miles uphill between Grand Crus Eichberg and the Pfersigberg towards Husseren-les-Châteaux. And when I say uphill, I do mean it. Dominated by the ruins of its three castles, and offering awesome views of the vineyards south of Colmar, Husseren must have been a very small village until somebody spotted its holiday-let potential.

Continue left through Husseren, and before proceeding to the unpronounceable village of Voegtlinshofen, you will pass Husseren's great winery Kuentz-Bas. Under the direction of Jean-Baptiste Adam, this small négociant grows its own vines biodynamically, and produces notably fine Rieslings from the two Grand Crus beneath the village. ① 03 89 49 30 24 ⁀ www.kuentz-bas.fr

To clamber amongst the ruins of Husseren's three castles, turn right off the route du Vin and cross over the village's rue Principale. Briefly follow route des Cinq Châteaux, and then fork right onto rue du Schlossberg. The restaurant Au Sapin Doré is the starting point for the forest footpaths that lead up towards the châteaux.

ABOVE
Picturebook houses in Eguisheim

The next village is Voegtlinshofen, a rather ghostly and uninspiring place, so after turning right into the village, turn left at the sign for Gueberschwihr. This road leads through Grand Crus Hatschbourg and then Goldert, weaving beneath stone walls reminiscent of those in the southern part of the Côte d'Or in Burgundy. Gueberschwihr is more interesting, and you will share its pretty medieval streets with far fewer tourists than you will those of Eguisheim, as most day-trippers from Colmar don't make it this far.

Lesser spotted stars

The next great wine estate is just over a mile away in Pfaffenheim. Continue straight through Gueberschwihr, and follow the road to the home of Alsace's quietest iconoclast, Jean-Pierre Frick (see page 350).

Near the N83, Pfaffenheim also boasts yet another great co-operative cellar. The Cave de Pfaffenheim & Gueberschwihr was created in 1957 and today includes some 230 growers, who together own a good proportion of the Goldert, Steinert, Hatschbourg and Zinnkoepflé Grand Crus. ✉ 59, rue du Chai ① 03 89 78 08 08

Pfaffenheim, or "Papanheim", became a centre of ecclesiastic power from the Middle Ages, its flourishing wine trade creating a wealth to which its many Renaissance buildings still bear witness. The church of St. Martin in the village centre is particularly curious, with its 13th century choir seeming to poke out from under its 19th century nave, like a little version of Basle Cathedral trying to escape.

Pfaffenheim also has Alsace's oldest signposted vineyard walk, which departs from outside the Mairie. More recently created is the *sentier des sanctuaires*, a path which follows a course through the sites linked to the history of religious faith in the village.

Rouffach

From Pfaffenheim, a country road leads south out of the village through the lower vineyards into Rouffach. The most ancient possession of the prince-bishops of Strasbourg, Rouffach remained the capital of ecclesiastical power in the Haut-Rhin until the French Revolution. The town's enormous church, *l'Eglise Notre-Dame de l'Assomption*, is often referred to as "the daughter of Strasbourg Cathedral".

There is a good tourist office on place de l'Eglise, which provides details of a walking tour of Rouffach in English. ℑ **03 89 78 53 15**

The famous and the fledgling

The winemaker you will have heard of in Rouffach is René Muré. The Muré estate takes its name from Clos St-Landelin, a superior parcel of south-exposed stony limestone soil on the southern edge of the Vorbourg Grand Cru, between Rouffach and neighbouring Westhalten. The Clos is a 15-hectare *monopole* belonging to the 22-hectare Muré estate. Muré also owns part of the larger Vorbourg, and some of Grand Cru Zinnkoepflé in Westhalten.

"Clos Saint-Landelin" has always appeared on Muré's labels alongside the appellation "Grand Cru Vorbourg" to which it is entitled, although in recent years the latter appellation has found itself relegated to the back label. The estate's most famous wines are the red Pinot Noirs it produces from this site: deep, spicy wines with an impressive ageing potential.

To visit René Muré, motorists turn off the N83 at the Westhalten junction, after which the estate is immediately on the right. Cyclists should follow the road out of Rouffach towards Westhalten (see below), then double back towards the N83 along the D18bis road. ✉ **30, rue de Rouffach** ℑ **03 89 47 64 20**

The alternative is to finish your tour where much of the region's great winemaking begins, at the Domaine de l'Ecole just beyond the town's ramparts behind the tourist office. This estate belongs to the Rouffach School of Agriculture, where some 200 viticulture students grow good Riesling, Pinot Gris and especially Gewurztraminer on the Grand Cru Vorbourg.

The last twenty years have seen a dramatic change in how viticulture is taught, and students are encouraged to respect the vineyard ecosystem, using technology simply to help the work of nature. Laboratory analysis is encouraged as an aid to, not a replacement for, observation and tasting. Drop in on Jean-Marc Bentzinger and his students to find out more. ✉ **8, Aux Remparts** ℑ **03 89 78 73 16**

Rouffach is also where the region's alternative annual agricultural event has traditionally taken place. Militant environmentalists like Jean-Pierre Frick have given life to the Foire Eco-Bio de Rouffach, which includes producers of all sorts of things organic, as well as alternative healers, musical entertainers and assorted exhibitions. From 2007, however, this is likely to take place in Colmar. ⌐ **www.ecobiorouffach.org**

Where to eat and when to stop

Deciding where to dine in Rouffach presents the same dilemma as choosing a winery as your last visit. The town is as well endowed gastronomically as it is with fine winemakers, but with the villages of Westhalten and then Soultzmatz just a few miles up the "Noble Valley", why stop here?

Rouffach's best restaurant belongs to Chef Philippe Bohrer of Hôtel à la Ville de Lyon. Having cooked for two French presidents, Philippe was far too important to speak to a young English writer, but the food here is very good, the prices surprisingly reasonable. ℑ **03 89 49 65 51** ✉ **1, rue Poincaré**

One of my favourite restaurants in the region, however, is L'Auberge du Cheval Blanc in neighbouring Westhalten. ✉ **20, rue de Rouffach** ℑ **03 89 47 01 16** ⌂ **www.auberge-chevalblc.com**

Chef Gilbert Koehler is living proof that you don't need a CV full of sexy restaurant names to be a top chef. The Koehler family have been winegrowers in Westhalten since time immemorial, opening their bistrot in 1770 to feed the village's hungry vineyard workers.

Two hundred years later, when Gilbert took over Le Cheval Blanc, things changed dramatically. The restaurant was expanded to include what had hitherto been part of the winery (which was moved over the road), and the style of cuisine changed from rustic to impeccably refined, efforts that earned L'Auberge a Michelin star in 1990. The attached cosy hotel was built in 1988, and Gilbert somehow still finds time to make and bottle his own wines, which he sells as the restaurant's house labels.

The Auberge's décor is classic chic with a wink at its rustic past. Gilbert definitely cooks Alsatian, with a spark of creativity that is all his own. The chef chuckles about modern "design cuisine", preferring a simple, elegant presentation of dishes that juxtapose no more than three distinct flavours.

Menus are €36 to €76. If you are visiting in the autumn, the chef's game dishes are particularly good. Otherwise, the *escalope de saumon* cooked like a *tarte flammée* is a delicious curiosity; or order the three-course homemade *foie gras* menu, the house speciality.

Closed Sunday evening, Monday, and Tuesday lunchtime.

Present this book for a free apéritif.

ABOVE
The church at Gueberswihr

TOP
The Châteaux above Hussener

BELOW
Chef-vigneron Gilbert Koehler in his vineyards above Soultzmatz

Beyond Rouffach

Follow rue Poincaré (D18bis) through Rouffach, and turn right into rue de Westhalten. This road skirts the foot of the Vorbourg Grand Cru, passing beneath Clos St-Landelin before entering the village. The Bestheim co-operative cellar dominates winemaking in Westhalten, specialising in the production of good Crémants d'Alsace. ℑ **03 89 78 09 09** ⌂ **www.bestheim.com**

And if you're already in Westhalten, then it is only another mile past the Zinnkoepflé Grand Cru into Soultzmatt, where everyone's favourite vigneron Seppi Landmann grows delicious Riesling, Pinot Gris and Gewurztraminer on this site. His Crémant is also very fine, and the *Vendanges Tardives* from unauthorised grape varieties such as the Sylvaner is amusingly contrived to test the resolve of the appellation authorities – and has so far found it lacking. ℑ **03 89 47 09 33** ✉ **20, rue de la Valleé**

Domaine Josmeyer

**76, rue Clémenceau
68920 Wintzenheim**

Phone 03 89 27 91 90
Fax 03 89 27 91 99
www.josmeyer.com
contact@josmeyer.com

BELOW
Balancing act:
Jean Meyer tastes wine
for blending

The Estate

Regarded as one of Alsace's finest *négociant* houses for over 100 years, Domaine Josmeyer recently decided instead of expanding its merchant activities, to stop them altogether. The need to buy grapes from other growers was a stumbling block to the estate's becoming fully biodynamic, so with this in mind, it signed long-term rental contracts with vineyard owners. This allowed the estate to work all of the 28 hectares of vines from which its wines are made according to its own impeccable standards.

The estate takes its name from Joseph O. S. Meyer, father of Jean Meyer, who today vinifies all of the Josmeyer wines. Since 1996, Jean's right hand-man Christophe Ehrhart has taken charge of vineyard work, preparing natural vine treatments from composted cow dung and decomposed willow branches.

Christophe has set himself the ambitious task of finding a European vine rootstock that resists the phylloxera louse. "Everyone grafts their vines onto American rootstocks," Christophe admits, "but they are too vigorous for our European plants. If a person eats five big meals every day, his health suffers, and it is the same with a vine. Diseases such as mould are attracted to the vine, not to attack it, but to feed off its excess and restore its natural balance.

"There is no magic in biodynamics, just logic," adds Christophe.

Moving from the vines to the winery, I found Jean Meyer busy tasting the young 2006 wines, deciding which vats to blend together. In an English as perfect as Christophe's, he explained the importance of this blending process:

"Each vat of wine is different, even those that have come from the same vineyard parcel. When blending, it is crucial to find the perfect partnerships; only in this way will you end up with a better wine."

Present this book for a 5% discount on wines bought.

UK agent:
Pol Roger UK
The estate is keen to help private customers to import their own wines.

Choice wines:

Riesling Grand Cru Brand 2004

The granitic soils of Turckheim's Brand give what Christophe Ehrhart describes as a "vertical wine", and its 2004 Riesling shows a typically austere nose of ground stones and lime fruits.

On the palate too the wine needs time to develop, with an intense mineral concentration and a rapier-like acidity that prolongs the wine's finish.

Best kept for a few years before drinking, this is a wine to partner with aromatic herbs and Japanese fish dishes.

Pinot Gris Grand Cru Brand 2001

This is a beautiful wine that fermented slowly over a long period and has only just begun to develop its secondary aromas. Puréed fruits combine with a mouth-watering freshness that is equally evident on the palate. A hint of spice mid-palate develops onto a long finish, where the wine's roundness and acidity are in perfect balance.

A great gastronomic wine, this Gris would be as comfortable with the fine and delicate as with the rich and powerful.

Riesling Grand Cru Hengst 2000

In contrast with the Brand, the limestone-based Hengst vineyard gives its wines a more "horizontal" character, typically showing more exuberance in their youth.

The nose is complex and full of contrasts: rhubarb, apricots, smoke and nettles… On the palate, the complexity translates into great breadth and length of flavour, and is characteristic of the Josmeyer dry wine style.

Try with fish cooked in sauce or with Mediterranean herbs.

Gewurztraminer Grand Cru Hengst 1995

Another complex, elegant wine, from a very ripe vintage, this Gewurz has benefited from its 10 years or so in bottle, allowing it time to develop aromas of acacia, kiwi fruit and white pepper.

On the palate, the first impression is of incense, followed by rounded apricot and mango flavours, with a finish that is long and refined.

Christophe Ehrhart regularly arranges press dinners where only Gewurztraminer is served, to show the grape's potential to partner with a range of interesting foods.

RIGHT & TOP
Christophe Ehrhart with cow
dung and other natural composts

Domaine Pierre Frick

5, rue de Baer
68250 Pfaffenheim

Phone 03 89 49 62 99
Fax 03 89 49 73 78
www.pierrefrick.com
contact@pierrefrick.com

The Estate

I fairly stumbled upon this winery in the last days of my Alsace tour, and the thought that I ever might have missed it is a frightening one. Pierre Frick began farming organically as early as 1970, and his son Jean-Pierre has practised biodynamic viticulture since 1981, making them the unsung godfathers of these two movements in Alsace.

Jean-Pierre is a curious character, showing an unusual mix of good humour and meticulous concentration, joking one minute, then earnestly taking notes on a new project the next. "I am a militant," he asserts. "People said I was crazy in the 1980s; it is only in the last few years that biodynamics has really become fashionable." But the innovations didn't end there. Tired of the problem of cork taint, Jean-Pierre decided to bottle all of his wines under stainless steel cap from 2002, a gutsy move for a grower whose principal clientele is French and therefore fiercely conservative. He also produces an entire range of wines without the addition of sulphur, labelled "wine without any additives". "I am not alone in making natural wines," says Jean-Pierre, "but many winemakers are still afraid to admit that they do, for fear of being branded as alternative."

The estate also explodes the myth that (good) organic and biodynamic wines need to be expensive: the average bottle price here is well under a tenner. Moreover, you are unlikely to leave Jean-Pierre's company without having tasted the whole range, including some old vintages. "There's no point leaving the *Vendanges Tardives* in the cellar," chuckles Jean-Pierre. "One day I'll kick the bucket, and I won't be able to take any of these with me."

It is a peculiar wonder of Alsace that such a fine estate with such a distinguished history has yet to be widely discovered. Jean-Pierre doesn't speak much English, but his charming wife and cellar companion Chantal does.

Present this book for a 5% discount on wines bought.

LEFT
Jean-Pierre Frick, the winemaking militant

OPPOSITE PAGE
BOTTOM
Jean-Pierre talks earnestly with his wife Chantal

Choice wines:

Pinot Blanc (100% Auxerrois) 2005 'without additives'
This grape variety is often presented as the first of the entry-level wines, a warm-up before the Rieslings and Gewurztraminers are uncorked. But Frick's is a great example of what can be achieved with the Pinot Blanc.

The debate about unsulphured wines is whether their very lack of additives causes them to resemble one another. Their flavours are characteristically savoury; often reminiscent of the salty tang found in Fino Sherries. But beyond these impressions, you can find butter and soft, ripe apple aromas in this Pinot. The wine is just off-dry, but with a fresh bracing acidity and wonderful balance of natural flavours. A great partner for tapas dishes.

"Oak-aged wines also resemble each other in some ways, and so do wines that undergo malolactic fermentations," says Jean-Pierre. "It is like reading Cyrillic script. Until you are familiar with the letters, everything is sure to look the same."

Gewurztraminer Grand Cru Steinert 2002 Vendanges Tardives
Owned by the bishoprics of Basle and Strasbourg in the 12th century, this lesser-known Grand Cru in Pfaffenheim is unusually rich in limestone and the wines need decanting to show the full breadth of their aromas.

The nose is very fresh, showing pure pineapple, mango and sweet melon aromas. The flavours are also exotic, of lychees with an interesting white pepper spice and a long, lightly nutty finish.

A great apéritif or partner for *foie gras*.

Sylvaner Bergweingarten 2001 "Perles Noires"
Another often overlooked grape, something extraordinary happened to the Sylvaner in the Bergweingarten vineyard in 2001. Darkened, withered grapes were harvested incredibly late and placed carefully into small buckets before being carried to the winery for a long, slow fermentation.

On the nose, the wine shows soft waxy aromas of ripe lemons and banana. On the palate the concentration of flavour and acidity is intense, with an enormous residual sugar level of over 200 grammes per litre, making this a Sélection des Grains Nobles style wine.

This is a "peaceful" wine that would partner well creamy cheeses.

Pinot Noir 1983
Comparable with a great old-style burgundy, I would love to see this Pinot in a blind tasting with some fine Côte d'Or 1983s.

With a light garnet colour and incredible freshness on the nose, the wine's aromas are a heady mix of incense and forest floor spice. Red fruit flavours are underpinned by the fresh acidity of a wine that, very unusually for a red, never underwent malolactic fermentation.

This wine deserves to be drunk with feathered game.

Accommodation

Obernai

Hôtel-Restaurant du Parc**** is the classiest joint in town, with every comfort you could wish for including two swimming pools. Prices start at about €120.
169, route d'Ottrott
Phone 03 88 95 50 08
Fax 03 88 95 37 29
www.hotel-du-parc.com

The **Hostellerie des Ducs d'Alsace***** is attached to Obernai's double Michelin-starred restaurant La Fourchette des Ducs. The hotel is surprisingly cheap at €55 to €75.
6, rue de la Gare
Phone 03 88 95 55 34
Fax 03 88 95 00 92
www.ducalsace.com

Hôtel La Diligence** in the town square has rooms for between €35 and €80, the cheapest appearing in translation as "the backside" of the building!
23, place du Marché
Phone 03 88 95 55 69
Fax 03 88 95 42 46
www.hotel-diligence.com

Andlau

Le Zinck Hôtel***,
13, rue de la Marne
Phone 03 88 08 27 30
www.zinckhotel.com
Daniel Zinck, brother of Pierre Zinck of Restaurant Le Relais de la Poste (see page 291), has turned the town's old mill house into a characterful hotel. All the rooms are decorated differently, and prices are between €50 and €100.

Otherwise try:
Hôtel-Restaurant*** Kastelberg
10, rue du Général-Koenig
Phone 03 88 08 97 83
www.kastelberg.com

Sélestat

There is a remarkable shortage of decent hotels in Sélestat. If your budget allows it, there is the **Hostellerie de l'Abbaye la Pommeraie*****, with its excellent restaurant-winstub duo (see page 303).

There are two others to try in the old town, both with rooms from about €55.
Hôtel Vaillant H***
Place de la République
Phone 03 88 92 09 46
Fax 03 88 82 95 01
www.hotel-vaillant.com

Auberge des Alliés
39, rue des Chevaliers
Phone 03 88 92 09 34
Fax 03 88 92 12 88
www.auberge-des-allies.com

Ribeauvillé

The first place I would try in Ribeauvillé is: **Domaine Jean Sipp**, which has a couple of excellent rooms from between €60 and €80.
60, rue de la Fraternité
Phone 03 89 73 60 02
Fax 03 89 73 82 38
www.jean-sipp.com

For around the same price, André Kientzler's sister Françoise owns **Hôtel de la Tour**** on the site of the old Kientzler winery in the centre of town.
1, rue de la Mairie
Phone 03 89 73 72 73
Fax 03 89 73 38 74
www.hotel-la-tour.com

A good slightly cheaper option is:
Hôtel-Restaurant** au Lion
6, place de la Sinne
Phone 03 89 73 67 69
Fax 03 89 73 80 64
www.au-lion.com

And for the best of the best, there's always:
Hôtel**** Le Clos Saint Vincent
Route de Bergheim
Phone 03 89 73 67 65
Fax 03 89 73 32 20
www.leclossaintvincent.com

Kaysersberg
There are plenty of good places to stay in Kaysersberg. The least expensive is **Hôtel Constantin***** right in the town centre, in an 18th century winemaker's house. Rooms are available from about €55, and the breaky (€7) is great.
10, rue du Pere
Phone 03 89 47 19 90

Otherwise try **Hôtel les Remparts*****. Run by the charming Kellers, this is the best place to stay if you're looking for advice on the area. The hotel is part of Horizons d'Alsace, which organises custom tours in the Kaysersberg valley. (**www.horizons-alsace.com**) Rooms are €65-€85. Try to get a room in 'the new building'.
4, rue de la Flieh
Phone 03 89 47 12 12
www.lesremparts.com

If money is no object, and the style appeals, try **Hôtel le Chambard** (see page 327), or give Madame Abbes a call to see if her wonderful gîte beside the River Weiss is available.
16, rue des Forgerons
Phone 03 89 41 20 76

Colmar
The most splendid and tranquil of Colmar's hotels is **Les Têtes******, set within a beautiful 17th century building in the old city. The restaurant too is highly recommended. Surprisingly, prices start at below €100.
19, rue de Têtes
Phone 03 89 24 43 43
Fax 03 89 24 58 34
www.la-maison-des-tetes.com

Next comes the **Best Western Grand Hôtel Bristol*****, which is attached to the even better restaurant Le Rendezvous de Chasse (see page 340). Prices are €75 to €100.
7, place de la Gare
Phone 03 89 23 59 59
Fax 03 89 23 92 26
www.grand-hotel-bristol.com

For something a little cheaper, try the charmingly rustic **Hôtel Turenne****. Expect to pay about €50 per night.
10, rue de Bâle
Phone 03 89 21 58 58
Fax 03 89 41 27 64
www.turenne.com

Rouffach
Attached to Rouffach's best restaurant is **Hôtel à la Ville de Lyon**. Prices here start at a very fair €50.
Phone 03 89 49 65 51
Fax 03 89 49 76 67
www.vdl-bohrer.com

Looming above La Ville de Lyon is the fantastically imposing **Château d'Isenbourg,** one of Alsace's most elegant and historic hotels. Rooms cost upwards of €115.
www.grandesetapes.fr/chateau_isenbourg
Phone 03 89 78 58 50
Fax 03 89 78 53 70

Or if continuing to Westhalten, book a room in **L'Auberge du Cheval Blanc**, where rooms are between €75 and €120 (see page 347).

Glossary

A

Appellation d'Origine contrôlée (AOC)
See page 14.

Assemblage
The process of wine blending; or a blended wine.

B

Barrique
A small oak barrel, with a capacity of 225 litres. The longer a wine spends in *barriques*, the more wood flavour it absorbs. The younger the *barriques*, the more flavour they also impart.

Biodynamic(s)
See page 13.

Blanc de blancs
A white wine made entirely from white-skinned grapes. In Champagne, the term means that the wine is only made from Chardonnay grapes.

Blanc de noirs
White wine made entirely from black-skinned grapes: the grapes' pulp gives white juice that is not stained by any contact with their dark skins during vinification. *Blanc de Noirs* champagne is made with the red Pinot Noir and Pinot Meunier grapes.

Botrytis
See 'noble rot', below.

Brut
Dry; applied to sparkling wines.

C

Chambre(s) d'hôte
Bed and breakfast.

Climat
A specific vineyard site. See Terroir, page 10.

Clos
Historically, a walled, often monastic vineyard; the term is frequently used to indicate a small, superior parcel of vines within a larger vineyard.

Commune
The wine growing area that surrounds a specific village.

Co-operative cellar
An organisation in which individual growers combine to make, label and sell wines from the grapes they harvest, under a single brand name. Growers who do not have their own winemaking facilities are thereby not obliged to sell their grapes to *négociant* houses (see below).

Crémant
Appellation-controlled sparkling wine made by the traditional method, in which the bubbles come from the wine's second, bottle, fermentation.

Cuvée
A blend.

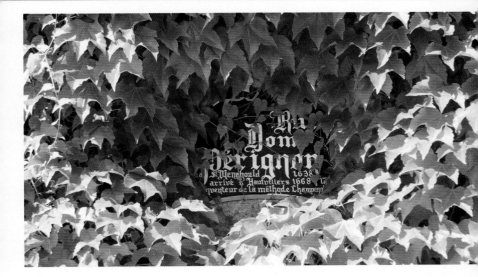

D

Demi-sec
Medium-dry.

Disgorgement (*dégorgement*)
See page 23.

Dosage
See page 23.

F

Finish
A wine's aftertaste; a useful benchmark for judging wine quality. See page 13.

G

Grand Cru
A superior vineyard site, defined by local *appellation contrôlée* regulations.

Green harvest
The removal of bunches of unripe grapes from the vines, in July and August, to reduce yields and concentrate flavours in the remaining fruit.

K

Kir
The Burgundian apéritif: *crème de cassis*, mixed with a larger measure of white wine, which is traditionally made from Burgundy's Aligoté grape.

L

Lees
The dead yeast cells left following a wine's fermentation. Many wines spend time ageing on their lees to add richness and complexity to their flavours.

Lieu-dit
A 'named' vineyard site that has no superior classification such as Premier or Grand Cru.

Liqueur d'éxpedition
See page 23.

Liqueur de tirage
See page 23.

M

Maceration
The grape juice's contact with grape skins before or during its fermentation, to give colour, flavour and tannins to the resulting wine.

Mairie
The mayor's office. Enormously powerful in local politics, their grandiose headquarters make excellent village landmarks by which to get your bearings!

Malolactic fermentation
Following a wine's alcoholic fermentation, in which sugar is converted into alcohol by yeast, malolactic fermentation is a bacterial process, converting the wine's sharp tasting malic acid to the softer lactic acid. A winemaker might either encourage or prevent malolactic fermentation, depending on the style of wine he wishes to create. Most red wines, and some whites, undergo malolactic fermentation.

Marc
Grape spirit, distilled from grape skins following their pressing.

Méthode traditionnelle
The method by which all quality sparkling wine in France is made; the bubbles in the wine must come from its second fermentation, in bottle. Once called *méthode champenoise*, this description is no longer permitted in France outside of the Champagne region.

Millésimé
Vintage dated.

Moelleux
Sweet.

Monopole
A vineyard with a single owner.

N

Négociant
A merchant winemaker who buys grapes or grape juice from other growers and finishes the winemaking process himself. Many *négociants* are themselves also vineyard owners. The finished wine is sold under the *négociant's* own brand label.

Noble Rot
A type of fungus, caused by *Botrytis cinerea*, which develops on the skins of grapes. Mist and humidity cause the rot to take hold in the mornings. It becomes 'noble' if afternoon sunshine is sufficient to halt its progress before it becomes a problem. The fungus sucks water from the grapes, shrivelling them and concentrating sugar, flavour and acidity. When the sun fails to burn off the damp in the afternoon, Botrytis develops into Grey Rot, which can cause off-flavours in the wine.

P

Phylloxera (vastatrix)
A louse that feeds off the roots of grape vines. It devastated the vineyards of Europe at the end of the 19th century. The pest was imported on vine cuttings from America, where the indigenous vines were naturally resistant. The eventual solution was to graft European vine varieties onto American rootstocks; a technique still practised by most of the world's winemakers.

Premier Cru
A superior vineyard classification; one which, in Burgundy and Champagne, is the next rung down the quality ladder from Grand Cru.

Prise de mousse
See page 22.

Pupitre
See page 23.

R

Récoltant-manipulant (RC)
A grower who makes wines only from his own harvest, as opposed to a *négociant* (see above).

Remuage
See page 23.

Residual sugar (RS)
The sugar left in wine after its alcoholic fermentation is finished.

S

Saignée ('skin contact')
The process by which red wine is 'bled off' after only a short period of contact between juice and grape skins. The skins impart flavour to the wine, but only a light colour. This is how all rosé wines are made in France, except in Champagne, where rosé may also come from a blend of white and red wines.

Sec
Literally translated as dry; when applied to a sparkling wine, the word '*sec*' generally means that it is slightly sweeter than the *brut* style.

Sélection des Grains Nobles
A sweet wine made in Alsace, from individually harvested 'nobly rotten' grapes. See page 275.

T

Table d'hôte
Set meals provided, usually as part of a bed and breakfast.

Terroir
See pages 10-13.

Tilleul
Lime blossom (as a tasting term).

V

Vendanges Tardives
A sweet, late harvest wine made in Alsace. See page 275.

Veraison
The moment in summer, usually in August, when black grapes lose their unripe green colour and begin to take on their eventual dark hue.

Vigneron
Winemaker.

Vin de garde
A wine that will benefit from considerable bottle ageing.

Index

A

Adam, Domaine Jean-Baptiste 328, 345
Adolphe of Nassau, King 320
Aldebert, Jackie and Jean-Marc 175
Alexandre de Bourgogne 245
Aligoté 186, 218
Allied-Domecq 35
Alliet, Philippe 141
Aloxe-Corton 190, 219, 224, 229, 236-237
Alsace 184, 269-279, 352-353
Alsace School of Viticulture 278
Amboise 104, 109-110, 116-117, 119, 122-123, 174
Ambonnay 28, 42, 48, 50-51, 56-57, 77
Amiot & Fils, Domaine Guy 255
Amirault, Domaine Yannick 152, 156-157
Ammerschwihr 328, 329, 334
Anagrus Atomus 170
Andlau 278, 285, 288-289, 291, 292-293, 352
Angers 98
Anjou 99
Anjou-Saumur 98
AOC (appellation d'origine contrôlée) 14
  Alsace 269, 272-273, 288
  Burgundy 179, 183, 185
  Champagne 64
  Loire Valley 101, 104, 107, 130-131
Armagnacs 284
Artigny 129, 136
Aube département 25
Aubert, Eric and Sylvie 60, 61
Auxerrois 273
Auxey-Duresses 190, 243, 244, 248
Avize 28, 63, 64, 72

Aÿ 21, 28, 52-53, 58, 60-61, 77
Aymmard-Claude family 234, 235
Azay-le-Rideau 104, 129, 130, 131, 134-135, 137, 174

B

Bachelet, Jean-Claude 245
Badier, Hervé 36, 40
Balzac, Honoré de 108, 130
Baradon-Michaudet, Champagne 65
Bardet, Jean 96
Barmes-Bucher, Domaine 343
Barr 283-284
Barthelmé family 343
Bartholdi, Auguste 331
Bas-Rhin 269, 278
Baudry, Domaine Bernard 141, 146-147, 226
Beaufort, Champagne André 51, 56-57
Beaujolais 101, 158, 182
Beaumont-en-Véron 150, 151
Beaune 184, 190, 218, 224, 230-233, 238-239, 246, 260, 265
Beblenheim 319, 322-323
Beck-Hartweg, Yvette and Michel 295
Becker, Jean 319
Bégouin, Sébastien 117
Belda, Benoit 168
Bellevue 79
Benais 153
Benedictine order 10
Bennwihr 278, 334
Bentzinger, Jean-Marc 346
Berger, Thierry 262
Bergheim 278, 306, 307, 308-309, 315, 320
Bernard, Saint 10, 11
Bernhard & Reibel, Domaine 295, 300-301
Bernstein 294

Bertagna, Domaine 206-207, 208
Berthaut, Domaine 194, 196
Berthelot, Gilles 130
Bestheim co-operative cellar 347
Beyer, Léon and family 272, 274, 339, 344
Bihler, Elliott 341
Billecart-Salmon, Champagne 52
Binner, Domaine 328-329
biodynamics 13, 55, 100, 258, 350
BIVB (Bureau Interprofessionel des Vins de Bourgogne) 210, 222
Bize, Domaine Simon 229
Blagny 245
Blanc de Blancs 24, 27, 63
Blanc de Noirs 24
Blanck, Domaine Paul 320, 324-325, 326
Bléger, Marc 314
Bléré 120
Bliard, Champagne Vincent 24, 78
Blienschwiller 294, 302
Blot, Jacky 121, 122, 123, 124, 125, 154
boating 77, 142, 165
Bohrer, Philippe 347
Boisset group 232
Bollinger, Champagne 28, 52
Bonnaire, Champagne 42, 63, 70-71
Bonnaventure, Pascale and Etienne 150
Bordeaux 14, 19
botrytis see 'noble rot'
Bott-Geyl, Domaine 319, 322-323
Bouchard Aîné et Fils 184, 232
Bougy, André 80
Bouillot, Louis 209

Boumier, Laurent and Georges 205
Bourgogne 186
Bourgogne Rouge 196
Bourgueil 100, 101, 104, 124, 131, 151-152, 156-160, 175
Bourré 126
Boursault 68
Bouvet-Ladubay 166
Bouvier, Domaine René 197, 200-201
Bouvier, Pascal 116
Bouzy 21, 28, 41-42, 46-47, 70, 76
Boxler, Domaine Justin 329
Boyer, Franck and Florence 214
Boyer, Gérard 89, 127
Brendel, Fabienne and Jean-Luc 326
Brenner, Gilbert 341
Bresse 187
Bretel, Valérie and Fabrice 172
Breton, Domaine Catherine & Pierre 153-154, 158-159, 160
Brochon 196
'The Brotherhood of the Horn' 281
Brun, Champagne Edouard 58
Brun, Champagne Roger 52, 58-59, 215
'brut' 24, 25
Bucer, Martin 296
Burgundy 19, 178-191
Butte, Domaine de la 124-125, 154
Bzikot, Domaine 253

C

Cabernet Franc 100, 101, 104, 109, 131, 140, 152, 163
Cabernet Sauvignon 101, 140, 152, 163
Canard-Duchêne 80
Candes-Saint-Martin 154
Carillon, Domaine 253
Casino de Santenay 256
Castellane, Champagne de 51, 53, 55
Catherine de Medici 119
Cave de Pfaffenheim & Gueberschwihr 345
Cave de Ribeauvillé 272
Cave des Vieilles Vignes
    Beaune 233
    Meursault 243
Cave des Vignerons de Saumur

164, 168-169
Cave des Vignerons des Hautes Côtes 239-240
Cave du Pays de Bourgueil 156
Cave Vinicole de Ribeauvillé 307
Cave Vinicole de Turckheim 330
Cave Vinicole Jean Geiler 331
Cave Vinicole Wolfberger 344
Caveau de l'Escargot de la Côte 205
Caveau de Puligny-Montrachet 253
Caveau de Vignerons d'Amboise 110
Caveau des Vignerons de Morey-Saint-Denis 205
Chablis 182
Chacé 164
Chagny 256
Chaintré 164
Chaintres, Château de 164, 170-171
Chalons, Jean-Pierre 174
Chalopin, Philippe 203
Chambertin 204
Chambes, Jean de 162
Chambolle-Musigny 178, 186, 190, 205, 206, 210-211, 214
Champagne 18-29
Champalou, Maison 108, 112-113, 116
Champignonnière, Chouzé-sur-Loire 154
Champigny 164
Chandon de Briailles, Domaine 228, 234-235
Chanliaud, Roland 238
Chardonnay
    Alsace 274
    Burgundy 186, 254
    Champagne 21, 24, 28, 38, 63
    Loire Valley 163
Charles the Fat 292
Charles II, Emperor 183
Charles VII 31, 99, 140, 162
Charles VIII 109
Charlopin, Philippe 194, 196, 242
Charolais 187
Charpentier, Champagne Jacky 69
Charruau family 164
Chassagne-Montrachet 190, 254, 255, 260-263
Chasselas 273

Chassigny 243
Châteaux-Thierry 22
Châtenois 295, 298, 300-301
Châtillon-sur-Marne 69
Chavy, Domaine Gérard 253
Chavy-Chouet, Hubert 243
cheese 26, 103, 181, 189, 196, 276, 342
Chenin 104
Chenin Blanc 100-101, 104, 107, 109, 130-131, 163
Chenonceaux 104, 118-120, 126
Chenôve 192, 193, 201
Chevaliers de Tastevin 141
Chevallier family 164
Chidaine, Domaine François 121
Chigny-les-Roses 28, 80, 84-85
Chinon 99, 100, 101, 104, 131, 138, 139-149, 158, 175
Chinon Blanc 140
Chinon Rouge 140
La Chocolaterie Thibaut, Pierry 62
Chorey-lès-Beaune 230
Chouilly 24, 72
Chouzé-sur-Loire 154
Churchill, Sir Winston 54
Cistercian order 10, 11, 206
CIVA (Conseil Interprofessionel des Vins d'Alsace) 332
CIVC (Comité Interprofessionel des Vins de Champagne) 24
Clair, Domaine Bruno 193
Clair, Françoise & Denis 255, 256, 257
Claudel, Eric and Martine 214
Clavelier, Bruno 208
Clavelier, Domaine Bruno 212-213
Clicquot-Ponsardin, Veuve 19, 23, 32, 63, 67, 68
climate 9-10, 20-21, 98, 132, 182-183, 271
Clos de l'Echo, Chinon 139, 141, 148
Clos Naudin, Domaine du 108
Clos Rougeard, Domaine du 164
Clouet, Paul 42
Clovis 31
Club Vosgien 276
Coates, Clive 212
Coche–Bizouard, Domaine 184, 243, 248-249, 251
Colin, Michel 263

Colmar 269, 271, 278, 331-332, 334, 340-341, 353
Combier distillery 165
Concoeur 208
Concours Européen des Villes & Villages Fleuris, 2005 64
Confrérie des Bons Etonneurs Rabelaisiens 141, 142, 143
Confrérie des Chevaliers du Tastevin 206
Cornu & Fils, Domaine Edmund 230
Corps des Carabiniers, Saumur 165
Corton 218, 230
Corton André 229
Côt (Malbec) 101, 104, 131
Côte Chalonnaise 182, 255, 256
Côte de Beaune 178, 185, 190
Côte de Nuits 178, 186, 190, 192-203, 204-215
Côte de Nuits-Villages 196
Côte des Blancs 21, 27, 28, 62-75
Côte d'Or 178, 182, 183-184, 186
Côteaux Champenois 21, 25, 26
Coudrain-Tribaut, Valérie 79
Coulaine 150-151
Couly-Dutheil family 139, 141
Courcel, Domaine 242
Couten, Jean 77
Couturier, Alain 96
Cramant 28, 42, 62-63, 70, 72
Cravant-les-Côteaux 141, 146
Crémant de Loire 100, 163
Crémants d'Alsace 274, 347
Crémants de Bourgogne 186, 209
Crème de Cassis 187, 218
crus 54
Cumières 22, 28, 69, 76-77, 77, 86
Cuvée Commodore 55
Cuvée Rosé Brut 51
cycling 9, 103, 104, 189, 190, 276, 278
bicycle hire 20, 54, 136, 180, 181-182, 256, 296

D
Daloz, Jean-Marie 239
Dambach-la-Ville 278, 292, 293, 294-295, 298-299
Damery 69

Decroix, Guillaume 131
Deiss, Domaine Marcel 275, 306, 308-309
Delagneau, Bruno 127
Delamotte, Champagne 51
Delattre, Damien 233
Delaunay Père et Fils 152
Delecheneau, Damien 122, 123
demi-sec 25, 107
Denis Père & Fils, Domaine 219
Descombes, Marie-Paule and Patrick 149
Desenne, Anne-Marie 152
Deuval, Emmanuel 97
Devilard, Philippe 251
Dézé, Stéphanie and Bertrand 161
Diane de Poitiers 119
Dijon 180-182, 182, 183
Distillerie Guillon 28, 41
Dopff au Moulin 318
Dormans 22, 68
Druet, Pierre-Jacques 153
Duguin, Christophe 148, 149
Dumangin, Jacky 80
Dumas, Alexandre 162
Duplessis-Mornay, Philippe 165
Dussourt, André and Paul 295
Dutheil family 175
Duval-Leroy 67

E
Ebermunster 296
Ebhardt, Bodo 305
Eblin, Jean-Michel 319
Echevronne 218
Ecole des Vins de Bourgogne 232
Ecole, Domaine de l' 34
Edelzwickers 273
Eguisheim 77, 278, 332, 342, 344, 345
Ehrhart, Christophe 348, 349
Eichoffen 294
Eleanor of Aquitaine 163
Emrchez, Amaury 75
Epernay 18, 21, 23, 24, 28, 51, 53-54, 60-61, 62, 91
Epfig 293, 298
Erasmus 296
Esmonin, Domaine Sylvie 197
Esvres 128-129, 132-133
Etichon, duke of Alsace 282
Exposition Universelle de Paris, 1889 54

F
Faiveley, François 209, 236
Faller, Colette and family 320
Faller, Domaine Léon 293
Faux de Verzy 28, 41
Ferber, Christine 330
Feuillatte, Nicholas 24
Fèvre, Ghislaine and Jean-Luc 137
Filliatreau, Domaine 164, 165
Fine de Champagne 25
Fixey 194, 195
Fixin 194, 195, 196
Flagey–Echézeaux 207
Flammé & Co. 320, 321, 327
Fleith-Eschard, René and Vincent 331
Fontevraud-l'Abbaye 104, 162-163, 172
Foreau, Philippe 108
Forest, Jean-Michel 137
Foucault brothers 164
Fougeray de Beauclair, Domaine 193, 196, 198-199, 205
Frick, Domaine Pierre 341, 345, 346, 350-351
Fringhian family 68
Frissant, Xavier 110
Fromagerie Gaugry 196
Funaro, Pasquale and Christiane 303

G
Gaertner, Philippe and Simone 329
Gagnard family 254
Gamay 101, 104, 109, 131, 186, 245
Gardet, Champagne 80, 84-85
Gelin, Domaine Pierre 194
Gente-Pont, Nathalie 250
Geoffroy, Champagne René 36, 77, 82-83
Gerbet, François 208
Germain, Fabrice and Corinne 263
Germaine 80
Gertwiller 284
Gevrey-Chambertin 178, 186, 190, 196-197, 200-201, 203, 264
Gewurztraminer 273, 274, 275, 283, 284
Gilg, Georges 291
Ginglinger, Paul and Michel 344

Giraud, Maurice 241-242
Gireudeau, Dominique 89
Gisselbrecht, Willy and family 295, 298-299
Gobillard & Fils, Champagne J.M. 78
Goess, Gilles 75
Gontran, King of Burgundy 183
Gosset family 139
Goulet, Joseph 40
Goutorbe, Champagne 52, 69
Goyard, Jean 60
Grand Cru
Alsace 273, 274-275, 284, 294
Burgundy 185-186, 190, 204, 205, 230, 254
Champagne 19, 28
Grange Tiphaine, Domaine de la 110, 118, 122-123
Gratien & Meyer 166
Gratien, Champagne Alfred 166
Gresser, André & Remy 285
Grolleau 101, 131, 163
Gros, Domaine A-F 241
Gros Frère & Soeur, Domaine 208
Grucker, Sylvie and Gilles 302
Grünewald, Matthias 331
Gueberschwihr 345
Guggenbuhl, Joëlle 339
Guillon, Thierry 41, 42
Guyot, Domaine Thierry 244
Guyot, Dr. 64

H
Haguenau, Nicolas de 331
Hardou, Romauld and Fanny 173
Hardouin, André and Jacques 108
Hauller, Louis & Claude 295
Haut-Koenigsbourg 278, 295, 305, 306
Haut-Rhin 278
Haut-Santenay 256, 257
Hautes-Côtes de Beaune 187, 189, 244
Hautes-Côtes de Nuits 187, 189, 190, 216, 218
Hautvillers 22, 28, 32, 77-78, 88
Hegner, Jean-Jacques 239
Heidsieck, Charles 32
Heiligenstein 273, 283
Henkell & Söhnlein 166

Henrion, Marielle 174
Henry II Plantagenet 99, 120, 140, 163
Hercher, Serge 61
Herin family 138, 139
Hering, Domaine 283
Heywang, Domaine 283
Holl, Gilbert 318
hot-air-balloon flights 119
Hotel-Dieu, Beaune 231, 232
Hudelot family 216-217
Hudelot-Baillet, Domaine 2, 210-211
Huët l'Enchansonne, Domaine 108, 113, 114-115
Hugel & Fils 272, 274, 317-318, 339, 344
Huguenot, Domaine 193
Humbrecht, Olivier and Margaret 336, 337
Hunawihr 316-317, 317, 336
Husseau 120, 121
Husseren-les-Châteaux 278, 345

I
INAO (Institut National des Appellations d'Origine) 56, 274
Ingersheim 330, 332, 334, 339
Itterswiller 293

J
Jacob, Domaine Lucien 218
Jacquart 24
Jaffelin Père & Fils, Domaine 219
Jaillant, Claude and Yvette 74
Javillier, Patrick 243
Jayer-Gilles, Domaine 218
Jeeper, Champagne 69
Jefferson, Thomas 243
Jessiaume Père et Fils, Domaine 256
Jeudi, Antoine 126
Jeune Talents award, Burgundy 200
Joan of Arc 31, 35, 99, 140
Joguet, Domaine Charles 141, 149
John II of France 184
Joliet Père & Fils 194
Josmeyer, Domaine 342, 343, 348-349
Jousselin, Daniel 173
Jung, Emile 270

K
Kaefferkopf 329
Katzenthal 329, 330, 332, 334-335
Kaysersberg 275, 278, 320, 321, 327, 328, 353
Kientz, Yves 295
Kientzel, Joseph and Carmen 314
Kientzheim 278, 286, 287, 295, 318-320, 324-325
Kientzler, André 307, 312-313
Kintzheim 278, 295, 296, 304-305
Kirchberg de Barr 283
Kirchberg de Ribeauvillé 283
Klevener de Heiligenstein (Traminer) 273, 283
Klipfel, Domaine 283
Klur, Domaine Clément 329, 330
Kniperlé 272
Koehler, Gilbert 347
Koehly family 304, 305
Kreydenweiss, Domaine Marc 285, 288-289
Kronenbourg 281
Krug 32, 64
Kuentz-Bas 345

L
La Grille 139
La Rochepot 190, 244, 245
Label Rouge culinary award 102
Ladoix-Serrigny 230
Lafagne, Madame 173
Laleure-Piot, Domaine 219
Lalou, René 35
Lambrays, Domaine des 205
Lammert, Olivier 327
Landmann, Armand 294
Landmann, Seppi 347
Landragin, Thierry 88
Languedoc 198
Lanson 65
Laplaigne, Laurent 36
Larmandier-Bernier, Champagne 67, 72
Latour, Louis 229
Launois, Champagne 51, 64, 65, 66
Laurent-Perrier 51, 55, 65
Laval, Champagne Georges 77
Le Mesnil-sur-Oger 21, 28, 51, 64-65, 66, 74
Le Montrachet 245

Le Vau 129, 132-133
Leclerc, Pascal 55
Leclerc-Briant, Champagne 55
Lefèvre, Champagne Etienne 40
Leflaive, Domaine 252, 253, 254, 258-259
Léger, Stéphane 262, 263
Leguin, Dominique 210
Lenoble, Martine 116
Leo IX, Pope Saint 344
Leonardo da Vinci 110
Lester, Krishna 164, 170, 171
Loire Valley 94-105, 174-175
Lorenz, Domaine Gustave 306
Losier, Dom 206
Louis XI 132
Louis XII 109
Ludes 28, 80
Lycée Viticole, Beaune 232
Lycée Viticole de la Champagne, Avize 63

M

Macé, Jean 319
Magny-les-Villers 218
Maignaut, Francis 136
Mailly, Champagne 24, 39, 41, 44-45
Maison Fossier, Reims 26
maisons troglodytiques 95, 109
Malbec see Côt
Malvoisie 129
Mann, Domaine Albert 343
Marc de Bourgogne 186, 189
Marc de Champagne 25, 26
Marc de Gewurztraminer 274
Marco, Louis-Félix 283
Mareuil-sur-Aÿ 52
Marey-lès-Fussey 217
Marguet Père & Fils, Champagne 51
Marlenheim 269
Marlot, Laurent 341
Marnay, Didier 154
Marne Valley 22, 27, 28, 68-69, 76-89
Marsannay-la-Côte 192, 193, 194, 196, 198-199, 200, 202
Maurice, Jean-Michel 229
May, Seigneur du 245
Menard, Stephane 290
Mercier 54, 80
Metz, Domaine Hubert 293
Meunier 70
Meursault 186, 190, 233, 243, 246, 248-249, 251, 252, 265
Meyer, Domaine Julien 294

Meyer, Jean 343, 348
Meyer, Nadine 84
Meyer-Thierry 339
Meyer–Fonné, Domaine 329, 334-335
Michelin stars 14
Michelon, Patrick 91
Milan, Champagne Jean 64
millésimé (vintage) wines 25
Mittelbergheim 278, 284-285, 286-287, 290-291
Mittnacht-Klack, Domaine 318
moelleux wines 107, 114
Moët & Chandon 19, 54, 65, 78, 80, 234
Moët Hennessy group 32, 34, 54
Moncontour, Château 108
Moncuit, Pierre 65, 74
Mons, Hervé 149
Mont-Sainte-Odile 278, 281, 282, 283
Montagne de Reims 21, 27, 28, 41
Montbazon 129-130, 136
Montchenot 89
Monthelie 250
Montlouis-sur-Loire 101, 104, 108, 120-121, 124, 127, 174
Montmorency family 245
Montsoreau 104, 154, 161, 162, 175
Morey, Domaine Bernard 254, 255
Morey, Domaine Jean-Marc 254, 260-261
Morey-Saint-Denis 178, 204-205
Mortet, Denis 196
Morvezen, Patrig 44, 45, 48
Mosnes 110
Mounier, Nathalie 243
Moyer, Dominique 121
Mumm, Champagne G.H. 34-35, 39-40
Munster 342
Muré, René 346
Muscat 273, 274, 284
mustard 180, 233
Mutigny 28
Muzard, Domaine Lucien 256

N

Nasti, Olivier and Emmanuel 275, 327
Nicolay, Manoir de 234, 235
Niedermorschwihr 329-330, 330

'noble rot' (botrytis) 101, 107, 131, 271, 275
Noble-Joué 104
Noisot, Captain Claude 196
Nothalten 293, 298
Nudant, Domaine 230
Nuits-Saint-Georges 208, 209, 215, 216, 222-223, 226, 264

O

Oberlin, Chrétien 332
Obernai 270, 271, 277, 280-281, 290, 352
Ocio, Bernard 60, 61
Oden, Servane 97
Odile, Sainte 282
Oed, John 338
Œuilly 68
Oger 64, 72
Oïsium (powdery mildew) 272
Ollivier, Patrice 198, 199
organic viticulture see viticulture
Orius 170
Ostertag, André 293, 294
Ottrott 281

P

Pages, Bernard 39
Paget, Domaine James and Nicholas 138
Paillard, Champagne Pierre 42, 46-47
Papet Père & Fils, Domaine 219
Parent, Domaine François 241
Parker, Robert 178-179
Parnay 164
Patriarch Père & Fils 184, 232, 243
Pelletier, Jean-Claude and Anne-Marie 49, 51
Pérignon, Dom Pierre 22, 23, 24, 32, 77, 88
Pernand-Vergelesses 190, 218-219, 224-225, 227
Pernod-Ricard 35
Perrault, Charles 139
Perreaut, Joël and Nicole 202
Perrier-Jouët, Champagne 54-55
Perrière, Manoir de la 194, 195
Perrières, Domaine des 288
Perrin, Emmanuel 314
Peters, Michaela 340
Petite Chapelle, Domaine de la 161

Peugeot, Laurent 117, 219, 238
Pfaffenheim 278, 345, 350-351
Pflixbourg 342
Philippe the Bold, Duke of Burgundy 184, 256
Philippon, Michel 215
Philipponnat, Champagne 52
phylloxera 24, 99, 103, 131, 132, 138, 140, 272, 348
Pibaleau, Domaine Pascal 131, 134-135
Picpoul de Pinet 198
Pierry 62
Pinguet, Noël 114
Pinon, François 108
Pinot Beurot, Burgundy 186, 218, 273
Pinot Blanc, Alsace 273, 274
Pinot Gris, Alsace 129, 186, 273, 274, 284
Pinot Meunier 21, 22, 24, 68, 129
Pinot Noir
  Alsace 274, 281
  Burgundy 179, 186, 188, 190, 198, 254
  Champagne 21, 22, 24, 40, 42, 46, 51, 67, 70, 72
  Loire Valley 101, 129
Pinot Noir rosé 193
Piper–Heidsieck, Champagne 35
Plouzeau, Caves 141, 144-145
poires tapées 138-139
Pol Roger, Champagne 54
Polisy 56
Pomerol 194
Pommard 190, 241-242, 246, 248, 260
Pommery, Champagne 34, 63
Pompelle, Fort de la 39
Ponsardin, Nicole-Barbe see Clicquot
Pont, Michel 219-220
Potel, Nicholas 209, 222
Pouilly-Fumé 101
Premier Cru
  Alsace 273
  Burgundy 186, 194, 207, 228, 232, 241, 255
  Champagne 19
Preuilly-sur-Chaise 148
Prieuré, Domaine du 229
Prudhon, Isabel and Bernard 245
Prunier & Fille, Domaine Michel 244

Puisais, Jacques 146
Puligny-Montrachet 186, 190, 243, 245, 248, 252-253, 258-259, 262, 265

Q
quetsch 276
Quinçay 138

R
Rabelais, François 141
Rambach, Jean-Claude 86, 87
Ramonet, Domaine 254
Rapet Père & Fils, Domaine 206, 224-225
Ratafia de Champagne 25, 26
Rateau, Jean-Claude 232
Reims 18, 21, 23, 24, 26, 28, 32-37, 38, 44, 90
La Reine Pédauque 229
Remoriquet, Domaine 209, 222-223
Rémy, St. 31
Retable d'Issenheim (Haguenau and Grünewald) 331, 333
Reuschle, Vincent 290
Ribeauvillé 278, 306, 307-309, 312-313, 352-353
Richard the Lionheart 163
Richarde, Empress 292
Rieffel, Domaine 285, 286-287
Riesling 274, 284
Rigny-Ussé 139
Rigollet, Jean-Claude 141, 148
Rilly-la-Montagne 28, 80-81
Ringmann, Matthias, Cosmographiae Introductio 296
Riquewihr 278, 317-318, 326
Robuchon, Joël 290
Rochcorbon 106-107
Rodern 305
Roederer, Louis 32, 67
Roguinet 151
Rollin, Nicholas 231
Rolly–Gassman, Maison 306
Romanée-Conti, Domaine de la 202
Romans 10
Rorschwihr 306
rosés 25, 51, 104, 193
Rossignol-Février, Domaine 242, 246-247
Rossignol-Jeanniard, Domaine 242
Rouffach 278, 346-347, 353

Rouge d'Ottrott 281
Rousseau, Armand 196
Rousseau Frères 129, 132-133
Rude, François, 'Napoléon' sculpture 194, 196
Ruff, Domaine Daniel 283
Ruinart, Champagne 19, 23, 32, 34, 38

S
Saché 130
Sacy, Champagne Louis de 40
Saint-Aubin 243, 244, 245, 260
Saint-Cyr-en-Bourg 164, 168-169
Saint-Emilion 194
Saint-Hilaire-Saint-Florent 166
Saint-Hippolyte 305, 314
Saint-Imoges 78-79, 80
Saint-Jean 256
Saint-Nicholas-de-Bourgueil 152, 154, 156
Saint-Romain 190, 243, 244
Salins, Guignone 231
Salon, Champagne 51, 65
Salon des Vins de Loire 98
Sancerre 100, 101
Sanger, Champagne 63
Santenay 190, 233, 255, 256, 260, 263
Saumur 163, 164, 165, 166-167, 168-169, 172-173, 175
Saumur-Champigny 99, 101, 104, 161, 163, 164
Sauvignon Blanc 101, 104, 110
Sauzet, Domaine Etienne 253
Savigny-lès-Beaune 185, 188, 189, 190, 218, 219, 220, 224, 228-229, 230, 234-235, 250, 265
Sazilly 141
Scherwiller 294, 295, 298
Schillinger, Jean-Yves 340
Schlossberg 324
Schmitter, Jacky 284
Schneider, Patrick and Antje 315
Schofitt, Domaine 332
Schwartz, Hélène and Thierry 286, 290
Schwendi, Marshall Lazare de 273, 331
sec 25, 107
sec-tendre 107
Seilly, Domaine 281
Sélection des Grain Nobles 275
Sélestat 296, 303, 352

Selosse, Domaine Jacques 63-64, 72
Selz, Albert 285
Senard, Domaine Comte 236-237
Senelet, Jean-Pierre 238
Sézanne 65
Sidan, Thierry 61
Sigolsheim 332
Sillery 28, 32, 38-39, 48-49
Sipp, Louis 307
The Sleeping Beauty 139, 140
Soultzmatt 347
Souzay-Champigny 164
Spesbourg 283
Stamm, Nicholas 281
Stein, Daniel 303
Steiner, Dr Rudolph 13
Stéphen-Liégeard 196
Stoeckel, Jean-Marie 315
Stoeffler, Domaine 284
Strasbourg 270, 277
swimming, Epernay 54
Sylvaner 273, 284, 286

T
Taille aux Loups, Domaine de la 121, 124-125
Tarlant, Champagne 68
Tastevinage 204, 206
Terregelesses, Domaine des 236
terroir 10-11
    Alsace 274
    Burgundy 185
    Champagne 21, 72
    Loire Valley 100, 102, 112, 114
Thann 336
Thevenot Lebrun, Domaine 217-218
Thieffry, Philippe 35
Thomas, Domaine Gérard 245
De Tigny family 170
Tinqueux 44
'Tokay d'Alsace' 273, 331-332
Tollot-Beaut, Domaine 230
Toudoire, August-Mareus 55
Tour de France 77, 137, 280
Touraine 98, 99, 101, 104
Touraine-Amboise 109
Touraine-Noble-Joué 128-129, 132-133
Tours 96, 96-97, 97, 104
Tours-sur-Marne 28, 51-52, 52
Traminer 273, 283
Tribaut, Champagne G. 78, 79
Trimbach family 272, 274, 307, 339, 344

Tulkki, Anneli 174
Turckheim 278, 330, 336-337, 338
Turgy, Champagne Michel 65

U
Urban II, Pope 69
Ussé 139, 140

V
Val de Brun, Domaine 164
Vallères 131
Valmer 109
Valois dukes 180, 184
Vauciennes 68
Vaugency, Henry de 64
Vazard, Philippe 48
Védrenne 209
Vendange Tardives, Alsace 275
Véretz 128
Vernou-sur-Brenne 108-109
Véron 104, 151
Vertuelle 41
Vertus 66-67, 72
Verzenay 35, 39-40, 41
Verzy 28, 40, 41
Veuve Clicquot see Clicquot-Ponsardin, Veuve
Villa Bissinger Champagne School, Aÿ 53
Villandry 131
Villars-Fontaine 216-217
Ville des Sacres 31
Ville-en-Selve 80
Villeneuve 164
Viller-aux-Bois 66, 67
Viller-Marmery 40
Villers-Allerand 81
Villers-sous-Châtillon 69
Vilmart, Champagne 80-81
Vin Sensation, Beaune 233
Vinay 67, 75
VINEXPO (Bordeaux) 2005 32
vins de pays 14
vins de table 14
Viticole de la Ville de Colmar, Domaine 332
viticulture 10-11, 80, 153, 179-180, 288, 334, 335, 346
    organic 13, 72, 77, 78, 100, 108, 134, 158, 212, 350
    Alsace 271-275, 278, 346
    Burgundy 14, 183-184
    Champagne 11, 18-29
    Loire Valley 64, 100-101
    see also biodynamics; wine types

Voegtlinshofen 345
Vogt family 37
Volnay 190, 241, 242, 246, 250
Vonville, Jean-Charles 281
Vosne-Romanée 178, 190, 207-208, 212-213, 214, 218
Vougeot 178, 185, 190, 204, 205, 206
Vouvray 100, 101, 104, 106, 107-108, 112, 114-115, 116, 158, 174

W
Wach, Benoît 296
Wach, Guy 285
Wagner, Pascal 258, 259
Wallerand, Julien 253
Wantz, Ehrhard 283
Weinbach, Domaine 320
Westhalten 353
Westhus, Jean de 296
Wettolsheim 278, 343
Weyden, Rogier van der 231
whisky 28, 41
Wiebelsberg 285
Willhelm I, Emperor 305
Williams, Frank 70
wine tasting 13-15
Wineck, Château de 329
Wintzenheim 332, 336, 342, 348-349
Wohlfahrt, Kathe 317

Z
Zellenberg 319
Zinck, Pierre 285, 291
Zind-Humbrecht, Domaine 316, 330, 336-337
Zotzenberg 284